COMPLETE HANDBOOK
TO
CRUISING

COMPLETE HANDBOOK
TO
CRUISING

by

DOUGLAS WARD

Executive Director
International Cruise Passengers Association

Berlitz Guides
A division of Macmillan S.A.

Acknowledgements

The design for this book was done by Philippe Aquoise, who also provided the vignettes, while Susan Alpert drew the ship silhouettes and cabin layouts.

"Fun Ship" cover photo courtesy of Carnival Cruise Lines, Miami.

PUBLISHER'S NOTE

The International Cruise Passengers Association has evaluated cruise ships since 1980, issuing annual reports on the world's cruise fleet. All opinions and ratings are strictly those of the author and not of the publisher, Berlitz, which makes this survey available in bookstores.

Contents

Foreword

by

James G. Godsman

President

Cruise Lines International Association

The fact is, if you're reading these words, you're in the company of millions of people who, like yourself, have expressed a strong interest in taking a cruise. Of course, if you've had the good fortune to take a cruise, you're probably thinking about your next one.

No matter what stage you are at in your decision-making process, you probably appreciate the value of your time and money. That's what makes a cruise vacation all the more rewarding. And that in turn explains the record-breaking number of people—more than 3 million—who will take a cruise this year.

Cruise vacations are the smart choice for many reasons:
THERE ARE NO HIDDEN COSTS!
EVERYTHING IS INCLUDED.

A cruise vacation is an all-inclusive package; that is, the price includes your accommodations, meals, daytime activities, night-time parties and entertainment, plus transportation. Thus, you'll know what your vacation will end up costing before you go.

You'll find a wide variety of options to choose from. You can cruise from three days to three months, and to virtually every port in the world.

Think of your ship as a floating resort that transports you in safety, comfort and style to new and exciting destinations, then compare it to other kinds of vacations. You'll be amazed at the value it represents and how affordable it really is.

YOU CAN DO EVERYTHING...OR NOTHING.

The wide open sea gives you a feeling of space and freedom few places can rival. There's plenty of room on the decks and in the public rooms. In fact, it may take you two or three days to explore all the space on board. Even then, you'll have new ports of call to scout—either on your own or with your ship-mates.

Every morning a list of daily activities will be delivered to your stateroom. You can join in exercise classes, sports contests and trivia quizzes. You can listen to a lecture, play in a bridge or backgammon tournament, drive golf balls, take a steam bath or sauna, swim, participate in a dance class, practise your tennis strokes, watch a feature movie, or even learn about computers.

Just like any resort, you can be off by yourself. Simply relax, lie back on a lounge chair, with your favorite book, soak up the rays, breathe the salt air and watch the sun reflect over the calm blue water.

YOU CAN COME BACK FROM YOUR CRUISE FIT
AND TRIM!

Do you know there are plenty of passengers who come on board to keep fit? Most ships will make special arrangements for salt-free, low-carbohydrate, weight-watching, or other diet preferences. Bountiful buffets feature fresh fruits and salads you can munch to your heart's content. Even the regular menu features lots of interesting items not loaded with calories.

There's plenty of opportunity to exercise, whether it's a leisurely stroll around the deck, participating in the daily aerobic, dancercize or calisthenic classes, or using the Nautilus equipment and free weights.

But nobody will stop you from indulging if that's what you want to do. With standard and unlimited fare like caviar and stuffed lobster, mealtimes are festive as well as tasty.

CRUISES ARE FOR EVERYONE!

A recent study showed that 60% of cruise passengers are under 55 years of age; 30% under 35. There are passengers who travel as families, as couples and as singles. There are doctors, lawyers, teachers, honeymooners, businessmen and women, corporate executives, secretaries, homemakers, bakers, bankers, aunts and uncles, and others just like you.

And there are plenty of opportunities to meet people and make new friends. The ambiance on the high seas—enhanced by the close-knit community of passengers and crew—is quite different from a land-based resort where guests do not share the experience with nearly the same intensity and spirit. Passengers tend to be out-going and congenial, yet sensitive to those who like their privacy.

Planning for a cruise is almost as much fun as taking one. This guide will help you create a mental picture of the whole wide range of cruise ships, plus all the activities they offer.

Of course, it's wise to ask the opinion of a professional travel agent, and CLIA-affiliated travel agents proudly display the blue, gold and white CLIA seal of our organization. Talk to one and be on your way to one of the greatest vacations of your life!

Cruise Lines International Association, or CLIA as it is commonly known, is the North American trade association for the industry. Most cruise lines operating in North America are members.

How to Use this Handbook

Ever since my very first Trans-Atlantic crossing, in July 1965, on Cunard's *Queen Elizabeth,* I have been captivated by passenger ships and the sea. More than 600 cruises, 80 Trans-Atlantic crossings and countless ships later, I am even more fascinated by every aspect of cruising and passenger-ship travel.

For the discerning vacationer, there simply is no better way to get away from it all than a cruise. Those who have cruised before will be unstinting in their praise of its joys. They may talk about a specific ship, line or cruise, but always with enthusiasm. So will you—that is, if you choose the right ship for the right reasons.

And that brings me to the purpose of this handbook: it is intended to be a primary and comprehensive source of information about cruising and the ships and companies that offer to take you away from the pressure, stresses and confines of daily life ashore. When you first start looking into the possibilities of taking a cruise, you will be confronted by an enormous and bewildering choice. Don't panic. Pick up this book and read it carefully. At the end you will be nearer to making the right choice and will leave for your cruise as well informed as most specialists in the industry! In fact, cruise/travel agents and personnel connected with the travel industry will also find this book a valuable reference source on ships and cruising.

The handbook is divided into two distinct sections. Part One, comprising 17 chapters and numerous charts and diagrams, introduces you to the world of cruising; helps you define what you are looking for in a cruise; tells you how and where to book and what kind of accommodation to choose; and provides valuable hints on what you should know before you go. There is a complete picture of life aboard ship and how to get the best from it: the world-famous cuisine, the background and history of cruising, nautical terminology, amusing anecdotes, who's who on board, advice about going ashore and a guide to shopping in the various ports of call. If you are looking for the cruise with a difference—along a river or an adventurous expedition—there is a brief look at these aspects, culminating with that ultimate travel experience: the world cruise, and other classic voyages.

Part Two contains a complete evaluation of 134 major ocean-going cruise ships of the world, plus three adventure cruise vessels. From large to small, from unabashed luxury to moderate and economy, they're all here. The ratings are a painstaking documentation of my personal work, much of it undertaken in strict secrecy. To keep this handbook up-to-date and accurate, I travel constantly world-wide. This means inspecting hundreds of ships (including areas that passengers would never normally see, but which are a necessary part of the total evaluation) and involves naturally, much on-board cruising as well.

The ratings are best used selectively—according to your personal tastes and preferences. If cuisine is important to you, or your concern is for keeping fit, then these aspects of the ratings will obviously be more significant for you than the overall score or the number of stars awarded. Particularly useful is the Pick-a-Ship chart at the beginning of Part Two which gives you an idea of the type of passenger to expect on board, the ambiance and whether the tone and style are formal, informal or casual. For instance, you might be looking for a young disco crowd, or perhaps want to avoid one. The attraction of cruising is the variety of opportunities available—and this handbook is intended to make it easier for you to choose.

As soon as new ships enter service, a survey is undertaken for the next edition of this handbook. This edition covers the state of the cruise industry through the fall of 1988.

This book is a tribute to everyone who has made my seafaring experiences possible, and to everyone who helped make this book a reality. In addition, I would like to give a brief mention to my mother and father, without whom I would never have gone cruising. With my love.

Douglas Ward
September 1988

Part One

The World of Cruising

Choosing Your Cruise

So, you've decided your next vacation will be a cruise. Good choice! But the decisions don't stop there. Bombarded with glossy cruise literature tempting you with every imaginable lure, you may find choosing the right cruise for you a difficult process.

How do you begin to select the cruise you'll enjoy most for the amount of money you want to spend? Price is, of course, the key word. The cost of a cruise provides a good guideline to the type of ambiance and passengers you'll find on board. And what you are prepared to spend will be a determining factor in the size, location and style of your ship-board accommodations.

Even aside from cost, ships are as individualistic as fingerprints; no two are the same and each ship can change its "personality" from cruise to cruise. Before you can establish exactly what you are looking for in your cruise vacation, you'll need to ask yourself several questions. Let's deal with each question in turn.

Where To?

Because itineraries vary widely, depending on ship and cruise, it is wise to make as many comparisons as possible by reading the cruise brochures and their descriptions of ports visited. If, for example, you are considering a Caribbean cruise, you'll have a choice of over two dozen itineraries.

Several ships may offer the same, or similar itineraries, simply because these have been tried and have proven successful, given the time allotted for the cruise, and the distance and geographical relationship of the ports featured. You can then narrow down the choice further by noting the time spent at each port, and whether the ship actually docks in port or lies at anchor. Then compare the size of each vessel and the facilities on board.

The recent trend and marketing strategy of some cruise lines is to offer "more ports" in a week than their competitors. This may be all right if you don't mind being ashore *every* day of your cruise. Indeed, there are several ships that feature seven or more ports in a week, which works out to at least one port a day on some of the Greek Isle cruises.

Such intensive "island-hopping" gives little time to explore a destination to the full before you have to nip back on board for a quick ride to the next port. While you see a lot in a week, by the end of the cruise you may need another week to unwind, and you'll be hard put to remember what you saw on which day. Ultimately, this is not the best way to cruise, except for those who want to see as much as possible in a short space of time.

Try to choose an itinerary that appeals to you, and then read about the proposed destinations and their attractions. The public library or your local bookstore are good information sources, and your cruise/travel agent will also be able to provide background on destinations and help you select an itinerary.

How Long?

The popular "standard" length of cruise is seven days, although it can vary from a one-day jamboree to "nowhere" to an exotic voyage lasting over 100 days. However, if you are new to cruising and want to "get your feet wet", you might do well to try a short trip of three or four days first. This will give you a good idea of what is involved, the kind of facilities and the life style on board.

At the same time, you should bear in mind that ships engaged in three- and four-day service are often of the older, less elegant variety. The standard of luxury is generally in direct proportion to the length of the cruise. Naturally, in order to operate the long, low-density voyages, cruise lines must charge high rates to cover the extensive preparations, special foods, port operations, fuel and other expenditures. So if you are seeking a truly luxurious cruise, a short one is not likely to live up to your expectations. The length of cruise you choose will depend on the time and money at your disposal and the degree of comfort you are seeking.

Which Ship?

There is a cruise and ship to suit every type of personality, so it is important to take into account your *own* personality when selecting a ship.

Ships basically come in four sizes— intimate (up to 10,000 grt*), small (between 10,000 and 20,000 grt), medium (between 20,000 and 30,000 grt) and large (over 30,000 grt). But whatever the dimensions, all ships offer the same basic ingredients: accommodations, food, activities, entertainment, good service and ports of call, although some do it better than others.

* Grt = gross registered tonnage—the weight of a ship in the water. (1 grt equals 100 cubic feet of enclosed space.)

If you like or need a lot of space around you, it is of little use booking a cruise on a small, intimate ship where you knock elbows almost every time you move. If you like intimacy, close contact with people and a homely ambiance, you may feel lost and lonely on a large ship, which inevitably will have a more impersonal atmosphere. If you are a novice in the world of cruises, choose a ship in the small or medium-size range. For an idea of the amount of space you'll have around you, look closely at the "Passenger Space Ratio" given in the evaluation of each ship in Part Two of this book. A passenger space ratio of 30 and above can be considered extremely spacious; between 20 and 30, moderately so; between 10 and 20 not very spacious; and below 10, fairly cramped.

A ship's country of registry or parent company location is often a clue to the national atmosphere you'll find on board, although there are many ships that are registered, for financial reasons, under a flag of convenience such as Liberia or Panama. The nationality of the officers or management usually sets the style and ambiance.

You can estimate the standard of service by looking at the crew to passenger ratio. Better service will be found on those ships that have a ratio of one crew member to every two passengers, or better.

The Pick-a-Ship chart at the beginning of Part Two will help you not only to compare the differences between the ships and lines, but will also indicate the ambiance and type of passengers you can expect to find aboard.

Theme Cruises
If you still think that all cruises are the same, the following list will give you some idea of available special theme cruises—offered by cruise lines to attract passengers of similar tastes and interests.

Adventure	Exploration	Pageantry
Archaeological	Fashion	Party
Art Lovers	Gourmet	Photography
Astronautical	Health & Fitness	Religious
Backgammon	Historical	River
Big Band	Hobby	Rock 'n' Roll
Bridge	Holistic Health	Schooner
Chess Tournament	Honeymoon	Seminar
Children's Educational	Jazz	Senior Citizen
Computer Science	Maiden Voyages	Singles
Cosmetology	Movie	Sports
Cruises to Nowhere	Murder Mystery	Theatrical
Diet & Nutrition	Music Festival	Trivial Pursuit
Economics	Naturalist	Wine Tasting
Educational	Oktoberfest	Yacht

Accommodations

Selecting your accommodations is the single most important decision you will have to make. So choose wisely, for if, when you get to the ship, you find your cabin is too small, you may not be able to change it or "upgrade" to a higher price category.

Although you may request a specific cabin when you book, many lines now designate cabins only at the point of embarkation. They will, however, guarantee the grade and rate requested.

Here are some tips to take into consideration when choosing your accommodations.

Price

The amount you pay for accommodations on a cruise is directly related to the size of the cabin, the location within the ship and the facilities provided. Some other factors are also taken into consideration when cruise lines grade their accommodations. There are no set standards within the cruise industry, each line implementing its own sys-tem according to ship size, age, construction and profit potential.

Before you select your cabin, decide how much you can afford to spend, including air fare (if applicable), on-board expenses (don't forget to include the estimated cost of shore excursions, port charges and tips), as this will determine the cabin categories available to you. It is advisable to choose the most expensive cabin you can afford, especially if it's your first cruise, as you *will* spend some time there. If it is too small (and most cabins *are* small), "cabin fever" could result, and the cruise may fall short of your expectations. Alternatively, it is better to book a low-grade cabin on a good ship than a high-grade cabin on a poor ship.

If you are a family of three or more and don't mind sharing a cabin, you'll achieve a substantial saving per person, so you may be able to go to a higher grade cabin without paying any extra.

With regard to cabins, it is generally true that you will get precisely what you pay for.

Size

Ships' cabins should be looked upon as hotel rooms *in miniature,* providing more or less the same facilities. With one difference—space. Ships necessarily have space limitations, and therefore tend to utilize every inch efficiently.

There is no such thing as an *average* cabin, as cabin size will depend on the space allocated to accommodation within a ship of given tonnage and dimensions. Generally, the larger the ship, the more generous it will be with regard to cabin space.

Remember that cruise ships are operated both for the pleasure of the passengers **and** for the profit of the cruise companies. This is why cabins on many new or modern ships are on the small side. The more cabins a ship can provide, the more fare-paying passengers can be carried, and the more revenue can be earned per cruise.

Ships of yesteryear offered more spacious cabins simply because there were fewer ports of call, greater distances between ports, generally less speed, and fewer passenger entertainment rooms. Thus, many people spent a considerable amount of time in their cabins, often using them for entertaining others.

Although most modern ships have smaller cabins, they are more than adequate for standard-length cruises leaving increased space in the public rooms for entertainment and social events.

Some cruise-line brochures are more detailed and specific than others when it comes to deck plans and cabin layout diagrams. Deck plans do not normally show the dimensions but they are drawn to scale, unless otherwise noted.

You can get a good idea of the space in a cabin by examining the cabin plan of the category you are interested in. By looking at the beds (each twin being between 2 feet and 3 feet wide and 6 feet long), you can easily figure out how much empty or utilized space (e.g. bathroom, closets, etc.) there is.

If the cabins appear to be the same size on the deck plan, it's because they *are* the same size, with the exception of suite rooms which will be marginally larger. This is particularly true on some of the newer ships, where all cabins are of a standard size.

Ask the cruise line, via your cruise/travel agent, for the square footage of the cabin you have selected, if it is not indicated on the deck plan. This will give you some idea of its size. Pace out one of your own rooms at home as a comparison.

Location

An "outside" cabin is preferable by far, especially if this is your introduction to cruising. An "inside" cabin has no portholes or windows, making it more difficult to orient yourself or gauge the weather or time.

Cabins in the center of a ship are more stable and noise- and vibration-free. Ships powered by diesels (this applies to most new and modern vessels) create and transmit vibration, especially toward the stern of the vessel.

Consider your personal habits when choosing the location of your cabin. For example, if you like to go to bed early, don't pick a cabin close to the disco. If you have trouble walking, don't select a cabin far away from the elevator, or worse still, on a lower deck where there is no elevator.

Generally, the higher the deck, the higher the cabin price and the better the service—a carry-over from trans-oceanic days, when upper-deck cabins and suites were sunnier and warmer.

Cabins at the bow (front) of a ship are slightly crescent-shaped, as the outer wall follows the curvature of the ship's hull. They are usually roomier and cheaper. However, these forward cabins can be subject to disturbing early morning sounds, such as the anchor being dropped at ports where the ship cannot dock.

Connecting cabins are fine for families or close friends, but remember that the wall between is unusually thin, and both parties can plainly hear anything that's being said next door.

If you book a deluxe upper-deck cabin, check the deck plan carefully; the cabin could have a view of lifeboats. Similarly, cabins on promenade decks may have windows which can easily be looked into by passing deck strollers.

If you select a cabin that is on one of the lower decks, be warned that engine noise and heat become more noticeable, especially at the aft end of the vessel.

Facilities

Cabins will provide some, or all, of the following features:

The Suite Life

Suites are the most luxurious and spacious of all ship-board accommodations. They usually comprise a separate lounge or sitting room, and a bedroom with a double, queen- or king-size bed, or large, movable twin beds.

The bathroom will be quite large (for a ship) and will feature a big bath tub and shower, plus a toilet, deluxe wash basin and even a bidet. Today, one ship actually boasts gold bathroom fittings in her best suites! Although that is the exception rather than the rule, the bathrooms attached to suites are usually superb.

Suites often contain a stereo system, television, video unit, refrigerator and a partially or fully stocked bar, and occupants command the very best of service around-the-clock. On a ship like the QE2, you'll find each suite room decorated in a different style, with authentic period furniture, beautiful drapes and fine furnishings throughout. On Royal Viking Line's ships, you'll be attended by a personal butler.

Suite rooms are ideal for a long voyage, when the ship's meandering course takes you across stretches of ocean for five or more days at a time. They are wonderful for impressing a loved one, and are good for entertaining in, too.

Many suites have their own balcony or verandah, although it would be wise to check the deck plan carefully in case the verandah faces the lifeboats or other apparatus. Suites are usually sheltered from noise and wind and also provide considerable privacy.

* Private bathroom (generally small and compact) with shower, wash basin and toilet. Higher-priced deluxe cabins and suites often feature fullsize bathtubs, while some may even have a private whirlpool bath and/or bidet—and much more space.
* Electrical outlets for personal appliances, usually U.S. standard, sometimes both 110 and 220 volt.
* Multi-channel radio; on some ships, television (regular or closed-circuit); video equipment.
* Two beds, or a lower and upper berth (plus, possibly, another one or two upper berths). Or a double, queen- or king-size bed (usually in suites or deluxe accommodations). On some ships, twin beds can be pushed together to form a double bed.
* Telephone, for inter-cabin or ship-to-shore communication.
* Depending on cabin size, a chair, or chair and table, or sofa and table, or a separate lounge/sitting area (higher-priced accommodations only).
* Refrigerator and bar (higher-priced accommodations only).
* Vanity/desk unit with chair or stool.
* Closet space and some drawer space, plus storage room under beds for suitcases.
* Bedside night stand/table unit.

Many first-time cruisers are surprised to find twin beds in their cabin. Double beds have been a comparative rarity on cruise ships except in the higher-priced suite rooms, at least until recently. On some ships, the twin beds may convert to sofas for daytime use, and at night are simply flipped over by the steward to become beds again.

The two beds are placed in one of two configurations: parallel to each other (with little space between beds) or in an ''L'' shape, which gives more floor space and the illusion that the cabin is larger, since one of the beds will be against the outer wall of the ship. The latter is preferable. On some newer ships, twin beds can be moved together to form what is essentially a double bed.

On some ships (especially older ones) you'll find upper and lower berths. A ''berth'' is simply a nautical term for a bed enclosed in a wooden or iron frame. A ''pullman berth'' tucks away out of sight during the day, usually into the bulkhead or ceiling. You climb up a short ladder at night to get into an upper berth.

Reading a Deck Plan

Learning to read a deck plan is a relatively easy matter. It is always laid out so that the bow (front part of the ship) faces to your right.

Traditionally, ships have always designated the central deck, which is equivalent to the main lobby of a hotel, as the ''Main Deck''. This is where you'll find the Purser's Office together with other principal business offices. Some modern ships, however, do not use the term Main Deck, preferring instead a name that sounds more exclusive and attractive.

All ships also have a Boat Deck, so called because this is where the ship's lifeboats are stowed, ever-ready but secured on their "davits".

Many ships of the past had a Promenade Deck, which featured an enclosed walkway along the length of the deck on one or both sides of the ship. The Promenade Deck was popular with passengers crossing the Atlantic for, when the weather was cold or foggy, they could still take their stroll; the "Prom Deck", as it was then known, was a place to be seen. It is always located between the Main Deck and the Boat Deck, except on some modern ships where "Boat" and "Promenade" may be interchangeable. When the new generation of specialized cruise ships came into being in the '70s, the Promenade Deck disappeared in favor of public entertainment lounges that spread across the full beam of the ship, and the name of the deck was changed. Some recent ships have returned to the idea of a Promenade Deck.

The uppermost decks are usually open and feature sunning space with multi-sports areas, including running or jogging tracks that may or may not encircle the ship.

The Restaurant Deck has undergone a metamorphosis, too. It used to be buried on one of the ship's lower decks so as to avoid the rolling motion of unstabilized ocean liners. Even on the most luxurious liners, there were often no portholes, because the deck was placed below the waterline. As cruising replaced transportation as the prime source of revenue, newer ships were designed with restaurants set high above the waterline. Big picture windows give diners a panoramic view of the port or surrounding sea. The Restaurant Deck can thus be either above or below Main Deck, depending on the ship and cruise line.

Traditionally, popular-priced cabins have been below Main Deck, with high-priced suites occupying space on one or two of the uppermost decks. Suites are always located where the view and privacy are best and the noise is least. In the latest ship designs, however, almost all accommodation areas are located above Main Deck in order to cut down on disturbing engine noise and vibration. Older ships designated their accommodation decks "A", "B", "C", "D", etc., while most modern cruise ships have given these decks more appealing names, such as "Acapulco", "Bimini", "Coral", "Dolphin" and so on, disguising the deck letter by using it as the first letter of a more exotic name.

On a deck plan, cabins will generally be shown as small rectangles or blocks, each with a number printed on it, so you'll be able to locate your own. Public rooms will either be drawn in detail or left as blank spaces. Elevators are usually indicated by the British term "lift", while any stairs will be shown as a small series of lines set closely together.

Typical Cabin Layouts

The following rates are typical of those you can expect to pay for a 7-day (a) and 10-day (b) Caribbean cruise on a modern cruise ship. The rates are per person, and are compiled from a composite listing of several representative lines, and include free roundtrip airfare, or low-cost air add-ons from principal North American gateways.

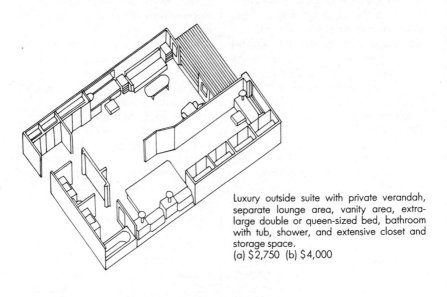

Luxury outside suite with private verandah, separate lounge area, vanity area, extra-large double or queen-sized bed, bathroom with tub, shower, and extensive closet and storage space.
(a) $2,750   (b) $4,000

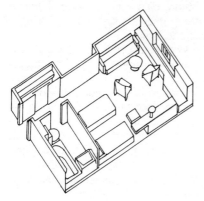

Deluxe outside cabin with lounge area, double or twin beds, bathroom with tub, shower, and ample closet and storage space.
(a) $2,250   (b) $2,850

Note that on some ships third- and fourth-person berths are available for families or friends wishing to share. These upper Pullman berths, not shown on these cabin layouts, would be recessed into the wall above the lower beds.

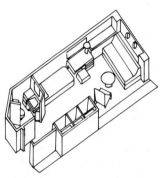

Large outside double, with bed and convertible daytime sofabed, bathroom with shower, and good closet space.
(a) $1,750 (b) 2,450

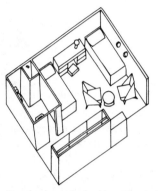

Standard outside double, with twin beds (plus a possible upper 3rd/4th berth), small sitting area, bathroom with shower, and reasonable closet space.
(a) $1,450 (b) $1,975

Inside double, with two lower beds that may convert into daytime sofabeds (plus a possible upper 3rd/4th berth), bathroom with shower, and fair closet space.
(a) $1,250 (b) $1,750

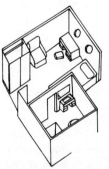

Outside or inside single, with bed and small sitting area, bathroom with tub or shower, and limited closet space.
(a) $1,650 (b) $2,450

Cruise Cuisine

Without doubt, food is the single most talked and written about aspect of the cruise experience. Some of the most sensual pleasures in life come from eating. And where is the person who is not aroused by the aroma of food being prepared, or charmed by a delicious, satisfying meal?

There is a special thrill that comes with dining out in a superb restaurant. So it is on board a luxury cruise ship, where gracious dining in elegant, friendly and comfortable surroundings enhances an appetite already sharpened by the bracing sea air.

Attention to consistent quality, presentation, and choice of menu in the tradition of Trans-Atlantic luxury liners has made cruise ships justly famous. Cruise lines know that you'll spend more time eating on board than anything else, so their intention is to cater to your palate in every way possible. With traditional favorites and special dishes from the great cuisines of the world, the temptation begins.

The cuisine will vary, naturally, depending on the nationality and regional influence of the Executive Chef, his staff and the country of registry or ownership. Thus, choosing a cruise and ship also involves thinking about the kind of food that will be served on board. Menus for luncheon and dinner are usually displayed outside the dining room each morning so you can preview the day's meals. When looking at the menu, one thing you'll never have to do is to consider the price—it's all included.

Depending on the ship and cruise, you could sit down to gourmet specialties such as duck *à l'orange,* beef Wellington, lobster thermidor or prime roast rib of Kansas beef. Or maybe French *chateaubriand,* Italian veal *scaloppini,* fresh sea bass in dill sauce, or rack of roast English lamb. To top off the meal there could well be chocolate mousse, kiwi tart, or that favorite standby—baked Alaska. And, you can always rely on your waiter to bring you a double portion!

Of course, these specialties may not be available on all ships. But, if you would like something that is not on the menu, see the Maitre d', give him 24 hours' notice (and a tip) and it's all yours.

Despite what the glossy brochures say, not all meals on all cruise ships are gourmet affairs. In general, however, cruise cuisine can be compared favorably to the kind of "banquet" food served in a first-class hotel. For a guide to the standard of cruise cuisine, service and presentation on a particular ship, refer to the ratings in Part Two.

One reason that the food on ships cannot always be a gourmet experience is that the galley (ship's kitchen) may have to turn out hundreds of meals at the same time. What you will find is a very fine selection of highly palatable, pleasing and complete meals served in very comfortable surroundings, in the company of friends. Add to this the possibility of a large picture window overlooking a shimmering, moonlit sea. Dining in such a romantic setting is a delightful and relaxed way to spend any evening.

The Executive Chef

Each ship has its own Executive Chef. He is responsible for planning the menus, ordering sufficient food (in conjunction with the Food Manager), organizing his staff and arranging meals.

When a cruise line finds a good Executive Chef, it is unlikely that they will part company. Many of the best ships have European chefs who are members of the prestigious *Confrérie de la Chaîne de Rôtisseurs,* the world's oldest gourmet society. Top food and beverage experts work together with their Executive Chefs, constantly striving for perfection in all aspects of the sea-going culinary tradition.

One of the principal aims of any good Executive Chef will be to make sure that menus are never repeated, even on long cruises. He will be inventive enough to offer dishes that will be new gastronomic experiences for his passengers. On long voyages, the Executive Chef will work with specially invited guest chefs to offer passengers a taste of the best in regional cuisines. Sometimes, he may also obtain fresh fish, seafood, fruit and local produce in "wayside" ports and incorporate them into the menu with a "Special of the Day" announcement.

The Dining Room

On many ships, the running and staffing of the dining room are contracted to an outside catering organization specializing in cruise ships. When this is the case, the cruise line simply gives the concessionaire a briefing on its requirements, and the entire operation, often including food purchase and supply, becomes the responsibility of the concessionaire. Ultimately, however, it's the Hotel Manager on board who watches over the cruise line's standards. Ships that are continually operating in waters away from their home country find that the professional catering companies do a good job and provide a degree of relief from the operation and staffing of their dining rooms.

Although a catering concession is likely to be more careful on quantity, the quality is usually to a high standard.

Ships that control their own catering staff and food are often those who go to great lengths to ensure that their passengers are highly satisfied.

Dining-Room Staff

The Maitre d' is an experienced host, with shrewd perceptions about compatibility; you can trust him when he gives you your table seating. If a table reservation has been arranged prior to boarding, you will find a table seating card in your cabin when you arrive. If this is not the case, you will need to make your reservations with the Maitre d' or one of his assistants. If you wish to reserve a prime table or location in the dining room, do it as soon after boarding as possible.

Unless you are with your own group of friends, you will be seated next to strangers in the dining room. Tables for two are a rarity, except on some small ships and on some of the upmarket liners. Most tables accommodate six or eight people. It would be wise to ask to be seated at a large table, for if you are a couple put at a table for four and you don't get along with your table partners, there's no one else to talk to. Meal times spent with incompatible table companions can make for a tedious cruise. Remember, also, that if the ship is full, it may be difficult to change tables after the start of the cruise.

Confide in the Maitre d' so that, if you are seated with table partners not to your liking, he will be able to make a change at the earliest opportunity and keep everybody happy.

If you are unhappy with any aspect of the dining room operation, the earlier you complain the better. Don't wait until the cruise is over and send a scathing letter to the cruise line, for then it is too late to do anything positive. See the people in charge—they are there to help you enjoy your meals during the cruise. They want your comments—good or bad.

Each table is assigned at least one waiter and one busboy or assistant waiter. On some ships, as many as 30 different nationalities may be represented among the dining-room staff. You will normally find them courteous, charming and very helpful. Many ships run special incentive programs, such as a "waiter of the month" competition. This helps keep the staff on their toes, especially if they want to be moved to the "best" tables in the dining room. The result is that passengers really do get fine service.

The best waiters are undoubtedly those from the exclusive European hotels or trained in hotel and catering schools. These highly qualified individuals will excel in "silver" service, will always be ready with the next course when you want it, and will know your likes and dislikes by the second night of the cruise. They normally work on the up-market ships, where dignified professionalism is evident everywhere in the dining room.

The Captain's Table

The Captain normally occupies a large table in or near the center of the dining room, seating eight or ten people picked from the passenger or "commend" list by the Maitre d'. Alternatively, the Captain may ask personal friends or important company officials to dine with him. If you are invited to the Captain's Table for dinner, it is gracious to accept and you'll have the chance to ask all the questions you like about ship-board life.

The Captain will not attend meals if he is required on the bridge. When there are two sittings, he may have dinner at the first sitting one night, and at the second, the following night. On some ships, the Captain's table guests are changed each day so that more passengers can enjoy the experience.

Senior Officers' Tables

Senior Officers also host tables, and if you are seated at such a table you'll have a fascinating time, especially as the senior officers tend to be less formal than the Captain.

Which Sitting?

Most ships in the luxury category, and some small ones, will offer an open, single sitting for meals, where you will be able to dine in unhurried style. The majority of ships, however, have two sittings. The first or main sitting is for those who like dining early and do not wish to linger over their meal. The second or late sitting is for those who enjoy a more leisurely meal. Those at the late sitting may not be hungry enough to eat yet again at the Midnight Buffet, since it begins about two hours after you will have finished dinner. You may also find that some of the better seats for the shows and at the movie theater have been taken by those on the first sitting. Some ships get around this problem by scheduling two performances for all shows at night—one for each sitting.

Most ships request that you enter the dining room not more than 15 minutes after the meal time has been announced, out of consideration for your fellow passengers, table companions and the dining room staff. This is especially true for those on the first sitting.

Special Requirements

If you are counting calories, are vegetarian or require a salt-free, sugar-restricted, macrobiotic or other special diet, let the cruise line know at the time of booking. The line will then pass the information to the ship, so that your particular needs can be met.

Because the food on cruises is considered "international" or French cuisine, be prepared for dishes that are liberally sprinkled with salt. Vegetables are often cooked with sauces containing dairy products, salt and sugar. A word with the Maitre d' should suffice.

Non-smokers who wish to be seated in a special section should tell the Maitre d' or his assistants when making their table reservations. Non-smokers should be aware that when "open seating" breakfasts and luncheons are featured in the dining room, smokers and non-smokers may be together. If smoke bothers you, be adamant; demand a table in a no-smoking area.

First, Second and Theme Nights

For new and experienced cruisers alike, the first evening at sea is exciting—like an opening night at the theater. Nowhere is there more a feeling of anticipation than at that first casual dinner when you get a foretaste of the feasting to come.

By contrast, the second night is a formal affair, for it is normally the Captain's Welcome Aboard Dinner. For this the Chef will pull out all the stops and introduce you to the realm of the gourmet. The dinner follows directly after the Captain's Cocktail Party, which takes place in one of the ship's larger lounges and is an excellent opportunity to get together with your fellow passengers and the ship's officers. Toward the end of the party, the Captain will give his customary welcome aboard speech and may introduce the senior members of his staff.

Some of the other nights of your cruise may be designated as special "theme" nights, when the waiters dress up fittingly and the menu is planned to suit the occasion.

Food Statistics
The amount of food and drink consumed during an average cruise is mind-boggling. Here is an idea of what would normally be carried aboard Cunard Line's famous *QE2* on a 10-day round-trip Trans-Atlantic sailing:

Item	Amount	Item	Amount	Item	Amount
Beef	25,000 lb	Milk	2,500 gallons	Dog biscuits	50 lb
Lamb	6,000 lb	Cream	3,000 quarts	Champagne	1,000 bottles
Pork	4,000 lb	Ice-cream	5,000 gallons	Assorted wines	1,200 bottles
Veal	3,000 lb	Eggs	6,250 dozen	Whiskey	1,000 bottles
Sausages	2,000 lb	Caviar	150 lb	Gin	600 bottles
Chicken	5,000 lb	Cereal	800 lb	Rum	240 bottles
Turkey	5,000 lb	Rice	3,000 lb	Vodka	120 bottles
Fresh vegetables	27,000 lb	Herbs/spices	50 lb	Brandy	240 bottles
Potatoes	30,000 lb	Jam/marmalade	700 lb	Liqueurs	360 bottles
Fish	1,400 lb	Tea bags	50,000	Sherry	240 bottles
Lobsters	1,500 lb	Tea (loose)	500 lb	Port	120 bottles
Crab	800 lb	Coffee	2,000 lb	Beer	12,000 bottles/cans
Canned fish	1,500 tins	Sugar	5,000 lb	Cigars	4,000
Fresh fruit	22,000 lb	Cookies	2,000 lb	Cigarettes	2,500 cartons
Frozen fruit	2,500 lb	Kosher food	600 lb	Tobacco	1,000 lb
Canned fruit	1,500 gallons	Baby food	600 jars		

A Typical Day

From morning till night, there's food a-plenty on even the most modest cruise ship. In fact, on some ships you can eat up to seven meals a day. Not long after the end of one meal, another is waiting in the wings.

Early risers will find piping hot coffee and tea on deck or at an outdoor café on a help-yourself basis from about 6 a.m. onward.

Full breakfast, featuring up to six courses and as many as 60 different items, can be taken in the main dining room. If you prefer a more casual meal, you may wish to have it *alfresco* or buffet style at the outdoor deck café. This is ideal after an early swim or if you don't wish to dress for the more formal atmosphere of the dining room. The choice is naturally more restricted than in the main dining room, but good nonetheless. Times will be given in your *Daily Program*.

A third possibility, especially for the romantics, is to have breakfast brought to your room. There's something rather special about waking up and eating breakfast without getting out of bed. Some ships offer a full choice of items, while others opt for the more simple, but usually well-presented, continental breakfast.

On many ships, mid-morning *bouillon* is an established favorite, often served on one of the open decks— a carry-over from the grand days of Trans-Atlantic steamship travel.

At lunch time, there are at least two choices: a hot lunch with all the trimmings in the dining room, or a buffet-style luncheon at the outdoor café, featuring light meals, salads and one or two hot dishes. On some days, this could well turn into a lavish spread, with enough food for a feast (special favorites are seafood and tropical fruits). And on some ships there'll be a separate hot dog and hamburger stand or pizzeria, where everything is cooked right in front of you.

At around 4 p.m. there will be another throwback from the heyday of the great liners: afternoon tea—in the best British tradition—complete with finger sandwiches, cakes and other goodies. This is often served in one of the main lounges to the accompaniment of live music (it may even be a "tea-dance") or recorded classical music. Normally, afternoon tea lasts about an hour. However, on some ships it only lasts about half an hour, in which case it is best to be on time or you risk missing out altogether.

Dinner, of course, is the main event of the evening, and, apart from the casual first and last nights, will be more formal in style.

If you enjoy wine with your dinner, you'll find an excellent choice on board. Upmarket ships will carry a selection of wines far more extensive than you'll find even in the better restaurants ashore, while other ships will provide some excellent inexpensive wines from the country of the ship's registry or ownership. It is wise to order your wine for the evening meal at lunch time, or at the very latest, as soon as you are seated, as the wine stewards tend to be extremely busy during the evening meal, and will need to draw their stock and possibly have it chilled.

If you are hungry again a few short hours after dinner, there's always the Midnight Buffet—without doubt the most famous of all cruise-ship meals. It really *is* at midnight (usually until 1 a.m.), but it still prompts the question "What time's the Midnight Buffet?"

It's a spread fit for a king, and, like dinner, may feature a different theme each night. For example, there could well be a King Neptune Seafood Buffet one evening, an Oriental Buffet the next, a Tropical Fruit Fantasy the third, and so on. And the desserts at each of these buffets are out of this world.

On one particular night (usually the next to last evening aboard) there will be a magnificent Gala Midnight Buffet, for which the chefs pull out all the stops. Beautifully sculpted ice-carvings will be on display, each fashioned from a 300-pound block of solid ice. Some ships stage an ice-carving demonstration just after the doors open for this Gala event.

Even if you are not hungry, stay up just to *see* this display of exquisite culinary art—it's something most people never forget.

In addition to or as an alternative to the Midnight Buffet, pizzas are often served for the late-night disco crowd or casino patrons.

During a typical day at sea, the ship's bars will open from about 10 a.m. to late into the night, depending on bar, location and number of patrons. Bar hours are given in the ship's *Daily Program*.

The Galley

The galley (kitchen for landlubbers) is the very heart of all food preparation on board. At any time of the day or night, there is constant activity—whether it's baking fresh bread and rolls at 2 a.m., making meals and snacks for passengers and crew round the clock, or decorating a cake for a passenger's birthday celebration.

The work force, from Executive Chef to pot-washer, must all work together as a team, each designated a specific role. There is little room for error.

Galley equipment has to be reliable, as it is in almost constant use, and failure of vital parts or complete units could upset service and successful operations. Regular inspections and maintenance help detect such things as faulty heating coils and elements that may cause problems or fail altogether.

Hygiene and correct sanitation are also vital in the galley, and consequently there is continual cleaning of equipment, utensils, bulkheads, floors and hands. Senior officers conduct regular inspections of the galley, equipment and personnel in order to maintain strict company standards.

Passenger ships sailing from U.S. ports or visiting them either regularly or occasionally are all subject to sanitation inspections by officials from the Department of Health and Human Services, under the auspices of the Centers for Disease Control.

It has been claimed that if the same standards were applied to hotels and restaurants in the U.S., as many as 75 per cent might fail the inspection over and over again.

On board many ships, a Hygiene Officer has the responsibility for overseeing health and sanitation standards. It is little wonder that many cruise lines are proud to show their galley(s) to passengers. A tour of the galley has proven to be a highlight on some of the smaller ships where the galley is not in constant use. On other, larger vessels, passengers are not permitted into the galley, in part, due to constant activity and washing down of decks, and in part, due to restrictions placed on the ship by its insurers. All personnel entering the galley are required to wear rubber-soled shoes or boots.

Cruising and the Disabled

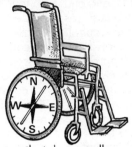

It is with growing awareness that cruise lines, port authorities, airlines and allied services are improving their facilities to enable those who are wheelchair-bound or otherwise disabled to enjoy a cruise to the full. At the last count, some 35 million people in America alone were registered disabled. Not all are in wheelchairs of course, but all provide unique problems—and good opportunities—that the cruise industry is slowly working to resolve.

The very design of ships is discouraging for disabled people. To keep out water or prevent it escaping from a flooded cabin or public area, raised edges or "lips" are frequently placed in doorways and across exit pathways. Furthermore, cabin doorways are often not wide enough to accommodate even a standard wheelchair.

Bathroom doorways are particularly troublesome in this regard, and the door itself, whether it opens outwards into the cabin or inwards into the bathroom, compounds the problems of maneuvering within a cramped space. Remember, too, that bathrooms on most ships are normally small and are full of plumbing and fixtures, often at odd angles—extremely awkward when you are trying to move about from the confines of a wheelchair.

It was once the policy of almost all cruise lines to discourage the disabled from taking a cruise or traveling anywhere by ship for reasons of safety, insurance and legal liability. But it is now becoming clear that a cruise is the *ideal* holiday for a disabled person because it provides a relaxed environment with plenty of social contact, ready-made entertainment and organized activities.

However, not all ships are as well fitted as others to accommodate disabled passengers. The Pick-a-Ship chart on p. 102 rates each ship according to the facilities it provides for the disabled.

Once you've decided on your ship and cruise, the next step is to select your accommodations. There are many grades of cabin, depending on size, facilities and location. Select a cruise line that permits you to choose a specific cabin, rather than one which merely allows you to select a price category, then assigns you a cabin just prior to your departure date or, worse still, at embarkation. The following tips will help you choose wisely:

* Book the best outside cabin you can afford.

* Choose a cabin that is close to an elevator. Remember that not all elevators necessarily go to all decks, so check the deck plan carefully. Smaller and older cruise vessels may not have any elevators, making access to many areas, including the dining room, difficult and sometimes almost impossible.

* Avoid, at all costs, a cabin down a little alleyway shared by several other cabins, even if the price is attractive. The space in these alleyways is extremely limited and entering one of these cabins in a wheelchair could be both frustrating and knuckle-bruising.

* Since cabins that are located amidships are less affected by the motion of the vessel, look for something in the middle of the ship if you're concerned about rough seas, no matter how infrequent.

* The larger (and therefore more expensive) the cabin, the more room you will have to maneuver. Nowhere is this more important than in the bathroom.

* If your budget allows, pick a cabin which has a bath rather than just a shower, as there will be much more room, especially if you are unable to stand comfortably.

* Ships over 20,000 grt will have more spacious alleyways, public rooms and (generally) cabins. Ships under 20,000 grt tend to have cabins that are somewhat confining and therefore difficult to maneuver in.

Wheelchair Guide to Embarkation Ports

Good Embarkation Ports
(Terminals with elevators, escalators and covered gangways)

Adelaide
Boston
Hong Kong
London (Tilbury)
Melbourne
Miami
Montreal
Naples
New York
Port Canaveral
Port Everglades (Fort Lauderdale)
San Francisco
San Juan
Southampton
Sydney
Tokyo
Vancouver (Canada Place Terminal)

Difficult Embarkation Ports
(Poor terminal facilities and, in most cases, uncovered, open gangways)

Acapulco
Baltimore
Civitavecchia
Genoa
Philadelphia
Piraeus
Rio de Janeiro
Singapore
Sydney
Vancouver (old piers)
Venice

* Meals on some ships may be served in your cabin, on special request, a decided advantage should you wish to avoid dressing for every meal.
* If you do want to join the other passengers in the dining room and your ship offers two sittings for meals, choose the second rather than the first. Then you can linger over dinner, secure in the knowledge that the waiter won't try to hurry you.
* Space at dining-room tables is somewhat limited on many ships. Therefore, when making table reservations, tell the Maître d' that you would like a table that leaves plenty of room for your wheelchair, so that it does not cause additional hardship for the waiters and there's room for them to get by.
* Even if you have found a cruise/travel agent who knows your needs and understands your requirements, follow up on all aspects of the booking yourself so that there will be no slip-ups when the day arrives for you to travel.
* Take your own wheelchair with you, as ships carry a very limited number of wheelchairs that are meant for emergency hospital use only.
* Hanging rails in the closets on most ships are too high for someone who is wheelchair-bound to reach. Certain ships, however, have cabins specially fitted out for disabled passengers, in which this and similar problem areas have been dealt with. In Part Two of this book, the ships which have special cabins are marked with a "Yes" under Cabins for the Disabled.
* Elevators on many ships are a constant source of difficulty for passengers in wheelchairs. Often the control buttons are located far too high to reach, especially those for the upper decks.
* Doors on upper decks that open onto a Promenade or Lido Deck are very strong, difficult to handle and have high sills. Unless you are ambulatory, or can get out of your wheelchair, these doors can be a source of annoyance, even when there's help around.
* Advise any airline you might be traveling with of any special needs well ahead of time so that arrangements can be made to accommodate you without last-minute problems.

Even if you've alerted the airline and arranged your travel accordingly, there's still one problem area that can remain when you arrive at your cruise embarkation port to join your ship: the actual boarding.

If you embark at ground level, the gangway to the ship may be level or inclined. It will depend on the embarkation deck of the ship and/or the tide in port.

Or you may be required to embark from an upper level of the terminal in which case the gangway could well be of the "floating" loading bridge type, such as those used at major airports. Some of these have floors that are totally flat, while others may have raised "lips" an inch or so in height, spaced every 3 feet. These are rather awkward, especially if the gangway is made steeper by a rising tide.

If the ship is at anchor, be prepared for an interesting but safe experience. The crew will lower you and your wheelchair into a waiting tender (ship-to-shore launch) and, after a short boat-ride, lift you out again onto a rigged gangway. If the sea is calm this performance proceeds uneventfully; if the sea is choppy, your embarkation could vary from exciting to harrowing—in any case something to write home about. Fortunately (or not) this type of embarkation is rare unless you are leaving a busy port with several ships all sailing the same day.

Passengers who suffer from a disability other than ambulatory, such as the blind, hearing-impaired and speech-impaired, present their own particular problem areas. Many of these can be avoided if the person is accompanied at all times by an ablebodied companion, experienced in attending to their special needs.

In any event, some cruise lines require the disabled to sign a waiver.

Whatever the disability, there is no doubt that the ship-board environment is very therapeutic, and a sensitive staff will make every effort to help their special passengers enjoy the cruise to the full.

Hearing-Impaired
More than 1.5 million Americans have a hearing loss of more than 40%. Those affected should be aware of problems on board ship:

a) hearing announcements on the public address system
b) use of telephone
c) poor acoustics in key areas (boarding tenders).

Wheelchair users with *limited mobility* should use a *collapsible* wheelchair. By limited mobility I mean a person able to get out of the wheelchair and step over a sill or walk with a cane, crutches or other walking device.

Booking Your Cruise

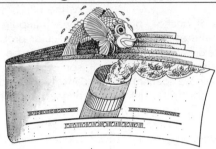

Cruise/Travel Agents

Many people think that cruise/travel agents charge for their services. They don't. They earn commission from cruise lines for booking their clients on a cruise.

Can you do your own booking direct with the cruise line? Yes, and no. Yes, you can book your cruise direct with a small number of cruise lines, and no because most cruise lines do not accept personal checks, thus in effect requiring you to book through a cruise/travel agent.*

A good cruise/travel agent will probably ask you to complete a "profile questionnaire". When this is done, the agent will go through it with you, perhaps asking some additional questions before making suggestions about the ships and cruises that seem to match your requirements.

Your cruise/travel agent will handle all matters relevant to your booking, and off you go. You may even find a nice flower arrangement in your cabin on arrival, or a bottle of wine or champagne for dinner one night, courtesy of the agency.

Consider a cruise/travel agent as your business advisor, and not merely as a ticket agent. As a business advisor, he will (or should) have the latest information on changes of itinerary, cruise fares, fuel surcharges, discounts and any other related items. He will also be able to arrange insurance in case you have to cancel prior to sailing.

A number of cruise-only agencies have sprung up in the last two or three years. While most are highly reputable, some are geared to selling a limited number of cruise lines, and may try to persuade you in their favor. This is because they may be receiving special "overrides" on top of their normal commission. If you have already chosen a ship and cruise, be firm and book exactly what you want, or change agencies. In the U.S.A. look for a member of NACOA—the National Association of Cruise Only Agents.

Many traditional travel agencies

* Fully 95% of cruise bookings are made by cruise/travel agents.

now have a special cruise section, with a knowledgeable consultant in charge. A good agent will help you solve the problem of cabin choice, but be firm in the amount you want to pay, or you may end up with a larger and more costly cabin than you had intended.

Cruise Lines International Association (CLIA), an organization of more than two dozen member lines, does an admirable job in providing regular training seminars for cruise/travel agents in the U.S. Agencies approved by CLIA display a gold circular emblem on the door.

Reservation

Rule number one: plan ahead and book early. After you have made the principal selection of ship, cruise, sailing date and cabin category, you'll be asked to give the agency a deposit. This will generally vary between 10 per cent for long cruises and 20 per cent for short cruises, depending on individual line policy.

At the time of your initial reservation, you should also make any special dining request known, such as your seating preference, whether you want the smoking or non-smoking section, or any special dietary requirements (see p. 27–28). Prices quoted in cruise brochures are based on tariffs current at the time the brochures are printed. All cruise lines reserve the right to change those prices in the event of tariff increases, fluctuating rates of exchange, fuel surcharges or other costs which are beyond the control of the cruise lines.

Confirmation of your reservation and cruise fare will be sent to you by your cruise/travel agent. The balance is normally requested 45–60 days prior to departure, depending on individual line policy. For a late reservation, you have to make your payment in full as soon as space is confirmed. Shortly after full payment has been received by the line, your cruise ticket and airline ticket (if applicable) will be issued, together with baggage tags and other relevant items.

When it arrives, *check your ticket.* In these days of automation, it is prudent to make sure that the ship, date and cruise you paid for are correctly noted on your ticket. Also verify any connecting flight times.

Fares

Your fare includes ship transportation, landing and embarkation charges, cabin accommodation, all meals, entertainment and service on board. With few exceptions, it does not include alcoholic beverages, laundry, dry cleaning or valet services, shore excursions, meals ashore, tips, port charges, optional on-board activities such as skeet shooting, bingo or horse racing, casino gambling, or special features or conveniences not specified in the cruise line's brochure.

In order to calculate the total cost of the cruise you've chosen, read the brochure and, with the help of your cruise/travel agent, write down the costs involved. Here are the approximate prices for a typical seven-day cruise on a well-rated, medium-sized ship, based on an outside two-bed cabin:

Cruise fare	$1,500	
Port charges	$ 30	(if not included)
Air add-on	$ 100	(if not included)
Gratuities	$ 50	
	$1,680 per person	

Divide this amount by seven and you'll get an approximate cost of $240 per person, per day.

Looking at the fares listed in current cruise line brochures is only the starting point. Because overcapacity exists in certain cruise markets, discounting and special incentives are widespread. Therefore, it is wise to enlist the eyes and ears of a good cruise/travel agent and check out current discount offers.

One way of saving money is to book well ahead, so that you can profit from one of the many variations on the "super savers" theme. Another method is to reserve a cabin grade, but *not* a specific cabin, booked as "tba" (to be assigned). Some lines will accept this arrangement and may even upgrade you on embarkation day if all the cabins in your grade have been sold. It is useful to know that usually the first cabins to be sold out are those at minimum and maximum rates.

Another way of economizing is to wait for a "stand-by" cabin on sailing day or a short time before-hand. Some lines offer stand-by fares up to 30 days prior to sailing (60 days for Trans-Atlantic crossings). They may confirm your booking, but will assign a cabin (some lines even assign the ship) on the day of embarkation. Those who can go suitcase in hand to the dockside might even be lucky enough to get aboard at minimum rate (or even less) and be assigned a high-grade cabin cancelled at the last moment.

For cruises to areas where there is year-round sunshine, there is an "on" and an "off" season. Naturally, the best cruise buys will be found in the off season, while the on season commands the highest prices. Some lines, however, offer a "shoulder" season, which is somewhere between the on and off seasons. Peak season is during the Christmas and New Year vacation. Better check with your cruise/travel agent who will get you the best rate for the time you wish to go.

Many cruise lines offer highly reduced rates for the third and fourth persons sharing the same cabin as two full-fare adults. Individual policy varies widely from line to line, so ask your cruise/travel agent for current third/fourth person rates. On some selected sailings, they might even go free.

Most cruise fares are listed as "ppd"—per person, double occupancy. If you are single, and wish to occupy a double cabin on your own, you may have to pay a single supplement. This can vary between 0 and 100 per cent over the ppd fare.

However, many lines will let you share a cabin at the standard ppd rate. The line will find you a cabin partner of the same sex, and you can both save money by sharing. The line cannot, however, guarantee you'll like your partner, and may also specify which cabin categories are available for sharing.

For those wishing to take their children (or grandchildren) on a cruise, there are some excellent bargains available. For children under 12, most lines offer a very low rate or a 50 per cent reduction on the minimum fare, while others offer special youth fares to anyone up to age 17. It pays to compare the children's rate with that for third/fourth adult in the cabin. One way or the other, the price will be extremely favorable. Infants under two usually travel free. Many ships have cots available for infants.

Cancellations / Refunds

Cruise lines generally accept cancellations notified more than 30 days before sailing, but all of them charge full fare if a no-show occurs on sailing day, whatever the reason. Other cancellation fees range from 10 to 100 per cent, depending on the cruise line and the length of trip.

In the event of a cancellation with sufficient notice due to serious medical problems, a doctor's letter should be obtained and is usually regarded sympathetically by most cruise lines.

Insurance

It is highly recommended that you take out cruise cancellation insurance. This can be obtained from your cruise/travel agent for a nominal charge. If your present medical insurance does not extend to travel overseas, you should look into extra coverage for the duration of your cruise.

Baggage insurance is also strongly advised when air travel is involved. The airline responsibility is limited, and the cruise line has no responsibility at all, even when baggage transfer arrangements are part of your overall fare.

Port Charges

These are assessed by individual port authorities and are normally shown with the cruise rates for each itinerary. Port charges will be part of your final payment, although they can change at any time up to the day of embarkation.

Air / Sea Packages

Where your cruise fare includes a one-way or round-trip (return) air ticket, airline arrangements usually cannot be changed without paying considerably more toward the fare. This is because cruise lines often book space on aircraft on a special group basis in order to obtain the most favorable rates.

In Europe, air/sea packages generally start at a major metropolitan airport, while some include first-class rail travel to the airport from outlying districts. In the U.S., it is no longer necessary to depart from a major city, since many cruise lines will include connecting flights from small suburban airports as part of the whole package.

There are many variations on the air/sea theme, but all have the same advantage of offering passengers an all-inclusive price, even down to airport-to-ship transfers and port charges.

Some cruise lines offer the flexibility of jetting out to join a ship in one port and flying home from another. This is especially popular for Mediterranean, Trans-Canal and long cruises. Cunard Line even has a Trans-Atlantic program that lets you cruise one way and then fly back. They have taken the idea even further by allowing you to return on specially selected supersonic Concorde flights, for an additional charge.

Another advantage of the air/sea package is that you only have to check in your baggage once—at the departure airport—for even the baggage transfer from plane to ship is handled for you. This does not include intercontinental fly/cruises, where you must claim your baggage at the airport on arrival in order to clear customs.

You may be able to hold an "open" return ticket, allowing you to make a pre- or post-cruise stopover. This depends on the type of contract that exists between a cruise line and its airline partner. Usually, however, you have no stop-overs en route nor can you even change flights. Many cruise lines book group space in order to benefit from special rates and in these cases you must abide by the restrictions placed on this kind of ticket by the airline concerned.

When the price of an air/sea package is all-inclusive, it is often presented as "free air" in publicity and advertising material. Of course, there is no such thing as a free air ticket—it is simply hidden in the overall cruise fare.

Some lines, instead of increasing their rates to include such "free air" packages, offer a subsidized fare that is attractive enough to get you interested in taking the cruise. Or if you live near the port and don't need an airline ticket, you get a reduction.

However, air tickets are not always included. Some lines simply don't believe in increasing their rates to cover "free air" or wish to avoid subsidizing airline tickets. These are, for the most part, upmarket lines that operate long distance cruises to some of the more exotic destinations.

Sail 'n' Stay Programs

A reasonably new concept in the cruise industry is that of going to a specific destination by ship, enjoying the cruise on the way. You then disembark (on an island in the Caribbean or South Pacific, for example) and stay a week or two. When the ship makes its return weekly or bi-weekly call, you get back on board for the remainder of the cruise.

The idea has been put to good use by an increasing number of cruise lines in conjunction with hotel and resort properties, adding yet another dimension to the cruise experience.

Sail 'n' Stay programs are on the increase as cruise lines diversify their offerings to cater to passengers who would like to have the best of both worlds.

It is also likely that cruise lines currently operating three- and four-day cruises to the Bahamas will build properties on Bahamian out islands, so that their passengers can extend their short cruise into a sail 'n' stay vacation.

The sail 'n' stay concept has yet to take hold in the Mediterranean market, although cruise vacation add-ons at resort or major city hotels are becoming increasingly popular.

Before You Go

Baggage

There is normally no limit to the amount of personal baggage allowed on board cruise ships, but closet space is limited, so take only those items that you intend to use. Allow some extra space for purchases during the cruise. Towels, soap and shower caps are provided on board.

It is important that all baggage be properly marked or tagged with the owner's name, ship, cabin number, sailing date and port of embarkation. Baggage tags will be provided by the cruise line along with your ticket. Baggage transfers from airport to ship are smooth and problem-free when handled by the cruise line.

Liability for loss or damage to baggage is contained in the passenger contract. If you are not adequately covered, it is advisable to take out insurance for this purpose. The policy should extend from the date of departure until two or three days after your return home. Coverage can be obtained from your cruise/travel agent or insurance agent.

Children

Yes, you *can* take children on a cruise. In fact, once you get them aboard you'll hardly see them at all, if you choose the right ship and cruise. Whether you have to share a cabin with them or whether they have their own separate, but adjoining, cabin, there's plenty to keep them occupied. If you do share a cabin with them, try to select one that's fairly spacious, even if it means upgrading.

A cruise for children is an educational experience. They'll tour the Bridge, meet senior officers, learn about navigation, radar and communications equipment and how the ship operates. They'll be exposed to different environments, experience many types of foods, travel to and explore new places and participate in any number of exciting activities.

On family-oriented ships, there will be a children's and teens' counselor who will run a very special program that is off-limits to adults. Most are designed to run simultaneously with adult programs.

For those who cruise with very

small children, baby-sitting may be available (see p. 49).

Cruise ships and lines that cater to families with children usually say so in their brochures. Also have a glance at the Pick-a-Ship chart on p. 102, for those vessels labeled as FAM under the heading Ambiance.

Cruise lines best geared to families with children include: Admiral Cruises, American Hawaii Cruises, CTC Lines, P&O, Canberra Cruises, Carnival Cruise Lines, Commodore Cruise Line, Cunard Line (the QE2 is especially well equipped to handle young children, with full-time nurses and real English nannies), Delta Queen Steamboat Company, Norwegian Cruise Line, Premier Cruise Lines, Royal Caribbean Cruise Line, SeaEscape.

Clothing

First, if you think you might not wear it, don't take it. Cabins on most ships are small, and closet space is at a premium. Unless you are going on an extended cruise, keep your luggage to a minimum. Most airlines have a limit of two suitcases at check-in or 44 pounds per person in tourist class. One large suitcase per person, plus a tote bag or carry-all for small items and toiletries is recommended.

For cruises to the Caribbean, South Pacific or other tropical areas, where the weather at any time of the year is warm to hot, with high humidity, casual wear should include plenty of light-weight, open-weave cottons and other natural fibers. Synthetic materials do not "breathe" as well and tend to retain heat. Take a light-weight sweater or two for ship-board wear in the evenings, when the air-conditioning will seem even more powerful after a day in the sun.

The same is true for cruises to the Mediterranean, Greek Isles or North Africa, although there will be little or no humidity for most of the year. Certain areas may be dusty, as well as dry. In these latitudes the weather can be changeable and rather cool in the evenings from October to March, so take along some extra sweaters.

On cruises to Alaska, the North Cape or the Norwegian Fjords, you'll need warm comfortable clothing, plus a raincoat or parka for the northernmost port calls. Cruises to Alaska and the Land of the Midnight Sun are only offered during the peak summer months, when the temperatures are pleasant and the weather is less likely to be inclement. Unless you are going to northern ports such as Leningrad during winter, you won't need your thermal underwear. However, you will need it if you are taking an adventure cruise to the Antarctic Peninsula or through the Northwest Passage. And overcoats, too.

In the Far East, clothing will depend on the season and time of year. The cruise information package that accompanies your tickets will give sensible recommendations.

For cruises that start in the depths of winter from a northern port (New York or Southampton, for example) and cruise south to find the sun, you will need to have light-weight cottons for southern wear, plus a few sweaters for the trip south.

There *are* rainstorms in the tropics. They are infrequent and don't last long, but they can give you a good soaking, so take some inexpensive, light-weight rainwear for shore excursions.

If you are going to a destination with a strong religious tradition such as Venezuela, Haiti, Dominican Republic, Colombia and many countries in the Far East, remember that the people may take offense at bare shoulders or shorts.

Aboard ship, dress rules are relaxed during the daytime, but evening wear is tasteful. Men should take a blazer or sports jacket and some ties for the dining room and for anytime the program states "informal". Trans-Atlantic passengers will feel out of place in casual clothing, so they should pack more elegant apparel.

If you are athletic, pack a tracksuit and/or shorts and top for the gymnasium. The ladies should take a leotard or two and tights for aerobics classes.

For the formal nights (there are usually two for every seven days at sea), ladies should wear their best long evening gown, elegant cocktail dress or smart pants suit. Gentlemen are expected to wear either a tuxedo (dinner jacket) or dark business suit. These "rules" are less rigid on short and moderately priced cruises.

Since there is normally a Masquerade Night on each cruise, you may wish to take along a costume. Or, you can create something entirely original on board out of a range of materials that most ships supply. A member of the Cruise Staff may help you, and there will most likely be a large display board full of photographs of past entries. Prizes are given for the most creative and original costume made on board.

No matter where in the world you are cruising, comfortable low- or flat-heeled shoes are a *must* for women aboard ship or ashore, except perhaps for the more formal nights aboard.

Light, airy walking shoes are by far the best. If you are cruising to the Caribbean or South Pacific and you are not used to the heat and high humidity, you may find your ankles swelling easily. In this case, tight-fitting shoes are definitely not recommended. For walking on deck or playing deck sports, rubber soles are best.

Customs

U.S.A.

This information, drawn from extensive regulations, should be used for general guidance only. For questions of interpretation or current practice, the following is not binding, and the opinion of a customs agent should be sought.

Returning residents. If you are a permanent resident of the U.S., you are allowed an exemption of a retail value of U.S.$400-worth of articles acquired outside the country*, providing you have been abroad at least 48 hours and have not claimed a duty-free exemption within 30 days.

Articles you acquire in excess of the U.S.$400 exemption, if under a maximum value of $1000, will be assessed at a flat duty rate of 10 per cent. Above $1000 in value, duty is assessed at the exact rate for the category of item brought in. Everything you have acquired abroad is subject to duty, including items which are worn or used. The goods must accompany you to qualify for exemption, and anything shipped home is subject to duty, with the exception of gifts worth under $50, based on the "fair retail value in the country of shipment". The outside of any gift package mailed to the U.S. should be clearly marked "unsolicited gift" and show the sender's name, the nature and value of the gift and the relationship of the recipient to you.

Gifts mailed in this manner need not be included in your customs declaration upon arrival in the U.S. Note, however, that "unsolicited gift" exemptions will not apply to items sent by you to yourself or to persons traveling with you.

Although it is permitted to send several separate gifts to the same person, a group of articles cannot be split into several shipments (for example, a creamer in one parcel and a sugar bowl in another), and still qualify for the exemption. If you are mailing items, you should arrange to have these sent one parcel per day, if addressed to the same person. Tobacco products, alcohol and perfumes containing alcohol cannot be included in gift packages; nor can $50 be applied as a duty-free deduction in a parcel valued for more than that.

No more than one U.S. quart of alcoholic beverages can be included in your $400 duty-free exemption for goods that accompany you, and then only if you are 21 years or older. Having reached that age, you can also bring in 100 cigars (not Cuban) and 200 cigarettes (one carton). Note, however, that some states have restrictions on the amount of cigarettes and liquor that residents can bring back. Families from one household traveling together may pool their exemptions.

Fruits, vegetables, plants, seeds, meats and pets must meet U.S. Department of Agriculture or Public Health Service requirements. Wildlife products such as furs, crocodile or alligator skins, require special documentation to enter the U.S.

On future trips abroad, remember to register dutiable items such as cameras, before departure. It is a simple step and avoids any discussion on returning about paying duty

*US$800 from the U.S. Virgin Islands including four liters (six quart bottles) of alcohol, providing one of them is Virgin Islands rum.

on "prior possessions". Registration can be done at local customs houses in major cities and ports, or at the airport, and is valid for life.

Non-residents. You are allowed to import into the U.S. for personal use, free of duty, 50 cigars or 200 cigarettes or 3 pounds of tobacco, plus one U.S. quart of alcoholic beverages (21 years or older). In addition, non-residents (including minors) are allowed to import gifts free of duty not exceeding U.S.$100 in value, provided that your stay in the U.S. is 72 hours or longer, and that you have not claimed the $100 gift exemption within the preceding six months.

Destination Europe

Customs regulations for all ports vary considerably from country to country. You are best advised to consult your travel agents or the Purser on board for up-to-date information on current allowances and regulations. These are usually liberal for cruise passengers.

Documents

A passport is the most practical proof of citizenship and identification. Although it is not required on all cruises, take it along, if you have one. Voter's registration cards and driver's licenses are acceptable normally but not considered valid proof of citizenship.

Non-U.S. citizens taking a cruise from an American port must have a valid B-2 multiple-entry (visitor's visa) stamped in their passports, in order to return to the U.S.

If you are cruising to areas other than the Bahamas, Bermuda, the Caribbean, Alaska, Hawaii or Canada, and most of Europe, you may need a tourist visa. Your cruise/travel agent or the cruise line will advise you and provide up-to-date information.

On cruises to the Orient particularly, but also other destinations in the Middle East and Africa, you may be required to hand in your passport at the Purser's Office prior to landing. This will enable the customs and immigration officials to "clear" the ship as soon as possible after arrival, and is standard. Your passports will be returned when the ship departs.

Medications

If you are planning a cruise that takes you away from your home country, make sure that you take along a supply of any medicines that you need. In many foreign countries it may be difficult or even impossible to find certain medications. Others may be sold under different brand names.

Those going on long cruises should ask their doctor for names of alternatives, should the medicine they are taking not be available.

The pharmacy aboard ship will stock certain standard remedies, but again, don't expect the ship to have a supply of unusual or obscure medicines.

Money Matters

Most cruise ships deal in U.S. dollars primarily, but also in British pounds, German marks or Australian dollars, depending on ship and location. For on-board expenses and transactions, major credit cards and traveler's checks are widely accepted, but not all lines take personal checks.

Many ships now allow passengers to sign for drinks at the bar, wine at meals and assorted other services. On some ships a convenient way to settle expenses is to set up a ship-board credit prior to sailing. This is especially useful on long voyages. Some cruise lines are now introducing their own credit cards or credit "passports", enabling you to charge "on-board" expenses, and even the cruise itself, to the card.

Pets

Pets are not normally carried by cruise ships, except on regular scheduled Trans-Atlantic services, such as on the *QE2*, which has 16 air-conditioned kennels (and even a British lamp post), cat containers, plus several special cages for birds.

Photography

It is hard to find any situation more ideal for photography than a cruise. Through your photographs you can relive your cruise and share your memories with others not so fortunate.

It is best to use low-speed film in tropical areas such as the Caribbean or South Pacific, as high-speed film is easily damaged by heat; low-speed film is less sensitive. Take plenty of film with you; standard sizes will be available in the ship's shop, although the selection will be limited. If you must purchase film during a port visit, try to buy from a store that is air-conditioned and check the expiry date on the box.

Keep your film as cool as possible, as the latent image on exposed film is fragile and easily affected by heat. There will be professional photographers on board who may develop your film for you, for a fee, of course.

When taking photographs at the various ports of call, respect the wishes of the local inhabitants. Ask permission to photograph someone close-up. Most will smile and tell you to carry on. But some people are superstitious or truly afraid of having their picture taken and will shy away from you quickly. Don't press the point.

Ship-to-Shore Communication

Each ship has a designated, internationally recognized call sign, which is a combination of several letters and digits and can be obtained from the cruise line. For each of the ships listed in Part Two of this book, the radio call sign is given, except for the six ships not yet in service. To receive a call during your cruise, simply give the call sign and name of the ship to those concerned before you leave. (See also p. 50.)

Tipping (Gratuities)

Many people find the whole question of tipping awkward and embarrassing. Use the information given here as a guideline, and add your own good judgement.

On some ships, suggestions regarding tips are subtly given, while on others, Cruise Directors sometimes get carried away and are far too dictatorial.

The industry standard for cruises is roughly as follows:

- Dining room waiter $2.50–3 per day, per person
- Busboy $1.50–2 per day, per person
- Cabin steward/stewardess $2.50–3 per day, per person

Any other gratuities should be given according to services rendered, just as in any first-class restaurant or hotel, for example to the Maître d', wine waiter, barman. On some ships, the barman's tip is added at once to your bar check when you sign.

Gratuities are customarily given on the last evening of a cruise of up to 14 days duration. For cruises of more than 14 days, you normally extend one half of the tip at the mid-point of the cruise and the remainder on your last evening at sea.

Envelopes for tipping will be available throughout the cruise from the Purser's Office, where you can also ask for advice on tipping.

Vaccinations

Vaccination requirements vary from country to country. Check with your cruise/travel agent or the cruise line for accurate up-to-the-minute information.

Work

Should you need to work while on board, secretarial help and limited office facilities may be available, together with recording equipment, film and slide projectors, screens and blackboards. Advance notice is advisable, or talk with the Purser when you get on board. Larger ships will be able to offer more office facilities and services than smaller vessels, of course.

Life Aboard

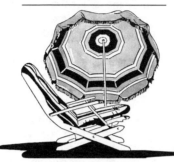

Air-Conditioning. On all modern cruise ships, cabin temperature is regulated by individually controlled thermostats, so it can be adjusted to your liking. The temperature in the public rooms is controlled automatically. On board, the air-conditioning is normally kept much cooler than you may be accustomed to, so don't forget a sweater or scarf.

Baby-Sitting. On many ships, cabin stewards, stewardesses and other staff members may be available as sitters for an hourly charge. Make arrangements at the Purser's Office.

Beauty Salon/Barber Shop. It is advisable to make any appointments for the beauty salon or barber shop as soon after boarding as possible, especially on cruises of short duration. Appointment times fill up rapidly, particularly before social evenings. Charges are comparable to those ashore. Hours of opening will be posted at the salon, and listed in the *Daily Program.*

Bridge Visits. Check the *Daily Program* for announcements of visits to the Bridge, for which appointment cards can be obtained from the Purser's Office or Cruise Staff Office. On some ships, Bridge visits are not allowed for reasons of security.

Cashless Cruising. On many ships, you can now cruise cash-free and settle your account with one easy payment. Often this is arranged by making an imprint of a credit card prior to departure, permitting you to sign for everything. Or you can pay by cash at the end of the cruise.

On some ships, it is no longer possible to pay cash at the bar, or in the shop aboard.

Before the end of the cruise, a detailed statement will be delivered to your cabin. Avoid lines by using a credit card for express check out.

Casino. A large number of vessels now feature a "full" casino, where blackjack, roulette and craps are played. Casino chips and change for the slot machines can be obtained from the cash booth in the casino. Children under 18 years of age are not allowed in the casino.

The ship's casino is closed in port due to international customs regulations; the taking of photographs in the casino is forbidden.

Communications. When the ship is at sea, you can call from your cabin (or the ship's Radio Room) to anywhere in the world: by radio-telephone (where a slight to moderate background noise might be noticed) or by satellite (which is as clear as your own home phone). Satellite calls are more expensive, but they are usually completed without delay. You can also call any other cabin or part of the ship. When the ship is in port you must use the local telephone facilities (often at the local post office).

Telegrams and telexes are accepted at the Purser's Office or Radio Room for transmission when the ship is at sea.

Daily Program. The *Daily Program* contains a list of the day's entertainment and social events. The publication covering the next day's events is normally delivered to your cabin in the evening, before you retire. It is important to read it carefully, so that you will know what, when and where things are happening on board. If you lose your *Daily Program,* you can obtain another from the Purser's Office or your cabin steward.

Deck Chairs. Deck chairs and cushions are available, free of charge on most ships, from the duty deck steward. Specific locations cannot normally be reserved, except on those ships where a charge is made, or by arrangement with the deck steward.

Disembarkation. During the final part of your cruise, the Cruise Director will give an informal talk on customs, immigration and disembarkation (sometimes called debarkation) procedures. At least one member of each family should attend this important talk. This will help simplify and speed up the procedure and avoid confusion at arrival time.

The night before your ship reaches its final destination (in most cases this will be a return to the port you sailed from) you will be given a customs form to fill out. Any duty-free items bought from the shop on board must be included in your allowance, so save the receipts in case a customs officer wishes to see them.

The night before arrival, your main baggage should be packed and placed outside your cabin on retiring or before 4 a.m. It will be collected, placed in a central baggage area and off-loaded on arrival. Remember to leave out any fragile items and liquor, together with the clothes you intend to wear for disembarkation and onward travel. Anything left in your cabin at this point will be considered hand baggage and has to be hand-carried off when you disembark.

Before leaving the ship, remember to claim any items you may have placed in the ship's safety deposit boxes and leave your cabin key in your cabin. Passengers cannot proceed ashore until all baggage has been off-loaded, and customs and/or immigration inspections or pre-inspections have been carried out on board.

In most ports, this normally takes about two to three hours from time of arrival. Therefore, do not plan to have people meet you when the ship arrives. They will not be allowed to board, and you can't get off until all formalities have been completed. Also, figure it will take at least three hours from time of arrival to make a connecting flight or other transportation arrangement.

Listen for announcements regarding disembarkation procedures and do not crowd the main disembarkation or gangway/lobby areas. Once off the ship, you will need to identify your baggage at pierside, before going through any main or secondary customs inspections. (Customs inspections or delay are usually minimal.) Porters will be available to assist you.

Drug Store. On some ships, there may be a separate drug store in which a fairly extensive range of standard items will be available, while on others the drug store will be a small section of the ship's main gift shop. Opening hours will be posted at the store and given in the *Daily Program.*

Electric Current. Most ships operating in U.S. waters have standard American 110 AC current and sockets. The newer and refurbished ships have both 110- and 220-volt AC outlets. A few older vessels may have 220-volt DC outlets, but transformers/converters are available.

Normally, electrical appliances may only be used if they operate on AC. Check with your cabin steward or stewardess before plugging in anything more powerful than an electric razor (such as a high-wattage hair dryer), just to make sure the cabin's circuitry can handle the load.

Engine Room. On virtually all passenger ships, the engine room is off-limits to passengers, and visits are not allowed, for insurance and security reasons.

On some ships, a technical information leaflet may be available from the Purser's Office. For more specific or detailed information, contact a member of the ship's engineering staff via the Purser's Office.

———•••———

Gift Shops. The gift shop/boutique/drug store provides a selection of souvenirs, gifts, toiletries and duty-free items, as well as a basic stock of essentials. Duty-free items —perfumes, watches, etc.,—will be very competitively priced, and may save you the hassle of shopping ashore. Opening hours will be posted at the store and given in the *Daily Program.*

Health and Fitness Facilities. Depending on the size of the ship, health and fitness facilities may include all or one or more of the following: gymnasium, weight room, sauna, solarium, exercise classes, jogging track, parcours, massage, swimming pool(s), whirlpool baths, nutrition lectures, herbal body wraps and scuba and snorkel instruction. For more information, check with your cruise/travel agent, or, when on board, contact the Cruise Director or Purser's Office.

Launch Service. Enclosed motor launches are used on those occasions when your cruise ship is unable to berth at a port or island. In such cases, a regular launch (tender) service operates between ship and shore for the duration of the port call. Details of the launch service will be given in the *Daily Program* and announced over the ship's P.A. system.

Laundrette. On some ships there are self-service laundrettes, equipped with washers, dryers and ironing facilities, all at no charge to the passenger. Supervisory staff may be available to assist you. (For laundry and dry-cleaning see Valet Service, p. 56.)

Library. Most cruise ships have a library offering a large selection of books, reference material and periodicals. A small deposit (refundable on return of the book) is often required should you wish to borrow a book from the library.

On many ships, the library is also the place to request games such as scrabble, backgammon and chess.

Lifeboat Drill. Safety at sea is the number one consideration of all members of the ship's crew. For any evacuation procedure to be totally effective and efficient, passengers must know precisely where to go in the unlikely event that an emergency arises. For this reason, and to acquaint passengers with general safety procedures, a lifeboat drill is held during the cruise. According to international maritime law, this must take place within 24 hours of embarkation.

There have been few incidents requiring the evacuation of passengers in past years. Indeed, travel by ship is one of the safest means of transportation. Even so, it cannot be stressed too strongly that attendance at lifeboat drill is not only required by the Captain, but also makes sense. You must know your boat station in the event of an emergency requiring evacuation of the vessel.

If others are lighthearted about the drill, don't let it affect your seriousness of purpose. Note your exit and escape pathways and learn how to put on your lifejacket correctly. The 20 minutes the drill takes is a good investment in playing safe.

Lifejackets will be found in your cabin. Instructions to get to your boat station will be on the back of your cabin or bathroom door.

Lost Property. Contact the Purser's Office immediately if you lose or find something on the ship. Notices are also posted on the bulletin boards.

Mail. You can buy stamps and post letters on board most ships. Some ships use the postal privileges and stamps of their flag of registration and others buy local stamps at the next port of call. Mail is usually taken ashore by the ship's port agent just before the ship sails for the next port.

Massage. Make your appointments for massage as soon as possible after boarding, in order to get a time of your choice. Larger ships have more staff, and therefore more flexibility in appointment times.

On some ships, massage service may be available in your cabin, if it is large enough to accommodate a portable massage table.

Medical Services (see also p. 46). A doctor and nursing staff are aboard ship at all times. Usually there is a fully equipped hospital in miniature. Standard fees are charged for treatment. Any existing health problems requiring treatment on board must be reported at the time of booking.

Movies. On most cruise ships, a movie theater is an essential part of the ship's public-room facilities. The movies are recent, selected often by the Cruise Director from a film or video leasing service.

Some recently built or modified ships have replaced or supplemented the movie theater with television sets in each cabin. News and events filmed on board are broadcast, as well as video movie features.

News and Sports Bulletins. The news and sports results are reported in the ship's newspaper or placed on the bulletin board, which is normally located near the Purser's Office or in the Library. For any sports results not listed, enquire at the Purser's Office, which may be able to obtain the results for you.

Photographs. Professional photographers are on board ship to take pictures of passengers throughout the cruise, including their arrival on the ship. They will also cover all the main events and major social functions such as the Captain's Cocktail Party.

All photographs can be viewed without any obligation to purchase. They will be displayed on photo boards either in the main foyer, or in a separate Photo Gallery. The color and quality of these pictures are usually excellent, and they are popular souvenirs of the trip. Duplicates may be obtained even after your cruise, from the shore-based headquarters of the photographic concessionaire.

Postcards and Writing Paper.
These are available either from the Writing Room, Library, Purser's Office or from your room steward upon request.

Purser's Office. Centrally located, this is the nerve center of the ship for general on-board information and problems. Opening hours are posted outside the office and given in the *Daily Program.* On some ships the Purser's Office is open 24 hours a day.

Religious Services. Interdenominational services are conducted on board, usually by the Captain or Staff Captain. A few older ships have a small private chapel. Sometimes denominational services are also offered by specially invited or fellow-passenger members of the clergy.

Room Service. Beverages and snacks are available at most hours. Liquor is normally limited to the hours when the ship's bars are open. Your room steward will advise you of the range of services that are offered.

Safety Aboard. Passenger safety is a high priority for all cruise lines. Crew members attend frequent emergency drills, lifeboat equipment is regularly tested, and fire-detection devices, alarm and fire-fighting systems are checked throughout the ship. If you spot fire or smoke, use the nearest fire alarm box, alert a member of staff or telephone the Bridge.

Sailing Time. In each port of call, the ship's sailing and all-aboard times will be posted at the gangway. The all-aboard time is usually half an hour before sailing (ships cannot wait for individual passengers who are delayed). On some ships, you will be given an identification card to be handed in at the gangway when you return from your visit ashore.

Sauna. Many ships offer a sauna, usually small and compact, occasionally unisex. Sometimes there is a small charge for its use, especially when combined with a massage. Towels are available at the sauna and there is a small changing area. Opening times will be posted at the sauna and in the information material in your cabin. Reservations are not necessary.

Seasickness. It's somewhat rare these days, even in rough weather. Ships have stabilizers—large underwater "fins" projecting from each side of the hull—to counteract any rolling motion. Nevertheless, you could be one of those who develop symptoms—anything from slight nausea or discomfort to actual vomiting. What do you do?

Seasickness is more than a state of mind. It has real physical causes, specifically an imbalance of a mechanism in the inner ear. The human body and brain are accustomed to motions of walking or riding on a non-moving surface. To have the surface itself move in another direction results in a signal to the brain that something's wrong.

Both old-time sailors and modern physicians have their own remedies, and you can take your choice or try them all:

1. When the first movement of the ship is noticed, get out on deck and start walking back and forth. The knees, which are a form of stabilizer for the human body, will start getting their feel of balance and counteraction. In other words, you'll be "getting your sea legs".

2. While on deck, focus your attention on a steady point, such as the horizon.

3. Get the breeze into your face, and suck on an orange or lemon if you have a queasy stomach.

4. Eat lightly. Don't make the mistake of thinking a heavy meal will keep your stomach well anchored. It won't.

5. A recommended preventive for seasickness is ginger in powder form. (Half a teaspoon, mixed in a glass of warm water or milk, drink before sailing.) It supposedly settles any stomach for a period of up to eight hours.

6. On board, Dramamine will be available in tablet form.

7. Now in widespread use is "the patch". This is Transderm V, available on prescription. It's like a small sticking plaster you put behind your ear, almost out of sight. For 72 hours it releases a minute quantity of a drug into the system which counteracts seasickness and nau-

sea. Any side effects are relatively harmless, but check with your physician or the ship's doctor.

8. If you are really in distress, the ship's doctor has an injection certain to solve all problems of discomfort. It might make you drowsy as well, but probably the last thing on your mind in any case would be staying awake at the ship's movie.

All of this being said, bear in mind that in addition to those stabilizers on the hull, the vast majority of cruises occur in warm, calm waters and most cruise ships spend a good deal of time along the coast or pull into port every day or two. The odds are all in your favor.

Security. All cabins are provided with keys, and it is recommended that you keep your cabin locked at all times when you are not there. Cruise lines are not responsible for money or valuables left in cabins and recommend you use a safety deposit box at the Purser's Office (see p. 56).

You will be issued a personal boarding pass when you embark. This serves as identification and must be shown at the gangway for security purposes each time you board or reboard the ship. If you misplace or lose it, you'll need to let the Purser's Office know immediately. The system of boarding passes is one of many ways in which cruise lines ensure the safety of their passengers.

Sports Facilities. Depending on their size, ships will offer a variety of on-board sports facilities. These will include some of the following: badminton, basketball practice area, golf driving cage, horseshoes, jogging track, miniature putting green, paddle tennis, quoits, ring toss, shuffleboard, skeet shooting, squash (rarely), table tennis, volleyball. Tournaments are normally arranged by the Sports Director or cruise staff. Check the *Daily Program* for times.

Sun. If your cruise takes you to the sun, remember that the closer you get to the Equator, the more potent and penetrating will be the rays. The rays are most harmful between noon and 2 p.m., when the sun is directly overhead.

Those taking short cruises to the Bahamas, the Caribbean or Mexico should beware of trying to get the best possible tan in a short space of time.

Use a protective sun cream in the 12 to 15 factor range, and re-apply it every time you go for a swim or soak in the pool or ocean. Start with only 15 minutes exposure at a time and gradually work your way up to an hour or so. It is far better to go home with a suntan than sunburn. If you do overdo it, seek immediate help from the ship's doctor, who is used to handling such cases, regrettably.

Swimming Pools. Depending on the cruise ship, there will be indoor or outdoor swimming pools aboard. They may be closed in port due to local health regulations and/or

cleaning. Hours of opening will be listed in the *Daily Program.* Diving is not normally allowed, since pools are shallow. Parents with young children should note that swimming pools on many ships are not supervised.

———••———

Twenty-Four-Hour Clock. On many European-owned ships, the twenty-four-hour clock is standard, in keeping with the practicality of its use in international travel. In spite of the initial strangeness of this system of time-telling, you will soon find it not only simple to use, but far less likely to lead to confusion.

Up to midday, the hours are shown as 0100–1200. Thereafter they go from 1300 to 2400. Thus, 1400 is 2 p.m., 1520 means 3.20 p.m., and so on.

———••———

Valet Service. This is available through your room steward or stewardess, and, depending on your cruise ship, can include dry-cleaning and pressing, or laundry only. For a list of charges, see your room steward or stewardess.

Valuables. A small number of ships have a lock box built into each cabin. However, items of special value should be kept in a safety deposit box available at the Purser's Office. Access to your valuables during the cruise is convenient and uncomplicated.

Visitors. Passes for visitors must be arranged in advance, preferably at the time of booking. Announcements will be made when it is time for all visitors to proceed ashore.

----•••----

Wine and Liquor. The cost of drinks on board ship is lower than on land. This is because ships have access to duty-free liquor. Drinks may be ordered in the dining room, at any of the ship's bars or from room service.

In the dining room, you can order wine with your meals from an extensive and reasonably priced wine list. If you like wine with your dinner, try to place your order at lunch time, as wine waiters are always at their busiest at the evening meal.

On some ships, a duty-free sales point will allow you to purchase wine and liquor for personal consumption in your cabin. Passengers are not normally permitted to bring this into the dining room or other public rooms, nor indeed any duty-free wine or liquor purchased in port. These regulations are naturally made to protect bar sales, which are a substantial source of on-board revenue for the cruise line.

Nautical Notes

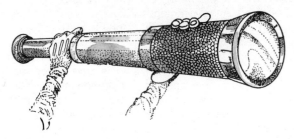

The world of ships is a world of its own. And associated with it is a whole language and culture which can sometimes be confusing—but always fascinating—to the newcomer. Here are a few tidbits of nautical information which may contribute to the pleasure of your cruise.

Rules of the Road

As the largest moving objects made by man, ships are subject to stringent international regulations. They must keep to the right in shipping lanes, and pass on the right (with certain exceptions). When circumstances are in doubt or shipping lanes crowded, ships often use their whistles, in the same way a car driver uses directional signals to show which way he will turn. When a ship passes another, one blast on the whistle means he is turning to starbóard (right). Two blasts means a turn to port (left). The other vessel acknowledges by repeating the same signal.

Ships also carry navigational running lights at night—green for starboard, red for port. In addition, two white lights are carried on the masts, the forward one lower than the aft.

Flags and pennants form another part of a ship's communication facilities and are displayed for identification purposes. Every time a country is visited, its national flag is shown. While entering and leaving a port, the ship flies a blue and yellow flag with vertical stripes to request a pilot, while a half red, half white flag (divided vertically) indicates that a pilot is ón board. Cruise lines and other passenger shipping lines also display their own "house" flag, proudly fluttering from the ship's main mast.

In the shipping industry, a ship's funnel or smokestack is another means of identification, each line having its own funnel design and colour scheme serving as a trademark or logo. The size, height and number of funnels were points worth advertising at the turn of the century. Most ocean liners of the time had four funnels and were known as "four-stackers".

In today's cruise industry, perhaps the most distinctive funnel design belongs to the gleaming white ships in the Royal Caribbean Cruise Line fleet, whose four vessels each have a nightclub/lounge perched part way up the stack itself, making the ships instantly identifiable. The view from one of these is outstanding.

But, aside from maritime law, there are customs at sea even more numerous, many of them older than any law. And superstition has always been an important element, as in this example quoted in the British *Admiralty Manual of Seamanship:* "The custom of breaking a bottle of wine over the stem of a ship when being launched originates from the old practice of toasting prosperity to a ship in a silver goblet of wine, which was then cast into the sea in order to prevent a toast of ill intent being drunk from the same cup. This practice proved too expensive and so was replaced in 1690 by the breaking of a bottle of wine over the stem."

On the Watch

A ship's working day is composed of six four-hour time periods called "watches". A complement of officers and crew in theory work the same watch round the clock— 4 hours on, followed by 8 hours off during any given 24-hour period.

To avoid permanently working the identical hours day after day, one of the four-hour time periods is split further into first and second "dog" watches of two hours each, as follows:

0000–0400 hours: midwatch
0400–0800 hours: morning watch
0800–1200 hours: forenoon watch
1200–1600 hours: afternoon watch
1600–1800 hours: first dog watch
1800–2000 hours: second dog watch
2000–2400 hours: evening watch

On board ship, time is traditionally recorded by the striking of bells to reflect the state of the watch. Each bell represents a half hour of time on watch and the duty is ended when 8 bells sound at midnight, 0400, 0800, 1200, etc.

Wind Speeds

A navigational announcement to passengers is normally made once or twice daily, giving the ship's position, temperature and weather information. You might be confused by the numbering system for wind velocity. The 12 velocities, known as "force" on the Beaufort scale, are as follows:

Force	Speed	Description
0	2 mph	calm
1	7 mph	light wind
2	11 mph	light breeze
3	16 mph	gentle breeze
4	20 mph	moderate breeze
5	25 mph	fresh breeze
6	30 mph	strong breeze
7	35 mph	moderate gale
8	45 mph	fresh gale
9	50 mph	strong gale
10	60 mph	whole gale
11	70 mph	storm
12	80 mph	hurricane

The Challenge of the North Atlantic

No award has inspired as much rivalry between shipping lines as the coveted Blue Riband, given to the liner making the fastest Trans-Atlantic crossing. Indeed, possession of the Blue Riband became a source of national pride.

Already in the late 1800s references to the award were recorded, but the first real mention was on August 1, 1900, when the *Illustrated London News* reported that the Blue Riband (blue ribbon) had been won by the Hamburg America Line passenger ship *Deutschland*.

Although the great passenger liners of the North Atlantic raced to beat the speed record, there was no material award until 1935, when the late Harold K. Hales, a Member of the British Parliament, offered a huge silver challenge trophy to the steamship line that established claim to the Blue Riband. So important did speed become, that national newspapers carried daily records of distance steamed by major ships, as well as the duration of each Trans-Atlantic crossing. Average speeds, although not revealed, were easily calculated from the figures provided.

Naturally the distance covered can vary with each crossing of the Atlantic. Since 1900 the shortest distance recorded for Blue Riband purposes was 2,807 nautical miles, between Sandy Hook and Queenstown, while the longest distance was 3,199 nautical miles, between Ambrose Light and Cherbourg. Since 1900, 12 ships have held the record westbound, and ten eastbound.

Some of the most illustrious passenger ships are listed among the holders of this prestigious award. For 22 years the Blue Riband was held by Cunard Line's *Mauretania,* passing briefly in 1929 to Germany's *Bremen* and in 1930 to that country's *Europa*. In 1933 the Italian *Rex* took over, only to lose it two years later to France's *Normandie*. Then came the *Queen Mary* to vie with the *Normandie*. Both kept the award for a year each, in 1936 and 1937, respectively, until in 1938 Cunard firmly held it with the *Queen Mary*. In 1952, the prize was taken by the new *United States*.

As current holder, the *United States* has the distinction of being the fastest liner ever to win the Blue Riband. Between July 3 and 7, 1952, during an eastbound crossing from Ambrose to Bishop Rock, an average speed of 35.59 knots was recorded, although it is claimed that in the process of achieving that speed mechanical damage was caused which made any repeat performance virtually out of the question.

No major passenger ship has been built since the early 1950s to challenge the speed record of the *United States,* although with the re-engining of Cunard's *QE2,* it is conceivable that she could someday attempt a "Blue Riband" crossing.

Ship Talk

Ships and the sea have their own special vocabulary, as shown below:

Abeam—off the side of the ship, at a right angle to its length.

Aft—near, toward or in the rear of the ship.

Alleyway—a passageway or corridor.

Amidships—in or toward the middle of the ship; the longitudinal center portion of the ship.

Astern—at or toward the stern (back) of the ship.

Backwash—motion in the water caused by the propeller(s) moving in a reverse (astern) direction.

Bar—sandbar, usually caused by tidal or current conditions near the shore.

Beam—width of the ship between its two sides at the widest point.

Bearing—compass direction, expressed in degrees, from the ship to a particular objective or destination.

Berth—dock, pier or quay. Also means bed on board ship.

Bilge—lowermost spaces of the infrastructure of a ship.

Bow—the forwardmost part of the vessel.

Bridge—navigational and command control center.

Bulkhead—upright partition (wall) dividing the ship into compartments.

Companionway—interior stairway.

Course—direction in which the ship is headed, in degrees.

Davit—a device for raising and lowering lifeboats.

Deadlight—a ventilated porthole cover to prevent light from entering.

Dock—berth, pier or quay.

Draft (or Draught)—measurement in feet from the ship's waterline to the lowest point of its keel.

Fantail—the rear or overhang of the ship.

Fathom—measurement of distance equal to 6 feet.

Free port—port or place that is free of customs duty and regulations.

Funnel—chimney, from which the ship's combustion gases are propelled into the atmosphere.

Galley—the ship's kitchen.

Gangplank/Gangway—the stairway or ramp link between ship and shore.

Gross registered ton (grt)—a measurement of 100 cubic feet of enclosed revenue earning space within a vessel. This is the standard system of measuring passenger ships used for classification by the Lloyds Register, the British ship survey and marine insurance society.

Helm—the apparatus for steering a ship.

House flag—the flag denoting the company to which a ship belongs.

Hull—the frame and body of the ship exclusive of masts or superstructure.

Leeward—the side which is sheltered from the wind.

Manifest—a list of the ship's passengers, crew and cargo.

Pitch—the alternate rise and fall of a ship's bow, which may occur when the ship is under way.

Port—the left side of a ship when facing forward.

Quay—berth, dock or pier.

Rudder—a fin-like device astern and below the waterline, for steering the vessel.

Screw—ship's propeller.

Smokestack—see under funnel.

Stabilizer—a gyroscopically operated retractable "fin" extending from either or both sides of the ship below the waterline to provide a more stable ride.

Starboard—the right side of the ship when facing forward.

Stern—the rearmost part of the ship, opposite the bow.

Tender—a smaller vessel, often a lifeboat, used to transport passengers between the ship and shore when the vessel is at anchor.

Wake—the track of agitated water left behind a ship when in motion.

Waterline—the line along the side of a ship's hull corresponding to the surface of the water.

Windward—the side toward which the wind blows.

Yaw—the erratic deviation from the ship's set course, usually caused by a heavy sea.

Quips and Quotes

Passengers cruising for the first time are supposedly the source of the questions below:

"Do the crew sleep on board?"
"Does this elevator go up as well as down?"
"Is the doctor qualified?"
"Are there two sittings at the Midnight Buffet?"
"What time's the Midnight Buffet?"
"Is dinner in the dining room?"
"Where's the bus for the walking tour?"
"When the ship's at anchor tomorrow, can we walk ashore?"
"Are the entertainers paid?"
"What time's the 2 o'clock tour?"
"Will the ship wait for the tour buses to get back?"
"Do we have to stay up until midnight to change our clocks?"
"Will I get wet if I go snorkeling?"
"Will this elevator take me to my cabin?"
"Do the Chinese do the laundry by hand?"
"How many fjords to the dollar?"
"Is the mail brought on by plane?"
"Does the ship dock in the middle of town?"
"Who's driving the ship if the Captain is at the cocktail party?"
"Is the island surrounded by water?"
"I'm married, but can I come to the Singles Party?"
"Should I put my luggage outside the cabin before or after I go to sleep?"
"Is the toilet flushed through a hole in the ship's bottom?"

Overheard in the dining room:
"Waiter, this vichyssoise is cold. Get me a hot one."
"If I put on weight, will I have to pay extra?"
"Was the fish caught this morning by the crew?"

Overheard on a Greek island cruise:
"Why did the Greeks build so many ruins?"

A nautical mile is one sixtieth of a degree of the earth's circumference and is equal to 6,080.2 feet. It is about 800 feet (or one seventh) longer than a land mile.

A knot is a unit of speed measuring one nautical mile per hour. Thus, when a ship is doing 20 knots (never 20 knots per hour), she is traveling 20 *nautical* miles per hour.

Love Boat

The famous television shows *The Love Boat* (U.S.A.) and *Dreamboat* (Germany) have given a tremendous boost to the concept of cruising as the ultimate romantic vacation, although what is shown on the screen does not quite correspond to reality. Indeed, the Captain of one of the ships featured in the television show, after being asked the difference between his real-life job as Captain and that of the master of *The Love Boat,* remarked: "On T.V. they can do a re-take if things aren't quite right first time round, whereas I have to get it right first time!"

The recurring theme behind the popular television shows is that of romance and romantic entanglements aboard ship. The concept is a good one, for ships are indeed romantic places. There is nothing quite like standing on the aft deck of a cruise ship with your loved one—hair blowing in the breeze—as you sail over the moonlit waters to yet another island paradise. Of course, a full moon only occurs once a month, so you'd better get the calendar out if you want the timing of *your* moonlit cruise to be perfect.

Speaking of moonlight and romance, it might interest male readers to know that during the past few years women have outnumbered them on many cruises by about eight to one. Someday, men are going to come to their senses, get rid of that "cruising isn't for me, there's nothing to do" notion, and find that the very opposite is true.

But there is no doubt that cruises are excellent opportunities to meet people of similar interests. So if it is romance you are looking for, and provided you choose the right ship—the odds are in your favor.

Latitude and Longitude

Latitude means distance north or south of the Equator. Longitude means distance east or west of the 0 degree at Greenwich, London. Both are recorded in degrees, minutes and seconds. At the Equator, one minute of longitude = 1 nautical mile, but as the meridians converge after leaving the Equator, meeting at the Poles, the size of a degree decreases.

Prefixes

ms   = motor ship (diesel power)
mv   = motor vessel (diesel power)
mts = motor twin screw (diesel power), or
mts = motor turbine ship (steam turbine power)
ss   = steam ship
sts = sail training ship
ts   = turbine steamer (steam turbine power), or
ts   = twin screw vessel
tsmv = twin screw motor vessel
tss = turbine steam ship, or turbine twin screw
ys   = yacht ship
RMS = Royal Mail Ship

Tonnage of Ships

Gross Registered Tonnage is the total of all permanently-enclosed spaces above and below decks, with certain exceptions such as the bridge, radio room, galleys, washing facilities and other specified areas above deck, and is the basis for harbor dues. New international regulations came into effect in 1982 requiring shipowners to re-measure the grt of their vessels.

Cruising Through the Ages

A Brief History

In 1835, a curious sample advertisement appeared in the first issue of the *Shetland Journal*. Under the heading "To Tourists", it proposed an imaginary cruise from England round Iceland and the Faroe Islands, and went on to suggest the pleasures of cruising under the Spanish sun in winter. The founder of the journal, Arthur Anderson, is thus said to have invented the cruising idea.

And it caught on. Writers such as Thackeray boarded ships for the excitement of the voyage, not necessarily just to reach a destination. The Victorians had discovered tourism, and they promoted the idea widely in their own society.

In 1881 the 2,376-ton P&O Line ship *Ceylon* was sold to the newly formed Oceanic Yachting Company for conversion into a profit-making pleasure yacht, capable of sailing round the world—the first passenger ship to do so. The ship continued its cruising career when sold to the Polytechnic Touring Association.

Cruising in a more modern sense began on March 12, 1889, when the 3,847-ton Orient liner *Chimborazo* sailed from England to the Mediterranean. From that year on, the Orient Line ran pleasure cruises to the Mediterranean, Norwegian Fjords and West Indies.

The first official world cruise was offered by Cunard Line in 1922–23 on the *Laconia* (19,680 grt)—a three-class ship that departed from New York. The itinerary included many of the ports of call still popular with world-cruise passengers today. The ship accommodated 350 persons in each of its first two classes, and 1,500 in third class, for a total capacity of 2,200 passengers, more than almost any ship today.

In the 1920s, cruising became the thing to do for the world's well-to-do. Being pampered in grand style was "in" and is still the underlying concept of cruising. The ship took you and your belongings anywhere, fed you, accommodated you, relaxed you and entertained you. At the time, it even catered for your servants, who, of course, accompanied you.

The cruise idyll was helped greatly by Prohibition. After all, just a few miles out at sea, liquor could be served in unlimited amounts. Cheap "booze cruises" were a good alternative to "bathtub gin".

During the late 1920s and well into the '30s, ships became floating luxury palaces, offering every amenity imaginable in this era of social elegance. One of the most beautiful, flowing staircases ever built was on board the French liner *Paris* (35,469 grt), constructed in 1921. It is reported that seagulls made this ship their 5-star favorite because of its *haute cuisine* garbage.

The 1930s saw a battle of the giants develop, as Great Britain, France, Germany and the U.S. built liners of unparalleled luxury, elegance, glamor and comfort. Each country wanted to have the biggest and best afloat. For a time, quality was somehow related to smokestacks. The more a ship had, the better. Although speed was always a factor, particularly on the Trans-Atlantic run, it now became a matter of national ambition.

After World War II, one of the most famous cruise liners of all time was Cunard's lovely *Caronia* (34,183 grt), conceived in 1948. She was designed and built to offer Trans-Atlantic service in the peak summer months only and spend the rest of the year doing long, expensive cruises. She had a single giant mast and one smokestack—the largest of her time—and her hull was painted in four shades of green, supposedly for heat resistance and easy identification. Lovingly known as the "Green Goddess", she was often referred to also as the "millionaires' ship". Famous for her extensive world cruises, she was one of the first ships to offer a private adjoining bathroom for every cabin—a true luxury.

In the autumn of 1958, the first commercial jet aircraft flew across the Atlantic and completely altered the economics of Trans-Atlantic travel. It was the last year that more passengers crossed the North Atlantic by sea than by air. In the early 1960s, the passenger shipping directories listed more than 100 ocean-going passenger shipping lines, with more than 30 ships doing Trans-Atlantic crossings for the better part of each year. Up until the 1960s, it was cheaper to cross the Atlantic by ship than by plane. The jets changed that rapidly, particularly with the introduction of the jumbos in the early 1970s.

Today, only one major superliner offers a regular Trans-Atlantic service—the elegant, modern Cunard liner *Queen Elizabeth 2* (66,451 grt). Built in 1969, and extensively refurbished in 1987, the *QE 2* offers more than two dozen crossings a year between New York and Southampton, with occasional calls at Cherbourg, Baltimore, Boston and Philadelphia. Besides the *QE 2*, there are several ships that offer a Trans-Atlantic crossing usually twice each year as part of repositioning from one cruise area to another.

The success of the jumbo jets

created a fleet of unprofitable and out-of-work passenger liners that seemed doomed for the scrap yards. Even the big "Queens", noted for their regular-as-clockwork weekly Trans-Atlantic service, were in jeopardy. The *Queen Mary* was withdrawn in September 1967. Her sister ship, the *Queen Elizabeth,* the largest passenger liner ever built, made her final crossing in October 1968. I was aboard for the last several voyages of this great ship.

The Trans-Atlantic shipping companies searched desperately for new employment for their ageing vessels, but few survived the ever-successful growth of jet aircraft. Ships were sold for a fraction of their value, and some lines simply went out of business.

Those that survived tried to mix Trans-Atlantic crossings with voyages south in search of the sun. The Caribbean was appealing. Cruising became an ideal alternative. An entire new industry was born, and new lines were formed exclusively for cruising. Then came smaller, highly specialized ships, capable of getting into the tiny ports of developing Caribbean islands, and constructed to carry sufficient passengers in a single class arrangement to make money.

Instead of cruising long distances south from ports such as New York, the new lines established their headquarters in Florida. They based their ships there, not only to escape the cold weather and rough seas, but to cut fuel costs in sailing to Caribbean ports. Cruising was reborn.

California became a base for cruises to the Mexican Riviera; Vancouver for Alaskan destinations in the summer. Flying passengers to the ports of embarkation was, of course, the next logical step, and there soon emerged a working relationship between cruise lines and airlines. The air/sea package came into being, as the cruise lines exploited the jumbo jets for their own purposes. Passengers can now be flown to join cruises almost anywhere in the world.

Then came the "sail 'n stay" packages, joint cruise and hotel vacations that were all included in the cruise fare. Cruising had become an integrated part of tourism, with ships and hotels offering comfort and relaxation and airlines providing the quick access.

Some of the old liners came out of "mothballs"—purchased by emerging cruise lines. Refurbished for warm-weather cruising operations, these ships are often almost completely new in internal design and fittings.

One of the finest examples of refurbishment of a famous Trans-Atlantic liner can be seen in the *Norway* (Norwegian Cruise Line), the former *France,* converted into a Caribbean cruise liner and occasional visitor to Scandinavia. The French can hardly recognize their former Trans-Atlantic flagship which first entered service in 1962, unfortunately just when passenger traffic on the North Atlantic run was declining. Other excellent examples of this type of conversion can be seen in

Princess's *Fair Princess* and *Dawn Princess* (the former Cunard passenger ships *Carinthia* and *Sylvania*), elegant after refurbishment in 1984.

By the late 1970s the cruise industry was growing at a rapid rate. It is still expanding today and is, in fact, the fastest-growing segment of the travel industry. An average of three brand-new cruise ships enter service each year, and that growth is expected to continue into the 1990s.

Cruising Today

Today's cruise concept hasn't changed a great deal from that of earlier days, although it has been improved and expanded. Cruises today feature more ports. Many modern ships are larger, on the whole, than their counterparts of yesteryear, yet the size of cabins has decreased in order to provide more space for entertainment and other public facilities.

Today's ships boast air-conditioning to keep the heat and humidity out, stabilizers to keep the ship on an even keel, an excellent level of maintenance and safety and more emphasis on health and fitness facilities.

Whatever you enjoy doing, you'll find it on a cruise. Although ships have long been devoted to eating and relaxation (with the maxim "Traveling slowly unwinds you faster"), cruise lines now offer all sorts of activities, learning and life-enrichment experiences that were not available in earlier years. And the places you can visit on a cruise are unlimited: Antarctica or Acapulco, Bermuda or Bergen, Dakar or Dubrovnik, Shanghai or St. Thomas, or even "nowhere" at all. All told, more than 300 ports are visited by the world's cruise fleet.

In 1987 over 3 million people (worldwide) took a cruise, packaged and sold by cruise lines through tour operators and cruise/travel agents.

The greatest number of cruise passengers are Americans, followed by Germans and British. Most cruising is in North American waters. While four times as many Americans still visit Europe on vacation than opt for a cruise, the latter is emerging as the ultimate, value-for-money escape. The most recent breakdown of passengers by nationality aboard cruise ships:

U.S.A.	2,800,000
West Germany	190,000
U.K.	120,000
Rest of Europe	175,000
Australia	100,000
Canada	75,000
Far East	50,000

In terms of popularity, the Caribbean is still at the forefront of warm-weather cruising, followed by the Aegean and Mediterranean (both of which offer not only sunshine but historical and archaeological interest). There is also a proliferation of short cruises from Florida and California—excellent for a short break and for introducing people to the concept of a longer cruise.

As more and more ships are built,

it is likely that some will have to move out of the Caribbean and develop new ports of call or home bases. This promises to make a wider range of voyages available to cruisers everywhere.

Cruising into the Future

Less than 10 per cent of U.S. vacationers have discovered cruising, industry analysts report, but more ships are being constructed because of an expected increase in popularity. This has led to an overcapacity of berths (or rather, less demand for) in certain cruising areas, which has kept prices modest and competitive for passengers. Since 85 per cent of those who take cruises are eager to go again, the overcapacity is expected to decline as the margin grows.

The average age of cruisers is decreasing, with almost 40 per cent of new cruise passengers under 35. Clearly, this has meant a revamping of on-board facilities and activities for many ships, the provision of more and better health and fitness facilities and programs, and a higher, more international standard of entertainment.

There is a definite trend towards "specialty" cruising, using smaller ships equipped to cater to young, active passengers, pursuing their hobbies or special interests. Cruise areas are developing for the islands of the South Pacific, the Far East, South America and East and West Africa.

As for ship design, current thinking in the industry follows two distinct avenues, both based on the "economy of scale", and the market. The "economy of scale" helps the operator to keep down the cost per passenger. This is the reason for the move toward either large ships that can carry 1,600 passengers or more, or smaller vessels that accommodate no more than 250 passengers.

This presumes some passengers will think "bigger is better", while others will "think small". Somehow, middle-sized ships are difficult to make profits on. Ships that have been delivered during the past few years are either large-capacity "jumbo" ships, or small-capacity "yacht-like" vessels. The ships under construction today are mainly for 1,200 to 2,000 passengers. Ships that can carry 3,000 to 4,000 passengers (or more) have been on the drawing board for some time, but no purchase orders have been written yet.

There are practical limitations to giant ships, such as draft restrictions and the likelihood of attracting the numbers needed to fill such huge vessels. Large ships can offer more facilities than small ships, but can't get into many ports. And a metropolis at sea poses a challenge for the cruise passenger who wants a quiet, restful vacation.

On the other hand, the "small is beautiful" concept has now taken a strong foothold, particularly in the luxury category. New specialist lines offer high-quality ships of limited capacity. A small-draft vessel can enter ports larger vessels can't even approach, and provides a highly personalized range of quality services. However, small ships aren't as stable if the weather is bad, which is why they tend to follow itineraries close to shore.

Some lines have expanded by "stretching" their ships. This is accomplished by taking a ship into dry dock, literally cutting it in half, and inserting a newly constructed midsection. This gives the vessel an instant increase in capacity, more accommodation space and enlarged public room facilities, with the bonus of maintaining the same draft.

Who's Who on Board

Consider that a cruise ship is a highly structured floating hotel, in which each crew member of the working society fills a well-defined role. A look at the chart on page 74–75 will clarify the hierarchy aboard ship. Authority starts with the Captain or General Manager and the chain of command works down through the ranks.

All members of the ship's company wear a uniform by which their station and function are instantly identifiable. Rank is also designated by the colors and insignia worn on the sleeves and epaulettes of the uniform itself.

General Manager

The policy rapidly gaining acceptance in the cruise industry is running each ship as a completely separate, self-contained business—distinct from the parent company's head office. The boss is a General Manager.

In companies with a General Manager for each ship, he is responsible for the complete day-to-day management of the vessel. Acting as a liaison between ship and head office, he has ultimate authority, even over the captains, although this is rarely exerted from the point of view of seamanship. In any unusual circumstance, the General Manager is consulted before an important decision affecting the safety and well-being of the vessel itself. In companies without an onboard General Manager, the Captain bears the responsibility.

The General Manager (or "G.M." as he is generally known) may either be a senior captain or an executive from head office with thorough knowledge of ship operations. On board, he is rarely noticed by passengers, as he is not in uniform and incognito. Once each voyage, the General Manager meets with the captains, all senior officers and department heads. Any problems that come up during the voyage are then dealt with.

Captain

The Captain is the master of the ship and has absolute dictatorial rights and control over his vessel, officers, crew and passengers. He is a seaman first, and manager of the ship second (except when the vessel carries a separate General Manager). He is also expected to be a generous and worthy host. When passenger ships are registered for insurance coverage (normally with Lloyds of London), the Captain's credentials and past record are reviewed together with the seaworthiness of the vessel itself.

Although on the Bridge there may be several officers with a master's certificate, the Captain still maintains unquestioned authority. He wears four gold bars on his sleeves and epaulettes.

Every ship has a log, a daily record in which are noted all navigational and pertinent nautical data, details of reports from various department heads and any relevant information on passengers or crew. Maritime law dictates that only the Captain is allowed to make daily entries in the log, a necessary but time-consuming part of his job. If a ship were to be abandoned, the log is the only record of the ship's operation, prevailing conditions, weather information and geographical locations that could be reviewed. The Captain normally attends numerous social functions during the course of a cruise, hosts a table in the dining room and is often seen during the day on walkabout inspection tours.

Staff Captain

The Staff Captain is second in command and can take over at any time if needed. As his title suggests, the Staff Captain is concerned not only with the Bridge, but also concentrates on the day-to-day running of the ship, its staff and crew, and all discipline.

In many companies the Staff Captain takes over when the regular Captain goes on leave, while in other companies there is a "floating" Captain who takes all the relief commands. The Staff Captain also wears four gold bars.

The Captain and Staff Captain work closely together, dividing the duties according to company policy and/or personal interest. At all times, one of the two must be on call, and most cruise lines insist that one or the other remains on board in any port of call.

Although the Captain earns a top salary, the Staff Captain is on almost the same scale. Yet, as a matter of interest, despite equal expertise, and the responsibility for a passenger count often three times as great, a ship's captain earns roughly half the salary of a jumbo jet pilot.

The airline captain has the added advantage of switching on an automatic pilot to handle almost every navigational task once aloft, and homes in on a runway through computer assistance and radar. His sea-going counterpart must be able to navigate manually and negotiate hidden reefs, sandbars, sunken vessels and marker buoys, and even hazards not recorded on any chart.

The sea-going Captain also has the awesome responsibility of docking, maneuvering and anchoring his ship, often in unfamiliar territory, in sometimes difficult weather conditions.

Bridge Officers

Besides the Captain and Staff Captain, other Bridge officers include the Chief Officer, First Officer, Second Officer and several Junior Officers. Their job is the navigation and safe conduct of the vessel at all times. The Bridge is manned 24 hours a day, even in port.

Also on the Bridge are the fire-detection systems, and controls for the fire and watertight doors, which can be activated by "compartments" in the event of a problem anywhere on the ship.

Chief Engineer

The Chief Engineer (almost always referred to as "Chief") has the ultimate responsibility for the mechanical well-being of a cruise ship. This includes overseeing not only the main and auxiliary engines, but also the generators, electrical systems, air-conditioning, heating, plumbing, ventilation and refrigeration systems.

He is thus trained in a multiplicity of on-board systems, and is, in fact, the only other person on board who can talk to the Captain on an equal footing. With regard to engineering and functional systems, he is

mechanical master. He wears four gold bars.

Chief Radio Officer

The function of the Chief Radio Officer is to keep the ship in constant touch with the outside world. The Radio Room is his domain, where all radio, telegraph, telex and satellite communication equipment is to be found. He may also be in charge of the automated telephone exchange and its switching equipment. He will have a staff of at least three.

Principal Medical Officer

On a large cruise ship, the medical department can be extremely busy, with anything up to 2,000 passengers and 1,000 crew to attend to. Hopefully, you will meet the doctor socially, and not professionally.

The hospital on many cruise ships is a miniature version of a hospital ashore, and may be equipped with operating theater, X-ray room, examination rooms, and several beds including an isolation unit. There is at least one fully qualified doctor on board every cruise ship plus a small nursing staff, physiotherapist, medical orderlies who may be petty officers, and maybe even a dentist.

Hotel Manager

As head of a "floating hotel" operation involving almost two thirds of the entire crew, the Hotel

Manager is in charge of overall passenger service, comfort, housekeeping, food, drink and information, just as in any first-class hotel ashore. He has several junior hotel officers and civilian staff to whom he delegates responsibility for the day-to-day running of various departments.

His most important associates and aides are the Purser and the Cruise Director. At one time, the Purser (called the Chief Purser on some ships) was responsible for the control of all passenger services. But with the increasing emphasis placed on food, recreation, comfort and entertainment, the new position of Hotel Manager has been developed.

If at any time during your cruise you have any unresolved problems or a request that has not been satisfied, contact the Hotel Manager or Deputy Hotel Manager through the Purser's Office.

Chief Purser

The Chief Purser's Office is the financial, business, accommodation and information center of any ship and will be found in a convenient location in the main "lobby" area amidships.

The Purser and his staff handle all money matters (including currency exchange), mail, telexes and telegrams; accept valuables for safekeeping; and provide a complete information service, sometimes around-the-clock. Thus the Purser is responsible for all passenger

and crew accounts, purchasing and requisitioning of supplies, shipboard concessions, the on-board printing of such items as the *Daily Program* and menus, and manning the telephone switchboard, if the ship does not have an automatic system. His domain also includes relations with customs and immigration officials in all ports of call.

The Purser has two main assistants: the Hotel Purser and the Crew Purser. The Hotel Purser is in charge of all passenger business, including accommodation (usually under the direction of a Berthing Officer), while the Crew Purser handles all matters relating to the ship's personnel and contracts.

If the ship is based in foreign waters, the Crew Purser also oversees crew changeovers, arranges flights, baggage and any other incidental crew matters. Many larger ships have two complete crews, one of which will be on leave while the other works the ship. Often, this works on a continuous rotation basis.

Concierge

On some luxury ships, such as those of Royal Viking Line, the Concierge acts as an invaluable liaison between ship and passenger. He may set up private parties, obtain opera or theater tickets, arrange special transportation in far-off ports of call, or simply obtain items that passengers cannot find themselves. His primary concern is the well-being and satisfaction of the ship's passengers.

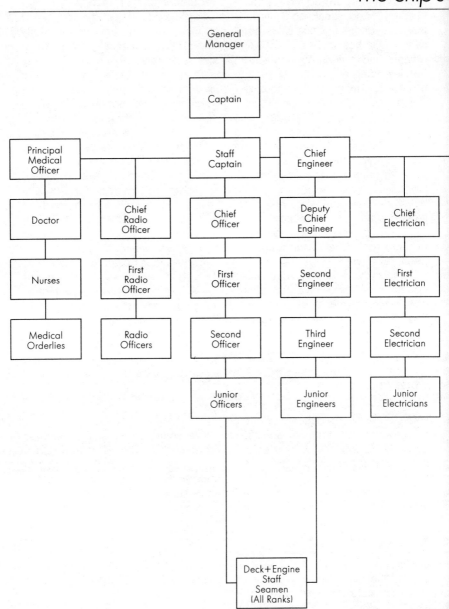

Company

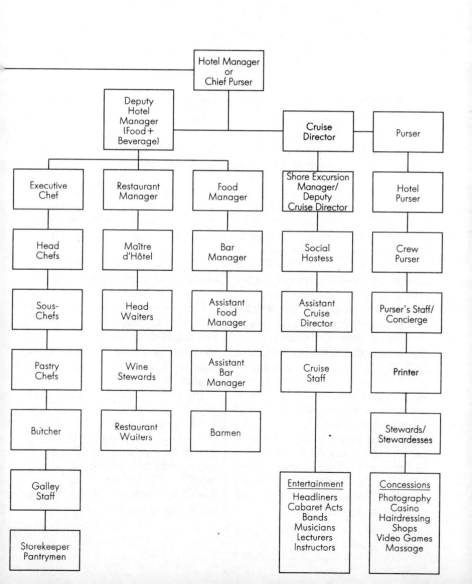

Deputy Hotel Manager

The Deputy Hotel Manager can take over from the Hotel Manager at any time, while his special domain is the food and beverage operation. On some ships, this is run by a concessionaire, who supplies not only the food, but the dining room and bar staff as well, in which case the Deputy Hotel Manager acts as an aide to both the Hotel Manager and the Purser.

Cruise Director

Without doubt the most visible man on board, the Cruise Director has the ultimate responsibility of planning and operating the passenger entertainment and activities program. He is the master of ceremonies for all ship-board functions and events, and oversees every area of leisure and recreation. The position is thus highly demanding.

Before each cruise, the Cruise Director sketches in all projected activities, entertainment and movies on a huge chart, showing the program in time slots throughout each day.

He has a number of helpers under his command, including the Cruise Staff and Hostesses, "headliner" and lesser entertainers, bands and musicians, lecturers, recreation, sports and health instructors and other support personnel.

On some larger ships, there may be one or more Assistant Cruise Directors or an Entertainment Manager, Stage Manager and Social Director. Cruise lines label their staff positions in different ways.

A Cruise Director must plan entertainment, movies and special theme nights with utter dexterity, taking care not to offend anyone in the process.

On the first full day of the cruise, he will usually invite all passengers to the main lounge to explain his entertainment program and will urge passengers to take advantage of the many events planned for the cruise. On short cruises, he may introduce his staff and give a brief ship orientation a short while after sailing.

Also at the start of each cruise, the Cruise Director gives a port lecture, usually with audio-visual aids. In this, he will advise passengers what to do ashore, describe the excursions available, and even offer advice on where to shop. But beware the Cruise Director that oversells certain stores, for he may be on commission!

The Cruise Director may be an officer (with two or three gold bar status), or he may be a "non-sailor" with a show-biz background. Certainly one of the qualities required for the job is an ability to deal with difficult entertainers, crew and, of course, obstreperous passengers!

The Cruise Director has an office, together with members of his Cruise Staff, through which he can be reached for anything relating to the entertainment and activities program on board. In Part Two of this book, you'll find an evaluation of the Cruise Director and his staff for each ship rated.

Going Ashore

Shore Excursions

For some people, the idea of a cruise may simply be to get away from it all. Indeed, no matter how many or what ports the ship visits, some never go ashore, but prefer instead to revel in the complete ship-board aspect of cruising. For these people, the ship is the ultimate destination, and they could just as well be on a cruise to nowhere.

For the vast majority, however, the ports offered on a cruise itinerary are important considerations, and the ship provides deluxe transportation. Shore excursions, both a challenge and a bane to cruise lines, are proving to be one of the most vital and attractive aspects of the total cruise experience. They are organized to be varied enough for everyone, from the young and active, to the elderly and infirm.

Today you need not feel the least bit uncomfortable or hesitant in strange or unusual surroundings, or intimidated by languages other than your own. If you don't want to miss the major sightseeing attractions in each port, you'll find the organized shore excursions the perfect answer. If you do not wish to be alone, they provide an ideal opportunity to meet fellow passengers with similar interests.

Cruise lines generally plan and oversee shore excursions assuming that you have not seen the place previously. They aim to show you the most beautiful, striking and fascinating aspects of a destination in a comfortable manner and at a reasonable price.

Tours are operated either by land, sea, or air. They are of varying duration: half-day sightseeing; full-day sightseeing, including lunch; evening outings, such as nightclub tours, including admission charges and one or more drinks; and overland excursions, often lasting several days and involving overnight stays in hotels.

On land, buses are often the principal choice of transportation, rather than taxis or private cars. This cuts the cost and allows the tour operator to narrow down the selection of guides to only those most competent, knowledgeable and fluent in English, while providing some degree of security and control.

In the case of air travel (usually in small aircraft or helicopters), operating companies and all equipment must be thoroughly inspected, as must their safety record.

If tours include overland segments and meals, the quality of any food to be served is taken into account, as are the food preparation areas and hygiene standards of personnel.

Shore excursions come under the heading of additional on-board expenses for passengers, and are considered as sources of on-board revenue by the cruise lines. Yet, most of the money generated by the sale of shore excursions never reaches the coffers of the cruise lines, but goes to third parties—the tour operators in the various ports of call. Only a tiny number of cruise lines include shore excursions in the cruise fare, generally those lines specializing in "adventure" or "expedition" type cruises to unusual and exotic destinations.

Interestingly, passengers often consider shore excursion prices as being high, unaware of the tremendous behind-the-scenes organization required, and the costs involved locally. A vast amount of time and money is spent by cruise lines setting up suitable shore excursion programs. The ship's Tour Office is the last link in the chain of operation of a successful tour program.

The Shore Excursion Department

The starting point is at the head office of a cruise line, in the Shore Excursion Department. At its head is the line's Shore Excursion Manager, a competent and knowledgeable individual who has the responsibility for setting up a successful program, sometimes worldwide. There may be several staff members involved in a department.

Shore Excursion Managers who work for lines operating worldwide have the greatest challenge, since each cruise may have a completely different itinerary. Those employed by lines that offer seasonal itineraries (for example Alaska/Mexican Riviera, or Caribbean/Mediterranean) have a smaller problem because the itinerary is unchanged for a complete cruising season.

Perhaps the most challenging of all jobs is setting up a comprehensive shore excursion program for a world cruise or exotic long voyage, where organizing shore excursions often involves meetings with various government tourism officials and complex overland and flight arrangements.

The Tour Operator

The shore tour operator is the next link in the chain. Few lines run their own shore excursions, instead they contract a tour operator for each port of call. He is then responsible for providing the best means of transportation, local guides, food, entrance tickets to public buildings, gardens, nightclubs, and other attractions that are part of the tour.

Cruise lines and tour operators work together in planning or suggesting tour itineraries, the tour operator offering the cruise line a "buying price per head" for the tour or tour package. The margin between the buying price and the selling price to the cruise passenger can be as little as 50 cents or as much as 50 per cent. The average mark-up is about 20–25 per cent, an amount far lower than most passengers imagine.

The Tour Manager

The ship's representative supervising the entire operation of the shore excursion program is the Tour Manager. As the eyes and ears of the cruise line, he can recommend to head office that the tour be suspended if it's not to his satisfaction—which gives him a good deal of authority with local tour operators.

The Tour Manager and his staff will be on the dockside despatching the tours in each port. Any last minute problems or questions can be raised at that time.

The Tour Office

The Tour Office is normally located in a central position on board, close to the Purser's Office, in the main lobby area. This is where you should go for information about the ports of call or to purchase your shore excursion tickets, and where you will find the Tour Manager and his staff. Please note that the staff cannot normally act as guides or interpreters.

At the Tour Office you'll find details of the tours and descriptive literature about the ports of call, with information on the history, language, population, currency, main sightseeing attractions, principal shopping areas, beaches and hotels, sports and watersports facilities, transport and principal eating establishments. For more specific information, see the Tour Manager or visit the ship's library. On many ships, special full-color port booklets or cruise guides may be available. Tour Office opening times will be listed at the office, and in the *Daily Program*.

Booking

Early booking of tours is highly recommended, especially if they are listed as "limited participation". This means that there is a restricted number of seats available, to be sold on a first come, first served basis. On some ships, where tours can be booked prior to the sailing date, you may find sell-outs occurring. So, visit the Tour Office as soon as you can after boarding and make your reservations early.

Payment is normally made via a ship's central billing system, by cash, traveler's check or credit card. Note that on most ships, personal checks aren't accepted.

The Tour Office usually develops

long lines shortly after the port lecture given by the Cruise Director. You can avoid a wait by reading through the descriptive tour literature and making your reservations before that talk.

On some ships, pre-booking forms for tours will either be forwarded with your cruise tickets and documents, or may be in your cabin on arrival. Pre-booking means that you can reserve (and in some cases pay for) tours before you board or before the Tour Office opens for general business.

For cancellations, most ships require a minimum of 24 hours notice before the advertised tour departure time. Refunds are at the discretion of the cruise line. However, should you be unable to go on a tour, or change your mind, you will be able, in most cases, to sell your ticket to another passenger. Tour tickets do not normally have names or cabin numbers on them, except those involving flights. However, before attempting to re-sell any tickets, it would be wise to check with the Tour Manager.

Selecting the Right Tour

As indicated previously, at the start of the cruise, the Cruise Director or Tour Manager will give an informal audio-visual lecture on the ports of call on your cruise, together with a brief description of the tours offered. Whether you are a novice or an experienced cruiser, make an effort to attend this talk. Remember to take pencil and paper with you to jot down any important points and the tours that interest you most.

Look carefully at the shore excursion literature and circle the tours that appeal to you. Then go to the Tour Office and ask any other questions you may have before you book. Here are a few guidelines:

* Tours are put together for general interest. If you want to see something that is not described in the tour literature, don't take the tour. Go on your own or with friends.

* Many sightseeing tours in the Caribbean cover the same ground. Choose one and then do something different in the next port. (The same is true of the history/archaeology tours in the Greek Isles.) It pays to use your time wisely and not to repeat the kind of visit you've already made.

* If you are a history buff, remember that most tours give very little in-depth history, and guides are often not acquainted with details beyond a superficial general knowledge. Pick up a pocket guide book to the area or check the ship's library.

* City tours are basically superficial. To get to know a city intimately, it is better to go it alone, or with a small group of friends. Travel by taxi or bus directly to the points that interest you most.

* If you enjoy diving or snorkeling, most Caribbean cruise ships offer dive-in excursions at a very reasonable cost, which includes flippers, mask and snorkel. Underwater cameras can often be rented, too. Instruction for novices is given on board.

Helpful Hints

Tours are timed to be most convenient for the greatest number of participants, taking into account meals on board. Where ships operate two dining-room sittings, passengers on the second breakfast sitting may find themselves having to rush in order to participate in a morning tour. Likewise, those on afternoon tours may have to hurry to get to the first sitting at dinner on time.

Departure times are listed in the descriptive tour literature and in your *Daily Program,* and will be announced over the ship's P.A. system. Don't be late, or you may be too late. There are absolutely no refunds if you miss the tour.

If you are hearing-impaired, make arrangements with the Tour Manager to assist you in departing for your tours at the correct times.

Only take along what is necessary. Leave any valuables on the ship, together with any money and credit cards you don't plan to use. People in groups are often targets for pickpockets in some of the major cities. Also, beware of the tour guide who gives you a colored disc to wear for ''identification''— he may be marking you as a ''rich'' tourist for local shopkeepers. It is easier and cheaper to remember your guide's name and the bus number.

Lost or misplaced tour tickets should be reported immediately to the Tour Manager. On most ships, tour tickets, once sold, become the sole responsibility of the purchaser,

and the cruise line is not generally able to issue replacements. If you place them on the dresser/vanity unit in your cabin, make sure they don't fall down the back, from where there is no possibility of retrieval. Since tour tickets are not cheap, place them in a clearly marked envelope right away and put them in your wallet or purse.

In a foreign port, convert a little money into local currency for minor expenses during any tour. This will be useful if you wish to buy a soft drink, for example, or wish to take a taxi to the ship, if you prefer to shop rather than go back on the bus.

Going Independently

If you do not like to tour with groups of people, you can, of course, go ashore on your own, and it's perfectly safe. In most areas of the world there are no restrictions on independent travel ashore, with the exception of the Soviet Union, China and areas of military importance.

Going ashore independently is ideal in the major cruise ports of the Caribbean, the Bahamas, Bermuda, Mexican Riviera, Canary Islands, Mediterranean, the Aegean ports and the islands of the South Pacific. In many of the South American ports, however, it would be wise to go with a friend, especially if you are unfamiliar with the language.

Indeed, in countries where the language is unknown to you, you should always carry some identification (but not your passport), the name of your ship and the area in which it is docked. If the ship is anchored and you take a launch ashore, take note of exactly where the landing place is by observing nearby landmarks, as well as writing down the location. This will be invaluable if you get lost and need to take a taxi back to the launch.

On most ships you'll be given an identification tag or boarding pass at the Purser's Office or gangway, which must be handed in each time you return to the ship. Remember that ships have schedules (and sometimes tides) to meet, and they will not wait for individual passengers who return late. If you are in a launch port in a tropical area and the weather changes for the worse, the ship's Captain could make a decision to depart early to avoid being hounded or hemmed in by an approaching storm—it has happened, especially in the Caribbean. If it does, locate the ship's agent for the port. (He'll try to get you back, and the experience will provide dinner conversation for months.)

If you are planning on going to a quiet, secluded beach to swim, first check with the Cruise Director or Tour Manager, as certain beaches may be considered off-limits because of a dangerous undertow. And, if you're thinking of going diving alone —don't! Not *anywhere,* even if you know the area well. Always go diving with at least one companion.

Naturally, going ashore independently does not have to mean going alone. You'll more than likely meet up with others with similar inten-

tions on board ship, who, like yourself, prefer their own group to the organized excursion.

Of course, you don't have to go off the ship in ports at all. You are perfectly free to come and go as you please. Sometimes, after several days at sea, it will feel just wonderful to stay aboard to enjoy the peace and calm, while everyone else, it seems, has deserted the ship.

Local Transport

In most cruise ports of the world, the same type of transportation is available for sightseeing. You can go by taxi, public bus, rental car, moped, motorcycle or bicycle.

Taxi. If you decide to hire a taxi for sightseeing, be prepared to negotiate the price in some countries, and don't pay until you get back to the ship or to your final destination. If you are with friends, hiring a taxi for a full- or half-day sightseeing trip can often work out far cheaper than renting a car and you avoid the hazards of driving. Naturally, prices do vary, according to where in the world you are, but if you can select a driver who speaks English, and his taxi is comfortable, even air-conditioned, you're ahead.

Be wary of taxi drivers who wear a badge that says "I speek Ingleesh" or even "I speak English", for it may be *all* the English they speak! To be certain, ask the driver a few questions, and make sure the price you negotiate is clear to both of you. Better still, if your driver speaks only a little English, write down the agreed fare and show it to him. Make sure you know what currency the number represents.

Bus. Getting around by public bus can be an inexpensive method of sightseeing and of becoming immersed in the local life. In most countries, public transportation is very safe, but there are those places where it pays to keep an eye on your wallet or purse. You will need a small amount of the local currency in order to travel on the bus system. This can be obtained on board your ship or at a local bank on arrival.

Rental Car. If you are planning on renting a car for any specific ports of call, try to do so ahead of your cruise, through your travel agent. This will not only save much precious time on your arrival in port, but will go a long way to ensuring that there will be a rental car available when you arrive.

Before departing for your cruise, check to see if your driving license is valid for the destination, as some countries may require you to obtain a local or visitor's license (for a fee) before allowing you to rent a car. Remember, also, to take along a major credit card, without which you will need to make a cash deposit.

Moped, Motorcycle and Bicycle. Mopeds and motorcycles will be available for hire in many ports. In places such as Bermuda, remember that roadside walls are of coral and limestone, and can give you a nasty scratch if you scrape them.

Bicycles are a favorite way of getting around in many parts of the world, especially in the Orient. They are inexpensive to rent, and you'll get some exercise as you pedal. One or two ships (and all hotel barges) have bicycles on board for passenger use.

The Shopping Scene

For many cruise passengers, shopping comes second only to eating in popularity. Indeed, one of the main joys of cruising is going ashore and shopping at leisure. Whether it's local craftwork, hand-made trinkets, articles of clothing, jewelry, or local liquor, there's something special in store at each destination.

In some places, you will find shopping a bargain compared with home, depending on the exchange rate. The best ports for shopping are, of course, those that are duty free, meaning that no customs duty is charged on items being bought. The Caribbean, being on the "doorstep" of the United States, has become known for its good value in shopping, with St. Thomas in the U.S. Virgin Islands the best known. Many people book a Caribbean cruise only if the itinerary includes St. Thomas.

Cruise lines are happy to go along with this. St. Thomas still offers prices that compare very favorably with those on the mainland, particularly liquor at duty-free prices. But don't forget that you'll have to carry that liquor home somehow. Alcoholic beverages can't be mailed home, but many other items can from St. Thomas or elsewhere. Mail packages only from a major island or port, where the postal service is reliable.

General Shopping Hints

A good general rule is: know in advance just what you are looking for, especially if your time is limited. But if time is no problem, browsing can be fun.

When shopping time is included in shore excursions, be careful of stores repeatedly recommended by the tour guides, who are likely to be receiving commissions from the merchants. Shop around and compare prices before you buy.

Excellent shopping hints and recommendations are often given in the Cruise Director's port lecture at the start of your cruise. But if you notice Cruise Directors "pushing" certain stores, it is possible that they, too, are on commission. They

Shopping by Destination

For those who like to anticipate their shopping, here is a brief list of the most popular items by major cruise destinations.

Africa. Chess sets, diamonds, pottery, rugs, straw goods, tapestries.
Alaska. Furs, moccasins, reindeer-leather goods, totem souvenirs, whalebone items.
Australia. Opals, sheepskin coats, woolen goods.
Barbados. English chinaware, English crystal.
Bermuda. English chinaware, crystal, porcelain, woolen sweaters.
Brazil. Leather goods, semi-precious stones.
Chile. Mapuche Indian rugs.
China. Antique Chinese bronzes, ginseng, ivory, jade, rugs, scroll paintings, tea, woodblock prints.
Colombia. Emeralds, pre-Columbian art (export permit required).
Denmark. Danish porcelain, furs, solid wood articles.
Dominican Republic. Amber.
Egypt. Alabaster articles, brass and copper articles, Egyptian cotton goods, silver jewelry, tapestries.
Greece. Hand-sewn fur capes, stoles, hand-woven wool rugs, honey, olive-wood articles.
Grenada. Shell jewelry, spices.
Haiti. Oil paintings, wood carvings.
Hong Kong. Antique Chinese bronzes, audio equipment, brocades and silks, cameras, carpets and rugs, chinaware, gems, hand-tailored clothes, leather goods, watches and clocks, woks.

India. Gold and silver jewelry, precious stones.
Israel. Brass and copper items, leather articles, olive-wood figurines.
Japan. Cameras, electronic gadgetry, watches, ceramics, pearls, toys.
Madeira. Embroidered goods, Madeira wine, orchids, wickerwork.
Martinique. French crystal, French perfume, Swiss watches.
Mexico. Hand-made leather sandals and shoes, leather articles, onyx chess sets, paper items, pottery.
Norway. Hand-knit wool clothing, pewter, reindeer skins, sealskin slippers.
Panama. Jade, French perfume, Swiss watches.
Portugal. Embroidery, knitware, pottery, shawls, tiles, wickerwork.
Puerto Rico. Jewelry, leather shoes.
St. Thomas. Cameras, gold, jewelry, liquor, Swiss watches.
Singapore. Antiques, batik, carpets, gold jewelry, hand-tailored clothes, ivory, jade, orchids, reptile-skin goods, silk.
Sweden. Furs, glassware, clothing, candles, suede, Lapp handicrafts.
Turkey. Carpets, hand-embroidered clothes, spices, suede and leather clothing.
U.S.S.R. Amber, caviar, dolls (*matryoshka* nest dolls), embroidery, fur hats, lacquered boxes, postage stamps, artisan work.
Venezuela. Coffee, gold jewelry, natural pearls.
Yugoslavia. Copperware, dolls, embroidery, lace, pottery.

do know, however, that the reputation of the cruise line is at stake if their suggestions are not in your best interests.

When shopping for local handicrafts, make sure that the item in question has indeed been made in the country. It can happen that the so-called local product has in fact been made in Taiwan, Hong Kong or other Far Eastern country. It pays to check.

You should also be wary of "bargain-priced" name brands, such as Gucci bags, Rolex or Omega watches, as they may well be counterfeit and of dubious quality. In the case of watches, check the guarantee.

If you have any specific questions, ask the Cruise Director, Tour Manager, or one of the Cruise Staff. Some shopping information may be available in descriptive port information literature available at the ship's Tour Office.

Keep in mind that the ship's shops are also duty-free, and, for the most part, competitive in price. The shops on board are closed while in port, however, due to international customs regulations.

Coastal and Inland Cruises (U.S.A.)

Coastal and inland vessels offer a change of style and pace from the big ocean-going liners. On these cruises, informality is the order of the day. Accommodating up to 160 passengers, the ships tend to be more like a private party or club—there's no pretentiousness. Unlike major cruise ships, these small vessels are rarely out of sight of land. Their owners seek out lesser-known cruise areas, offering in-depth visits to destinations inaccessible to larger ships.

During the last few years, there has been a tremendous growth in this segment of the cruise market, and bookings remain strong, but with fewer discounts or "fly-free" incentives offered. If you prefer a small country inn to a large resort, this type of cruise will appeal to you.

You cruise in relaxed comfort at up to 12 knots. Life is serene, but because the vessels are of American registry, there's no casino on board. In fact, all public room facilities are limited, some lines even inviting you to bring your own alcoholic beverages with you. As far as

entertainment goes, passengers are usually left to their own devices, although there may be a piano aboard. Most of these vessels are in port during the evening, so you can go ashore for the local nightlife.

Getting ashore is easy, and passengers can be off in a matter of a few minutes, with no waiting at the gangway.

Accommodations consist of all-outside cabins, each with its own large picture window, and, though not elaborate, with its own private bathroom. The cabins are small, but quite cozy, although closet space is very limited, so take only what you absolutely need. The only drawback to all-outside cabins is that some open directly onto the deck—not convenient when it rains. The quietest cabins are at the bow of the vessel. Also, tall passengers should be aware that the overall length of beds on most of these vessels is 6 feet maximum.

The principal evening event on board is dinner in the dining room, which accommodates all passengers at one time. This can even be a family-style affair with passengers seated at long tables, and the food passed around. The cuisine is American, with fresh local specialties favored.

There are usually four decks on these vessels, and no elevators. Stairs can be a little on the steep side, and are not recommended for people with walking difficulties. This kind of cruise is ideal for those who do not like crowds, but like a family-type cruise experience in pleasant surroundings. The maxim "You just relax, we'll move the scenery" is very appropriate here.

Coastal and inland cruise vessels are not featured in Part Two of this book since they are small and specialized with limited facilities. But, here is a list of the cruise lines and their ships.

Coastal and Inland Cruises—USA

CRUISE LINE/OPERATOR	NAME	BUILT	LENGTH (feet)	PASS. CAP.	CREW	CRUISE AREAS
American Canadian Caribbean Line	Caribbean Prince	1983	116	80	38	C/E/F
American Canadian Caribbean Line	New Shoreham II	1979	150	72	35	A/E/F
American Cruise Lines	Charleston	1987	220	140	66	D/E
American Cruise Lines	New Orleans	1985	220	140	60	D/M
American Cruise Lines	Savannah	1985	220	140	66	D/E
Clipper Cruise Line	Nantucket Clipper	1984	207	108	51	A/C/D/E
Clipper Cruise Line	Newport Clipper	1983	207	108	51	A/C/D/E
Clipper Cruise Line	Yorktown Clipper	1988	207	138	69	A/C/D/E
Exploration Cruise Lines	Colonial Explorer	1984	192	96	49	A/I
Exploration Cruise Lines	Glacier Bay Explorer	1970	125	62	32	J
Exploration Cruise Lines	Great Rivers Explorer	1982	152	92	44	G/J
Exploration Cruise Lines	Majestic Explorer	1982	152	88	44	K
Exploration Cruise Lines	North Star	1966	295	156	80	J
Exploration Cruise Lines	Pacific Northwest Explorer	1980	143	80	44	G/J

Key: A = U.S. Virgin Islands   E = U.S. East Coast   J = Alaska/Inside Passage
B = Bahamas   F = Saguenay/Quebec   K = Tahiti
C = Southern Caribbean   G = Panama Canal Zone   M = Mississippi River
D = Colonial South   I = Pacific Northwest

PASS. CAP. = Passenger Capacity

River Cruising

Steamboating—U.S.A.

Most famous of all river cruises in the U.S.A. are those aboard the steamboats of the mighty Mississippi River. Mark Twain, an outspoken fan of Mississippi cruising, once said: "When man can go 700 miles an hour, he'll want to go seven again".

The grand traditions of the Steamboat Era are faithfully carried on by the *Delta Queen* and *Mississippi Queen* (Delta Queen Steamboat Company), both of which are powered by steam engines that drive huge wooden paddlewheels on the stern.

The smaller 180-passenger *Delta Queen,* whose life began on Scotland's Clydeside in 1926, is now on the National Register of Historic Places. She gained much attention when President Carter spent a week aboard her in August 1979.

A half-century younger, the 400-passenger *Mississippi Queen* was built at a cost of some $27 million in 1976 in Jefferson, Indiana, from where nearly 5,000 steamboats originated during the 19th century.

(The exterior of the *Mississippi Queen* was designed by James Gardner of London, creator of Cunard's *QE2.*) Each steamboat features one of the rarest of musical instruments—a real "steam piano", driven by the engine.

Aboard one of these steamboats, you'll find yourself stepping back into history and American folklore. Charm and old-world graciousness surround you, as do delightful woods, brass and flowing staircases. And once a year, the two boats rival each other in the Great Steamboat Race—a 10 day extravaganza when the *Delta Queen* battles bigger sister *Mississippi Queen* in a boat-against-boat, crew-against-crew and passenger-against-passenger spectacular.

You can go steamboating from two to 12 nights, and during the course of a year there are several theme cruises, with big bands and lively entertainment. The boats traverse the Mississippi and Ohio rivers. It's a great life on the river, away from the congestion of roads and airports. No immigration or customs formalities in the heartland of America, of course.

Other River Cruising

Cruising down one of the world's great rivers is an experience in itself—quite different from sailing on an open sea. Whether you want to cruise down the historic Nile, the stately Volga, the magnificent Rhine, the "blue" Danube or the "yellow" Yangtze—to say nothing of the Don and the Dnieper—there's a cruise just waiting for you.

River cruises provide a constant change of scenery—even country, are always close to land and offer the chance to visit cities and areas inaccessible to large ships. Indeed, watching the scenery slip past your floating hotel is one of the most refreshing ways to absorb the beauty that has inspired poets and artists over countless centuries. A cruise on the Danube, for example, will take you through four countries.

Although small when compared to ocean-going cruise ships, river vessels do have a unique and friendly international atmosphere. The most modern vessels offer the discreet luxury of a floating hotel, often including a swimming pool, several public rooms, dining room and an observation lounge. Although cabins are small (with limited closet space), they are quite comfortable for a one-week journey. They are clean and tidy, as well as functional. Informality is the order of the day. And, because rivers are calm by nature, you can't get seasick.

In Europe, river cruising has reached a highly sophisticated level, and you can be assured of good service and meals of a consistently high European standard. Dining is pleasant, although not quite a gourmet experience. Typical rates range from $800 to more than $2,000 per person for a one-week cruise, including meals, cabin with private facilities, side trips and airport/railway transfers. (See chart p. 91.)

Barge Cruising—Europe

Smaller than river vessels, and accurately called boats, "hotel barges" ply the inland waterways and canals of Europe from April to November, when the weather is generally good. Barge cruises are usually of 3-, 6-, or 13-days duration, and offer a completely relaxed, unstructured vacation in a completely informal atmosphere, for a small number of passengers. The barges motor along in the daytime, and moor early each evening, so that you can pay a visit to the local village, and get a restful night's sleep.

Hotel barges are beautifully fitted out—with rich wood paneling, full carpeting, and custom-built furniture and tastefully chosen fabrics. Each barge has a dining room/lounge-bar and is equipped with your total comfort in mind. Each barge captain takes pride in his vessel, often supplying rare memorabilia to be incorporated into the decor.

With locally grown fresh foods,

usually purchased and prepared each day by a loving crew, you'll live well and be treated like a house guest.

Most barges can also be chartered exclusively—just take your family and friends, for example.

The waterways of France, especially, offer beauty, tranquility and diverse interest, and barge cruising is an excellent way of exploring an area not previously visited. Most cruises include a visit to a famous vineyard and wine cellar, as well as side-trips to places of historic, architectural or scenic interest. You will be accompanied by a crew member familiar with the surrounding countryside. You can even go hot-air ballooning over the local countryside, and land to a welcome glass of champagne and a flight certificate.

Depending on which barge and area you choose (my favorite is the Burgundy area of France), dining aboard will range from home-style cooking to truly outstanding nouvelle cuisine, with all the trimmings. Hotel barges have English or English-speaking French crews.

Barging on the canals often means going through a constant succession of locks. Nowhere is this more enjoyable and entertaining than in the Burgundy region of France where, between Dijon and Macon, a barge can negotiate as many as 54 locks in a six-day cruise. Interestingly, all lock-keepers in France are women!

Typical rates range from $600 to more than $3,000 per person for a six-day cruise. Rates include cabin with private facilities, all meals, excellent wines, beverages, use of bicycles, side trips and airport/railway transfers.

Major Cruise Rivers of the World

RIVER	WHERE	DURATION (in days)	FROM	TO
Amazon*	South America (Brazil)	9–15	Manaus	Barbados/ Ft. Lauderdale/ St. Thomas
Danube	Europe (Austria)	7	Vienna	Cernavoda
		7	Vienna	Rousse
		7	Passau/Budapest/Passau	
Nile	Middle East (Egypt)	3/4/7	Luxor	Aswan
		10–15	Cairo	Aswan
Orinoco*	South America (Brazil)	7	Barbados	Barbados
Rhine	Europe	6–8	Amsterdam	Basle
Sepik	Melanesia (New Guinea)	3–16	Madang	Ambunti
Volga	Russia	8	Kazan	Rostov-on-Don

*Note that Amazon and Orinoco cruises are combined with a Caribbean cruise itinerary and are featured on ocean-going cruise vessels.

Adventure Cruising

"The risk one runs in exploring a coast in these unknown and icy seas is so very great that I can be so bold to say no man will ever venture farther than I have done and that the lands to the south will never be explored."

So wrote Captain James Cook in 1774. His voyage was a feat of great courage, for not only did he enter an unknown sea, but his ship, the *Resolution,* was far too fragile a vessel (462 tons) to undertake such a trip. Yet there is no landscape quite so breathtaking and compelling as the polar regions of the south, and no experience so unforgettable as a visit there. Today's Captain Cooks have the curiosity and drive to move into "adventure cruising".

With so many opportunities to cruise in the Caribbean, Mediterranean, Alaskan and Mexican Riviera areas, it may seem surprising to discover a small group of enthusiasts heading out for strange and remote waters. But there are countless virtually untouched areas to be visited and explored by the more adventurous.

On an adventure cruise, passengers take an active role in every aspect of the expedition. Naturalists and lecturers are aboard each ship to provide background information and regional observations about wildlife.

Because of the briefings, lectures and a laboratory at sea, there is a cultural and intellectual element not found on other cruise ships. The ships themselves are designed and equipped to sail in ice-laden waters, and yet have a shallow enough draft to glide over coral reefs.

The adventure cruise vessel nevertheless provides elegant and comfortable surroundings for up to 200 passengers, a highly trained and knowledgeable staff and first-class food. Without traditional cruise ports to stop at, the ship must be self-sufficient and capable of long-range cruising.

Adventure cruising was pioneered in the late 1960s by Lars-Eric Lindblad, a Swedish-American who was determined to turn travel into adventure by opening up parts of the world tourists had never visited.

After chartering several vessels for adventure cruises to Antarctica, he arranged the design and construction of a ship capable of going to virtually anywhere in the world in comfort and safety. In 1969, the *Lindblad Explorer* was launched.

In the years that followed, the ship earned an enviable reputation in adventure travel. Lindblad's company sold the ship to Salén-Lindblad Cruising in 1982. They subsequently resold the vessel to Society Expeditions, who renamed her the *Society Explorer,* but kept its role in joint marketing of the ship's unusual cruise programs.

Adventure Cruise Areas

The principal adventure cruise areas of the world are: Alaska and the Aleutians, Amazonia and the Orinoco, Antarctica, Australasia, Chilean Fjords, Galapagos Archipelago, Indonesia, Melanesia, Northwest Passage, Polynesia and the South Pacific. Baha California and the Sea of Cortez, Greenland, the Red Sea, East Africa, the Reunion Islands and the Seychelles, West Africa and the Ivory Coast and the South China Seas and China Coast are other adventure cruise destinations growing in popularity.

In order to put together their special cruise expeditions, the staff at Lindblad Travel, Salén-Lindblad Cruising, Society Expeditions and Special Expeditions turn to various knowledgeable sources and advisors. Scientific institutions are consulted, experienced world explorers are questioned, and naturalists provide up-to-date reports on wildlife sightings, migrations and other natural phenomena. Although there are days scheduled for relaxing, unwinding or for preparing for the events of the days ahead, participants are kept active both physically and mentally. And speaking of physical activity, it is unwise to consider such an adventure cruise if you are not 100% ambulatory.

As this book goes to press, it is understood that both Lindblad Travel and Salén-Lindblad Cruising (the two are not related) have ordered new, high-tech expedition cruise vessels, capable of taking up to 200 passengers to the most fascinating and remote areas of the world. Both vessels will have ice-hardened hulls for cruising in Arctic and Antarctic waters.

Cousteau's Zodiac

Essential to most adventure cruise vessels is a small armada of inflatable rubber boats known as Zodiacs. These agile craft, developed by Jacques Cousteau especially for expedition work, serve as landing craft for the mother ship. They hold up to 15 people and can penetrate deep into otherwise inaccessible areas.

The adventure cruise ship is seldom "alongside" a dock and is more likely to be found at anchor in a small inlet or bay. For use as a diving base in warm waters, such as around Australia's Great Barrier Reef, the Zodiac is ideal and is safe and unsinkable. And, if hemmed in by ice in the Antarctic, the Zodiac is light enough to be lifted onto the ice floe and carried to the next stretch of open water.

Until these are ready for delivery (sometime in 1990) these two companies charter other vessels for specific programs, as well as sell into the two ships operated by Society Expeditions—the *Society Explorer* and *World Discoverer*. So, if you've wanted a taste of real adventure, an expedition cruise might be just the ticket for you. Better get your waterproof clothing ready for the cruise of a lifetime.

Lindblad Travel—reportedly has a new ship on order, as indicated earlier.

Salén-Lindblad Cruising—In addition to its new ship on order, the company also sells special expedition programs on the *Island Explorer* (Indonesia), *Melanesian Discoverer* (New Guinea) and the *Kimberley Explorer* (Australia), all three of which are high-tech catamaran-type vessels, completely outfitted for in-depth adventuring.

Society Expeditions—owns and operates the *Society Explorer* and *World Discoverer*, both of which are true expedition cruise vessels, featuring fine luxury appointments and full creature comforts (see profile section for details).

Special Expeditions—operates the *Polaris*, a true expedition vessel, featuring fine luxury appointments and full creature comforts (see profile section for details).

In Search of the Northwest Passage
In 1984, Salén-Lindblad Cruising made maritime history by successfully negotiating a westbound voyage through the Northwest Passage, a 41-day epic which started from St. John's, Newfoundland, and ended at Yokohama, Japan. The expedition cruise had taken two years of planning, and was sold out days after it was announced.

The search for a Northwest Passage to the Orient attracted brave explorers for more than 400 years. Despite numerous attempts and loss of life, including Henry Hudson in 1610, a "white passage" to the east remained an elusive dream. Amundsen's 47-ton ship, the *Gjoa*, successfully navigated the route in 1906, taking three years to do so. It was not until 1943 that a Canadian ship, the *St. Roch*, became the first vessel in history to make the passage in a single season. The *Lindblad Explorer* became the 34th vessel, and the first cruise ship, to complete the incredibly difficult voyage.

The World Cruise

The World Cruise

The ultimate classic voyage for any traveler is a world cruise. A world cruise is normally the complete circumnavigation of the earth in a continuous one-way voyage. Ports of call are programmed for interest and diversity, and the whole trip can run as long as four months.

A world cruise is a voyage usually in warm waters with crisp, clear days, sparkling nights, delicious food, tasteful entertainment, superb accommodations, delightful company and unforgettable memories. It is for some the cultural, social and travel experience of a lifetime, and for the few who can afford it, an annual event!

The concept of the world cruise became popular in the 1920s, although it has existed since the 1880s. The first round-the-world voyage was made by Ferdinand Magellan in 1539.

A world cruise on today's ships means stabilized, air-conditioned comfort, luxury cabins, and extraordinary sightseeing and excursions ashore.

A world cruise gives you the opportunity to indulge yourself. Although at first the idea may sound extravagant, it need not be, and fares can be as low as $100 per day for a voyage of up to four months. And you can book just a segment if you prefer.

How much a round-the-world voyage costs will depend on your choice of ship and accommodations. For 1989, double occupancy cruise fares will vary from about $8,000 to more than $100,000 per person. QE2's penthouse split-level suites, for example, can cost $360,000 each!

Planning and Preparation

Few enterprises can match the complexity of planning a world cruise. Enough food must be ordered for every meal, and shore-based chefs contracted to board and help with local specialty dishes. Several hundred professional entertainers, lecturers, bands and musicians must all be booked about a year in advance. Airline tickets must be arranged for personnel flying in to join the ship—in the right port, and at the right time.

Crew changeovers during the cruise must be organized. On a ship the size of Cunard's *QE2*, there will be two major crew changes on the three-month-long voyage. This normally requires chartering a jumbo jet to and from the ship.

Because a modern world cruise ship has to be totally self-contained, a warehouse-full of spare parts (electrical, plumbing and engineering supplies, for example) must be anticipated, ordered, loaded and stored somewhere aboard ship.

For just about every ship-board department, the same fundamental consideration applies. For, once at sea, it will be impossible to pick up a replacement projector bulb, air-conditioning belt, table tennis ball or saxophone reed.

The Cruise Director will have his hands full planning entertainment and social events for a long voyage —not like the "old days" when an occasional game of bingo, horse racing, or the daily tote would satisfy his passengers.

Other preparations aboard include reserving of fuel at various ports on the itinerary. A cruise line must give advance notice of the date and time that pilots will be needed, together with requirements for tugs and docking services, customs and immigration authorities, or meeting local dignitaries and the press. Then there's the organization of dockside labor and stevedoring services at each port of call, plus the planning and contracting of bus or transportation services, for both shore excursion participants and those wishing to explore places on their own.

The complexity of the preparations requires the concerted efforts of many departments and people on every continent to bring about, with exact timing, the ultimate cruising experience—round the world.

Other Classic Voyages

Voyages to exotic destinations— China, the Orient, South Pacific, Africa and the Indian Ocean or around South America—offer all the delights associated with a world cruise. The cruise can be shorter and hence less expensive, yet offer the same excellent service, elegance and comfort, splendid food, delightful ambiance and fellow passengers.

An exotic voyage can be a totally self-contained cruise to a spe-

Going Posh
This colloquialism for "grand" or "first rate" has its origin in the old days of constant steamship travel between England and India. Passengers would, at some cost, book their round trip passage as "*Port Outward, Starboard Home*". This would secure cabin bookings on the cooler side of the ship while crossing the unbearably hot Indian Ocean in the sun. Abbreviated as P.O.S.H., the expression soon came to be applied to first-class passengers who could afford that luxury.
(From Brewers Dictionary of Phrase & Fable, Cassell Ltd., 1981 Edition.)

cific destination, lasting anything from 14 days to 100. Or you can book a segment of a world cruise to begin at one of its ports of call, getting off at another port. "Segmenting" is ideal for those who wish to be a part of a world cruise, but have neither the time nor the money for the prolonged extravagance of a three- to four-month cruise.

Necessarily, segment cruising will involve flying either to or from your cruise, or both. You can join your special cruise at such ports as Genoa, Rio de Janeiro, Acapulco, Honolulu, Sydney, Hong Kong, Singapore, Bangkok, Bombay or Athens, depending on ship and cruise.

Ships that already cruise worldwide during the year offer the most experienced world cruises or segments. Although most of these accommodate a maximum of 750 passengers, they often run at about 75 per cent capacity round the world, thus providing passengers with far more space than normal.

World Cruise Fleet

Although the best known ships offering round-the-world or other extended cruises are luxury class (HI), some offer moderate (MOD), even economy (LOW), prices. The following list includes ships currently scheduled for world or extended cruises, and others that have offered them in the past few years.

SHIP	CRUISE LINE/OPERATOR	GRT	PRICE
Azerbaydzhan	Black Sea Shipping	16,900	LOW
Belorussiya	Black Sea Shipping	16,900	LOW
Canberra	P&O Canberra Cruises	44,807	MOD
Danae	Costa Cruises	16,300	MOD
Europa	Hapag-Lloyd Line	33,819	HI
Kazakhstan	Black Sea Shipping	16,631	LOW
Maxim Gorki	Black Sea Shipping	25,022	MOD
Mermoz	Paquet Cruises	13,691	MOD
Odessa	Black Sea Shipping	13,757	LOW
Queen Elizabeth 2	Cunard Line	66,451	HI
Royal Viking Sea	Royal Viking Line	28,078	HI
Royal Viking Sky	Royal Viking Line	28,078	HI
Royal Viking Sun	Royal Viking Line	38,000	HI
Sagafjord	Cunard Line	24,474	HI
Sea Princess	Princess Cruises	27,670	MOD
Taras Shevchenko	Black Sea Shipping	20,027	LOW
Vasco da Gama	Neckermann Seereisen	24,562	MOD

Part Two

Cruise Ship Directory
and Ratings

How to Use this Directory

In this section, I have listed 148 ocean-going cruise ships currently in service. All except 10 new or reconstructed ships not yet rated, plus 1 tall ship and 3 expedition cruise vessels, have been examined from over 400 separate inspection points based on personal sailings and visits. For the sake of simplicity, I have channeled the inspections into 20 major sections. With a possible 100 points per section, maximum score for any ship is a theoretical 2,000 points. The 3 expedition cruise vessels and 1 tall ship cannot be judged according to the same criteria as the other ships, because of their special-purpose construction, but I have given them stars in the same way as the others, as an appraisal of quality.

If you have only the vaguest idea of what kind of cruise or ship you wish to take, I suggest you first consult the "Pick-a-Ship" chart on p. 102–110. In this general listing of cruise ships and the kind of ambiance and fellow passengers you'll find on board, there are 201 vessels listed. Of these, there are 53 that I have chosen not to grade or describe in detail. This is simply because of lack of space. A few were still under construction or not available for inspection at the time this revision was being completed.

The stars beside the name of the ship at the top of each page relate directly to the numerical score achieved in the evaluation (Overall Rating). The highest number of stars awarded is five (★), the lowest is one. A plus (+) indicates that a ship deserved just that little bit more than the number of stars given.

Overall Rating	Number of Stars	Minimum Average Score
1801 and above	★★★★★+	90.0
1751–1800	★★★★★	87.5
1676–1750	★★★★+	83.7
1601–1675	★★★★	80.0
1551–1600	★★★+	77.5
1501–1550	★★★	75.0
1401–1500	★★	70.0
1400 or less	★	under 70.0

Cruise lines are in the business of creating and selling products of excellence, and thus the common factor of all cruise ships is quality. Therefore, in appraising and grading such an industry, it is inevitable that scores will be on the high side and the difference in score from one ship to another perhaps very little. If you were to look at it in terms of school marks, you would expect to find most ships in the "A" and "B" brackets. Or, according to my system, of 134 cruise ships evaluated, 111 have achieved three stars or more.

This is where smaller detail and the comments on each ship will help you determine what is best for *you*.

Needless to say, there is no such thing as a standard cruise ship. They come in all sizes and shapes, internal layout, facilities and appointments. The one thing all ships have in common is gross registered tonnage, often abbreviated to grt. This is an international measurement used for ship classification and insurance purposes.

Since size is often the key to the kind of facilities, level of comfort—and, of course, number of passengers—on board, I have found it convenient to divide the ships into four categories based on their grt.

Grt	Classification	Category	No. of Ships Evaluated
Up to 10,000	Intimate	1	31
10,000–20,000	Small	2	41
20,000–30,000	Medium	3	36
Over 30,000	Large	4	26

At the end of the ship-by-ship evaluations, you will find my final rating results broken down into these categories. Also shown is a silhouette of a ship typical of the category. These will be drawn in proportion to one another to indicate their comparative size.

In future editions of this Complete Handbook to Cruising, I will further update and revise, since constant change and dynamic growth are intrinsic features of this industry.

"Pick-a-Ship" Chart

This at-a-glance chart will help you compare cruise ships and select those that interest you most. You can then turn to the ratings and evaluations which follow for an in-depth look at each vessel. Certain ships included in this chart, such as small coastal vessels or Soviet ships catering mainly to Eastern European passengers, have not been rated or evaluated in depth.

Key

Ship Name
Given in alphabetical order.

Cruise Line/Operator
The owner, chartering company and/or operator.

Cruise Length
Usual length of cruise in days.
Var. = various itineraries and cruise lengths.
Line = this ship operates on a fixed "line" voyage either year-round or seasonally.

Departure Day
Given for those ships with year-round or scheduled seasonal sailing days.

Price Range
Given to indicate what you can expect to pay per person, per day, based on the minimum full published tariff rate available.
LOW = Low—up to $175 per person, per day.
MOD = Moderate—$175 to $250 per person, per day.
HI   = High—over $250 per person, per day.

Tone/Lifestyle
CAS = Casual, relaxed dress code, completely informal.
INF   = Informal, moderately conservative, resort attire suggested.
FOR = Formal, elegant, conservative and "correct" attire requested.

Ambiance
FUN = Fun—lively party action cruises, recommended for singles and young couples seeking fun and plenty of life.
FAM = Family—ideal for families with children of all ages.
CPL = Couples—and those not seeking action at all hours.

102

MAT = Mature—conservative, quality cruising for the discerning passenger.

EDU = Educational—for adventure/expedition/educational cruisers interested in life enrichment.

Cabin Insulation Rating
On a scale of 1–10, with 10 being highest and most soundproof. Each rating takes into account the general noise level and degree of insulation between cabins. This is a composite rating taken from cabins on several decks.

Sports/Health Facilities
On a scale of 1–10, with 10 being the highest score. The rating reflects gymnasium/health and fitness facilities and equipment, instruction programs and degree of professionalism.

Disabled Access Rating
On a scale of 1–10, with 10 being the highest score. Each rating takes into account the ship itself, public areas and access, cabin access, and the accessibility of open decks and gangways. In addition, asterisks have been added:

* = this ship has no or low (less than ½″) *sill/lip* into cabin.
** = this ship has no *sill/lip* into both cabin and bathroom.

SHIP NAME	TON-NAGE	CRUISE LINE/OPERATOR	CRUISE LENGTH	DEPARTURE DAY	PRICE RANGE	TONE/LIFESTYLE	AMBIANCE	CABIN IN-SULATION RATING	SPORTS/HEALTH FACILITIES	DISABLED ACCESS RATING
Achille Lauro	23,629	Star Lauro Line/TFC Cruises	var.	var.	LOW	CAS	FUN/FAM	7	3	3*
• Adjaria	5,035	Black Sea Shipping	7	Tue.	LOW	CAS	CPL	3	1	2
Adriana	4,590	Jadrolinija	7–22	var.	LOW	INF	FUN/FAM	7	3	3*
Aegean Dolphin	11,200	Dolphin Hellas Shipping	7	Sat.	LOW	CAS	FAM/CPL	4	3	3*
Albatross	10,026	Dolphin Hellas Shipping	7	Sat.	LOW	CAS	FAM/CPL	5	4	3*
Alexandr Pushkin	20,502	Baltic Shipping	var.	var.	LOW	CAS	FUN/FAM	6	5	4*
• Alla Tarasova	5,035	Murmansk Shipping	line	var.	LOW	CAS	CPL	3	1	1
Americana	19,203	Ivaran Lines	46–48	var.	MOD	INF	CPL/MAT	7	1	3
Amerikanis	19,904	Chandris Fantasy Cruises	1/6/7	var.	LOW	INF	FUN/FAM	6	4	4*
Antonina Nezhdanova	3,941	Far Eastern Shipping	var.	var.	MOD	INF	CPL/MAT	4	2	1*
• Aquanaut Ambassador	2,573	Aquanaut Cruises	var.	var.	LOW	CAS	FAM/CPL	3	1	
Argonaut	4,500	Epirotiki Lines	var.	var.	LOW	INF	CPL	5	1	2
Arkona	18,834	Deutsche Seereederei/Seetours	12–17	var.	MOD	INF	CPL	7	4	6
• Armenia	5,035	Black Sea Shipping	line	var.	LOW	CAS	CPL	3	1	1
Atalante	13,113	Mediterranean Sun Lines	7/14	Sat.	LOW	CAS	FUN/FAM	4	2	2
Atlantic	33,800	Premier Cruise Lines	3/4	Fri/Mon	LOW	CAS	CPL	7	7	8*
Atlas	16,000	Epirotiki Lines	7	Fri.	LOW	CAS	FAM/CPL	6	3	4
Ausonia	12,750	Siosa Lines	7	Sat.	LOW	CAS	FAM/CPL	6	3	3
• Ayvasovsky	7,127	Soviet Danube Shipping	line	var.	LOW	CAS	FUN/CPL	4	2	3
Azerbaydzhan	16,631	Black Sea Shipping	var.	var.	LOW	CAS	CPL	5	4	4*
The Azur	14,717	Chandris Fantasy Cruises	7–12	var.	LOW	CAS	CPL	6	7	4*
Azure Seas	21,486	Admiral Cruises	3/4	Fri/Mon	LOW	CAS	FUN/CPL	6	5	4
• Baikal	5,035	Far Eastern Shipping	line	var.	LOW	CAS	CPL	3	1	1
• Bashkiria	5,035	Black Sea Shipping	7	Tue.	LOW	CAS	CPL	3	1	1
Belorussiya	16,900	Black Sea Shipping	var.	var.	LOW	CAS	FAM/CPL	5	4	4*
Berlin	9,570	Deilmann Reederei	var.	var.	MOD	INF	CPL	7	3	4*
Bermuda Star	23,395	Bermuda Star Line	7	Sat.	LOW	INF	FAM/CPL	7	4	5**
Black Prince	11,209	Fred Olsen Cruises	var.	var.	LOW	INF	CPL	7	6	5*
Britanis	25,245	Chandris Fantasy Cruises	2/5/7	var.	LOW	INF	FUN/FAM	7	5	5**

Buccaneer	1,574	Galapagos Cruises	7	Tue.	LOW	CAS	EDU	3	1	1
Canberra	44,807	P&O Canberra Cruises	14/21	Sat.	LOW	INF	FAM/CPL	7	7	5*
Carib Vacationer	2,435	Vacation Liners	7	Sat.	LOW	CAS	FAM/CPL	2	0	1
Caribe I	17,434	Commodore Cruise Lines	7	Sat.	LOW	INF	FUN/FAM	5	4	4*
Carla Costa	20,477	Costa Cruises	7	Sat.	LOW	INF	FUN/FAM	5	4	4*
Carnivale	27,250	Carnival Cruise Lines	3/4	Fri/Mon	LOW	CAS	FUN/FAM	6	5	5
Celebration	47,262	Carnival Cruise Lines	7	Sat.	LOW	CAS	FUN/FAM	8	7	9**
City of Mykonos	4,755	Cycladic Cruises	3/4	Fri/Mon	LOW	CAS	FUN/FAM	3	1	1
City of Rhodos	8,000	Cycladic Cruises	3/4	Fri/Mon	LOW	CAS	FUN/FAM	2	1	1'
Constitution	30,090	American Hawaii Cruises	3/4/7	var.	MOD	CAS	FAM/CPL	5	4	6*
Coral Princess	9,639	China Navigation/Swire Group	var.	var.	LOW	INF	CPL	3	2	2
Costa Riviera	31,500	Costa Cruises	7	Sat.	LOW	INF	FUN/FAM	7	6	7*
Crown del Mar	8,963	Crown Cruise Line	2/5	Fri/Mon	LOW	CAS	FUN/FAM	10	9	10**
Crown Odyssey	34,242	Royal Cruise Line	var.	var.	MOD	FOR	CPL/MAT	5	4	4*
Cunard Countess	17,593	Cunard Line	7	Sat.	LOW	CAS	FUN/FAM	5	4	4*
Cunard Princess	17,495	Cunard Line	7/10/11	var.	LOW	CAS	FUN/FAM	3	3	1
Dalmacija	5,651	Jadrolinija	14	Sat.	LOW	CAS	CPL	6	4	5**
Danae	16,300	Costa Cruises	11	var.	MOD	INF	CPL	6	5	5**
Daphne	16,000	Costa Cruises	7	Sat.	LOW	INF	CPL	8	5	5*
Dawn Princess	25,000	Princess Cruises	9-14	var.	MOD	INF	FAM/CPL	4	2	2
Dimitri Shostakovich	9,878	Estonian Shipping	14	Tue.	LOW	CAS	CPL	3	5	3
Discovery I	12,244	Discovery Cruises	1	Daily	LOW	CAS	FUN/FAM	4	3	4
Dolphin IV	13,007	Dolphin Cruise Line	3/4	Fri/Mon	LOW	CAS	FUN/FAM	5	4	5*
Emerald Seas	24,458	Admiral Cruises	3/4	Fri/Mon	LOW	CAS	FUN/FAM	4	2	3
Enrico Costa	16,495	Costa Cruises	7	Sun.	LOW	CAS	FAM/CPL	6	4	6*
Eugenio Costa	30,567	Costa Cruises	10	var.	LOW	INF	FAM/CPL	10	9	10**
Europa	33,819	Hapag-Lloyd Line	var.	var.	HI	FOR	MAT	8	4	4*
Explorer Starship	8,282	Exploration Cruise Lines	7	Sun.	HI	INF	CPL/MAT	8	5	5*
Fair Princess	25,000	Princess Cruises	7-28	var.	MOD	INF	FAM/FAM	6	5	5*
FairStar	23,764	P&O Sitmar Cruises	8-28	var.	LOW	CAS	FUN/FAM	8	5	5*
Fantasy	70,000	Carnival Cruise Lines	7	Sat.	LOW	CAS	FUN/FAM	6	5	5*
Fedor Dostoyevsky	20,158	Black Sea Shipping/Transocean	var.	var.	MOD	CAS	CPL	8	7	7

	Ship	Tonnage	Cruise Line								
	Fedor Shalyapin	21,406	Black Sea Shipping	var.	var.	LOW	CAS	CPL	7	3	4
•	Felix Dzerjinsky	5,035	Far Eastern Shipping	line	var.	LOW	CAS	CPL	3	1	1
	Festivale	38,175	Carnival Cruise Lines	7	Sun.	LOW	CAS	FUN/FAM	7	5	6*
	Funchal	9,845	Fritidskryss	14	Sun.	LOW	INF	CPL	5	3	4*
•	Galapagos Explorer	2,143	Galapagos Cruises	var.	var.	LOW	CAS	EDU	3	1	1
	Galaxias	5,500	Global Cruises	var.	var.	LOW	CAS	CPL	4	2	2
	Galileo	28,083	Chandris Fantasy Cruises	2/5	Fri/Sun	LOW	INF	FUN/FAM	7	5	7*
•	Georg Ots	9,878	Estonian Shipping	7	var.	LOW	CAS	CPL	4	3	2
	Golden Odyssey	10,563	Royal Cruise Line	7/14/16	var.	MOD	FOR	CPL/MAT	7	3	5*
	Gruziya	16,631	Black Sea Shipping	var.	var.	LOW	CAS	CPL	5	4	4*
	Holiday	46,052	Carnival Cruise Lines	7	Sat.	LOW	CAS	FUN/FAM	7	7	9**
•	Ilich	8,000	Fritidskryss	4	Tue/Fri	LOW	CAS	FAM/CPL	4	2	3
	Illiria	3,751	Blue Aegean Cruises/Tauck Tours	7	Sat.	MOD	CAS	CPL	3	1	1
	Independence	30,090	American Hawaii Cruises	7	Sat.	MOD	CAS	FAM/CPL	5	4	6
•	Isabela II	20,000	Galapagos Cruises	7	Tue.	MOD	CAS	EDU	7		
	Island Princess	20,000	Princess Cruises	7	Sat.	MOD	INF	CPL/MAT	8	6	8*
•	Istra	5,634	Jadrolinija	var.	var.	LOW	CAS	CPL	3	1	1
	Ivan Franko	20,064	Black Sea Shipping	var.	var.	LOW	CAS	FAM/CPL	4	4	4*
	Jason	5,250	Epirotiki Lines	3/4/7	var.	LOW	CAS	CPL	4	2	2
•	Jin Jiang	14,812	Shanghai Shipping	4	Sun.	LOW	CAS	FAM/CPL	5	2	3*
•	Jubilee	47,262	Carnival Cruise Lines	7	Sun.	LOW	CAS	FUN/FAM	7	7	9**
	Jupiter	9,000	Epirotiki Lines	7	Fri.	LOW	CAS	FAM/CPL	4	2	3*
	Kazakhstan	16,631	Black Sea Shipping	7–14	Sat.	LOW	CAS	FAM/CPL	5	4	4*
•	Khabarovsk	5,035	Far Eastern Shipping	line	var.	LOW	CAS	CPL	3	1	1
	Kirgistan	3,219	Black Sea Shipping	line	var.	LOW	CAS	CPL	3	1	1
	Klavdia	3,941	Murmansk Shipping	line	var.	LOW	CAS	CPL	3	1	1
•	Kolkida	5,035	Black Sea Shipping	line	var.	LOW	CAS	CPL	3	1	1
•	Konstantin Chernenko	12,800	Far Eastern Shipping	var.	var.	LOW	CAS	CPL	3	2	3*
•	Konstantin Simanov	12,800	Far Eastern Shipping	var.	var.	LOW	CAS	CPL	3	2	3*
	La Palma	11,608	Intercruise	7	Sat.	LOW	CAS	FUN/FAM	5	3	3*
•	Latvia	5,035	Black Sea Shipping	var.	var.	LOW	CAS	CPL	3	1	1
	Leonid Brezhnev	16,900	Black Sea Shipping/CTC	var.	var.	LOW	INF	FAM/CPL	5	4	4*

Ship	Tonnage	Company	Days	Departs	Price	Style	Program	col1	col2	col3
• Leonid Sobinov	21,846	Black Sea Shipping	var.	var.	LOW	CAS	FAM/CPL	6	3	3*
• Lev Tolstoi	9,878	Black Sea Shipping	14	Tue.	LOW	CAS	CPL	4	2	3
• Litva	5,035	Black Sea Shipping	line	var.	LOW	CAS	CPL	3	1	1
• Lyubov Orlova	3,941	Far Eastern Shipping	line	var.	LOW	CAS	CPL	3	1	1
Majestic	17,370	Premier Cruise Lines	3/4	Thu/Sun	LOW	CAS	FUN/FAM	5	4	5*
Mardi Gras	27,250	Carnival Cruise Lines	3/4	Thu/Sun	LOW	CAS	FUN/FAM	6	5	4
• Mariya Ermalova	3,941	Murmansk Shipping	line	var.	LOW	CAS	CPL	3	1	2
• Mariya Savina	3,941	Far Eastern Shipping	line	var.	LOW	CAS	CPL	3	1	1
• Mariya Ulyanova	5,035	Far Eastern Shipping	line	var.	LOW	CAS	CPL	3	1	1
Maxim Gorki	25,022	Black Sea Shipping/Phoenix	var.	var.	LOW	INF	FAM/CPL	7	5	7*
Maxim's des Mers	1,590	Maxim's des Mers	7	Sun.	HI	FOR	MAT	7	1	1
• Mediterranean Sky	14,941	Karageorgis Lines	var.	var.	MOD	CAS	CPL/EDU	4	2	2
Mermoz	13,804	Paquet Cruises	7-14	var.	MOD	INF	CPL	6	4	3
Mikhail Sholokhov	9,878	Far Eastern Shipping	16	var.	LOW	CAS	CPL	4	2	2*
• Mikhail Suslov	9,878	Far Eastern Shipping	line	var.	LOW	CAS	CPL	4	2	2*
• Moldavia	3,219	Black Sea Shipping	line	var.	LOW	CAS	CPL	3	1	1
Monterey	21,051	Aloha Pacific Cruises	7	Sat.	MOD	CAS	FAM/CPL	5	3	5*
Neptune	4,000	Epirotiki Lines	3/4	Fri/Mon	LOW	CAS	FAM/CPL	3	1	2
Nieuw Amsterdam	33,930	Holland America Line	7	Sat.	LOW	FOR	MAT	9	8	9*
Noordam	33,930	Holland America Line	7	Sat.	LOW	FOR	MAT	9	8	9*
Nordic Prince	23,200	Royal Caribbean Cruise Line	7/8/10	var.	MOD	INF	FAM/CPL	6	6	7*
• North Star	3,095	Exploration Cruise Lines	3/4/7	var.	MOD	CAS	CPL	4	1	1
• Norway	70,202	Norwegian Cruise Line	7	Sat.	MOD	INF	FUN/FAM	9	9	8*
Ocean Islander	6,179	Ocean Cruise Lines	7	Sun.	LOW	INF	CPL	5	1	2*
Ocean Pearl	12,456	Ocean Cruise Lines	14	var.	MOD	INF	CPL/EDU	7	5	5*
Ocean Princess	12,183	Ocean Cruise Lines	7	Sun.	LOW	INF	CPL	6	3	3*
• Ocean Spirit	8,666	Ocean Quest	7	Sat.	LOW	CAS	FUN	4	7	2
Oceanic	39,241	Premier Cruise Lines	3/4	Fri/Mon	LOW	CAS	FUN/FAM	8	6	8*
Oceanos	14,000	Epirotiki Lines	7/14	var.	LOW	CAS	CPL	5	2	3*
Odessa	13,757	Black Sea Shipping/Transocean	var.	var.	LOW	CAS	CPL	5	3	4*
Odysseus	9,272	Epirotiki Lines	3/4/7	Fri/Mon	LOW	CAS	FUN/FAM	5	3	3*
• Olga Androvskaya	3,941	Far Eastern Shipping	line	var.	LOW	CAS	CPL	3	1	1

Ship		Line	line	var.	LOW	CAS	CPL	3	1	1
• Olga Sadovskaya	3,941	Far Eastern Shipping	7	var.	LOW	CAS	CPL	3	1	1
• Orient Express	12,343	Orient Express/British Ferries	7	Sat.	LOW	CAS	FAM/CPL	4	2	6
Orpheus	5,092	Epirotiki Lines	14–16	var.	LOW	INF	CPL/CDU	5	1	3
Pacific Princess	20,000	Princess Cruises	7/12/14	var.	MOD	INF	CPL/MAT	8	6	8*
Pegasus	17,500	Epirotiki Lines	3/4/10/11	var.	LOW	CAS	FAM/CPL	5	4	4
Polaris	2,214	Special Expeditions	var.	var.	HI	INF	EDU	5	1	1
Queen Elizabeth 2	66,451	Cunard Line	5/var.	var.	MOD	FOR	MAT	9	10	10*
Queen of Bermuda	23,879	Bermuda Star Line	7	Sat.	LOW	INF	FAM/CPL	7	5	6**
Regent Sea	22,785	Regency Cruises	7	Sun.	LOW	INF	FAM/CPL	8	4	6**
Regent Star	24,214	Regency Cruises	7	Sun.	LOW	INF	FAM/CPL	8	4	6*
Regent Sun	25,500	Regency Cruises	7	Sun.	LOW	INF	FAM/CPL	9	6	7*
Romanza	7,537	Chandris Fantasy Cruises	7	Sat.	LOW	CAS	FAM/CPL	5	1	2
Rotterdam	38,645	Holland America Line	var.	var.	LOW	FOR	MAT	9	7	7*
Royal Princess	44,348	Princess Cruises	10/11/14	var.	MOD	FOR	CPL/MAT	9	7	9**
Royal Viking Sea	28,078	Royal Viking Line	var.	var.	MOD	FOR	MAT	9	8	8*
Royal Viking Sky	28,078	Royal Viking Line	var.	var.	MOD	FOR	MAT	9	8	8*
Royal Viking Star	28,078	Royal Viking Line	var.	var.	MOD	INF	MAT	9	8	8*
Royal Viking Sun	38,000	Royal Viking Line	var.	var.	HI	FOR	MAT	10	10	10*
Sagafjord	25,147	Cunard Line	var.	var.	MOD	FOR	MAT	10	8	9**
• Santa Cruz	1,052	Galapagos Cruises	3/4	var.	LOW	CAS	EDU	3	1	1
Scandinavian Saga	10,000	SeaEscape	1/4	Daily/Sun	LOW	CAS	FUN/FAM	4	3	3
Scandinavian Sky	8,139	SeaEscape	1/2	Daily/Thu	LOW	CAS	FUN/FAM	3	1	3
Scandinavian Star	10,513	SeaEscape	1/2	Daily	LOW	CAS	FUN/FAM	3	2	3
Scandinavian Sun	9,903	SeaEscape	1	Daily	LOW	CAS	FUN/FAM	4	1	2
Sea Goddess I	4,260	Cunard Line	var.	var.	HI	FOR	MAT	9	4	4*
Sea Goddess II	4,260	Cunard Line	var.	var.	HI	FOR	MAT	9	4	4*
• Sea Nymph	3,967	Mediterranean Ionian Cruises	7	Sat.	LOW	CAS	FUN/FAM	3	1	1
Sea Princess	27,670	Princess Cruises	10–14	var.	MOD	FOR	CPL/MAT	9	6	8*
Sea Venture	8,500	Sea Venture Cruises	7/10/11	var.	MOD	INF	CPL/MAT			
Seabourn Pride	9,000	Seabourn Cruise Line	11–24	var.	HI	FOR	MAT			
SeaBreeze	21,900	Dolphin Cruise Lines	7	Sun.	LOW	CAS	FUN/FAM	6	5	4
Seaward	40,000	Norwegian Cruise Line	7	Sat.	LOW	INF	FUN/FAM	8	8	7*

Ship	Tonnage	Cruise Line	Days	Day	Price	Cabin	Style			
Shota Rustaveli	20,499	Black Sea Shipping	var.	var.	LOW	CAS	FAM/CPL	5	4	4*
Sky Princess	46,314	Princess Cruises	10/12	var.	MOD	INF	FAM/CPL	8	8	9**
Skyward	16,254	Norwegian Cruise Line	7	Sun.	LOW	CAS	FUN/FAM	5	5	5*
Society Explorer	2,398	Society Expeditions	var.	var.	HI	INF	EDU	2	1	2
Song of America	37,584	Royal Caribbean Cruise Line	7	Sun.	MOD	INF	FAM/CPL	8	7	7*
Song of Norway	23,005	Royal Caribbean Cruise Line	7	Sun/Wed	MOD	INF	FAM/CPL	6	6	7*
Southward	16,609	Norwegian Cruise Line	3/4	Fri/Mon	LOW	CAS	FUN/FAM	5	5	5*
Sovereign of the Seas	73,192	Royal Caribbean Cruise Line	7	Sat.	MOD	INF	FAM/CPL	8	8	8*
Star Princess	62,500	Princess Cruises	10	var.	MOD	INF	FAM/CPL	9	9	9**
Stardancer	26,747	Admiral Cruises	7	Fri.	LOW	INF	FAM/CPL	7	9	8*
Starward	16,107	Norwegian Cruise Line	7	Sun.	LOW	CAS	FUN/CPL	5	5	5*
Stella Maris	4,000	Sun Line Cruises	3-14	var.	MOD	INF	CPL/MAT	4	1	1*
Stella Oceanis	6,000	Sun Line Cruises	3/4/7	var.	MOD	INF	CPL	5	2	2*
Stella Solaris	17,832	Sun Line Cruises	4-12	var.	MOD	FOR	MAT	6	4	5*
Sun Viking	18,556	Royal Caribbean Cruise Line	7/10/14	var.	MOD	INF	FAM/CPL	7	4	6*
Sunward II	14,100	Norwegian Cruise Line	3/4	Fri/Mon	LOW	CAS	FUN/FAM	5	4	4*
• Tadzikistan	3,219	Black Sea Shipping	line	var.	LOW	CAS	CPL	3	1	1*
• Talin	3,219	Murmansk Shipping	line	var.	LOW	CAS	CPL	3	1	1
Taras Shevchenko	20,027	Black Sea Shipping	var.	var.	LOW	CAS	FAM/CPL	4	4	4*
Tropicale	36,674	Carnival Cruise Lines	7	Sun.	LOW	CAS	FUN/FAM	7	5	7**
Turkmenia	5,035	Far Eastern Shipping	line	var.	LOW	CAS	CPL	3	1	1
Universe	18,100	World Explorer Cruises	14	Sun.	MOD	INF	CPL/EDU	6	2	4*
• Uzbekistan	3,219	Black Sea Shipping	line	var.	LOW	CAS	CPL	3	1	1
Vasco da Gama	24,562	Arcalia Shipping (Neckermann Seereisen)	var.	var.	MOD	INF	CPL	6	7	5*
Veracruz	10,595	Bermuda Star Line	7	Sat.	LOW	CAS	FAM/CPL	3	2	3
The Victoria	14,917	Chandris Fantasy Cruises	7	Mon.	LOW	CAS	FAM/CPL	5	4	5*
Viking Princess	7,029	Crown Cruise Line	1/2	Daily	LOW	CAS	FUN/FAM	4	1	2
Vistafjord	24,292	Cunard Line	var.	var.	MOD	FOR	MAT	10	8	9**
Westerdam	42,090	Holland America Line	7	Sun.	MOD	FOR	CPL/MAT	9	8	9**
Wind Song	5,037	Windstar Sail Cruises	7	Sat/Sun	MOD	INF	MAT	9	5	3*
Wind Spirit	5,037	Windstar Sail Cruises	7	Fri.	MOD	INF	MAT	9	5	3*
Wind Star	5,037	Windstar Sail Cruises	7	Sat.	MOD	INF	MAT	9	5	3*

	LENGTH -FT	CRUISE LINE/OPERATOR	CRUISE LENGTH	DEPARTURE DAY	PRICE RANGE	TONE/ LIFESTYLE	AMBIANCE	CABIN IN-SULATION RATING	SPORTS/ HEALTH FACILITIES	DISABLED ACCESS RATING
● Winston Churchill	8,658	DFDS Seaways	9	var.	LOW	CAS	CPL	4	2	2
● World Discoverer	3,153	Society Expeditions	var.	var.	HI	INF	EDU	6	2	3
● World Renaissance	11,724	Epirotiki Lines	10/11/14	var.	LOW	INF	CPL	7	4	4*

WINDJAMMER TALL SHIPS:	LENGTH -FT	CRUISE LINE/OPERATOR	CRUISE LENGTH	DEPARTURE DAY	PRICE RANGE	TONE/ LIFESTYLE	AMBIANCE	CABIN IN-SULATION RATING	SPORTS/ HEALTH FACILITIES	DISABLED ACCESS RATING
● Amazing Grace	243	Windjammer Barefoot Cruises	7/14/21	Sun.	LOW	CAS	FUN	2	1	1
● Fantome	282	Windjammer Barefoot Cruises	6	Mon.	LOW	CAS	FUN	3	1	1
● Flying Cloud	208	Windjammer Barefoot Cruises	6	Mon.	LOW	CAS	FUN	3	1	1
● Mandalay	236	Windjammer Barefoot Cruises	13	Mon.	LOW	CAS	FUN	3	1	1
● Polynesia	248	Windjammer Barefoot Cruises	6	Mon.	LOW	CAS	FUN	3	1	1
● Sea Cloud	316	Sea Cloud Cruises	var.	var.	HI	FOR	MAT	6	1	1
● Yankee Clipper	197	Windjammer Barefoot Cruises	6	Mon.	LOW	CAS	FUN	3	1	1

CATAMARAN CRUISERS	LENGTH -FT	CRUISE LINE/OPERATOR	CRUISE LENGTH	DEPARTURE DAY	PRICE RANGE	TONE/ LIFESTYLE	AMBIANCE	CABIN IN-SULATION RATING	SPORTS/ HEALTH FACILITIES	DISABLED ACCESS RATING
● Executive Explorer	98	Catamaran Cruises	var.	var.	MOD	CAS	EDU	4	1	1
● Island Explorer	860	Spice Island Cruises	var.	var.	HI	CAS	EDU	4	1	1
● Melanesian Discoverer	860	Melanesian Tourist Services	var.	var.	MOD	CAS	EDU	4	1	1

● = This ship is either a Soviet ship principally for Europeans, or a small coastal vessel and is not included in the Ratings/Profile section.

How a Ship is Evaluated

More than 400 separate items are taken into consideration during the evaluations. These in turn are brought under 20 major headings for the purpose of this part of the book. The list below includes many of the angles from which each ship is inspected before I arrive at a specific score.

Since the first edition of this handbook, I have further refined the evaluation system and categories, changing things only where necessary for the benefit and effectiveness of the final ratings.

The results, comments and ratings are strictly personal, and are intended to guide you in formulating your own opinions and cruise plans.

• **Ship Appearance and Condition**
1) Aesthetic appearance, styling, lines, stature and condition
2) Bow rake, stern type, funnel design
3) Condition of hull and exterior paint
4) Condition, fit and finish of decking materials
5) Condition of lifeboats and davits
6) Condition of liferafts and other live-preserving equipment
7) Safety, smoke detection, fire and watertight door apparatus
8) Escape route markings and signs
9) Exterior stairways and condition
10) Gangways and launch/tender access points

• **Cleanliness**
1) Public rooms, restrooms and elevators
2) Floor coverings, carpeting
3) Ceilings, bulkheads, wall coverings
4) Stairways, passageways, door-ways, other access points
5) Passenger accommodations
6) Galleys, food preparation areas and food staff
7) Food and beverage storage rooms, refrigeration units
8) Crew stairways and alleyways
9) Crew accommodations, communal facilities
10) Outside deck areas and lifeboats

- **Passenger Space**
  1) Amount of common passenger spaces
  2) Open deck, sheltered deck, sunning areas and promenades
  3) Swimming pools, deck furniture and condition
  4) Access points and doorways
  5) Outdoor observation spaces
  6) Public room spaces
  7) Lobbies, stairways and passage-ways
  8) Public restrooms and facilities
  9) Passenger cabins, bathrooms
  10) Condition of all common passenger spaces

- **Passenger Comfort Level**
  1) Interior appointments and fittings
  2) Lighting, heating and ventilation flow in public areas
  3) Air-conditioning (including "comfort zone") system
  4) Cabin ventilation, controls and efficiency
  5) Deck layout, direction signs and passenger flow
  6) Interior noise and vibration levels
  7) Ventilation and smoke extraction
  8) Public restroom facilities
  9) Seating design, comfort and avail-ability in public areas
  10) Passenger space ratio, density

- **Furnishings/Decor**
  1) Overall appearance and condition
  2) Interior design and decor
  3) Color combinations and appeal
  4) Quality, fit and finish of materials
  5) Choice of fabrics, color and condition
  6) Durability and practicality of furnishings
  7) Carpet color and practicality
  8) Carpet fit, seams, edging
  9) Ceilings and treatments
  10) Artwork, quality and suitability

- **Cruise Cuisine**
  1) Menu planning, combinations
  2) Culinary creativity, variety and appeal
  3) Quality and freshness of ingredients
  4) Taste and palatability
  5) Presentation and balance
  6) Breakfast, luncheon, deck buffets
  7) Midnight buffets, late-night snacks
  8) Appetizers, soups, pastas, entrees, salads, desserts, bread, pastries
  9) Decorative elements, ice carvings
  10) Special dietary considerations

- **Food Service**
  1) Overall dining room service
  2) Restaurant manager, Maitre d', assistants, headwaiters
  3) Table waiters, assistant waiters/busboys
  4) Table set-ups and presentation
  5) Linen, china and cutlery choice, quality and condition
  6) Buffet staff—attitude, service
  7) Public room food service
  8) Afternoon tea/coffee service
  9) Correct temperature of plates/service
  10) Dining room decor, colors, lighting and ambiance

- **Beverages/Service**
  1) Wine list, choice, prices
  2) Alcoholic beverages—variety, quality, pricing
  3) Non-alcoholic beverages—variety, quality, pricing
  4) Wine waiters, professionalism, knowledge, service
  5) Bar Staff—professionalism, knowl-edge, service
  6) Public room service staff—profes-sionalism, knowledge, service
  7) Afternoon tea/coffee service
  8) Self-service items
  9) Glassware and non-glass items
  10) Beverage hustling

- **Accommodations**
  1) Cabin dimensions, accessibility
  2) Space and its use
  3) Insulation, noise and vibration level
  4) Furniture quality and condition
  5) Beds and berths—size, design, comfort level
  6) Closets and hanging space
  7) Drawer and other storage space
  8) Lighting, air-conditioning, heating
  9) Audio/visual systems and quality
  10) Bathroom size, fixtures, fittings

- **Cabin Service**
  1) Steward/stewardess service, attention and attitude
  2) Language and communication
  3) Appearance and dress
  4) Efficiency and professionalism
  5) Visibility and availability
  6) Promptness, speed and accuracy
  7) Linen provision and change
  8) In-cabin meal service
  9) Attention to cleanliness
  10) Extra attention to detail

- **Itineraries/Destinations**
  1) Itinerary/route planning
  2) Balance of sea days/port days
  3) Number and diversity of destinations
  4) Major destination attractions
  5) Geographical location and climate
  6) Historical, cultural and social attraction
  7) Dockside areas, access and cleanliness
  8) Transportation availability
  9) Time allotted in ports of call
  10) Ship-to-shore operation

- **Shore Excursion Program**
  1) Port lectures and information
  2) Descriptive literature
  3) Shore Excursion Manager and staff
  4) Variety, content and balance of shore excursions
  5) Availability and pricing of excursions
  6) Transportation/guide quality
  7) Timing of shore excursions/meals
  8) Special needs and private excursion/transportation arrangements
  9) Overall operation and performance
  10) Overall satisfaction level

- **Entertainment**
  1) Quality, variety and appeal of professional shows
  2) Quality and content of production spectaculars
  3) Professional entertainment/cabaret
  4) Stage and technical production proficiency
  5) Lighting, set design and use
  6) Sound systems, volume levels and acoustics
  7) Music, bands and soloists
  8) Dance music, suitability and quality
  9) Movies, videos, theatre productions
  10) Timing of shows and events

- **Activities Program**
  1) Variety, content and timing of activities
  2) Mind-enrichment lectures and demonstrations
  3) Cocktail parties and social functions
  4) Balance of indoor and outdoor activities
  5) Sports and games activities
  6) Staff attitude in running activities
  7) Staff performance
  8) Originality and creativity
  9) Singles and special interest activities
  10) Children's and teens' programs

- **Cruise Director/Cruise Staff**
  1) Appearance and dress
  2) Visibility and social contact
  3) Stage prescence and professionalism
  4) Microphone technique
  5) Pre-show warm-ups and games
  6) Port lectures and other briefings
  7) Control, diplomacy, administration and problem handling technique
  8) Gangway prescence and visibility
  9) Entertainment value
  10) Professionalism and visibility

- **Ship's Officers**
  1) Captain and senior officers
  2) Appearance and dress
  3) Control, respect and authority
  4) Social contact and visibility
  5) Availability to passengers
  6) Staff control, discipline and guidance
  7) Language and communication skills
  8) Politeness and pleasantness
  9) Staff morale and attitude
  10) Company and product knowledge

- **Fitness/Sports facilities**
  1) Health/fitness spa and facilities
  2) Swimming pools and whirlpools— size and cleanliness
  3) Gymnasium and equipment
  4) Sauna, massage, changing rooms
  5) Parcours, running and jogging circuits
  6) Exercise instruction program
  7) Instructors and consultants
  8) Lectures, classes and activities
  9) Watersports programs
  10) Outdoor sports/games programs

- **Overall Ship Facilities**
  1) Public rooms/restrooms
  2) Lounges and bars
  3) Open decks and sunning spaces
  4) Health and fitness facilities
  5) Sports equipment and facilities
  6) Casino operations
  7) Shops and boutiques
  8) Hairdressing and beauty services
  9) Medical facilities
  10) Smoking/no-smoking provision and enforcement

- **Value for Money**
  1) Brochure description and accuracy
  2) Product expectation and delivery
  3) Product delivery for singles
  4) Ship operational level
  5) Standard of service
  6) Cruise environment and ambiance
  7) Destination value
  8) Competitive analyses
  9) Pricing realism
  10) Perceived value per diem

- **Total Cruise Experience**
  1) Brochure presentation, readability and product description
  2) Air/sea arrangements
  3) Ticketing and other documentation
  4) Transportation arrangements
  5) Embarkation and disembarkation
  6) Pre- and post-cruise packages
  7) Overall on-board facilities
  8) Overall on-board staff
  9) Overall on-board services
  10) Overall passenger satisfaction level

Ratings and Evaluations

In this section, 134 ships are examined in detail. Technical and specific information on each ship is given first, followed by a point by point evaluation of the various aspects of the vessel. Finally, the ship, its good points and bad, are summed up under Comments.

Explanatory Notes

Cruise Line/Operator
Note that the cruise line and operator may be different, depending on whether the company that owns the vessel markets and operates it, or whether it is chartered by the cruise line to another operator. Charters of this nature are common for Soviet-owned ships, which is why under the heading Cruise Line/Operator there may be differences between the Pick-a-Ship chart and the Ratings and Evaluations section.

Passenger Capacity
The number of passengers a ship can carry is given in two ways: two berths per cabin occupied, plus all single cabins; and all available berths filled.

Passenger Space Ratio
Achieved by dividing the gross registered tonnage by the number of passengers carried (Passenger Capacity), based also on two berths per cabin occupied, plus all single cabins; and all available berths filled.

Cabins for the Disabled
Cabins specifically designed and outfitted to accommodate passengers with mobility problems.

The Cruise Fleet

Admiral Cruises:
Azure Seas
Emerald Seas
Stardancer

Aloha Pacific Cruises:
Monterey

American Canadian Caribbean Line:
Caribbean Prince
New Shoreham II

American Cruise Lines:
Charleston
New Orleans
Savannah

American Hawaii Cruises:
Constitution
Independence

Bermuda Star Line:
Bermuda Star
Queen of Bermuda
Veracruz

Carnival Cruise Lines:
Carnivale
Celebration
Festivale
Holiday
Jubilee
Mardi Gras
Tropicale

Chandris Fantasy Cruises:
Amerikanis
The Azur
Britanis
Galileo
Romanza
The Victoria

Clipper Cruise Line:
Nantucket Clipper
Newport Clipper
Yorktown Clipper

Commodore Cruise Lines:
Caribe I

Costa Cruises:
Carla Costa
CostaRiviera
Danae
Daphne
Enrico Costa
Eugenio Costa

Crown Cruise Line:
Crown del Mar
Viking Princess

Cunard Line:
Cunard Countess
Cunard Princess
Queen Elizabeth 2
Sagafjord
Sea Goddess I
Sea Goddess II
Vistafjord

Cycladic Cruises:
City of Mykonos
City of Rhodos

Deilmann Reederei:
Berlin

Discovery Cruises:
Discovery I

Dolphin Cruise Line:
Dolphin IV
SeaBreeze

Dolphin Hellas Shipping:
Aegean Dolphin
Albatross

Epirotiki Lines:
Argonaut
Atlas
Hermes
Jason
Jupiter
Neptune
Oceanos
Odysseus
Orpheus
Pegasus
World Renaissance

Exploration Cruise Lines:
Colonial Explorer
Glacier Bay Explorer
Great Rivers Explorer
Explorer Starship
Majestic Northwest Explorer
North Star
Pacific Northwest Explorer

Fred Olsen Lines:
Black Prince

Fritidskryss:
Funchal

Hapag-Lloyd Line:
Europa

Holland America Line:
Nieuw Amsterdam
Noordam
Rotterdam
Westerdam

Intercruise:
La Palma

Ivaran Lines:
Americana

Jadrolinija:
Adriana
Dalmacija
Istra

Maxim's des Mers:
Maxim's des Mers

Mediterranean Sun Lines:
Atalante

Norwegian Cruise Line:
Norway
Norwegian Star
Seaward
Skyward
Southward
Starward
Sunward II

Ocean Cruise Lines:
Ocean Islander
Ocean Pearl
Ocean Princess

Orient Express:
Orient Express

P&O Canberra Cruises:
Canberra

P&O Princess Cruises:
Dawn Princess
Fair Princess
Island Princess
Pacific Princess
Royal Princess
Sea Princess
Sky Princess
Star Princess

P&O Sitmar Cruises:
FairStar

Paquet Cruises:
Mermoz

Premier Cruise Lines:
Atlantic
Majestic
Oceanic

Regency Cruises:
Regent Sea
Regent Star
Regent Sun

Royal Caribbean Cruise Line:
Nordic Prince
Song of America
Song of Norway
Sovereign of the Seas
Sun Viking

Royal Cruise Line:
Crown Odyssey
Golden Odyssey

Royal Viking Line:
Royal Viking Sea
Royal Viking Sky
Royal Viking Star
(until Apr. 1989)
Royal Viking Sun

Seabourn Cruise Line:
Seabourn Pride

Sea Cloud Cruises:
Sea Cloud

SeaEscape Cruises:
Scandinavian Saga
Scandinavian Sky
Scandinavian Star
Scandinavian Sun

Sea Venture Cruises:
Sea Venture

Siosa Lines:
Ausonia

Society Expeditions:
Society Explorer
World Discoverer

Special Expeditions:
Polaris

Swan Hellenic Cruises:
Orpheus

Vacation Liners:
Carib Vacationer

Windjammer Barefoot Cruises:
Amazing Grace
Fantome
Flying Cloud
Mandalay
Polynesia
Yankee Clipper

Windstar Sail Cruises:
Wind Song
Wind Spirit
Wind Star

World Explorer Cruises:
Universe

**SHIPS UNDER FULL
LONG-TERM CHARTER:**

Jahn Reisen:
Vistamar

Neckermann Reisen:
Vasco da Gama

Phoenix Seereisen:
Maxim Gorki

Seetours:
Adriana

Transocean Cruise Lines:
Fedor Dostoyevsky
Odessa

1) Please note that Soviet-registered ships (owned by seven companies under the Morflot umbrella and often chartered to western operators) are not listed.

2) Only ocean-going cruise ships are listed. Correct as of January, 1989.

Achille Lauro ★★

Principal Cruising Areas:
Mediterranean/Indian Ocean/South Africa

Ship	mv Achille Lauro		
Cruise Line/Operator	Star Lauro Line		
Former Names	Willem Ruys		
Gross Registered Tonnage	23,629		
Built	N.V. de Schelde (Holland)		
First Entered Service	1947		
Last Refurbished	1984		
Country of Registry	Italy		
Radio Call Sign	IBHE		
Satellite Telephone Number	1150152		
Length 624 ft./190.1 m.	Beam 82 ft./24.9 m.		
Engines	8×Sulzer diesels		
Passenger Decks	8		
Number of Crew	325		
Passenger Capacity (basis 2)	788		
Passenger Capacity (all berths)	1,372		

Passenger Space Ratio (basis 2)			29.9
Passenger Space Ratio (all berths)			17.2
Officers Italian		Service Staff European	
Total Cabins 381		Cabin Door Width 27"	
Outside 230	Inside 151		Single 79
Wheelchair Accessible Cabins			No
Dining Rooms 1			Sittings 2
Number of Elevators 5		Door Width 30"	
Electric Current in Cabins			220 AC
Casino Yes		Slot Machines Yes	
Swimming Pools Outside 2			Inside No
Whirlpools			No
Gymnasium Yes	Sauna Yes	Massage Yes	
Cinema/Theatre Yes		Number of Seats 320	
Cabin TV No			Library No
Children's Facilities/Playroom			Yes

Ratings

Ship Appearance/Condition	68
Interior Cleanliness	72
Passenger Space	72
Passenger Comfort Level	72
Furnishings/Decor	66
Cruise Cuisine	77
Food Service	75
Beverages/Service	72
Accommodations	68
Cabin Service	76
Itineraries/Destinations	72

Shore Excursion Program	62
Entertainment	72
Activities Program	62
Cruise Director/Cruise Staff	70
Ship's Officers/Staff	72
Fitness/Sports Facilities	68
Overall Ship Facilities	72
Value for Money	72
Total Cruise Experience	75
Overall Rating	**1415**
Average	**70.7**

Comments

Distinctive vintage ship with blue hull/still has her original engines and two impressive tall blue funnels/very expansive open deck and sunning space/good wooden decking and polished rails/tasteful, but well-worn, old-world interior decor, mostly in heavy, subdued colors/acres of polished wood and trim/lovely balconied theatre/numerous public rooms to choose from/spacious Lido Deck suites have private balconies/standard cabins are small/homely and attractive dining room/very good pasta every day, otherwise food choice limited/bubbly Italian service/ship provides inexpensive cruising in the Mediterranean and around Africa, but there's little finesse.

Adriana ★★

Principal Cruising Areas:
Mediterranean/Scandinavia

Ship	ms Adriana	Passenger Space Ratio (basis 2)	18.3
Cruise Line/Operator	Jadrolinija	Passenger Space Ratio (all berths)	14.5
Former Names	Aquarius	Officers Yugoslavian	Service Staff Yugoslavian
Gross Registered Tonnage	4,590	Total Cabins 137	Cabin Door Width 24″
Built	United Shipping Yard (Greece)	Outside 119 Inside 18	Single No
First Entered Service	1972	Wheelchair Accessible Cabins	No
Last Refurbished	1988	Dining Rooms 1	Sittings 2
Country of Registry	Yugoslavia	Number of Elevators 1	Door Width 30″
Radio Call Sign	SZXF	Electric Current in Cabins	125 AC
Satellite Telephone Number	–	Casino Yes	Slot Machines Yes
Length 340 ft./103.7 m.	Beam 45 ft./13.5 m.	Swimming Pools Outside 1	Inside No
Engines	2×Pielstick diesels	Whirlpools	No
Passenger Decks	6	Gymnasium No Sauna No	Massage No
Number of Crew	125	Cinema/Theatre Yes	Number of Seats 100
Passenger Capacity (basis 2)	250	Cabin TV No	Library No
Passenger Capacity (all berths)	316	Children's Facilities/Playroom	No

Ratings

Ship Appearance/Condition	80	Shore Excursion Program	68
Interior Cleanliness	78	Entertainment	71
Passenger Space	78	Activities Program	68
Passenger Comfort Level	78	Cruise Director/Cruise Staff	69
Furnishings/Decor	79	Ship's Officers/Staff	70
Cruise Cuisine	76	Fitness/Sports Facilities	64
Food Service	77	Overall Ship Facilities	73
Beverages/Service	72	Value for Money	78
Accommodations	76	Total Cruise Experience	78
Cabin Service	77	**Overall Rating**	**1488**
Itineraries/Destinations	78	**Average**	**74.4**

Comments

Fairly smart-looking ship with second mast atop funnel/well-maintained vessel has good teak decking and polished rails, but there's not much sunning space/nice interior decor, with clean, crisp colors, but pegboard ceilings in some areas spoil it/good artwork throughout/cabins are not large, and have little closet and drawer space, but have tasteful wood trim/dining room set low down, but is light and cheerful/food typically continental/this is a chic small ship that provides a very comfortable cruise experience in surroundings that are quite adequate.

Aegean Dolphin ★★★ +

Principal Cruising Areas:
Mediterranean

Ship	mv Aegean Dolphin	Passenger Space Ratio (basis 2)	20.0
Cruise Line/Operator	Dolphin Hellas Shipping	Passenger Space Ratio (all berths)	16.6
Former Names	Alkyon/Narcis	Officers Greek	Service Staff Chinese
Gross Registered Tonnage	11,200	Total Cabins 289	Cabin Door Width 24"
Built	Perama Shipyards (Greece)	Outside 201	Inside 88	Single No
First Entered Service	1973	Wheelchair Accessible Cabins	No
Last Refurbished	1988	Dining Rooms 1	Sittings 2
Country of Registry	Greece	Number of Elevators 2	Door Width 30"
Radio Call Sign	SWEO	Electric Current in Cabins	220 AC
Satellite Telephone Number	1130627	Casino Yes	Slot Machines Yes
Length 462 ft./140.8 m.	Beam 67 ft./20.5 m.	Swimming Pools Outside 1	Inside No
Engines	2×Pielstick diesels	Whirlpools	No
Passenger Decks	9	Gymnasium Yes Sauna Yes Massage Yes	
Number of Crew	190	Cinema/Theatre Yes Number of Seats 136	
Passenger Capacity (basis 2)	558	Cabin TV Yes	Library Yes
Passenger Capacity (all berths)	672	Children's Facilities/Playroom	No

Ratings

Ship Appearance/Condition	82	Shore Excursion Program	75
Interior Cleanliness	82	Entertainment	75
Passenger Space	81	Activities Program	73
Passenger Comfort Level	82	Cruise Director/Cruise Staff	78
Furnishings/Decor	82	Ship's Officers/Staff	78
Cruise Cuisine	76	Fitness/Sports Facilities	79
Food Service	77	Overall Ship Facilities	80
Beverages/Service	74	Value for Money	80
Accommodations	80	Total Cruise Experience	81
Cabin Service	79	**Overall Rating**	**1572**
Itineraries/Destinations	78	**Average**	**78.6**

Comments

Profile looks really smart after recent extensive conversion/limited open deck and sunning space when ship is full/public rooms include an excellent showroom, laid out amphitheatre-style/Belvedere Lounge set high atop the ship and forward, features a piano bar/contemporary decor/but too many mirrors/mostly outside cabins are reasonably spacious for size of ship and have picture windows instead of portholes/bathrobes provided for all passengers/dining room, set low down, is bright and cheerful, but rather cramped/only two tables for two/food is typically continental/features dialysis station/service quite attentive/this ship will cruise you in comfortable surroundings, at a decent price, but lacks finesse.

Albatross ★ ★ ★ +

Principal Cruising Areas:
Aegean/Mediterranean

Ship	mv Betsy Ross	Passenger Space Ratio (basis 2)		26.9
Cruise Line/Operator	Dolphin Hellas Shipping	Passenger Space Ratio (all berths)		20.7
Former Names	Betsy Ross/Allegro/Leda/Najia	Officers Greek		Service Staff Greek
Gross Registered Tonnage	10,026	Total Cabins 186		Cabin Door Width 26"
Built	Swan, Hunter (UK)	Outside 169	Inside 17	Single No
First Entered Service	1956	Wheelchair Accessible Cabins		No
Last Refurbished	1988	Dining Rooms 1		Sittings 2
Country of Registry	Greece	Number of Elevators 2		Door Width 30"
Radio Call Sign	SVIZ	Electric Current in Cabins		220 AC
Satellite Telephone Number	1130470	Casino Yes		Slot Machines Yes
Length 451 ft./137.4 m.	Beam 59 ft./17.9 m.	Swimming Pools Outside 1		Inside No
Engines	4×DRG diesels	Whirlpools		No
Passenger Decks	5	Gymnasium Yes	Sauna Yes	Massage Yes
Number of Crew	190	Cinema/Theatre Yes		Number of Seats 97
Passenger Capacity (basis 2)	372	Cabin TV No		Library Yes
Passenger Capacity (all berths)	484	Children's Facilities/Playroom		No

Ratings

Ship Appearance/Condition	78	Shore Excursion Program	78
Interior Cleanliness	82	Entertainment	81
Passenger Space	78	Activities Program	72
Passenger Comfort Level	78	Cruise Director/Cruise Staff	78
Furnishings/Decor	81	Ship's Officers/Staff	81
Cruise Cuisine	79	Fitness/Sports Facilities	70
Food Service	79	Overall Ship Facilities	73
Beverages/Service	78	Value for Money	78
Accommodations	79	Total Cruise Experience	82
Cabin Service	80	**Overall Rating**	**1568**
Itineraries/Destinations	83	**Average**	**78.4**

Comments

Classic fifties exterior styling/royal blue hull with narrow red band/well-planned itineraries/ship is nicely refurbished with lively contemporary decor, splashy colors and too many mirrors/dining room has big picture windows, but metal ceiling planks reflect sound, making it noisy/food is continental cuisine/good open deck and sunning space/cabins are quite comfortable, with good closet space/bathrobes and toiletry kits provided in all cabins/smartly-dressed officers and crew/this ship provides good-value-for-money cruising to some much-sought-after destinations.

Alexandr Pushkin ★★★

Principal Cruising Areas:
Australasia / South Pacific

Ship		ms Alexandr Pushkin
Cruise Line/Operator		Baltic Shipping
Former Names		–
Gross Registered Tonnage		20,502
Built	Matthias Thesen Werft (E. Germany)	
First Entered Service		1965
Last Refurbished		1975
Country of Registry		USSR
Radio Call Sign		UERU
Satellite Telephone Number		–
Length 580 ft./176.7 m.	Beam 77 ft./23.4 m.	
Engines		2×Sulzer diesels
Passenger Decks		8
Number of Crew		340
Passenger Capacity (basis 2)		504
Passenger Capacity (all berths)		793

Passenger Space Ratio (basis 2)		40.6
Passenger Space Ratio (all berths)		25.8
Officers Soviet	Service Staff E. European	
Total Cabins 252*	Cabin Door Width 26"	
Outside 240	Inside 12	Single No
Wheelchair Accessible Cabins		No
Dining Rooms 1		Sittings 2
Number of Elevators 3	Door Width 32"	
Electric Current in Cabins		220 AC
Casino Yes	Slot Machines Yes	
Swimming Pools Outside 2	Inside No	
Whirlpools		No
Gymnasium Yes	Sauna Yes	Massage Yes
Cinema/Theatre Yes	Number of Seats 130	
Cabin TV No	Library Yes	
Children's Facilities/Playroom		Yes

* 141 cabins without facilities

Ratings

Ship Appearance/Condition	78
Interior Cleanliness	76
Passenger Space	78
Passenger Comfort Level	76
Furnishings/Decor	75
Cruise Cuisine	74
Food Service	76
Beverages/Service	74
Accommodations	76
Cabin Service	78
Itineraries/Destinations	80

Shore Excursion Program	73
Entertainment	75
Activities Program	68
Cruise Director/Cruise Staff	76
Ship's Officers/Staff	76
Fitness/Sports Facilities	78
Overall Ship Facilities	76
Value for Money	81
Total Cruise Experience	78
Overall Rating	**1522**
Average	**76.1**

Comments

Classic ocean liner styling/good, but cluttered deck space/nice woods used throughout/popular indoor pool and solarium/pleasant but spartan interior decor/most public rooms located on one deck makes layout easy/lively casino action/four suites are good, but other mostly outside cabins are somewhat small and lacking/141 budget cabins without facilities do at least have a washbasin/dining is family-style/little choice of food/attentive but inflexible service/good ship for families with children/especially good for young, active singles/interesting itineraries/this ship provides a fun cruise experience for the young Australasian set, at a modest price.

Americana

Principal Cruising Areas:
South America/USA

Ship	ms Americana	Passenger Space Ratio (basis 2)	221.5
Cruise Line/Operator	Ivaran Lines	Passenger Space Ratio (all berths)	180.5
Former Names	–	Officers Norwegian	Service Staff S. American
Gross Registered Tonnage	19,203	Total Cabins 54	Cabin Door Width 26"
Built	Hyundai Heavy Industries (Korea)	Outside 42 Inside 12	Single 20
First Entered Service	1988	Wheelchair Accessible Cabins	No
Last Refurbished	–	Dining Rooms 1	Sittings 1
Country of Registry	Norway	Number of Elevators 2	Door Width 36"
Radio Call Sign	LADX2	Electric Current in Cabins	110/220 AC
Satellite Telephone Number	1311131	Casino Yes	Slot Machines Yes
Length 578 ft./176.1 m. Beam 85 ft./25.9 m.		Swimming Pools Outside 1	Inside No
Engines	1×MAN diesel	Whirlpools	1
Passenger Decks	6	Gymnasium Yes Sauna Yes	Massage Yes
Number of Crew	44	Cinema/Theatre No	Number of Seats –
Passenger Capacity (basis 2)	88	Cabin TV No	Library Yes
Passenger Capacity (all berths)	108	Children's Facilities/Playroom	No

Ratings*

Ship Appearance/Condition	–	Shore Excursion Program	–
Interior Cleanliness	–	Entertainment	–
Passenger Space	–	Activities Program	–
Passenger Comfort Level	–	Cruise Director/Cruise Staff	–
Furnishings/Decor	–	Ship's Officers/Staff	–
Cruise Cuisine	–	Fitness/Sports Facilities	–
Food Service	–	Overall Ship Facilities	–
Beverages/Service	–	Value for Money	–
Accommodations	–	Total Cruise Experience	–
Cabin Service	–	**Overall Rating**	–
Itineraries/Destinations	–	**Average**	–

Comments

Incredible space ratio (see above) due to the fact that this is a brand new freighter-cruise ship with excellent passenger facilities that are placed astern of the 1120-capacity container section/elegant and beautifully-finished interior/two owner's suites are lavish, with separate bedroom and living room, and big picture windows on two sides/other cabins are quite lovely, well appointed, and feature restful decor/good number of single cabins/generous sheltered and open sunning space/elegant dining room has beautiful table settings/well-stocked library—necessary for long voyages/decidedly for the passenger with time to spare, this is the ultimate in contemporary freighter travel. (Not rated at press time.)

Amerikanis ★★★ +

Principal Cruising Areas:
Bermuda / Caribbean

Ship	ss Amerikanis		
Cruise Line / Operator	Chandris Fantasy Cruises		
Former Names	Kenya Castle		
Gross Registered Tonnage	19,904		
Built	Harland & Wolff (UK)		
First Entered Service	1952		
Last Refurbished	1987		
Country of Registry	Panama		
Radio Call Sign	3FIH2		
Satellite Telephone Number	–		
Length 576 ft. / 175.5 m.	Beam 74 ft. / 22.5 m.		
Engines	2 × H & W turbines		
Passenger Decks	8		
Number of Crew	400		
Passenger Capacity (basis 2)	609		
Passenger Capacity (all berths)	609		

Passenger Space Ratio (basis 2)			32.6
Passenger Space Ratio (all berths)			32.6
Officers Greek	Service Staff International		
Total Cabins 306	Cabin Door Width 28"		
Outside 212	Inside 94		Single 3
Wheelchair Accessible Cabins			No
Dining Rooms 2			Sittings 2
Number of Elevators 2	Door Width 35"		
Electric Current in Cabins			110/220 AC
Casino Yes		Slot Machines Yes	
Swimming Pools Outside 2			Inside No
Whirlpools			No
Gymnasium Yes	Sauna Yes		Massage Yes
Cinema / Theatre Yes		Number of Seats 115	
Cabin TV Yes			Library Yes
Children's Facilities / Playroom			Yes

Ratings

Ship Appearance / Condition	78
Interior Cleanliness	82
Passenger Space	78
Passenger Comfort Level	80
Furnishings / Decor	78
Cruise Cuisine	80
Food Service	80
Beverages / Service	78
Accommodations	78
Cabin Service	80
Itineraries / Destinations	81

Shore Excursion Program	74
Entertainment	78
Activities Program	71
Cruise Director / Cruise Staff	72
Ship's Officers / Staff	75
Fitness / Sports Facilities	70
Overall Ship Facilities	76
Value for Money	84
Total Cruise Experience	83
Overall Rating	**1556**
Average	**77.8**

Comments

Charming, much-loved older vessel with classic liner profile / extremely well maintained / outstandingly clean engine room / good open deck and sunning space / plenty of spacious public rooms and facilities to choose from, although colors are a little somber / lovely marble fireplace in disco / fine statuary and other artworks aboard / very spacious cabins have real heavy-duty furnishings, solid doors and plenty of closet and drawer space / two good dining rooms / good quality food served well by attentive multi-national staff / excellent-value-for-money cruising at a very realistic price / this ship provides a far better standard and experience than you might expect.

Antonina Nezhdanova

Principal Cruising Areas:
Antarctica / South America / Orient

Ship	ms Antonina Nezhdanova		Passenger Space Ratio (basis 2)		41.0
Cruise Line / Operator	Far East Shipping		Passenger Space Ratio (all berths)		20.9
Former Names	–		Officers Soviet	Service Staff East European	
Gross Registered Tonnage	3,941		Total Cabins 48	Cabin Door Width 24"	
Built	Brodgradiliste Uljanik (Yugoslavia)		Outside 48	Inside No	Single No
First Entered Service	1978		Wheelchair Accessible Cabins		No
Last Refurbished	1988		Dining Rooms 1		Sittings 1
Country of Registry	USSR		Number of Elevators 0	Door Width –	
Radio Call Sign	ESWY		Electric Current in Cabins		220 AC
Satellite Telephone Number	–		Casino No	Slot Machines No	
Length 328 ft. / 100 m.	Beam 53 ft. / 16.2 m.		Swimming Pools Outside 1		Inside No
Engines	2 × Uljanik diesels		Whirlpools		No
Passenger Decks	6		Gymnasium No	Sauna Yes	Massage No
Number of Crew	100		Cinema / Theatre Yes	Number of Seats 75	
Passenger Capacity (basis 2)	96		Cabin TV No		Library Yes
Passenger Capacity (all berths)	188		Children's Facilities / Playroom		No

Ratings

Ship Appearance / Condition	82		Shore Excursion Program	78
Interior Cleanliness	81		Entertainment	76
Passenger Space	81		Activities Program	74
Passenger Comfort Level	80		Cruise Director / Cruise Staff	80
Furnishings / Decor	80		Ship's Officers / Staff	80
Cruise Cuisine	78		Fitness / Sports Facilities	68
Food Service	76		Overall Ship Facilities	–
Beverages / Service	79		Value for Money	80
Accommodations	78		Total Cruise Experience	80
Cabin Service	78		**Overall Rating**	**1489**
Itineraries / Destinations	80		**Average**	**74.4**

Comments

Very intimate ship with well-balanced profile is one of a series of eight identical sisters / has ice-hardened hull suitable for expedition cruising / excellent open deck space / recently underwent extensive refurbishment / has outdoor observation deck and enclosed promenade deck for inclement weather / charming forward music lounge has wooden dance floor / rich, highly polished wood paneling throughout / lovely winding brass-railed main staircase / good cinema-lecture room / comfortable dining room has ocean views / limited choice of food, but service is friendly and quite attentive / cabins are compact and spartan, but most can accommodate four persons / this ship is small, yet comfortable / chartered to western operators for expedition-style cruises.

Argonaut ★★★

Principal Cruising Areas:
Aegean/Mediterranean

Ship	mts Argonaut	Passenger Space Ratio (basis 2)	25.6
Cruise Line/Operator	Epirotiki Lines	Passenger Space Ratio (all berths)	19.5
Former Names	Orion/Vixen	Officers Greek	Service Staff Greek
Gross Registered Tonnage	4,500	Total Cabins 88	Cabin Door Width 26"
Built Frieder, Krupp Germaniawerft (W. Germ.)		Outside 88 Inside No	Single No
First Entered Service	1929	Wheelchair Accessible Cabins	No
Last Refurbished	1986	Dining Rooms 1	Sittings 1
Country of Registry	Greece	Number of Elevators 1	Door Width 30"
Radio Call Sign	SWXZ	Electric Current in Cabins	110 AC/220 DC
Satellite Telephone Number	–	Casino No	Slot Machines No
Length 340 ft./103.6 m. Beam 47 ft./14.3 m.		Swimming Pools Outside 1	Inside No
Engines	2×Krupp diesels	Whirlpools	No
Passenger Decks	4	Gymnasium No Sauna No	Massage No
Number of Crew	100	Cinema/Theatre No	Number of Seats –
Passenger Capacity (basis 2)	176	Cabin TV No	Library Yes
Passenger Capacity (all berths)	231	Children's Facilities/Playroom	No

Ratings

Ship Appearance/Condition	82	Shore Excursion Program	84
Interior Cleanliness	85	Entertainment	76
Passenger Space	72	Activities Program	75
Passenger Comfort Level	81	Cruise Director/Cruise Staff	70
Furnishings/Decor	82	Ship's Officers/Staff	78
Cruise Cuisine	78	Fitness/Sports Facilities	50
Food Service	77	Overall Ship Facilities	72
Beverages/Service	75	Value for Money	78
Accommodations	80	Total Cruise Experience	80
Cabin Service	78	**Overall Rating**	**1531**
Itineraries/Destinations	78	**Average**	**76.5**

Comments

Lovely small vintage ship built originally as private yacht for American owner/warm, intimate and informal atmosphere/gorgeous woods and wood trim used throughout/homely decor in the limited public rooms/beautiful winding center stairway/ extensive artworks featured throughout/large, single-sitting dining room/good Mediterranean food and attentive warm service/interesting itineraries/ship provides a very pleasant cruise experience for the discerning traveler.

Arkona ★★★+

Principal Cruising Areas:
Baltic/Mediterranean/Scandinavia

Ship	ms Arkona	Passenger Space Ratio (basis 2)		39.0
Line/Operator	Deutsche Seereederei/Seetours	Passenger Space Ratio (all berths)		37.6
Former Names	Astor/Berlin	Officers E. German	Service Staff E. European	
Gross Registered Tonnage	18,834	Total Cabins 285	Cabin Door Width 24″	
Built Howaldtswerke Deutsche Werft (W. Germ.)		Outside 189	Inside 96	Single No
First Entered Service	1981	Wheelchair Accessible Cabins		No
Last Refurbished	1984	Dining Rooms 1		Sittings 2
Country of Registry	East Germany	Number of Elevators 6	Door Width 30″	
Radio Call Sign	Y5CC	Electric Current in Cabins		220 AC
Satellite Telephone Number	–	Casino No	Slot Machines No	
Length 538 ft./163.9 m.	Beam 74 ft./22.5 m.	Swimming Pools Outside 1		Inside 1
Engines	4×Mann diesels	Whirlpools		No
Passenger Decks	8	Gymnasium Yes	Sauna Yes	Massage Yes
Number of Crew	240	Cinema/Theatre No	Number of Seats –	
Passenger Capacity (basis 2)	482	Cabin TV No		Library Yes
Passenger Capacity (all berths)	500	Children's Facilities/Playroom		No

Ratings

Ship Appearance/Condition	85	Shore Excursion Program		76
Interior Cleanliness	82	Entertainment		75
Passenger Space	83	Activities Program		76
Passenger Comfort Level	82	Cruise Director/Cruise Staff		76
Furnishings/Decor	84	Ship's Officers/Staff		76
Cruise Cuisine	78	Fitness/Sports Facilities		80
Food Service	78	Overall Ship Facilities		80
Beverages/Service	76	Value for Money		80
Accommodations	81	Total Cruise Experience		80
Cabin Service	78	**Overall Rating**		**1588**
Itineraries/Destinations	82	**Average**		**79.4**

Comments

Well-constructed modern ship, with somewhat squarish, yet handsome, profile/good open deck and sunning space, with gorgeous teakwood decking and rails/beautifully-appointed interior fittings and decor, with much rosewood paneling and trim/has good meetings facilities/the Arkona Restaurant is lovely, with restful, elegant decor/food is good, though choice is rather limited/Boat Deck suite rooms are simply lovely/other cabins are well appointed and decorated, but have compact bathrooms/excellent fitness center/good traditional European hotel service/dialysis machines and trained staff carried/this ship presently cruises under German charter during the summer, and features good-value-for-money cruising in contemporary comfort with European passengers.

Atalante ★

Principal Cruising Areas:
Aegean/Mediterranean

Ship	ms Atalante	Passenger Space Ratio (basis 2)	30.6
Cruise Line/Operator	Mediterranean Sun Lines	Passenger Space Ratio (all berths)	19.0
Former Names	Tahitien	Officers Greek	Service Staff Greek
Gross Registered Tonnage	13,113	Total Cabins 217	Cabin Door Width 26"
Built Arsenal de la Marine Nationale (France)		Outside 162 Inside 55	Single No
First Entered Service	1953	Wheelchair Accessible Cabins	No
Last Refurbished	1976	Dining Rooms 1	Sittings 2
Country of Registry	Greece	Number of Elevators 0	Door Width –
Radio Call Sign	SUKA	Electric Current in Cabins	220 AC
Satellite Telephone Number	–	Casino No	Slot Machines No
Length 548 ft./167.2 m. Beam 67 ft./20.4 m.		Swimming Pools Outside 2	Inside No
Engines	2×B&W diesels	Whirlpools	No
Passenger Decks	5	Gymnasium Yes Sauna No	Massage No
Number of Crew	200	Cinema/Theatre No	Number of Seats –
Passenger Capacity (basis 2)	428	Cabin TV No	Library Yes
Passenger Capacity (all berths)	689	Children's Facilities/Playroom	No

Ratings

Ship Appearance/Condition	66	Shore Excursion Program	60
Interior Cleanliness	66	Entertainment	62
Passenger Space	72	Activities Program	60
Passenger Comfort Level	64	Cruise Director/Cruise Staff	62
Furnishings/Decor	66	Ship's Officers/Staff	64
Cruise Cuisine	68	Fitness/Sports Facilities	52
Food Service	70	Overall Ship Facilities	63
Beverages/Service	68	Value for Money	62
Accommodations	66	Total Cruise Experience	64
Cabin Service	67	**Overall Rating**	**1290**
Itineraries/Destinations	68	**Average**	**64.5**

Comments

Passenger-car liner has small, squat funnel amidships/ship has an awkward layout/plenty of open deck and sunning space, but outdoor decking well worn/interior decor old and worn, yet vaguely comfortable/public rooms limited/dining room low down and musty/food is fair, that's all—with little choice/cabins small and rather spartan/limited closet space/nightlife is disco-loud/there's no finesse anywhere/this ship is for the young, budget-minded cruiser wanting to party and travel without much service.

Atlantic ★★★★

Principal Cruising Areas:
Bahamas

Ship	star/ship Atlantic	Passenger Space Ratio (basis 2)	37.5
Cruise Line/Operator	Premier Cruise Lines	Passenger Space Ratio (all berths)	22.8
Former Names	–	Officers Greek	Service Staff International
Gross Registered Tonnage	36,500	Total Cabins 549	Cabin Door Width 24″
Built	C.N.I.M. (France)	Outside 380	Inside 169 Single 14
First Entered Service	1982	Wheelchair Accessible Cabins	Yes
Last Refurbished	1988	Dining Rooms 1	Sittings 2
Country of Registry	Liberia	Number of Elevators 4	Door Width 30″
Radio Call Sign	ELAJ4	Electric Current in Cabins	110 AC
Satellite Telephone Number	–	Casino Yes	Slot Machines Yes
Length 672 ft./205 m.	Beam 90 ft./27.5 m.	Swimming Pools Outside 1	Inside 1
Engines	2×GM diesels	Whirlpools	3
Passenger Decks	9	Gymnasium Yes Sauna Yes	Massage Yes
Number of Crew	550	Cinema/Theatre Yes	Number of Seats 251
Passenger Capacity (basis 2)	972	Cabin TV No	Library Yes
Passenger Capacity (all berths)	1600	Children's Facilities/Playroom	Yes

Ratings

Ship Appearance/Condition	81	Shore Excursion Program	80
Interior Cleanliness	81	Entertainment	80
Passenger Space	84	Activities Program	77
Passenger Comfort Level	83	Cruise Director/Cruise Staff	80
Furnishings/Decor	80	Ship's Officers/Staff	80
Cruise Cuisine	82	Fitness/Sports Facilities	82
Food Service	82	Overall Ship Facilities	82
Beverages/Service	83	Value for Money	84
Accommodations	83	Total Cruise Experience	82
Cabin Service	82	**Overall Rating**	**1628**
Itineraries/Destinations	80	**Average**	**81.4**

Comments

Slab-sided ex-Home Lines ship has stubby bow and squat funnel/outdoor deck space is excellent/interior is spacious, with plenty of public rooms/decor garish in places, but generous in stainless steel and teak wood trim/good observation lounge/nice indoor-outdoor pool area, but tiling is cracked and worn/good duty-free shopping/spacious cabins are generously equipped and very comfortable/nice dining room, set low down, but tables are close together/food quality good/service is multinational/will provide a good cruise experience for families with children at the right price—and recently changed owners, joining Premier Cruise Lines (Walt Disney World), introducing their typical style. This ship was rated when operated by Home Lines.

Atlas ★★★

Principal Cruising Areas:
Aegean / Caribbean / Mediterranean

Ship	tts Atlas
Cruise Line / Operator	Epirotiki Lines
Former Names	Ryndam / Waterman
Gross Registered Tonnage	˚16,000
Built	Wilton-Fijenoord (Holland)
First Entered Service	1951
Last Refurbished	1973
Country of Registry	Greece
Radio Call Sign	SYMB
Satellite Telephone Number	1130166
Length 510 ft. / 155.5 m.	Beam 70 ft. / 21.3 m.
Engines	2×GE turbines
Passenger Decks	8
Number of Crew	300
Passenger Capacity (basis 2)	578
Passenger Capacity (all berths)	742

Passenger Space Ratio (basis 2)		27.7
Passenger Space Ratio (all berths)		21.6
Officers Greek		Service Staff Greek
Total Cabins 289		Cabin Door Width 24"
Outside 185	Inside 104	Single 28 *
Wheelchair Accessible Cabins		No
Dining Rooms 1		Sittings 2
Number of Elevators 2		Door Width 30"
Electric Current in Cabins		220 AC
Casino No		Slot Machines No
Swimming Pools Outside 2		Inside 1
Whirlpools		No
Gymnasium Yes	Sauna Yes	Massage Yes
Cinema / Theatre Yes		Number of Seats 300
Cabin TV No		Library Yes
Children's Facilities / Playroom		No

* with added upper

Ratings

Ship Appearance / Condition	76
Interior Cleanliness	80
Passenger Space	78
Passenger Comfort Level	74
Furnishings / Decor	78
Cruise Cuisine	78
Food Service	79
Beverages / Service	76
Accommodations	76
Cabin Service	78
Itineraries / Destinations	80

Shore Excursion Program	78
Entertainment	76
Activities Program	75
Cruise Director / Cruise Staff	78
Ship's Officers / Staff	78
Fitness / Sports Facilities	73
Overall Ship Facilities	76
Value for Money	78
Total Cruise Experience	78
Overall Rating	**1543**
Average	**77.1**

Comments

Largest ship in the Epirotiki fleet / has interesting, almost contemporary profile / plenty of open deck area and sunning space / good sheltered promenade deck / lots of public rooms to choose from, though the interior decor is rather subdued / cheerful dining room, set low down / typical continental food / good basic service, but lacks finesse / upper grade cabins are spacious / others are somewhat compact, yet quite adequate and comfortable / this ship provides a decent cruise experience in comfortable, but not elegant, surroundings / best of all is the superb itinerary and value.

Ausonia ★★★

Principal Cruising Areas:
Mediterranean / Scandinavia

Ship	ts Ausonia	Passenger Space Ratio (basis 2)		24.7
Cruise Line/Operator	Siosa Lines	Passenger Space Ratio (all berths)		20.4
Former Names	–	Officers Italian	Service Staff Italian	
Gross Registered Tonnage	12,750	Total Cabins 258	Cabin Door Width 26"	
Built	Cantieri Riuniti dell'Adriatico (Italy)	Outside 201	Inside 57	Single No
First Entered Service	1957	Wheelchair Accessible Cabins		No
Last Refurbished	1986	Dining Rooms 1	Sittings 2	
Country of Registry	Italy	Number of Elevators 1	Door Width 30"	
Radio Call Sign	IBAX	Electric Current in Cabins		220 AC
Satellite Telephone Number	–	Casino No	Slot Machines No	
Length 520 ft./158.4 m.	Beam 66 ft./20.1 m.	Swimming Pools Outside 2	Inside No	
Engines	2×diesels	Whirlpools		No
Passenger Decks	8	Gymnasium No	Sauna No	Massage No
Number of Crew	215	Cinema/Theatre Yes	Number of Seats 125	
Passenger Capacity (basis 2)	516	Cabin TV No	Library No	
Passenger Capacity (all berths)	625	Children's Facilities/Playroom		No

Ratings

Ship Appearance/Condition	80	Shore Excursion Program	70
Interior Cleanliness	81	Entertainment	75
Passenger Space	76	Activities Program	72
Passenger Comfort Level	80	Cruise Director/Cruise Staff	72
Furnishings/Decor	79	Ship's Officers/Staff	78
Cruise Cuisine	78	Fitness/Sports Facilities	60
Food Service	80	Overall Ship Facilities	78
Beverages/Service	78	Value for Money	78
Accommodations	77	Total Cruise Experience	80
Cabin Service	79	**Overall Rating**	**1531**
Itineraries/Destinations	80	**Average**	**76.5**

Comments

Well-maintained ship with classic, swept-back lines and profile/very clean/good open deck and sunning space/much upgraded public areas are light and spacious/recently added Ballroom is pleasantly decorated in blues and creams/small, compact, but comfortable, cabins/dining rooms set high up, with good ocean views/friendly, efficient Italian service throughout/good continental food, with plenty of pasta/midnight pizza parties very popular/this ship offers a regular Mediterranean service in very comfortable surroundings and true Italian flair.

Azerbaydzhan ★★★

Principal Cruising Areas:
Aegean/Baltic/Mediterranean/
Scandinavia

Ship	ms Azerbaydzhan
Cruise Line/Operator	Black Sea Shipping
Former Names	–
Gross Registered Tonnage	16,900
Built	Wartsila (Finland)
First Entered Service	1976
Last Refurbished	1986
Country of Registry	USSR
Radio Call Sign	UFZX
Satellite Telephone Number	–
Length 515 ft./156.9 m.	Beam 72 ft./21.9 m.
Engines	2×Pielstick diesels
Passenger Decks	8
Number of Crew	240
Passenger Capacity (basis 2)	460
Passenger Capacity (all berths)	692

Passenger Space Ratio (basis 2)		36.7
Passenger Space Ratio (all berths)		24.4
Officers Soviet	Service Staff East European	
Total Cabins 230	Cabin Door Width 26"	
Outside 114	Inside 116	Single No
Wheelchair Accessible Cabins		No
Dining Rooms 2*		Sittings 2
Number of Elevators 2	Door Width 30"	
Electric Current in Cabins		220 AC
Casino No	Slot Machines No	
Swimming Pools Outside 1		Inside No
Whirlpools		No
Gymnasium No	Sauna Yes	Massage Yes
Cinema/Theatre Yes	Number of Seats 145	
Cabin TV No		Library Yes
Children's Facilities/Playroom		No

* no smoking in one

Ratings

Ship Appearance/Condition	81		Shore Excursion Program	66
Interior Cleanliness	80		Entertainment	72
Passenger Space	78		Activities Program	70
Passenger Comfort Level	80		Cruise Director/Cruise Staff	72
Furnishings/Decor	79		Ship's Officers/Staff	76
Cruise Cuisine	76		Fitness/Sports Facilities	78
Food Service	78		Overall Ship Facilities	78
Beverages/Service	78		Value for Money	80
Accommodations	76		Total Cruise Experience	78
Cabin Service	78		**Overall Rating**	**1534**
Itineraries/Destinations	80		**Average**	**76.7**

Comments

Fairly sleek-looking ship with squarish funnel/recently underwent complete refurbishment, which added a new nightclub, cinema, and a few more cabins/pleasant interior decor that is fairly bright, but not elegant/12 large suites are nicely furnished, and have wood-paneled walls/other cabins are small and sparingly furnished, but quite adequate and comfortable/steep gangway in most ports/plain, but cozy dining room with attentive waitress service, but there's no finesse/this ship will provide a good cruise experience for a modest price/mainly European passengers.

The Azur ★★★+

Principal Cruising Areas:
Aegean/Caribbean/Mediterranean

Ship	mv The Azur	Passenger Space Ratio (basis 2)		22.1
Cruise Line/Operator	Chandris Fantasy Cruises	Passenger Space Ratio (all berths)		22.1
Former Names	Eagle/Azur	Officers Greek	Service Staff International	
Gross Registered Tonnage	14,717	Total Cabins 335	Cabin Door Width 24"	
Built	Dubigeon-Normandie (France)	Outside 152	Inside 183	Single 10
First Entered Service	1970	Wheelchair Accessible Cabins		No
Last Refurbished	1987	Dining Rooms 1		Sittings 2
Country of Registry	Panama	Number of Elevators 1	Door Width 27"	
Radio Call Sign	3EPR5	Electric Current in Cabins		220 AC
Satellite Telephone Number	1332515/1110252	Casino Yes	Slot Machines Yes	
Length 466 ft./142.0 m.	Beam 74 ft./22.5 m.	Swimming Pools Outside 2	Inside No	
Engines	2×Pielstick diesels	Whirlpools		No
Passenger Decks	7	Gymnasium Yes	Sauna No	Massage No
Number of Crew	340	Cinema/Theatre Yes	Number of Seats 175	
Passenger Capacity (basis 2)	665	Cabin TV No	Library Yes	
Passenger Capacity (all berths)	665	Children's Facilities/Playroom		Yes

Ratings

Ship Appearance/Condition	80	Shore Excursion Program		80
Interior Cleanliness	81	Entertainment		76
Passenger Space	78	Activities Program		70
Passenger Comfort Level	80	Cruise Director/Cruise Staff		72
Furnishings/Decor	81	Ship's Officers/Staff		76
Cruise Cuisine	81	Fitness/Sports Facilities		82
Food Service	80	Overall Ship Facilities		78
Beverages/Service	80	Value for Money		85
Accommodations	80	Total Cruise Experience		82
Cabin Service	80	**Overall Rating**		**1583**
Itineraries/Destinations	81	**Average**		**79.1**

Comments

Smart, but somewhat stubby-looking ship has twin funnels set well aft/excellent recent major refurbishment/generous open deck space for sunning/plenty of public rooms, with light, contemporary decor/most cabins nicely refurbished, and decorated in earth tones/charming dining room has ocean views on three sides through big picture windows/courteous staff and service/lively casino action/excellent sports facilities and extensive "Fantasea" watersports program ashore (Caribbean itinerary)/typically good food and service/this ship will appeal to the young, active set looking for a good cruise experience at a most reasonable price.

Azure Seas ★★★

Principal Cruising Areas:
Mexican Riviera

Ship	ss Azure Seas
Cruise Line/Operator	Admiral Cruises
Former Names	Calypso/Southern Cross
Gross Registered Tonnage	21,486
Built	Harland & Wolff (UK)
First Entered Service	1955
Last Refurbished	1984
Country of Registry	Panama
Radio Call Sign	H8MW
Satellite Telephone Number	–
Length 604 ft./184.0 m.	Beam 78 ft./23.7 m.
Engines	4×H&W turbines
Passenger Decks	9
Number of Crew	370
Passenger Capacity (basis 2)	734
Passenger Capacity (all berths)	734

Passenger Space Ratio (basis 2)		29.0
Passenger Space Ratio (all berths)		29.0
Officers International	Service Staff International	
Total Cabins 367	Cabin Door Width 23″	
Outside 222	Inside 145	Single No
Wheelchair Accessible Cabins		No
Dining Rooms 1		Sittings 2
Number of Elevators 2	Door Width 28″	
Electric Current in Cabins		110/220 AC
Casino Yes	Slot Machines Yes	
Swimming Pools Outside 1		Inside No
Whirlpools		1
Gymnasium Yes	Sauna Yes	Massage No
Cinema/Theatre Yes	Number of Seats 254	
Cabin TV No		Library Yes
Children's Facilities/Playroom		No

Ratings

Ship Appearance/Condition	78
Interior Cleanliness	77
Passenger Space	78
Passenger Comfort Level	77
Furnishings/Decor	80
Cruise Cuisine	76
Food Service	76
Beverages/Service	77
Accommodations	78
Cabin Service	78
Itineraries/Destinations	72

Shore Excursion Program	66
Entertainment	72
Activities Program	70
Cruise Director/Cruise Staff	72
Ship's Officers/Staff	74
Fitness/Sports Facilities	72
Overall Ship Facilities	70
Value for Money	80
Total Cruise Experience	78
Overall Rating	**1501**
Average	**75.0**

Comments

Older, lengthy ship is easily distinguished by its aft solitary funnel/well maintained, although showing her age in places/good open deck and sunning space/Mexican themed decor around the ship/dining room set low down, but warm and cheerful/food good for short cruises/service reasonable, but there's no finesse/cabins are comfortable and nicely decorated though not large/lots of activity in the huge casino/this ship is an action-filled party ship/casual dress and casual everything, it's a lot of fun for a modest price.

Belorussiya ★★★

Principal Cruising Areas:
Australasia/Orient/South Pacific

Ship	ms Belorussiya	Passenger Space Ratio (basis 2)	36.4
Cruise Line/Operator	Black Sea Shipping	Passenger Space Ratio (all berths)	21.9
Former Names	–	Officers Soviet	Service Staff East European
Gross Registered Tonnage	16,900	Total Cabins 232	Cabin Door Width 26"
Built	Wartsila (Finland)	Outside 117 Inside 115	Single No
First Entered Service	1976	Wheelchair Accessible Cabins	No
Last Refurbished	1986	Dining Rooms 2*	Sittings 2
Country of Registry	USSR	Number of Elevators 1	Door Width 30"
Radio Call Sign	UDDP	Electric Current in Cabins	220 AC
Satellite Telephone Number	–	Casino Yes	Slot Machines Yes
Length 515 ft./156.9 m.	Beam 72 ft./21.9 m.	Swimming Pools Outside 1	Inside No
Engines	2×Pielstick diesels	Whirlpools	No
Passenger Decks	8	Gymnasium Yes Sauna Yes	Massage Yes
Number of Crew	250	Cinema/Theatre Yes	Number of Seats 143
Passenger Capacity (basis 2)	464	Cabin TV No	Library Yes
Passenger Capacity (all berths)	770	Children's Facilities/Playroom	No
		* no smoking in one	

Ratings

Ship Appearance/Condition	81	Shore Excursion Program	68
Interior Cleanliness	81	Entertainment	72
Passenger Space	80	Activities Program	70
Passenger Comfort Level	81	Cruise Director/Cruise Staff	72
Furnishings/Decor	81	Ship's Officers/Staff	77
Cruise Cuisine	76	Fitness/Sports Facilities	78
Food Service	78	Overall Ship Facilities	78
Beverages/Service	74	Value for Money	83
Accommodations	78	Total Cruise Experience	81
Cabin Service	78	**Overall Rating**	**1549**
Itineraries/Destinations	82	**Average**	**77.4**

Comments

Smart-looking modern ship with square, contemporary funnel/recently underwent extensive $15 million refurbishment/added are a new nightclub, cinema, and new cabins/smart interior decor/new suites on Boat Deck are very large and well equipped/ other cabins are compact, but adequate/ two dining rooms are quite attractive/food is reasonable, but choice is limited/service is good, but there's no finesse, and communication is difficult/however, this ship will provide a comfortable cruise at an extremely low price.

Berlin ★★★★

Principal Cruising Areas:
Caribbean/Mediterranean/Scandinavia

Ship	mv Berlin
Cruise Line/Operator	Deilmann Reederei
Former Names	Princess Mahsuri
Gross Registered Tonnage	9,570
Built Howaldtswerke Deutsche Werft (W. Germ.)	
First Entered Service	1980
Last Refurbished	1986
Country of Registry	West Germany
Radio Call Sign	DLRC
Satellite Telephone Number	1120251
Length 460 ft./140.2 m.	Beam 57 ft./17.3 m.
Engines	2×MAK diesels
Passenger Decks	8
Number of Crew	212
Passenger Capacity (basis 2)	432
Passenger Capacity (all berths)	470

Passenger Space Ratio (basis 2)		22.1
Passenger Space Ratio (all berths)		20.3
Officers German		Service Staff German
Total Cabins 216		Cabin Door Width 24"
Outside 162	Inside 54	Single No
Wheelchair Accessible Cabins		No
Dining Rooms 1		Sittings 2
Number of Elevators 2		Door Width 30"
Electric Current in Cabins		220 AC
Casino Yes		Slot Machines Yes
Swimming Pools Outside 1		Inside No
Whirlpools		No
Gymnasium Yes	Sauna Yes	Massage Yes
Cinema/Theatre Yes		Number of Seats 120
Cabin TV No		Library Yes
Children's Facilities/Playroom		No

Ratings

Ship Appearance/Condition	84	Shore Excursion Program	78
Interior Cleanliness	83	Entertainment	78
Passenger Space	81	Activities Program	76
Passenger Comfort Level	83	Cruise Director/Cruise Staff	75
Furnishings/Decor	82	Ship's Officers/Staff	80
Cruise Cuisine	81	Fitness/Sports Facilities	80
Food Service	82	Overall Ship Facilities	81
Beverages/Service	78	Value for Money	78
Accommodations	82	Total Cruise Experience	82
Cabin Service	82	**Overall Rating**	**1608**
Itineraries/Destinations	82	**Average**	**80.4**

Comments

Very attractive contemporary profile, with clean lines/1986 midsection stretch has added more cabins and a new nightclub/very crisp and tidy throughout/elegant, tasteful European decor and furnishings/elegant dining room has big picture windows/attentive, professional European service with a smile/cabins are extremely comfortable and well appointed/each has its own television/intimate, highly personable atmosphere/continental passenger mix/this ship will provide a real deluxe cruise experience in elegant, contemporary surroundings, for the more discerning European passenger.

Bermuda Star ★★★ +

Principal Cruising Areas:
Bermuda/Mexican Riviera

Ship	ss Bermuda Star	Passenger Space Ratio (basis 2)		32.8
Cruise Line/Operator	Bermuda Star Line	Passenger Space Ratio (all berths)		32.8
Formerly	Veendam/Monarch Star/Argentina	Officers European	Service Staff International	
Gross Registered Tonnage	23,395	Total Cabins 364	Cabin Door Width 26"	
Built	Ingalls Shipbuilding (USA)	Outside 270	Inside 94	Single 3
First Entered Service	1958	Wheelchair Accessible Cabins		No
Last Refurbished	1988	Dining Rooms 1		Sittings 2
Country of Registry	Panama	Number of Elevators 3	Door Width 30–33"	
Radio Call Sign	3FMG2	Electric Current in Cabins		110 AC
Satellite Telephone Number	–	Casino Yes	Slot Machines Yes	
Length 617 ft./188.0 m.	Beam 84 ft./25.6 m.	Swimming Pools Outside 1		Inside No
Engines	4×GE turbines	Whirlpools		No
Passenger Decks	8	Gymnasium Yes	Sauna Yes	Massage Yes
Number of Crew	300	Cinema/Theatre Yes	Number of Seats 200	
Passenger Capacity (basis 2)	713	Cabin TV No		Library Yes
Passenger Capacity (all berths)	713	Children's Facilities/Playroom		No

Ratings

Ship Appearance/Condition	78	Shore Excursion Program		78
Interior Cleanliness	80	Entertainment		77
Passenger Space	79	Activities Program		76
Passenger Comfort Level	80	Cruise Director/Cruise Staff		76
Furnishings/Decor	80	Ship's Officers/Staff		78
Cruise Cuisine	78	Fitness/Sports Facilities		75
Food Service	79	Overall Ship Facilities		78
Beverages/Service	77	Value for Money		81
Accommodations	78	Total Cruise Experience		80
Cabin Service	78	**Overall Rating**		**1565**
Itineraries/Destinations	79	**Average**		**78.2**

Comments

Nice ocean liner profile with big, but false, funnel/stable sea ship that is well maintained/interior not glamorous, though very pleasant/homely ambiance/spacious cabins, with solid, heavy-duty furniture and fittings/large casino is ugly and underused/ dining room set low down and needs more light/service is attentive/food is quite good, but choice is limited/this ship will provide a very decent cruise experience, at a down-to-earth price.

Black Prince ★★★ +

Principal Cruising Areas:
Iberia / Mediterranean / Scandinavia

Ship	ms Black Prince
Cruise Line / Operator	Fred Olsen Cruises
Former Names	–
Gross Registered Tonnage	11,209
Built	Lubeck Fender Werke (W. Germany)
First Entered Service	1966
Last Refurbished	1987
Country of Registry	Philippines
Radio Call Sign	DUAT
Satellite Telephone Number	1700235
Length 465 ft./141.7 m.	Beam 66 ft./20.1 m.
Engines	2×Pielstick diesels
Passenger Decks	7
Number of Crew	176
Passenger Capacity (basis 2)	450
Passenger Capacity (all berths)	520

Passenger Space Ratio (basis 2)	24.9
Passenger Space Ratio (all berths)	21.6
Officers European	Service Staff Filipino
Total Cabins 246	Cabin Door Width 26"
Outside 173 Inside 73	Single 57
Wheelchair Accessible Cabins	2
Dining Rooms 2	Sittings Open
Number of Elevators 2	Door Width 30"
Electric Current in Cabins	240 AC
Casino Yes	Slot Machines Yes
Swimming Pools Outside 2	Inside No
Whirlpools	No
Gymnasium Yes Sauna Yes	Massage Yes
Cinema/Theatre No	Number of Seats –
Cabin TV No	Library Yes
Children's Facilities/Playroom	No

Ratings

Ship Appearance/Condition	79		Shore Excursion Program	74
Interior Cleanliness	82		Entertainment	76
Passenger Space	74		Activities Program	72
Passenger Comfort Level	80		Cruise Director/Cruise Staff	74
Furnishings/Decor	82		Ship's Officers/Staff	80
Cruise Cuisine	82		Fitness/Sports Facilities	78
Food Service	81		Overall Ship Facilities	78
Beverages/Service	78		Value for Money	80
Accommodations	80		Total Cruise Experience	82
Cabin Service	81		**Overall Rating**	**1575**
Itineraries/Destinations	82		**Average**	**78.7**

Comments

Solidly built gleaming white ship with a new, somewhat boxy profile after an extensive refurbishment/painted bow decor is unattractive, and the two "sails" mounted topside serve no purpose/stern features a popular new 60' hydraulic "marina park" and free-float swimming pool surround that extends from the mother ship/outside suites are lovely/other cabins are small, but well equipped, and tastefully decorated/large number of single cabins/new bi-level show lounge is a nice addition/two main dining rooms have big picture windows, while a third is an informal open-air area on Marquee Deck/good indoor fitness center/this ship combines traditional Fred Olsen cruise values with a contemporary, yet intimate, friendly ship, and with lots of repeat passengers.

Britanis ★ ★ ★ +

Principal Cruising Areas:
Caribbean / South America

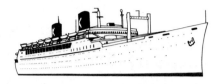

Ship	ss Britanis	Passenger Space Ratio (basis 2)	28.2
Cruise Line/Operator Chandris Fantasy Cruises		Passenger Space Ratio (all berths)	27.2
Former Names Monterey/Matsonia/Lurline		Officers Greek Service Staff International	
Gross Registered Tonnage 26,141		Total Cabins 463 Cabin Door Width 26–30″	
Built Bethlehem Shipbuilders (USA)		Outside 159 Inside 304 Single No	
First Entered Service 1932		Wheelchair Accessible Cabins No	
Last Refurbished 1987		Dining Rooms 2 Sittings 2	
Country of Registry Panama		Number of Elevators 3 Door Width 31″	
Radio Call Sign HPEN		Electric Current in Cabins 110 AC/220 DC	
Satellite Telephone Number 1332531		Casino Yes Slot Machines Yes	
Length 642 ft./195.6 m. Beam 79 ft./24.0 m.		Swimming Pools Outside 1 Inside No	
Engines 4×Bethlehem turbines		Whirlpools No	
Passenger Decks 8		Gymnasium Yes Sauna Yes Massage Yes	
Number of Crew 530		Cinema/Theatre Yes Number of Seats 208	
Passenger Capacity (basis 2) 926		Cabin TV No Library Yes	
Passenger Capacity (all berths) 960		Children's Facilities/Playroom No	

Ratings

Ship Appearance/Condition	79	Shore Excursion Program	73
Interior Cleanliness	81	Entertainment	77
Passenger Space	77	Activities Program	68
Passenger Comfort Level	78	Cruise Director/Cruise Staff	75
Furnishings/Decor	78	Ship's Officers/Staff	76
Cruise Cuisine	81	Fitness/Sports Facilities	74
Food Service	80	Overall Ship Facilities	75
Beverages/Service	79	Value for Money	81
Accommodations	78	Total Cruise Experience	81
Cabin Service	80	**Overall Rating**	**1551**
Itineraries/Destinations	80	**Average**	**77.5**

Comments

Vintage former ocean liner with classic profile is one of few with two funnels/solid, well-constructed ship that has tremendous charm and character/despite her age, she is surprisingly well maintained/public rooms have high ceilings, are spacious, even majestic/dining room is attractive, even though set low down/food is better than you might expect, with good buffet spreads/attentive service from a staff eager to please/cabins are mostly inside, but are quite large and comfortable/this ship offers excellent value for money, and delivers far more than one would imagine.

Canberra ★★★★

Principal Cruising Areas:
Caribbean/Iberia/Mediterranean/
World Cruise

Ship	ss Canberra
Cruise Line/Operator	P&O Canberra Cruises
Former Names	–
Gross Registered Tonnage	44,807
Built	Harland & Wolff (UK)
First Entered Service	1961
Last Refurbished	1988
Country of Registry	Great Britain
Radio Call Sign	GBVC
Satellite Telephone Number	1440205
Length 818.5 ft./249.4 mBeam 102.5 ft./31.2 m.	
Engines	2×AEI turbines
Passenger Decks	10
Number of Crew	805
Passenger Capacity (basis 2)	1399
Passenger Capacity (all berths)	1626

Passenger Space Ratio (basis 2)		32.0
Passenger Space Ratio (all berths)		27.5
Officers British	Service Staff British/Goanese	
Total Cabins 780*	Cabin Door Width 26″	
Outside 462	Inside 318	Single 161
Wheelchair Accessible Cabins		No
Dining Rooms 2		Sittings 2
Number of Elevators 6	Door Width 40″	
Electric Current in Cabins		220 AC
Casino Yes		Slot Machines Yes
Swimming Pools Outside 3		Inside No
Whirlpools		No
Gymnasium Yes	Sauna No	Massage Yes
Cinema/Theatre Yes	Number of Seats 400	
Cabin TV No		Library Yes
Children's Facilities/Playroom		Yes

* 236 cabins without facilities

Ratings

Ship Appearance/Condition	80	Shore Excursion Program	78
Interior Cleanliness	81	Entertainment	79
Passenger Space	81	Activities Program	80
Passenger Comfort Level	82	Cruise Director/Cruise Staff	77
Furnishings/Decor	79	Ship's Officers/Staff	79
Cruise Cuisine	79	Fitness/Sports Facilities	79
Food Service	81	Overall Ship Facilities	81
Beverages/Service	80	Value for Money	81
Accommodations	78	Total Cruise Experience	82
Cabin Service	82	**Overall Rating**	**1602**
Itineraries/Destinations	83	**Average**	**80.1**

Comments

Reassuringly large/streamlined styling with midships bridge and twin aft funnels/aging but well-maintained ship with good sea manners/expansive open deck sunning space, and real British-style deck chairs/recent upgrading changed some public rooms, added new features and decor/my favorite is the "Crow's Nest Bar"/the two dining rooms now sport softer decor/British and "colonial" cuisine/luxury suites are lovely, with fine wood furniture/wide range of other cabins/some cabins share nearby bathroom facilities/those on "B" Deck have obstructed views/efficient, courteous service/excellent for families with children/laundrette on every deck/this ship will cruise you in comfortable, if plain, surroundings, at an affordable price, in good British style.

Carib Vacationer ★

Principal Cruising Areas:
Caribbean

Ship		ms Carib Vacationer
Cruise Line/Operator		Vacation Line
Formerly	Vacationer/Nassau/Kieller Forge	
Gross Registered Tonnage		2,435
Built	De Merwede (Holland)	
First Entered Service		1971
Last Refurbished		1982
Country of Registry		Holland
Radio Call Sign		n/a
Satellite Telephone Number		–
Length 250 ft./76.2 m.	Beam 42.5 ft./12.9 m.	
Engines		1×MWM diesel
Passenger Decks		4
Number of Crew		23
Passenger Capacity (basis 2)		148
Passenger Capacity (all berths)		173

Passenger Space Ratio (basis 2)		16.4
Passenger Space Ratio (all berths)		14.0
Officers Dutch	Service Staff European	
Total Cabins 74	Cabin Door Width 22"	
Outside 74	Inside No	Single No
Wheelchair Accessible Cabins		No
Dining Rooms 1		Sittings 1
Number of Elevators 0		Door Width –
Electric Current in Cabins		220 AC
Casino No	Slot Machines No	
Swimming Pools Outside 1		Inside No
Whirlpools		No
Gymnasium No	Sauna No	Massage No
Cinema/Theatre No	Number of Seats –	
Cabin TV No		Library No
Children's Facilities/Playroom		No

Ratings

Ship Appearance/Condition	75
Interior Cleanliness	82
Passenger Space	72
Passenger Comfort Level	71
Furnishings/Decor	68
Cruise Cuisine	68
Food Service	74
Beverages/Service	70
Accommodations	68
Cabin Service	68
Itineraries/Destinations	76

Shore Excursion Program	62
Entertainment	50
Activities Program	60
Cruise Director/Cruise Staff	64
Ship's Officers/Staff	66
Fitness/Sports Facilities	50
Overall Ship Facilities	60
Value for Money	66
Total Cruise Experience	73
Overall Rating	**1343**
Average	**67.1**

Comments

Cute little vessel that doesn't pretend to be either pretty or glamorous/funnel sits right over the stern/plain and basic interior appointments, yet comfortable as long as you don't expect too much/multi-functional public rooms/food is barely adequate— better to eat ashore/cabins are small and functional, but there's little closet space/minuscule swimming pool/this ship offers a "no-frills" cruise for those on a very low budget/completely informal in every way.

Caribe I ★★★

Principal Cruising Areas:
Caribbean

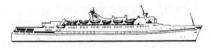

Ship	ms Caribe I
Cruise Line/Operator	Commodore Cruise Line
Former Names	Olympia
Gross Registered Tonnage	22,979
Built	A. Stephen & Son (UK)
First Entered Service	1953
Last Refurbished	1988
Country of Registry	Panama
Radio Call Sign	3EIC2
Satellite Telephone Number	–
Length 611 ft./186.2 m.	Beam 80 ft./24.3 m.
Engines	2×Deutz diesels
Passenger Decks	8
Number of Crew	370
Passenger Capacity (basis 2)	876
Passenger Capacity (all berths)	1160

Passenger Space Ratio (basis 2)		26.2
Passenger Space Ratio (all berths)		19.8
Officers European	Service Staff International	
Total Cabins 443	Cabin Door Width 28–32"	
Outside 217	Inside 226	Single 10
Wheelchair Accessible Cabins		1
Dining Rooms 1		Sittings 2
Number of Elevators 3	Door Width 36"	
Electric Current in Cabins		110 AC
Casino Yes	Slot Machines Yes	
Swimming Pools Outside 1		Inside No
Whirlpools		2
Gymnasium Yes	Sauna No	Massage No
Cinema/Theatre Yes	Number of Seats 166	
Cabin TV No		Library Yes
Children's Facilities/Playroom		No

Ratings

Ship Appearance/Condition	78	Shore Excursion Program	74
Interior Cleanliness	78	Entertainment	76
Passenger Space	74	Activities Program	76
Passenger Comfort Level	79	Cruise Director/Cruise Staff	76
Furnishings/Decor	76	Ship's Officers/Staff	78
Cruise Cuisine	78	Fitness/Sports Facilities	77
Food Service	80	Overall Ship Facilities	74
Beverages/Service	78	Value for Money	76
Accommodations	77	Total Cruise Experience	79
Cabin Service	79	**Overall Rating**	**1539**
Itineraries/Destinations	76	**Average**	**76.9**

Comments

Solid former ocean liner profile/new conventional funnel/excellent sea manners/rather crowded open deck space when full/polished teak decking is lovely/indoor promenade deck popular with strollers/lovely old-world dining room has original oil paintings on veneered walls/food is plentiful, and good/public rooms are "stacked" on several decks/layout is awkward fore-and-aft arrangement/new two-tier nightclub is delightful/large casino has exciting action/cabins are quite roomy, with good closet space/service is friendly, but not polished/this ship will cruise you in comfortable, though not elegant, surroundings, with lots of fun, at a modest price.

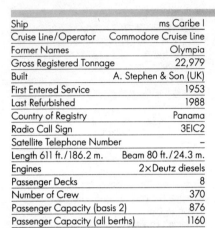

Carla Costa ★★★ +

Principal Cruising Areas:
Caribbean

Ship	ms Carla Costa
Cruise Line/Operator	Costa Cruises
Former Names	Princess Carla/Flandre
Gross Registered Tonnage	20,477
Built	Ateliers et Chantiers de France (France)
First Entered Service	1952
Last Refurbished	1988
Country of Registry	Italy
Radio Call Sign	ICCO
Satellite Telephone Number	–
Length 600 ft./182.8 m.	Beam 80 ft./24.3 m.
Engines	2×SWD diesels
Passenger Decks	7
Number of Crew	370
Passenger Capacity (basis 2)	748
Passenger Capacity (all berths)	748

Passenger Space Ratio (basis 2)	27.4
Passenger Space Ratio (all berths)	27.4
Officers Italian	Service Staff Italian
Total Cabins 378	Cabin Door Width 26"
Outside 195 Inside 183	Single No
Wheelchair Accessible Cabins	No
Dining Rooms 1	Sittings 2
Number of Elevators 5	Door Width 22–31"
Electric Current in Cabins	127/220 AC
Casino Yes	Slot Machines Yes
Swimming Pools Outside 2	Inside No
Whirlpools	No
Gymnasium Yes Sauna Yes	Massage Yes
Cinema/Theatre Yes	Number of Seats 145
Cabin TV No	Library Yes
Children's Facilities/Playroom	No

Ratings

Ship Appearance/Condition	78	Shore Excursion Program	76
Interior Cleanliness	77	Entertainment	76
Passenger Space	76	Activities Program	72
Passenger Comfort Level	79	Cruise Director/Cruise Staff	76
Furnishings/Decor	78	Ship's Officers/Staff	80
Cruise Cuisine	81	Fitness/Sports Facilities	73
Food Service	81	Overall Ship Facilities	76
Beverages/Service	79	Value for Money	82
Accommodations	79	Total Cruise Experience	81
Cabin Service	80	**Overall Rating**	**1560**
Itineraries/Destinations	80	**Average**	**78.0**

Comments

Solidly built former ocean liner with classic styling/good open deck space/Lido Deck contains most public rooms/suites are very large/other cabins are quite roomy for two, crowded with more/dining room is set low down and is cheerful/new art-deco decor is quite elegant/food is Italian, with excellent pasta/good service/small, but popular pizzeria/cheerful ambiance and good Italian service on board/this ship provides a comfortable cruise experience for a reasonable price, but don't expect elegance, for this is an informal ship for relaxed, fun-filled cruising with a jolly, Italian crew.

Carnivale ★★★+

Principal Cruising Areas:
Bahamas

Ship	tss Carnivale	Passenger Space Ratio (basis 2)	28.7
Cruise Line/Operator	Carnival Cruise Lines	Passenger Space Ratio (all berths)	20.2
Formerly Queen Anna Maria/Empress of Britain		Officers Italian Service Staff International	
Gross Registered Tonnage	27,250	Total Cabins 482 Cabin Door Width 26–30"	
Built Fairfield Shipbuilding (UK)		Outside 217 Inside 265 Single No	
First Entered Service	1956	Wheelchair Accessible Cabins	No
Last Refurbished	1984	Dining Rooms 1	Sittings 2
Country of Registry	Panama	Number of Elevators 4 Door Width 36"	
Radio Call Sign	HOKL	Electric Current in Cabins 110 AC/220 DC	
Satellite Telephone Number	–	Casino Yes Slot Machines Yes	
Length 640 ft./195.0 m. Beam 87 ft./26.5 m.		Swimming Pools Outside 3 Inside 1	
Engines	2×GT turbines	Whirlpools	No
Passenger Decks	9	Gymnasium Yes Sauna Yes Massage Yes	
Number of Crew	550	Cinema/Theatre Yes Number of Seats 180	
Passenger Capacity (basis 2)	950	Cabin TV No Library Yes	
Passenger Capacity (all berths)	1350	Children's Facilities/Playroom Yes	

Ratings

Ship Appearance/Condition	79	Shore Excursion Program	76
Interior Cleanliness	78	Entertainment	76
Passenger Space	77	Activities Program	75
Passenger Comfort Level	80	Cruise Director/Cruise Staff	78
Furnishings/Decor	78	Ship's Officers/Staff	78
Cruise Cuisine	76	Fitness/Sports Facilities	80
Food Service	78	Overall Ship Facilities	74
Beverages/Service	75	Value for Money	80
Accommodations	79	Total Cruise Experience	81
Cabin Service	78	**Overall Rating**	**1551**
Itineraries/Destinations	75	**Average**	**77.5**

Comments

Solidly built former ocean liner, with midships funnel in distinctive Carnival colors/nice original woods and polished brass throughout the interior/delightful enclosed promenade decks/rather stimulating interior colors/wide range of cabins, some with warm, rich wood furniture/very busy casino/beverage staff are real hustlers/this ship features lively party cruises that appeal to real active types who really don't want to relax/the food could stand improvement; otherwise an excellent operation.

Celebration ★★★★

Principal Cruising Areas:
Caribbean

Ship	ms Celebration	Passenger Space Ratio (basis 2)	31.5
Cruise Line/Operator	Carnival Cruise Lines	Passenger Space Ratio (all berths)	25.5
Former Names	–	Officers Italian	Service Staff International
Gross Registered Tonnage	47,262	Total Cabins 750	Cabin Door Width 22"
Built	Kockums (Sweden)	Outside 460	Inside 290	Single No
First Entered Service	1987	Wheelchair Accessible Cabins	No
Last Refurbished	–	Dining Rooms 2	Sittings 2
Country of Registry	Liberia	Number of Elevators 8	Door Width 33"
Radio Call Sign	ELFT8	Electric Current in Cabins	110 AC
Satellite Telephone Number	1240526	Casino Yes	Slot Machines Yes
Length 748 ft./227.9 m.	Beam 92 ft./28.0 m.	Swimming Pools Outside 2	Inside No
Engines	2×Sulzer diesels	Whirlpools	2
Passenger Decks	10	Gymnasium Yes Sauna Yes	Massage Yes
Number of Crew	670	Cinema/Theatre No	Number of Seats –
Passenger Capacity (basis 2)	1500	Cabin TV Yes	Library Yes
Passenger Capacity (all berths)	1850	Children's Facilities/Playroom	Yes

Ratings

Ship Appearance/Condition	85	Shore Excursion Program	77
Interior Cleanliness	86	Entertainment	83
Passenger Space	85	Activities Program	81
Passenger Comfort Level	85	Cruise Director/Cruise Staff	81
Furnishings/Decor	84	Ship's Officers/Staff	81
Cruise Cuisine	76	Fitness/Sports Facilities	83
Food Service	78	Overall Ship Facilities	85
Beverages/Service	75	Value for Money	85
Accommodations	85	Total Cruise Experience	83
Cabin Service	82	**Overall Rating**	**1640**
Itineraries/Destinations	80	**Average**	**82.0**

Comments

One of Carnival's new breed of high-rise megaships which are somehow attractive/sports the line's distinctive wing-tipped funnel/flamboyant interior decor in public rooms is stimulating, not restful, except for the beautiful, quiet Admiral's Library/superb nautically-themed decor in Wheelhouse Bar-Grill/double-width indoor promenade deck/lots of public entertainment rooms/good open deck space/swimming pools are small/cabins are sizeable and comfortable/especially good are ten suites with private balconies on Verandah Deck/two dining rooms are somewhat cramped/food is best for quantity, not quality/huge casino/this ship offers dazzle and sizzle for the whole family/excellent choice for a first cruise, if you like lots of people and action.

City of Mykonos ★★

Principal Cruising Areas:
Aegean

Ship	mts City of Mykonos
Cruise Line/Operator	Cycladic Cruises
Former Names	San Marco
Gross Registered Tonnage	4,755
Built	Cantieri Riuniti dell'Adriatico (Italy)
First Entered Service	1956
Last Refurbished	1987
Country of Registry	Greece
Radio Call Sign	SVYW
Satellite Telephone Number	. –
Length 370 ft./112.7 m.	Beam 52 ft./15.8 m.
Engines	2×GM turbines
Passenger Decks	4
Number of Crew	90
Passenger Capacity (basis 2)	280
Passenger Capacity (all berths)	370

Passenger Space Ratio (basis 2)		17.0
Passenger Space Ratio (all berths)		12.9
Officers Greek		Service Staff Greek
Total Cabins 140	Cabin Door Width 24"	
Outside 115	Inside 25	Single No
Wheelchair Accessible Cabins		No
Dining Rooms 1		Sittings 2
Number of Elevators 0		Door Width –
Electric Current in Cabins		220 AC
Casino No		Slot Machines No
Swimming Pools Outside 1		Inside No
Whirlpools		No
Gymnasium No	Sauna No	Massage No
Cinema/Theatre No	Number of Seats –	
Cabin TV No		Library Yes
Children's Facilities/Playroom		No

Ratings

Ship Appearance/Condition	78		Shore Excursion Program	64
Interior Cleanliness	79		Entertainment	62
Passenger Space	68		Activities Program	62
Passenger Comfort Level	76		Cruise Director/Cruise Staff	70
Furnishings/Decor	76		Ship's Officers/Staff	72
Cruise Cuisine	75		Fitness/Sports Facilities	50
Food Service	78		Overall Ship Facilities	66
Beverages/Service	71		Value for Money	70
Accommodations	75		Total Cruise Experience	75
Cabin Service	77		**Overall Rating**	**1420**
Itineraries/Destinations	76		**Average**	**71.0**

Comments

Small, smart-looking ship, with nice lines/ recently upgraded interior decor and colors/ship is cramped when full/very limited public room space/cabins are small, but adequate for short cruises/charming dining room is intimate, but noisy/food is typically Mediterranean in style, and choice is limited/staff are reasonably attentive, but not overly friendly/this ship offers Aegean cruising in adequate surroundings, nothing more.

City of Rhodos ★

Principal Cruising Areas:
Aegean

Ship	mts City of Rhodos	Passenger Space Ratio (basis 2)	19.0
Cruise Line/Operator	Cycladic Cruises	Passenger Space Ratio (all berths)	15.7
Former Names	Oriental	Officers Greek	Service Staff Greek
Gross Registered Tonnage	8,000	Total Cabins 205	Cabin Door Width 22"
Built	Society Española (Spain)	Outside 135 Inside 70	Single No
First Entered Service	1966	Wheelchair Accessible Cabins	No
Last Refurbished	1980	Dining Rooms 1	Sittings 2
Country of Registry	Greece	Number of Elevators 0	Door Width –
Radio Call Sign	SYXO	Electric Current in Cabins	220 AC
Satellite Telephone Number	–	Casino No	Slot Machines No
Length 435 ft./132.5 m.	Beam 60 ft./18.2 m.	Swimming Pools Outside 1	Inside No
Engines	2×B&W diesels	Whirlpools	No
Passenger Decks	5	Gymnasium No Sauna No	Massage No
Number of Crew	100	Cinema/Theatre No	Number of Seats –
Passenger Capacity (basis 2)	420	Cabin TV No	Library No
Passenger Capacity (all berths)	510	Children's Facilities/Playroom	No

Ratings

Ship Appearance/Condition	74	Shore Excursion Program	64
Interior Cleanliness	74	Entertainment	64
Passenger Space	64	Activities Program	62
Passenger Comfort Level	74	Cruise Director/Cruise Staff	70
Furnishings/Decor	68	Ship's Officers/Staff	70
Cruise Cuisine	73	Fitness/Sports Facilities	50
Food Service	76	Overall Ship Facilities	62
Beverages/Service	71	Value for Money	64
Accommodations	74	Total Cruise Experience	70
Cabin Service	74	**Overall Rating**	**1373**
Itineraries/Destinations	75	**Average**	**68.6**

Comments

Long, but rather unattractive profile, rebuilt from former ferry/very high-density ship is cramped/has only two main public rooms plus dining room/cabins are small and barely adequate, except for suites on Andros deck/public rooms are aft, away from cabins, but decor needs attention/small swimming pool, and not much open deck space for sunning/dining room is mildly attractive but the food definitely isn't/service is adequate, but there's not even a flicker of finesse/this ship caters to those who cruise the Aegean on a limited budget, don't mind noise, crowded places, or mediocre food.

Constitution ★ ★ ★ +

Principal Cruising Areas:
Hawaii

Ship	ss Constitution		Passenger Space Ratio (basis 2)	38.6
Cruise Line/Operator	American Hawaii Cruises		Passenger Space Ratio (all berths)	30.0
Former Names	–		Officers American	Service Staff American
Gross Registered Tonnage	30,090		Total Cabins 397	Cabin Door Width 26"
Built	Bethlehem Shipbuilders (USA)		Outside 178 Inside 219	Single 16
First Entered Service	1951		Wheelchair Accessible Cabins	No
Last Refurbished	1988		Dining Rooms 2	Sittings 2
Country of Registry	USA		Number of Elevators 4	Door Width 31"
Radio Call Sign	KAEG		Electric Current in Cabins	110 AC
Satellite Telephone Number	–		Casino No	Slot Machines No
Length 682 ft./207.8 m.	Beam 89 ft./27.1 m.		Swimming Pools Outside 2	Inside No
Engines	2×DRG turbines		Whirlpools	No
Passenger Decks	9		Gymnasium No Sauna Yes	Massage Yes
Number of Crew	350		Cinema/Theatre Yes	Number of Seats 144
Passenger Capacity (basis 2)	778		Cabin TV No	Library Yes
Passenger Capacity (all berths)	1000		Children's Facilities/Playroom	Yes

Ratings

Ship Appearance/Condition	78		Shore Excursion Program	78
Interior Cleanliness	82		Entertainment	78
Passenger Space	82		Activities Program	76
Passenger Comfort Level	82		Cruise Director/Cruise Staff	76
Furnishings/Decor	81		Ship's Officers/Staff	80
Cruise Cuisine	78		Fitness/Sports Facilities	72
Food Service	80		Overall Ship Facilities	76
Beverages/Service	76		Value for Money	80
Accommodations	78		Total Cruise Experience	80
Cabin Service	80		**Overall Rating**	**1573**
Itineraries/Destinations	80		**Average**	**78.6**

Comments

Distinctive, solidly constructed vessel is one of the few two-funnel ships still operating/ expansive open deck space for sunworshippers, set around two outdoor pools/ American-built, crewed and registered, this ship has good facilities for meetings/ public areas are spacious/wide range of cabins to choose from, all of which offer ample room to move in, plus decent closet and drawer space/heavy-duty furniture and fittings/two dining rooms are set low down, but have cheerful decor/food is typically American-Polynesian in style/service is attentive, and comes with a smile/this ship features Hawaii cruising in comfortable surroundings reminiscent of times past.

CostaRiviera ★★★★

Principal Cruising Areas:
Caribbean

Ship	ss CostaRiviera	Passenger Space Ratio (basis 2)	32.0
Cruise Line/Operator	Costa Cruises	Passenger Space Ratio (all berths)	32.0
Former Names	Guglielmo Marconi	Officers Italian	Service Staff Italian
Gross Registered Tonnage	31,500	Total Cabins 492	Cabin Door Width 25"
Built	Cantieri Riuniti dell'Adriatico (Italy)	Outside 297	Inside 195	Single 1
First Entered Service	1963	Wheelchair Accessible Cabins	No
Last Refurbished	1985	Dining Rooms 1	Sittings 2
Country of Registry	Italy	Number of Elevators 7	Door Width 26–36"
Radio Call Sign	IBBG	Electric Current in Cabins	110/220 AC
Satellite Telephone Number	1150146	Casino Yes	Slot Machines Yes
Length 700 ft./213.3 m.	Beam 94 ft./28.6 m.	Swimming Pools Outside 3	Inside No
Engines	2×CRDA turbines	Whirlpools	3
Passenger Decks	8	Gymnasium Yes Sauna Yes Massage Yes	
Number of Crew	500	Cinema/Theatre Yes	Number of Seats 186
Passenger Capacity (basis 2)	984	Cabin TV No	Library Yes
Passenger Capacity (all berths)	984	Children's Facilities/Playroom	No

Ratings

Ship Appearance/Condition	80	Shore Excursion Program	76
Interior Cleanliness	82	Entertainment	82
Passenger Space	81	Activities Program	80
Passenger Comfort Level	82	Cruise Director/Cruise Staff	80
Furnishings/Decor	81	Ship's Officers/Staff	80
Cruise Cuisine	80	Fitness/Sports Facilities	81
Food Service	80	Overall Ship Facilities	82
Beverages/Service	79	Value for Money	84
Accommodations	80	Total Cruise Experience	82
Cabin Service	81	**Overall Rating**	**1609**
Itineraries/Destinations	76	**Average**	**80.4**

Comments

Reconstructed former ocean liner tries for streamlined yacht look, though it doesn't quite gel/built up fore and aft decks/ expansive open deck and sunning space/ contemporary interior styling, colors and appointments/delightfully Italian in character and ambiance/excellent public rooms, with lots of nooks and crannies to hide in/excel- lent pizzeria/cabins are quite spacious and tastefully furnished, but bathrooms are small/bubbly dining room/fine Italian food, with excellent pasta, pizza and buffets/ good service with a smile/this ship will cruise you in very comfortable surroundings for a modest price, and is lots of fun.

Crown del Mar

Principal Cruising Areas:
Bahamas / Mexico

Ship	mv Crown del Mar	Passenger Space Ratio (basis 2)	22.3
Cruise Line / Operator	Crown Cruise Line	Passenger Space Ratio (all berths)	20.5
Former Names	Las Palmas de Gran Canarias	Officers Norwegian	Service Staff International
Gross Registered Tonnage	10,000	Total Cabins 224	Cabin Door Width 22"
Built	Unión Naval de Levante (Spain)	Outside 138	Inside 86	Single No
First Entered Service	1967	Wheelchair Accessible Cabins	No
Last Refurbished	1988	Dining Rooms 1	Sittings 1
Country of Registry	Panama	Number of Elevators 1	Door Width 31"
Radio Call Sign	n/a	Electric Current in Cabins	110 AC
Satellite Telephone Number	–	Casino Yes	Slot Machines Yes
Length 429 ft./130.7 m.	Beam 63 ft./19.2 m.	Swimming Pools Outside 1	Inside No
Engines	2×Burmeister & Wain diesels	Whirlpools	2
Passenger Decks	5	Gymnasium No Sauna No	Massage No
Number of Crew	195	Cinema/Theatre No	Number of Seats –
Passenger Capacity (basis 2)	448	Cabin TV Yes	Library Yes
Passenger Capacity (all berths)	486	Children's Facilities/Playroom	No

Ratings

Ship Appearance/Condition	–	Shore Excursion Program	–
Interior Cleanliness	–	Entertainment	–
Passenger Space	–	Activities Program	–
Passenger Comfort Level	–	Cruise Director/Cruise Staff	–
Furnishings/Decor	–	Ship's Officers/Staff	–
Cruise Cuisine	–	Fitness/Sports Facilities	–
Food Service	–	Overall Ship Facilities	–
Beverages/Service	–	Value for Money	–
Accommodations	–	Total Cruise Experience	–
Cabin Service	–	**Overall Rating**	–
Itineraries/Destinations	–	**Average**	–

Comments

After an extensive refurbishment, this former Spanish ferry sports a sleek new cruise ship look/new twin funnels/most public rooms set below accommodation decks, except for two forward observation lounges/soft earth tone colors used in decor/charming dining room is set low down, but has ocean views/cuisine and service are good/attentive staff throughout/outdoor topdeck area for light grill meals/"Oh Gee's" piano bar is popular nightspot/active casino/attractive Vista Mar observation lounge has sweeping stairway to upstairs lounge and library/this ship will provide a very comfortable cruise experience, with good value as a bonus. (Not rated at press time.)

Crown Odyssey ★★★★★

Principal Cruising Areas:
Worldwide

Ship	ms Crown Odyssey	Passenger Space Ratio (basis 2)		32.5
Cruise Line/Operator	Royal Cruise Line	Passenger Space Ratio (all berths)		28.0
Former Names	–	Officers Greek		Service Staff Greek
Gross Registered Tonnage	34,242	Total Cabins 526		Cabin Door Width 25"
Built	Meyer Werft (W. Germany)	Outside 412	Inside 114	Single No
First Entered Service	1988	Wheelchair Accessible Cabins		4
Last Refurbished	–	Dining Rooms 1		Sittings 2
Country of Registry	Greece	Number of Elevators 4		Door Width 36"
Radio Call Sign	SVZG	Electric Current in Cabins		110 AC
Satellite Telephone Number	1130633	Casino Yes		Slot Machines Yes
Length 615.1 ft./187.5 m.	Beam 92 ft./28.0 m.	Swimming Pools Outside 1		Inside 1
Engines	4×MAK diesels	Whirlpools		4
Passenger Decks	10	Gymnasium Yes	Sauna Yes	Massage Yes
Number of Crew	470	Cinema/Theatre Yes		Number of Seats 215
Passenger Capacity (basis 2)	1052	Cabin TV No		Library Yes
Passenger Capacity (all berths)	1221	Children's Facilities/Playroom		No

Ratings

Ship Appearance/Condition	92	Shore Excursion Program	86
Interior Cleanliness	95	Entertainment	87
Passenger Space	92	Activities Program	84
Passenger Comfort Level	93	Cruise Director/Cruise Staff	86
Furnishings/Decor	93	Ship's Officers/Staff	85
Cruise Cuisine	87	Fitness/Sports Facilities	88
Food Service	85	Overall Ship Facilities	92
Beverages/Service	85	Value for Money	92
Accommodations	94	Total Cruise Experience	93
Cabin Service	88	**Overall Rating**	**1788**
Itineraries/Destinations	91	**Average**	**89.4**

Comments

Superb new ship with impressive profile/ fine attention to detail and quality evident everywhere/spacious layout with lavish public rooms/generous warm woods and marble used throughout/ample open decks/outdoor promenade deck/genuine theatre with superb sound system is refreshing/stunning indoor spa and pool/ apartments and suites are spacious and gracious/other cabins are very large/all come fully equipped and beautifully furnished/classic, though noisy, dining room features stained-glass ceiling/this ship exudes quality, style and charm, for a moderately decent price/you'll be pampered with refined living at sea aboard this majestic new ship.

Cunard Countess ★★★ +

Principal Cruising Areas:
Caribbean

Ship	mv Cunard Countess
Cruise Line/Operator	Cunard Line
Former Names	–
Gross Registered Tonnage	17,593
Built	Burmeister & Wain (Denmark)
First Entered Service	1976
Last Refurbished	1986
Country of Registry	Great Britain
Radio Call Sign	GUNP
Satellite Telephone Number	1140330
Length 536 ft./163.3 m.	Beam 75 ft./22.8 m.
Engines	2×B&W diesels
Passenger Decks	8
Number of Crew	350
Passenger Capacity (basis 2)	790
Passenger Capacity (all berths)	956

Passenger Space Ratio (basis 2)		22.2
Passenger Space Ratio (all berths)		18.4
Officers British	Service Staff International	
Total Cabins 398	Cabin Door Width 24"	
Outside 249	Inside 149	Single No
Wheelchair Accessible Cabins		No
Dining Rooms 1		Sittings 2
Number of Elevators 2	Door Width 31"	
Electric Current in Cabins		110/220 AC
Casino Yes	Slot Machines Yes	
Swimming Pools Outside 1		Inside No
Whirlpools		2
Gymnasium Yes	Sauna Yes	Massage No
Cinema/Theatre Yes	Number of Seats 126	
Cabin TV No		Library Yes
Children's Facilities/Playroom		No

Ratings

Ship Appearance/Condition	81		Shore Excursion Program	80
Interior Cleanliness	77		Entertainment	80
Passenger Space	75		Activities Program	82
Passenger Comfort Level	80		Cruise Director/Cruise Staff	83
Furnishings/Decor	76		Ship's Officers/Staff	84
Cruise Cuisine	78		Fitness/Sports Facilities	80
Food Service	79		Overall Ship Facilities	81
Beverages/Service	78		Value for Money	83
Accommodations	76		Total Cruise Experience	82
Cabin Service	80		**Overall Rating**	**1597**
Itineraries/Destinations	82		**Average**	**79.8**

Comments

Ship has fine modern profile, with clean lines and distinctive swept-back red funnel/ good public rooms and attractive, contemporary decor with astronautical theme throughout/could be cleaner/excellent indoor-outdoor entertainment center/cabins are small, space-efficient units but with tinny metal fixtures and very thin walls/ pleasant dining room has large picture windows/reasonable banquet food standard/ good, cheerful service that lacks finesse/ recommended for a destination-oriented first cruise experience in comfortable surroundings, at an excellent and realistic price.

Cunard Princess ★★★+

Principal Cruising Areas:
Trans-Canal/Bermuda/Mexican Riviera

Ship	mv Cunard Princess		Passenger Space Ratio (basis 2)		21.7
Cruise Line/Operator	Cunard Line		Passenger Space Ratio (all berths)		18.1
Former Names	Cunard Conquest		Officers British	Service Staff International	
Gross Registered Tonnage	17,495		Total Cabins 403	Cabin Door Width 24"	
Built	Burmeister & Wain (Denmark)		Outside 270	Inside 133	Single 1
First Entered Service	1977		Wheelchair Accessible Cabins		No
Last Refurbished	1985		Dining Rooms 1		Sittings 2
Country of Registry	Bahamas		Number of Elevators 2	Door Width 31"	
Radio Call Sign	C6CG		Electric Current in Cabins		110/220 AC
Satellite Telephone Number	1104111		Casino Yes	Slot Machines Yes	
Length 536 ft./163.3 m.	Beam 75 ft./22.8 m.		Swimming Pools Outside 1		Inside No
Engines	2×B&W diesels		Whirlpools		2
Passenger Decks	8		Gymnasium Yes	Sauna Yes	Massage No
Number of Crew	350		Cinema/Theatre Yes	Number of Seats 130	
Passenger Capacity (basis 2)	805		Cabin TV No		Library Yes
Passenger Capacity (all berths)	962		Children's Facilities/Playroom		No

Ratings

Ship Appearance/Condition	81		Shore Excursion Program	81
Interior Cleanliness	77		Entertainment	80
Passenger Space	75		Activities Program	83
Passenger Comfort Level	80		Cruise Director/Cruise Staff	82
Furnishings/Decor	76		Ship's Officers/Staff	84
Cruise Cuisine	78		Fitness/Sports Facilities	80
Food Service	80		Overall Ship Facilities	81
Beverages/Service	78		Value for Money	83
Accommodations	76		Total Cruise Experience	82
Cabin Service	80		**Overall Rating**	**1599**
Itineraries/Destinations	82		**Average**	**79.9**

Comments

Twin sister to *Cunard Countess*, with same contemporary profile and balanced good looks/good open deck space for sun-worshippers/could be cleaner/plentiful public rooms with attractive, nautical-themed decor/excellent indoor-outdoor entertainment center/pleasant dining room with sea views from big picture windows/ reasonable food standard/service attentive and with a smile, but lacks finesse/cabins are small and compact, but with tinny metal fixtures, very thin walls, and little closet space/however, this ship provides a very comfortable first cruise experience at an excellent price, to well-chosen destinations.

Dalmacija ★★

Principal Cruising Areas:
Mediterranean/Scandinavia

Ship	ms Dalmacija	Passenger Space Ratio (basis 2)	19.0
Cruise Line/Operator	Jadrolinija	Passenger Space Ratio (all berths)	18.2
Former Names	–	Officers Yugoslavian	Service Staff Yugoslavian
Gross Registered Tonnage	5,650	Total Cabins 148	Cabin Door Width 26"
Built	Brodogradiliste Uljanik (Yugoslavia)	Outside 93 Inside 55	Single No
First Entered Service	1965	Wheelchair Accessible Cabins	No
Last Refurbished	1987	Dining Rooms 1	Sittings 2
Country of Registry	Yugoslavia	Number of Elevators 0	Door Width –
Radio Call Sign	YTND	Electric Current in Cabins	220 AC
Satellite Telephone Number	–	Casino No	Slot Machines No
Length 387 ft./117.9 m. Beam 54 ft./16.4 m.		Swimming Pools Outside 1	Inside No
Engines	2×Sulzer diesels	Whirlpools	No
Passenger Decks	5	Gymnasium No Sauna No Massage No	
Number of Crew	112	Cinema/Theatre No Number of Seats –	
Passenger Capacity (basis 2)	296	Cabin TV No	Library Yes
Passenger Capacity (all berths)	310	Children's Facilities/Playroom	No

Ratings

Ship Appearance/Condition	74	Shore Excursion Program	72
Interior Cleanliness	72	Entertainment	70
Passenger Space	68	Activities Program	68
Passenger Comfort Level	71	Cruise Director/Cruise Staff	70
Furnishings/Decor	71	Ship's Officers/Staff	72
Cruise Cuisine	72	Fitness/Sports Facilities	66
Food Service	75	Overall Ship Facilities	68
Beverages/Service	73	Value for Money	70
Accommodations	71	Total Cruise Experience	73
Cabin Service	76	**Overall Rating**	**1428**
Itineraries/Destinations	76	**Average**	**71.4**

Comments

Smart, classic small ship profile/good open deck and sunning space, except when full/this is a cozy vessel that doesn't pretend to be glamorous/clean and tidy throughout/limited public rooms are cleanly decorated/small, sparsely furnished cabins have very tiny bathrooms/pleasant dining room and service, but English is hardly spoken/reasonably friendly staff/food choice rather limited/rather cramped when full/caters primarily to European passengers looking for a destination-oriented cruise in comfortable, but not elegant, surroundings, at a modest price.

Danae ★★★★

Principal Cruising Areas:
Mediterranean/World Cruise

Ship	mts Danae		Passenger Space Ratio (basis 2)	39.3
Cruise Line/Operator	Costa Cruises		Passenger Space Ratio (all berths)	39.3
Former Names	Akrotiki Express/Port Sydney		Officers Italian	Service Staff European
Gross Registered Tonnage	16,300		Total Cabins 207	Cabin Door Width 25"
Built	Harland & Wolff (UK)		Outside 188	Inside 19	Single No
First Entered Service	1956		Wheelchair Accessible Cabins	No
Last Refurbished	1984		Dining Rooms 1	Sittings 1
Country of Registry	Panama		Number of Elevators 2	Door Width 22–31"
Radio Call Sign	SYVK		Electric Current in Cabins	220 AC
Satellite Telephone Number	1330220		Casino Yes	Slot Machines Yes
Length 532 ft./162.1 m.	Beam 74 ft./22.5 m.		Swimming Pools Outside 2	Inside No
Engines	2×B&W diesels		Whirlpools	No
Passenger Decks	7		Gymnasium Yes	Sauna Yes	Massage Yes
Number of Crew	250		Cinema/Theatre Yes	Number of Seats 275
Passenger Capacity (basis 2)	414		Cabin TV No	Library Yes
Passenger Capacity (all berths)	414		Children's Facilities/Playroom	Yes

Ratings

Ship Appearance/Condition	81		Shore Excursion Program	79
Interior Cleanliness	82		Entertainment	80
Passenger Space	80		Activities Program	78
Passenger Comfort Level	82		Cruise Director/Cruise Staff	78
Furnishings/Decor	82		Ship's Officers/Staff	80
Cruise Cuisine	81		Fitness/Sports Facilities	78
Food Service	81		Overall Ship Facilities	80
Beverages/Service	79		Value for Money	79
Accommodations	82		Total Cruise Experience	82
Cabin Service	81		**Overall Rating**	**1609**
Itineraries/Destinations	84		**Average**	**80.4**

Comments

Solidly built ship with good lines/high quality of interior appointments/spacious public rooms, although decor somewhat conservative/spacious, traditional theatre has three audio channels for simultaneous translation for international conventions/cabins are a good size, have heavy-duty furniture and fittings, and lots of closet and drawer space/very good open deck space for sunning/Italian-European cuisine in the dining room, which is quite nicely appointed/friendly service/nice old-world ambiance/this ship will provide a fine-tuned cruise experience for discerning Europeans.

Daphne ★★★★

Principal Cruising Areas:
Alaska / Caribbean

Ship	mts Daphne	Passenger Space Ratio (basis 2)	40.2
Cruise Line / Operator	Costa Cruises	Passenger Space Ratio (all berths)	40.2
Formerly	Therisos Express / Port Melbourne	Officers Italian	Service Staff European
Gross Registered Tonnage	16,330	Total Cabins 203	Cabin Door Width 25"
Built	Swan, Hunter (UK)	Outside 183　Inside 20	Single No
First Entered Service	1955	Wheelchair Accessible Cabins	No
Last Refurbished	1988	Dining Rooms 1	Sittings 2
Country of Registry	Panama	Number of Elevators 2　Door Width 22–31"	
Radio Call Sign	SYWK	Electric Current in Cabins	110/220 AC
Satellite Telephone Number	1330277	Casino Yes	Slot Machines Yes
Length 532 ft./162.1 m.　Beam 74 ft./22.5 m.		Swimming Pools Outside 1	Inside No
Engines	2 × Doxford diesels	Whirlpools	2
Passenger Decks	7	Gymnasium Yes　Sauna Yes　Massage Yes	
Number of Crew	250	Cinema / Theatre Yes　Number of Seats 275	
Passenger Capacity (basis 2)	406	Cabin TV No	Library Yes
Passenger Capacity (all berths)	406	Children's Facilities / Playroom	No

Ratings

Ship Appearance / Condition	82	Shore Excursion Program	79
Interior Cleanliness	82	Entertainment	79
Passenger Space	80	Activities Program	77
Passenger Comfort Level	83	Cruise Director / Cruise Staff	80
Furnishings / Decor	80	Ship's Officers / Staff	81
Cruise Cuisine	81	Fitness / Sports Facilities	80
Food Service	82	Overall Ship Facilities	80
Beverages / Service	80	Value for Money	80
Accommodations	83	Total Cruise Experience	82
Cabin Service	81	**Overall Rating**	**1614**
Itineraries / Destinations	82	**Average**	**80.7**

Comments

Identical in outward appearance to sister *Danae,* this ship's interior decor is quite different / well-maintained vessel / bright, contemporary colors in public rooms / lovely theatre and dining room / friendly, attentive European service throughout / food is very good, especially the pasta / excellent outdoor deck and sunning space / spacious cabins with good, solid fittings and heavy-duty doors / there's plenty of closet and drawer space / bathrooms are a good size too / this is a very comfortable ship that maintains an air of intimacy / good value cruising.

Dawn Princess ★★★★

Principal Cruising Areas:
Australasia/Caribbean/Mediterranean/
Scandinavia/South Pacific

Ship	tss Dawn Princess
Cruise Line/Operator	Princess Cruises
Former Names	FairWind/Sylvania
Gross Registered Tonnage	25,000
Built	John Brown & Co. (UK)
First Entered Service	1957
Last Refurbished	1984
Country of Registry	Liberia
Radio Call Sign	ELPH
Satellite Telephone Number	1241217
Length 608 ft./185.3 m.	Beam 80 ft./24.3 m.
Engines	2×Brown turbines
Passenger Decks	11
Number of Crew	440
Passenger Capacity (basis 2)	906
Passenger Capacity (all berths)	1100

Passenger Space Ratio (basis 2)	27.5
Passenger Space Ratio (all berths)	22.7
Officers Italian Service Staff Italian/Portuguese	
Total Cabins 459	Cabin Door Width 24"
Outside 231 Inside 228	Single No
Wheelchair Accessible Cabins	No
Dining Rooms 2	Sittings 2
Number of Elevators 3	Door Width 36"
Electric Current in Cabins	110 AC
Casino Yes	Slot Machines Yes
Swimming Pools Outside 3	Inside No
Whirlpools	No
Gymnasium Yes Sauna Yes	Massage Yes
Cinema/Theatre Yes	Number of Seats 330
Cabin TV No	Library Yes
Children's Facilities/Playroom	Yes

Ratings

Ship Appearance/Condition	82	Shore Excursion Program	78
Interior Cleanliness	83	Entertainment	80
Passenger Space	78	Activities Program	80
Passenger Comfort Level	82	Cruise Director/Cruise Staff	80
Furnishings/Decor	81	Ship's Officers/Staff	83
Cruise Cuisine	80	Fitness/Sports Facilities	78
Food Service	82	Overall Ship Facilities	80
Beverages/Service	78	Value for Money	82
Accommodations	80	Total Cruise Experience	82
Cabin Service	80	**Overall Rating**	**1612**
Itineraries/Destinations	83	**Average**	**80.6**

Comments

Twin sister to *Fair Princess,* this former ocean liner has classic steamship profile/well maintained/excellent Promenade Deck/crowded open decks when full/quality fittings and furnishings everywhere/art-deco decor is dated, but very comfortable/excellent woods throughout/beautiful library/ excellent dining room operation/plenty of good pasta dishes/Italian service is attentive, but not overly friendly/cabins are quite spacious, and well equipped/this ship is good for families, or for the older passenger wanting to cruise in comfortable, homely surroundings, at a moderate price.

Discovery I ★★

Principal Cruising Areas:
Bahamas

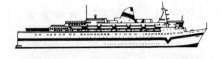

Ship	Discovery I
Cruise Line/Operator	Discovery Cruises
Formerly	Venus Venturer/Scan. Sea/Blenheim
Gross Registered Tonnage	12,244
Built	Upper Clyde Shipbuilders (UK)
First Entered Service	1970
Last Refurbished	1986
Country of Registry	Panama
Radio Call Sign	3EJM3
Satellite Telephone Number	–
Length 490 ft./149.3 m.	Beam 66 ft./20.1 m.
Engines	2×Pielstick diesels
Passenger Decks	6
Number of Crew	340
Passenger Capacity (basis 2)	200
Passenger Capacity (all berths)	1300

Passenger Space Ratio (basis 2)		61.2
Passenger Space Ratio (all berths)		9.4
Officers Spanish	Service Staff International	
Total Cabins 100	Cabin Door Width 24"	
Outside 100	Inside No	Single No
Wheelchair Accessible Cabins		No
Dining Rooms 3		Sittings 2
Number of Elevators 1	Door Width 30"	
Electric Current in Cabins		110/220 AC
Casino Yes		Slot Machines Yes
Swimming Pools Outside 1		Inside No
Whirlpools		No
Gymnasium Yes	Sauna Yes	Massage Yes
Cinema/Theatre No	Number of Seats –	
Cabin TV No		Library No
Children's Facilities/Playroom		Yes

Ratings

Ship Appearance/Condition	76
Interior Cleanliness	79
Passenger Space	75
Passenger Comfort Level	78
Furnishings/Decor	76
Cruise Cuisine	78
Food Service	78
Beverages/Service	77
Accommodations	72
Cabin Service	76
Itineraries/Destinations	60

Shore Excursion Program	50
Entertainment	73
Activities Program	71
Cruise Director/Cruise Staff	71
Ship's Officers/Staff	74
Fitness/Sports Facilities	80
Overall Ship Facilities	76
Value for Money	80
Total Cruise Experience	80
Overall Rating	**1480**
Average	**74.0**

Comments

Nicely-proportioned outer styling, except for somewhat stubby stern/contemporary interior decor is rather bright/good open deck and sunning space set around small pool/limited cabins are compact and utilitarian/large casino area on two decks is very busy/lively party atmosphere/good for families with children/best fitness facilities of all one-day ships/food is good, but choice is limited/caters to over a thousand day-passengers but accommodates only 200 in cabins/good value for money for a real fun day out, but remember it's not like a cruise of longer duration.

Dolphin IV ★★★

Principal Cruising Areas:
Bahamas

Ship	ss Dolphin IV		Passenger Space Ratio (basis 2)		23.1
Cruise Line/Operator	Dolphin Cruise Line		Passenger Space Ratio (all berths)		19.0
Former Names	Ithaca/Amelia de Mello/Zion		Officers Greek	Service Staff International	
Gross Registered Tonnage	13,007		Total Cabins 281	Cabin Door Width 24"	
Built	Deutsche Werft (W. Germany)		Outside 206	Inside 75	Single No
First Entered Service	1956		Wheelchair Accessible Cabins		No
Last Refurbished	1986		Dining Rooms 1		Sittings 2
Country of Registry	Panama		Number of Elevators 1	Door Width 27"	
Radio Call Sign	HOOG		Electric Current in Cabins		110/220 AC
Satellite Telephone Number	–		Casino Yes	Slot Machines Yes	
Length 501 ft./152.7 m.	Beam 65 ft./19.8 m.		Swimming Pools Outside 1		Inside No
Engines	2×DRG turbines		Whirlpools		1
Passenger Decks	7		Gymnasium Yes	Sauna No	Massage No
Number of Crew	260		Cinema/Theatre No	Number of Seats –	
Passenger Capacity (basis 2)	562		Cabin TV No		Library No
Passenger Capacity (all berths)	684		Children's Facilities/Playroom		Yes

Ratings

Ship Appearance/Condition	79		Shore Excursion Program	72
Interior Cleanliness	80		Entertainment	74
Passenger Space	74		Activities Program	71
Passenger Comfort Level	78		Cruise Director/Cruise Staff	73
Furnishings/Decor	82		Ship's Officers/Staff	76
Cruise Cuisine	78		Fitness/Sports Facilities	72
Food Service	80		Overall Ship Facilities	77
Beverages/Service	77		Value for Money	82
Accommodations	78		Total Cruise Experience	81
Cabin Service	79		**Overall Rating**	**1534**
Itineraries/Destinations	71		**Average**	**76.7**

Comments

Attractive-looking older ship with pleasing lines, even with its noticeable centre-sag/open deck and sunning area cramped due to high density/new contemporary public rooms are well decorated in clean, contemporary colors/new larger shopping arcade/revamped showroom is good/ charming dining room has warm ambiance/ food reasonably good/service moderately good, but is hurried and without finesse/ cabins are small, but comfortable and quite adequate/entertainment weak/ship good for short, fun cruises for the young, active set.

Emerald Seas ★★★

Principal Cruising Areas:
Bahamas

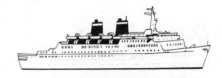

Ship	ss Emerald Seas	Passenger Space Ratio (basis 2)	30.5
Cruise Line/Operator	Admiral Cruises	Passenger Space Ratio (all berths)	23.2
Formerly Atlantis/Roosevelt/Leilani/La Guardia		Officers International Service Staff International	
Gross Registered Tonnage	24,458	Total Cabins 396 Cabin Door Width 26"	
Built Federal Shipbuilding (USA)		Outside 278 Inside 118 Single No	
First Entered Service	1944	Wheelchair Accessible Cabins	No
Last Refurbished	1985	Dining Rooms 1 Sittings 2	
Country of Registry	Panama	Number of Elevators 3 Door Width 36"	
Radio Call Sign	3FCV	Electric Current in Cabins	110 AC
Satellite Telephone Number	–	Casino Yes Slot Machines Yes	
Length 622 ft./189.5 m. Beam 75 ft./22.8 m.		Swimming Pools Outside 1 Inside No	
Engines	2×DRG turbines	Whirlpools	No
Passenger Decks	9	Gymnasium No Sauna No Massage No	
Number of Crew	400	Cinema/Theatre Yes Number of Seats 158	
Passenger Capacity (basis 2)	800	Cabin TV No Library No	
Passenger Capacity (all berths)	1050	Children's Facilities/Playroom	No

Ratings

Ship Appearance/Condition	80	Shore Excursion Program	70
Interior Cleanliness	82	Entertainment	78
Passenger Space	81	Activities Program	76
Passenger Comfort Level	81	Cruise Director/Cruise Staff	76
Furnishings/Decor	80	Ship's Officers/Staff	76
Cruise Cuisine	77	Fitness/Sports Facilities	71
Food Service	79	Overall Ship Facilities	69
Beverages/Service	76	Value for Money	82
Accommodations	81	Total Cruise Experience	80
Cabin Service	79	**Overall Rating**	**1544**
Itineraries/Destinations	70	**Average**	**77.2**

Comments

Classic, proud liner styling/extremely strong hull built to US Navy specifications/one of the few two-funnel ships still in service/superbly maintained, but engine plant needs replacing/very good open deck and sunning space/interior decor conservative and somber/public rooms reasonable, nothing special/cabins, however, are delightfully spacious/cabin decor dark, but soothing/excellent large bathrooms/dining room is old-world, but cheerful/food is reasonably good/ship offers a fine short cruise experience, and the ship's staff provide a big plus.

Enrico Costa ★★

Principal Cruising Areas:
Mediterranean

Ship	ts Enrico Costa	Passenger Space Ratio (basis 2)		21.3
Cruise Line/Operator	Costa Cruises	Passenger Space Ratio (all berths)		16.1
Former Names	Provence	Officers Italian	Service Staff Italian	
Gross Registered Tonnage	16,495	Total Cabins 386*	Cabin Door Width 26"	
Built	Swan, Hunter (UK)	Outside 184	Inside 202	Single No
First Entered Service	1950	Wheelchair Accessible Cabins		No
Last Refurbished	1976	Dining Rooms 1		Sittings 2
Country of Registry	Italy	Number of Elevators 2	Door Width 30"	
Radio Call Sign	ICEI	Electric Current in Cabins		220 DC
Satellite Telephone Number	–	Casino No	Slot Machines No	
Length 579 ft./176.4 m.	Beam 73 ft./22.2 m.	Swimming Pools Outside 3		Inside No
Engines	2×Parsons turbines	Whirlpools		No
Passenger Decks	7	Gymnasium No	Sauna No	Massage No
Number of Crew	300	Cinema/Theatre Yes	Number of Seats 85	
Passenger Capacity (basis 2)	772	Cabin TV No		Library No
Passenger Capacity (all berths)	1019	Children's Facilities/Playroom		Yes

* 75 cabins without facilities

Ratings

Ship Appearance/Condition	72	Shore Excursion Program	70
Interior Cleanliness	73	Entertainment	70
Passenger Space	67	Activities Program	68
Passenger Comfort Level	72	Cruise Director/Cruise Staff	72
Furnishings/Decor	71	Ship's Officers/Staff	75
Cruise Cuisine	78	Fitness/Sports Facilities	64
Food Service	78	Overall Ship Facilities	64
Beverages/Service	77	Value for Money	66
Accommodations	73	Total Cruise Experience	72
Cabin Service	77	**Overall Rating**	**1434**
Itineraries/Destinations	75	**Average**	**71.7**

Comments

Traditional, but dated ocean liner styling/ large single yellow funnel/many coats of exterior paint hide her age/solidly built vessel/public rooms are crowded with large, ugly chairs and well-worn fabrics/two dining rooms noisy, but comfortable/good bubbly Italian service and food, with excellent pasta/cabins are compact but comfortable/75 cabins without private facilities/good wood paneling and trim throughout the ship adds warmth/this ship caters primarily to budget-minded European passengers looking for a Mediterranean cruise without the trimmings.

Eugenio Costa ★★★ +

Principal Cruising Areas:
Caribbean/Mediterranean/Scandinavia/
South America

Ship	ts Eugenio Costa
Cruise Line/Operator	Costa Cruises
Former Names	–
Gross Registered Tonnage	30,567
Built	Cantieri Riuniti dell'Adriatico (Italy)
First Entered Service	1966
Last Refurbished	1987
Country of Registry	Italy
Radio Call Sign	ICVV
Satellite Telephone Number	1150116
Length 713 ft./217.3 m.	Beam 96 ft./29.2 m.
Engines	4×De Laval turbines
Passenger Decks	9
Number of Crew	475
Passenger Capacity (basis 2)	844
Passenger Capacity (all berths)	1158

Passenger Space Ratio (basis 2)		36.2
Passenger Space Ratio (all berths)		26.3
Officers Italian		Service Staff Italian
Total Cabins 422		Cabin Door Width 28"
Outside 238	Inside 184	Single No
Wheelchair Accessible Cabins		No
Dining Rooms 1		Sittings 2
Number of Elevators 5		Door Width 36"
Electric Current in Cabins		127/220 AC
Casino No		Slot Machines No
Swimming Pools Outside 3		Inside No
Whirlpools		No
Gymnasium Yes	Sauna Yes	Massage Yes
Cinema/Theatre Yes		Number of Seats 230
Cabin TV No		Library Yes
Children's Facilities/Playroom		Yes

Ratings

Ship Appearance/Condition	82
Interior Cleanliness	80
Passenger Space	80
Passenger Comfort Level	82
Furnishings/Decor	78
Cruise Cuisine	79
Food Service	81
Beverages/Service	78
Accommodations	80
Cabin Service	81
Itineraries/Destinations	80

Shore Excursion Program	76
Entertainment	78
Activities Program	74
Cruise Director/Cruise Staff	74
Ship's Officers/Staff	76
Fitness/Sports Facilities	75
Overall Ship Facilities	80
Value for Money	79
Total Cruise Experience	80
Overall Rating	**1573**
Average	**78.6**

Comments

Finely proportioned liner with graceful, flowing lines/sports twin slender funnels aft/well-built ship ideally suited to long voyages/superb teakwood decking outdoors/vastly upgraded public rooms and facilities in recent $18 million refurbishment program, in which 69 new cabins were added/spacious and gracious public rooms with new contemporary decor/good range of cabins, well appointed, but some still without private facilities/plenty of open and sheltered deck and sunning space/good Italian food and excellent European service in each of three dining rooms/this ship is now very comfortable throughout, and provides good-value cruising in moderately elegant style.

Europa ★★★★★+

Principal Cruising Areas:
Worldwide

Ship	ms Europa	Passenger Space Ratio (basis 2)		56.4
Cruise Line/Operator	Hapag-Lloyd Line	Passenger Space Ratio (all berths)		56.4
Former Names	–	Officers W. German	Service Staff European	
Gross Registered Tonnage	33,819	Total Cabins 316	Cabin Door Width 27"	
Built	Bremer Vulkan (W. Germany)	Outside 260	Inside 56	Single 32
First Entered Service	1982	Wheelchair Accessible Cabins		1
Last Refurbished	1987	Dining Rooms 1		Sittings 2
Country of Registry	W. Germany	Number of Elevators 4	Door Width 36"	
Radio Call Sign	DLAL	Electric Current in Cabins		110/220 AC
Satellite Telephone Number	1120756	Casino No	Slot Machines No	
Length 655 ft./199.9 m.	Beam 94 ft./28.6 m.	Swimming Pools Outside 2		Inside 1
Engines	2×MAN diesels	Whirlpools		No
Passenger Decks	12	Gymnasium Yes	Sauna Yes	Massage Yes
Number of Crew	300	Cinema/Theatre Yes	Number of Seats 238	
Passenger Capacity (basis 2)	600	Cabin TV Yes		Library Yes
Passenger Capacity (all berths)	600	Children's Facilities/Playroom		No

Ratings

Ship Appearance/Condition	95	Shore Excursion Program	92
Interior Cleanliness	97	Entertainment	86
Passenger Space	95	Activities Program	84
Passenger Comfort Level	95	Cruise Director/Cruise Staff	83
Furnishings/Decor	94	Ship's Officers/Staff	86
Cruise Cuisine	88	Fitness/Sports Facilities	95
Food Service	88	Overall Ship Facilities	95
Beverages/Service	87	Value for Money	90
Accommodations	96	Total Cruise Experience	95
Cabin Service	90	**Overall Rating**	**1823**
Itineraries/Destinations	92	**Average**	**91.1**

Comments

Beautifully designed ship with sleek, well-balanced lines/traditional features and service/immaculate maintenance/exuberant good taste abounds everywhere/superb open and sheltered deck and sunning space, including a nude-sunbathing deck/exquisite interior decor, with relaxing colors/numerous public rooms to choose from/Belvedere Lounge is one of the most elegant afloat/every cabin is superb, extremely spacious, equipped with everything, and highlighted by restful wood paneling/impeccable personal service/dining room is spacious, but should ideally be one sitting/superb indoor health spa and pool/ship provides a most elegant cruise experience in luxurious, spacious surroundings/in the pursuit of excellence, grace and tradition, this ship is unbeatable.

Explorer Starship ★★★★

Principal Cruising Areas:
Alaska / Caribbean

Ship	ms Explorer Starship	Passenger Space Ratio (basis 2)		33.3
Cruise Line/Operator	Exploration Cruise Lines	Passenger Space Ratio (all berths)		31.2
Former Names	Begonia	Officers Norwegian		Service Staff Filipino
Gross Registered Tonnage	8,282	Total Cabins 124	Cabin Door Width 24"	
Built	Lloyd Werft (W. Germany)	Outside 124	Inside No	Single No
First Entered Service	1986	Wheelchair Accessible Cabins		No
Last Refurbished	–	Dining Rooms 1		Sittings 2
Country of Registry	Bahamas	Number of Elevators 2	Door Width 30"	
Radio Call Sign	C6B14	Electric Current in Cabins		220 AC
Satellite Telephone Number	1104154	Casino Yes		Slot Machines Yes
Length 415 ft./126.4 m. Beam 52.5 ft./16.0 m.		Swimming Pools Outside 1		Inside No
Engines	2×Wichman diesels	Whirlpools		1
Passenger Decks	8	Gymnasium Yes Sauna Yes		Massage No
Number of Crew	140	Cinema/Theatre No	Number of Seats –	
Passenger Capacity (basis 2)	248	Cabin TV Yes		Library Yes
Passenger Capacity (all berths)	265	Children's Facilities/Playroom		No

Ratings

Ship Appearance/Condition	82	Shore Excursion Program	78
Interior Cleanliness	87	Entertainment	76
Passenger Space	86	Activities Program	76
Passenger Comfort Level	86	Cruise Director/Cruise Staff	76
Furnishings/Decor	85	Ship's Officers/Staff	78
Cruise Cuisine	81	Fitness/Sports Facilities	78
Food Service	80	Overall Ship Facilities	81
Beverages/Service	78	Value for Money	81
Accommodations	84	Total Cruise Experience	84
Cabin Service	81	**Overall Rating**	**1620**
Itineraries/Destinations	82	**Average**	**81.0**

Comments

Excellent conversion, with twin, tall funnels/ somewhat squat, boxy outward appearance hides an elegant, well-appointed interior/ earth-tone colors throughout most of ship/ tiered showroom is extremely comfortable, with good sightlines from all seats/ delightful dining room, colors and ambiance/ good, creative food/ excellent service from a very warm staff/ good sheltered and open deck and sunning space/ compact health spa/ fully equipped cabins are lovely/ fine quality furnishings throughout/ this ship will provide a destination-oriented cruise in supremely comfortable surroundings.

Fair Princess ★★★★

Principal Cruising Areas:
Alaska/Australasia/Mexican Riviera/
South Pacific

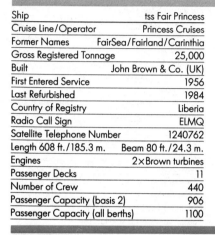

Ship	tss Fair Princess
Cruise Line/Operator	Princess Cruises
Former Names	FairSea/Fairland/Carinthia
Gross Registered Tonnage	25,000
Built	John Brown & Co. (UK)
First Entered Service	1956
Last Refurbished	1984
Country of Registry	Liberia
Radio Call Sign	ELMQ
Satellite Telephone Number	1240762
Length 608 ft./185.3 m.	Beam 80 ft./24.3 m.
Engines	2×Brown turbines
Passenger Decks	11
Number of Crew	440
Passenger Capacity (basis 2)	906
Passenger Capacity (all berths)	1100

Passenger Space Ratio (basis 2)		27.5
Passenger Space Ratio (all berths)		22.7
Officers Italian	Service Staff Italian/Portuguese	
Total Cabins 459	Cabin Door Width 24"	
Outside 231	Inside 228	Single No
Wheelchair Accessible Cabins		No
Dining Rooms 2		Sittings 2
Number of Elevators 3	Door Width 36"	
Electric Current in Cabins		110 AC
Casino Yes	Slot Machines Yes	
Swimming Pools Outside 3		Inside No
Whirlpools		No
Gymnasium Yes	Sauna Yes	Massage Yes
Cinema/Theatre Yes	Number of Seats 270	
Cabin TV No		Library Yes
Children's Facilities/Playroom		Yes

Ratings

Ship Appearance/Condition	82
Interior Cleanliness	83
Passenger Space	78
Passenger Comfort Level	82
Furnishings/Decor	80
Cruise Cuisine	80
Food Service	82
Beverages/Service	78
Accommodations	80
Cabin Service	80
Itineraries/Destinations	82

Shore Excursion Program	78
Entertainment	80
Activities Program	80
Cruise Director/Cruise Staff	80
Ship's Officers/Staff	83
Fitness/Sports Facilities	78
Overall Ship Facilities	80
Value for Money	82
Total Cruise Experience	82
Overall Rating	**1610**
Average	**80.5**

Comments

Solidly constructed former ocean liner, with classic steamship lines and profile/open deck and sunning space good, but crowded when full/superb refurbishment of Promenade Deck interior/dated, but elegant, art-deco interior decor/tastefully furnished throughout/has popular Pizzeria/dining room set low down, but is an excellent operation/excellent pasta dishes/attentive Italian staff/good facilities for families with children/cabins are generally spacious, with heavy-duty furnishings and fittings/this ship, although high-density, represents excellent cruising value, with service-oriented Italian crew and style.

FairStar ★ ★ ★

Principal Cruising Areas:
Australasia / South Pacific

Ship	tss FairStar	Passenger Space Ratio (basis 2)	22.1
Cruise Line / Operator	P&O Sitmar Cruises	Passenger Space Ratio (all berths)	13.9
Former Names	Oxfordshire	Officers Italian Service Staff Italian / Indonesian	
Gross Registered Tonnage	23,764	Total Cabins 488*	Cabin Door Width 24"
Built	Fairfield Shipbuilding (UK)	Outside 165 Inside 323	Single No
First Entered Service	1957	Wheelchair Accessible Cabins	No
Last Refurbished	1986	Dining Rooms 2	Sittings 2
Country of Registry	Liberia	Number of Elevators 4	Door Width 26"
Radio Call Sign	5MXH	Electric Current in Cabins	115 AC
Satellite Telephone Number	–	Casino Yes	Slot Machines Yes
Length 609 ft./185.6 m.	Beam 78 ft./23.7 m.	Swimming Pools Outside 1	Inside No
Engines	2×Parsons turbines	Whirlpools	No
Passenger Decks	10	Gymnasium Yes Sauna No Massage No	
Number of Crew	458	Cinema / Theatre Yes Number of Seats 360	
Passenger Capacity (basis 2)	976	Cabin TV No	Library Yes
Passenger Capacity (all berths)	1548	Children's Facilities / Playroom	Yes

* 68 cabins without private facilities

Ratings

Ship Appearance / Condition	76	Shore Excursion Program	74
Interior Cleanliness	77	Entertainment	72
Passenger Space	74	Activities Program	73
Passenger Comfort Level	77	Cruise Director / Cruise Staff	79
Furnishings / Decor	74	Ship's Officers / Staff	78
Cruise Cuisine	80	Fitness / Sports Facilities	61
Food Service	80	Overall Ship Facilities	73
Beverages / Service	77	Value for Money	78
Accommodations	73	Total Cruise Experience	76
Cabin Service	76	**Overall Rating**	**1509**
Itineraries / Destinations	81	**Average**	**75.4**

Comments

Well-constructed ship has classic lines and profile / open deck space limited / densely packed / lacks elegance and glamor, but makes up in spirit and boisterous atmosphere / good for the whole family—children will love it / 9:30 p.m. curfew for children / public rooms comfortable, adequate / too many duty-free shops / suites on Boat Deck are quite large / other cabins fine for two, crowded with more / bathrooms are incredibly tiny / plenty of tables for two in the two dining rooms / excellent, busy Pizzeria / take books to read as there's no library / good-value-for-money cruising for "down-under" passengers who want a lively, fun-filled cruise / lacks finesse, but who cares?

Fantasy

Principal Cruising Areas:
Caribbean

Ship	ms Fantasy	Passenger Space Ratio (basis 2)	34.1
Cruise Line/Operator	Carnival Cruise Line	Passenger Space Ratio (all berths)	26.9
Former Names	–	Officers Italian	Service Staff International
Gross Registered Tonnage	70,000 (estimated)	Total Cabins 1025	Cabin Door Width 22"
Built	Wartsila (Finland)	Outside 625　Inside 400	Single No
First Entered Service	Late 1989	Wheelchair Accessible Cabins	No
Last Refurbished	–	Dining Rooms 2	Sittings 2
Country of Registry	Panama	Number of Elevators 14	Door Width 36"
Radio Call Sign	n/a	Electric Current in Cabins	110 AC
Satellite Telephone Number	n/a	Casino Yes	Slot Machines Yes
Length 865 ft./263.6 m.　Beam 105 ft./32.0 m.		Swimming Pools Outside 3	Inside No
Engines	6×Pielstick diesels	Whirlpools	6
Passenger Decks	14	Gymnasium Yes　Sauna Yes	Massage Yes
Number of Crew	1000	Cinema/Theatre No	Number of Seats –
Passenger Capacity (basis 2)	2050	Cabin TV Yes	Library Yes
Passenger Capacity (all berths)	2600	Children's Facilities/Playroom	Yes

Ratings

Ship Appearance/Condition	–	Shore Excursion Program	–
Interior Cleanliness	–	Entertainment	–
Passenger Space	–	Activities Program	–
Passenger Comfort Level	–	Cruise Director/Cruise Staff	–
Furnishings/Decor	–	Ship's Officers/Staff	–
Cruise Cuisine	–	Fitness/Sports Facilities	–
Food Service	–	Overall Ship Facilities	–
Beverages/Service	–	Value for Money	–
Accommodations	–	Total Cruise Experience	–
Cabin Service	–	**Overall Rating**	–
Itineraries/Destinations	–	**Average**	–

Comments

The first of three identical Wartsila-built megaships for Carnival will reflect the same basic design as other recent ships in the fleet/expansive open deck areas/forward observation lounge has glass skylight/ dramatic three-deck-high glass-enclosed spa facility/banked jogging track/five cabin categories/26 outside suites have whirlpool bathtubs/double-wide indoor promenade decks/lavish multi-tiered show-room/public entertainment lounges, bars and clubs galore/gigantic casino promises non-stop action/two huge dining rooms/ same Carnival service expected. (Not rated at presstime.)

Fedor Dostoyevsky ★★★★+

Principal Cruising Areas:
Baltic/Mediterranean/Scandinavia

Ship	ms Fedor Dostoyevsky
Cruise Line/Operator	Black Sea Shipping
Former Names	Astor
Gross Registered Tonnage	20,158
Built Howaldtswerke Deutsche Werft (W. Germ.)	
First Entered Service	1986
Last Refurbished	–
Country of Registry	USSR
Radio Call Sign	n/a
Satellite Telephone Number	n/a
Length 580 ft./176.7 m.	Beam 74 ft./22.5 m.
Engines	4×Sulzer diesels
Passenger Decks	7
Number of Crew	250
Passenger Capacity (basis 2)	590
Passenger Capacity (all berths)	650

Passenger Space Ratio (basis 2)		34.2
Passenger Space Ratio (all berths)		31.0
Officers Soviet	Service Staff East European	
Total Cabins 295	Cabin Door Width 24"	
Outside 199	Inside 96	Single No
Wheelchair Accessible Cabins		No
Dining Rooms 1		Sittings 2
Number of Elevators 3	Door Width 30"	
Electric Current in Cabins		220 AC
Casino No	Slot Machines No	
Swimming Pools Outside 1		Inside 1
Whirlpools		No
Gymnasium Yes	Sauna Yes	Massage Yes
Cinema/Theatre No	Number of Seats –	
Cabin TV Yes		Library Yes
Children's Facilities/Playroom		Yes

Ratings

Ship Appearance/Condition	88
Interior Cleanliness	88
Passenger Space	87
Passenger Comfort Level	88
Furnishings/Decor	88
Cruise Cuisine	85
Food Service	83
Beverages/Service	81
Accommodations	84
Cabin Service	84
Itineraries/Destinations	88

Shore Excursion Program	82
Entertainment	79
Activities Program	77
Cruise Director/Cruise Staff	80
Ship's Officers/Staff	85
Fitness/Sports Facilities	86
Overall Ship Facilities	86
Value for Money	86
Total Cruise Experience	87
Overall Rating	**1686**
Average	**84.3**

Comments

Very attractive ship with raked funnel/finest ship in the Soviet-owned fleet/everything is top quality/fine teakwood decking and rails/almost worldwide itineraries/supremely comfortable and varied public rooms and facilities/wood-paneled tavern is a favorite retreat/mix of traditional and contemporary styling/well-designed interior fitness center and pool/exquisite dining room is one of the nicest afloat/food and service are good/cabins are well appointed and very tastefully decorated in pastel colors/plenty of closet and drawer space/continental atmosphere/mostly European passengers/this ship provides style, comfort and elegance, and a fine cruise experience. (This ship was rated as Astor; a new rating will be given in the next edition.)

Fedor Shalyapin ★★

Principal Cruising Areas:
Mediterranean / Scandinavia

Ship	ts Fedor Shalyapin	Passenger Space Ratio (basis 2)	37.1
Cruise Line / Operator	Black Sea Shipping	Passenger Space Ratio (all berths)	26.7
Former Names	Franconia / Ivernia	Officers Soviet	Service Staff East European
Gross Registered Tonnage	21,406	Total Cabins 292	Cabin Door Width 27"
Built	John Brown & Co. (UK)	Outside 159	Inside 133	Single No
First Entered Service	1955	Wheelchair Accessible Cabins	No
Last Refurbished	1982	Dining Rooms 2	Sittings 2
Country of Registry	USSR	Number of Elevators 3	Door Width 36"
Radio Call Sign	UZLA	Electric Current in Cabins	110/220 AC
Satellite Telephone Number	–	Casino No	Slot Machines No
Length 608 ft. / 185.3 m.	Beam 80 ft. / 24.3 m.	Swimming Pools Outside 1	Inside No
Engines	2 × Brown turbines	Whirlpools	No
Passenger Decks	7	Gymnasium Yes	Sauna Yes	Massage No
Number of Crew	380	Cinema / Theatre Yes	Number of Seats 260
Passenger Capacity (basis 2)	576	Cabin TV No	Library Yes
Passenger Capacity (all berths)	800	Children's Facilities / Playroom	Yes

Ratings

Ship Appearance / Condition	78	Shore Excursion Program	68
Interior Cleanliness	76	Entertainment	75
Passenger Space	73	Activities Program	72
Passenger Comfort Level	76	Cruise Director / Cruise Staff	72
Furnishings / Decor	75	Ship's Officers / Staff	71
Cruise Cuisine	75	Fitness / Sports Facilities	66
Food Service	76	Overall Ship Facilities	63
Beverages / Service	73	Value for Money	70
Accommodations	78	Total Cruise Experience	74
Cabin Service	77	**Overall Rating**	**1464**
Itineraries / Destinations	76	**Average**	**73.2**

Comments

Well-built older ship with classic steamship profile / looking the worse for wear / ship is not very clean / two good indoor promenades / furniture and fittings worn and in need of refurbishing / public rooms rather poor with the exception of the Music Salon and Theatre / dining room set low down, is unappetizing, as is the food, of which there is little choice / staff rather perfunctory and inflexible / appeals mainly to low-budget continental European passengers / cabins are reasonable, but decor is rather worn / although the price is right, this ship is not up to western standards / mediocre.

Festivale ★ ★ ★ +

Principal Cruising Areas:
Caribbean

Ship			tss Festivale
Cruise Line/Operator			Carnival Cruise Lines
Former Names		S.A. Vaal/Transvaal Castle	
Gross Registered Tonnage			38,175
Built		John Brown & Co. (UK)	
First Entered Service			1961
Last Refurbished			1986
Country of Registry			Panama
Radio Call Sign			HPFG
Satellite Telephone Number			–
Length 760 ft./231.6 m.		Beam 90 ft./27.4 m.	
Engines			4×Parsons turbines
Passenger Decks			9
Number of Crew			570
Passenger Capacity (basis 2)			1148
Passenger Capacity (all berths)			1432

Passenger Space Ratio (basis 2)		33.3
Passenger Space Ratio (all berths)		26.7
Officers Italian		Service Staff International
Total Cabins 580	Cabin Door Width 26–30"	
Outside 272	Inside 308	Single No
Wheelchair Accessible Cabins		No
Dining Rooms 1		Sittings 2
Number of Elevators 4		Door Width 36"
Electric Current in Cabins		110 AC
Casino Yes		Slot Machines Yes
Swimming Pools Outside 2		Inside No
Whirlpools		No
Gymnasium Yes	Sauna Yes	Massage Yes
Cinema/Theatre Yes	Number of Seats 202	
Cabin TV No		Library Yes
Children's Facilities/Playroom		Yes

Ratings

Ship Appearance/Condition	84
Interior Cleanliness	84
Passenger Space	78
Passenger Comfort Level	81
Furnishings/Decor	80
Cruise Cuisine	78
Food Service	80
Beverages/Service	78
Accommodations	80
Cabin Service	81
Itineraries/Destinations	80

Shore Excursion Program	75
Entertainment	76
Activities Program	78
Cruise Director/Cruise Staff	80
Ship's Officers/Staff	80
Fitness/Sports Facilities	71
Overall Ship Facilities	80
Value for Money	83
Total Cruise Experience	81
Overall Rating	**1588**
Average	**79.4**

Comments

Classic ocean-going conversion with well-balanced profile/looks like a real liner/superb refurbishment left much of the original wood and brass interior intact/very well maintained and very clean throughout/contemporary colors blend well, but are too bold/good public rooms/dining room, located low down, is bright and cheerful, but noisy/cabins are spacious, with plenty of closet and drawer space/large cabins are good for those with children/attentive staff, but English is a problem for some/food is a letdown/service is good, but without finesse/real fun ship experience, with lively casino action/good ship for singles and young at heart/moderate rates and good value for money/excellent choice for your first cruise experience.

Funchal ★★★ +

Principal Cruising Areas:
Caribbean / Mediterranean / Scandinavia

Ship	ms Funchal	Passenger Space Ratio (basis 2)	24.2
Cruise Line/Operator	Fritidskryss	Passenger Space Ratio (all berths)	21.2
Former Names	–	Officers Swedish	Service Staff European
Gross Registered Tonnage	9,846	Total Cabins 222	Cabin Door Width 24"
Built	Helsingor Skibsvog (Denmark)	Outside 134 Inside 88	Single 38
First Entered Service	1961	Wheelchair Accessible Cabins	No
Last Refurbished	1986	Dining Rooms 1	Sittings 1
Country of Registry	Panama	Number of Elevators 2	Door Width 24"
Radio Call Sign	3EHK4	Electric Current in Cabins	220 AC
Satellite Telephone Number	1330320	Casino Yes	Slot Machines Yes
Length 498 ft./151.7 m. Beam 62 ft./18.8 m.		Swimming Pools Outside 1	Inside No
Engines	2×SWD diesels	Whirlpools	No
Passenger Decks	6	Gymnasium Yes Sauna Yes	Massage No
Number of Crew	155	Cinema/Theatre No	Number of Seats –
Passenger Capacity (basis 2)	406	Cabin TV No	Library Yes
Passenger Capacity (all berths)	460	Children's Facilities/Playroom	No

Ratings

Ship Appearance/Condition	80	Shore Excursion Program	76
Interior Cleanliness	81	Entertainment	74
Passenger Space	75	Activities Program	73
Passenger Comfort Level	79	Cruise Director/Cruise Staff	80
Furnishings/Decor	80	Ship's Officers/Staff	78
Cruise Cuisine	80	Fitness/Sports Facilities	72
Food Service	80	Overall Ship Facilities	72
Beverages/Service	78	Value for Money	76
Accommodations	80	Total Cruise Experience	80
Cabin Service	80	**Overall Rating**	**1554**
Itineraries/Destinations	80	**Average**	**77.7**

Comments

This tidy-looking ship has a classic, well-balanced profile/very warm and attentive staff/twin sheltered promenade decks/public rooms are well laid out, with lots of good wood paneling and wood trim throughout/cabins are compact, but well appointed, and decorated in colors that are pleasing to the eye/dining room is very tastefully decorated/food is surprisingly good, as is the service/popular with Europeans, this ship offers a destination-oriented cruise experience in comfortable surroundings, ideally suited to singles and couples.

Galaxias ★ ★

Principal Cruising Areas:
Caribbean / Mediterranean

Ship	mts Galaxias
Cruise Line / Operator	Global Cruises
Former Names	Galaxy / Scottish Coast
Gross Registered Tonnage	5,500
Built	Harland & Wolff (UK)
First Entered Service	1957
Last Refurbished	1987
Country of Registry	Panama
Radio Call Sign	SXCO
Satellite Telephone Number	–
Length 342 ft. / 104.2 m.	Beam 52 ft. / 15.8 m.
Engines	2 × B&W diesels
Passenger Decks	6
Number of Crew	140
Passenger Capacity (basis 2)	286
Passenger Capacity (all berths)	286

Passenger Space Ratio (basis 2)		19.2
Passenger Space Ratio (all berths)		19.2
Officers Greek		Service Staff Greek
Total Cabins 143		Cabin Door Width 22″
Outside 112	Inside 31	Single No
Wheelchair Accessible Cabins		No
Dining Rooms 1		Sittings 2
Number of Elevators 0		Door Width –
Electric Current in Cabins		220 AC
Casino Yes		Slot Machines Yes
Swimming Pools Outside 1		Inside No
Whirlpools		No
Gymnasium No	Sauna No	Massage No
Cinema / Theatre No		Number of Seats –
Cabin TV No		Library No
Children's Facilities / Playroom		No

Ratings

Ship Appearance / Condition	76	Shore Excursion Program	70
Interior Cleanliness	78	Entertainment	70
Passenger Space	72	Activities Program	70
Passenger Comfort Level	75	Cruise Director / Cruise Staff	72
Furnishings / Decor	75	Ship's Officers / Staff	75
Cruise Cuisine	76	Fitness / Sports Facilities	60
Food Service	78	Overall Ship Facilities	70
Beverages / Service	75	Value for Money	72
Accommodations	76	Total Cruise Experience	80
Cabin Service	78	**Overall Rating**	**1476**
Itineraries / Destinations	78	**Average**	**73.8**

Comments

Clean, crisp-looking small white ship has recent change of owners / limited facilities make it confining for anything longer than a few days / deck space is reasonable / the few public rooms have been refurbished, but still sport rather plain ceilings / earth-tone colors used to good effect, creating a sense of spaciousness / most cabins are outside and are quite comfortable, with tasteful Mediterranean colors and wood trim / cabins located above disco are noisy / dining room has porthole windows for sea view, and is quite cheerful / food is decidedly Greek, with limited choice / service is attentive / this ship is crowded when full, but offers a reasonably pleasant cruise experience as long as you don't expect too much.

Galileo ★★★+

Principal Cruising Areas:
Bahamas/Bermuda/Mexico

Ship	ss Galileo	Passenger Space Ratio (basis 2)	26.0
Cruise Line/Operator	Chandris Fantasy Cruises	Passenger Space Ratio (all berths)	25.0
Former Names	Galileo Galilei	Officers Greek	Service Staff International
Gross Registered Tonnage	28,083	Total Cabins 543	Cabin Door Width 26"
Built	Cantieri Riuniti dell'Adriatico (Italy)	Outside 300	Inside 243	Single 6
First Entered Service	1963	Wheelchair Accessible Cabins	No
Last Refurbished	1987	Dining Rooms 1	Sittings 2
Country of Registry	Panama	Number of Elevators 3	Door Width 36"
Radio Call Sign	3FIP2	Electric Current in Cabins	110/220 AC
Satellite Telephone Number	1331154	Casino Yes	Slot Machines Yes
Length 700 ft./213.3 m.	Beam 93 ft./28.3 m.	Swimming Pools Outside 2	Inside No
Engines	4×De Laval turbines	Whirlpools	No
Passenger Decks	8	Gymnasium Yes Sauna Yes	Massage Yes
Number of Crew	580	Cinema/Theatre Yes	Number of Seats 220
Passenger Capacity (basis 2)	1080	Cabin TV No	Library Yes
Passenger Capacity (all berths)	1120	Children's Facilities/Playroom	Yes

Ratings

Ship Appearance/Condition	82	Shore Excursion Program	77
Interior Cleanliness	82	Entertainment	79
Passenger Space	82	Activities Program	77
Passenger Comfort Level	81	Cruise Director/Cruise Staff	81
Furnishings/Decor	78	Ship's Officers/Staff	78
Cruise Cuisine	81	Fitness/Sports Facilities	74
Food Service	80	Overall Ship Facilities	80
Beverages/Service	80	Value for Money	85
Accommodations	79	Total Cruise Experience	82
Cabin Service	80	**Overall Rating**	**1598**
Itineraries/Destinations	80	**Average**	**79.9**

Comments

Long, sleek, well-balanced profile, with rakish bow and rounded stern/former ocean liner is a very stable ship/superb, expansive sheltered and open deck and sunning space/public rooms have high ceilings/large casino with lots of action/showroom configuration needs attention/charming twin garden lounges/wide selection of cabin sizes/a few cabins underneath the disco are noisy/new forward suites are spacious and well appointed/dining room has good ambiance/very good food and choice/lavish buffets/friendly, attentive service throughout/this ship delivers a far better cruise experience than expected, at very realistic rates that are excellent value for money/highly recommended for a first cruise experience.

Golden Odyssey ★★★★

Principal Cruising Areas:
Alaska/Mediterranean/Far East/
South Pacific

Ship	ms Golden Odyssey	Passenger Space Ratio (basis 2)	22.9
Cruise Line/Operator	Royal Cruise Line	Passenger Space Ratio (all berths)	22.9
Former Names	–	Officers Greek	Service Staff Greek
Gross Registered Tonnage	10,563	Total Cabins 227	Cabin Door Width 24"
Built	Helsingor Skibsvog (Denmark)	Outside 181 Inside 46	Single No
First Entered Service	1974	Wheelchair Accessible Cabins	No
Last Refurbished	1987	Dining Rooms 1	Sittings 2
Country of Registry	Greece	Number of Elevators 2	Door Width 24"
Radio Call Sign	SXTD	Electric Current in Cabins	110 AC
Satellite Telephone Number	1130420	Casino Yes	Slot Machines Yes
Length 427 ft./130.1 m.	Beam 63 ft./19.2 m.	Swimming Pools Outside 1	Inside No
Engines	2×MAK diesels	Whirlpools	No
Passenger Decks	7	Gymnasium Yes Sauna Yes	Massage Yes
Number of Crew	200	Cinema/Theatre Yes	Number of Seats 154
Passenger Capacity (basis 2)	460	Cabin TV No	Library Yes
Passenger Capacity (all berths)	460	Children's Facilities/Playroom	No

Ratings

Ship Appearance/Condition	85	Shore Excursion Program	84
Interior Cleanliness	88	Entertainment	82
Passenger Space	82	Activities Program	80
Passenger Comfort Level	86	Cruise Director/Cruise Staff	81
Furnishings/Decor	88	Ship's Officers/Staff	81
Cruise Cuisine	82	Fitness/Sports Facilities	78
Food Service	82	Overall Ship Facilities	82
Beverages/Service	82	Value for Money	81
Accommodations	84	Total Cruise Experience	83
Cabin Service	82	**Overall Rating**	**1658**
Itineraries/Destinations	85	**Average**	**82.9**

Comments

Sleek-looking ship has balanced, compact contemporary profile/elegant, intimate ship with tremendously loyal following/very clean throughout/highly attentive staff offer real personal service/recent refurbishment is very well done/cabins are now very tastefully furnished and decorated, with generous closet and drawer space/very nice dining room/food is fine quality throughout/the line's attention to detail is outstanding/this is a gem of a ship that offers highly personal service in intimate, very comfortable surroundings, at a moderate price.

Gruziya ★★★

Principal Cruising Areas:
Baltic/Mediterranean/Scandinavia

Ship	ms Gruziya
Cruise Line/Operator	Black Sea Shipping
Former Names	–
Gross Registered Tonnage	16,900
Built	Wartsila (Finland)
First Entered Service	1975
Last Refurbished	1988
Country of Registry	USSR
Radio Call Sign	UUFC
Satellite Telephone Number	–
Length 515 ft./156.9 m.	Beam 72 ft./21.9 m.
Engines	2×Pielstick diesels
Passenger Decks	8
Number of Crew	250
Passenger Capacity (basis 2)	432
Passenger Capacity (all berths)	640

Passenger Space Ratio (basis 2)		39.1
Passenger Space Ratio (all berths)		26.4
Officers Soviet	Service Staff East European	
Total Cabins 226	Cabin Door Width 26"	
Outside 116	Inside 110	Single No
Wheelchair Accessible Cabins		No
Dining Rooms 2		Sittings 2
Number of Elevators 2	Door Width 30"	
Electric Current in Cabins		220 AC
Casino Yes	Slot Machines Yes	
Swimming Pools Outside 1		Inside No
Whirlpools		No
Gymnasium Yes	Sauna Yes	Massage Yes
Cinema/Theatre Yes	Number of Seats 143	
Cabin TV No		Library Yes
Children's Facilities/Playroom		No

Ratings

Ship Appearance/Condition	81	Shore Excursion Program	68
Interior Cleanliness	81	Entertainment	72
Passenger Space	78	Activities Program	70
Passenger Comfort Level	81	Cruise Director/Cruise Staff	72
Furnishings/Decor	80	Ship's Officers/Staff	76
Cruise Cuisine	75	Fitness/Sports Facilities	78
Food Service	77	Overall Ship Facilities	78
Beverages/Service	74	Value for Money	81
Accommodations	77	Total Cruise Experience	80
Cabin Service	78	**Overall Rating**	**1536**
Itineraries/Destinations	79	**Average**	**76.8**

Comments

Smart-looking contemporary profile with swept-back squarish funnel/recently underwent an extensive refurbishment program which added a new nightclub, cinema and new cabins/open deck and sunning space crowded when ship is full/smart interior decor, but uninteresting ceiling treatments in public rooms/two dining rooms (one is no-smoking) have light decor and big picture windows/food is attractive, but choice rather limited/service is good, but lacks finesse, although staff are eager to please/top-grade suites are very spacious and welcoming/other cabins are compact, yet comfortable/this ship caters mainly to Europeans, who know the value of cruising on this type of Soviet-owned vessel.

Holiday ★★★★

Principal Cruising Areas:
Caribbean

Ship	ms Holiday
Cruise Line/Operator	Carnival Cruise Lines
Former Names	–
Gross Registered Tonnage	46,052
Built	Aalborg Vaerft (Denmark)
First Entered Service	1985
Last Refurbished	–
Country of Registry	Panama
Radio Call Sign	3EYK3
Satellite Telephone Number	1330633
Length 727 ft./221.5 m.	Beam 92 ft./28.0 m.
Engines	2×Sulzer diesels
Passenger Decks	9
Number of Crew	660
Passenger Capacity (basis 2)	1452
Passenger Capacity (all berths)	1760

Passenger Space Ratio (basis 2)		31.7
Passenger Space Ratio (all berths)		26.2
Officers Italian	Service Staff International	
Total Cabins 726	Cabin Door Width 22"	
Outside 447	Inside 279	Single No
Wheelchair Accessible Cabins		No
Dining Rooms 2		Sittings 2
Number of Elevators 8	Door Width 33"	
Electric Current in Cabins		110 AC
Casino Yes		Slot Machines Yes
Swimming Pools Outside 2		Inside No
Whirlpools		2
Gymnasium Yes	Sauna Yes	Massage Yes
Cinema/Theatre No	Number of Seats –	
Cabin TV Yes		Library Yes
Children's Facilities/Playroom		Yes

Ratings

Ship Appearance/Condition	86	Shore Excursion Program	74
Interior Cleanliness	86	Entertainment	82
Passenger Space	86	Activities Program	80
Passenger Comfort Level	84	Cruise Director/Cruise Staff	80
Furnishings/Decor	82	Ship's Officers/Staff	81
Cruise Cuisine	76	Fitness/Sports Facilities	82
Food Service	78	Overall Ship Facilities	84
Beverages/Service	75	Value for Money	82
Accommodations	84	Total Cruise Experience	82
Cabin Service	81	**Overall Rating**	**1619**
Itineraries/Destinations	74	**Average**	**80.9**

Comments

Bold, high-rise yet attractive ship with short bow and stubby stern/distinctive, swept-back wing-tipped funnel/numerous public rooms on two entertainment decks/good passenger flow/stunning multi-tiered showroom/bright colors in all public rooms/double-wide indoor promenade/excellent casino with non-stop action/cabins are quite spacious, and attractively decorated/ especially nice are ten large suites with private balconies/every outside cabin has large picture windows/two dining rooms have low ceilings and raised center sections/food is quantity, not quality/service is average, and hurried/prompt service for drinks, but intimidating/plenty of entertainment/this ship is ideal for a first cruise for the active set, at an attractive price.

Illiria ★★★★

Principal Cruising Areas:
Canada / Mediterranean

Ship	mv Illiria	Passenger Space Ratio (basis 2)		29.4
Cruise Line/Operator	Blue Aegean Cruises	Passenger Space Ratio (all berths)		19.8
Former Names	–	Officers Greek		Service Staff Greek
Gross Registered Tonnage	3,852	Total Cabins 68		Cabin Door Width 24"
Built	Cantieri Riuniti dell'Adriatico (Italy)	Outside 58	Inside 10	Single 5
First Entered Service	1962	Wheelchair Accessible Cabins		No
Last Refurbished	1981	Dining Rooms 1		Sittings 2
Country of Registry	Greece	Number of Elevators 0		Door Width –
Radio Call Sign	SWAE	Electric Current in Cabins		220 AC
Satellite Telephone Number	1130413	Casino No		Slot Machines No
Length 333 ft./101.4 m.	Beam 48 ft./14.6 m.	Swimming Pools Outside 1		Inside No
Engines	2×GMT diesels	Whirlpools		No
Passenger Decks	5	Gymnasium No	Sauna No	Massage No
Number of Crew	90	Cinema/Theatre No		Number of Seats –
Passenger Capacity (basis 2)	131	Cabin TV No		Library Yes
Passenger Capacity (all berths)	194	Children's Facilities/Playroom		No

Ratings

Ship Appearance/Condition	81	Shore Excursion Program	80
Interior Cleanliness	83	Entertainment	81
Passenger Space	80	Activities Program	78
Passenger Comfort Level	81	Cruise Director/Cruise Staff	80
Furnishings/Decor	81	Ship's Officers/Staff	82
Cruise Cuisine	79	Fitness/Sports Facilities	78
Food Service	80	Overall Ship Facilities	80
Beverages/Service	78	Value for Money	81
Accommodations	80	Total Cruise Experience	82
Cabin Service	80	**Overall Rating**	**1606**
Itineraries/Destinations	81	**Average**	**80.3**

Comments

A real gem of a ship/small and compact/ spotlessly clean throughout/impeccably maintained/specializes in expedition-style cruises under charter to various organizations and tour packagers/well appointed, but has limited public rooms/superb artworks/elegant interior decor and furnishings/charming dining room reminiscent of classical Greece/food is continental/fine attentive service by all-Greek crew/cabins are reasonably spacious for ship size, and have wood trim/this ship will provide a very comfortable expedition cruise experience for those seeking to get close to the natural world.

Independence ★★★ +

Principal Cruising Areas:
Hawaii

Ship	ss Independence
Cruise Line/Operator	American Hawaii Cruises
Former Names	–
Gross Registered Tonnage	30,090
Built	Bethlehem Shipbuilders (USA)
First Entered Service	1951
Last Refurbished	1988
Country of Registry	USA
Radio Call Sign	KPHI
Satellite Telephone Number	1502244
Length 682 ft./207.8 m.	Beam 89 ft./27.1 m.
Engines	2×Bethlehem turbines
Passenger Decks	9
Number of Crew	350
Passenger Capacity (basis 2)	752
Passenger Capacity (all berths)	1000

Passenger Space Ratio (basis 2)		40.0
Passenger Space Ratio (all berths)		30.0
Officers American		Service Staff American
Total Cabins 388		Cabin Door Width 26"
Outside 166	Inside 222	Single 24
Wheelchair Accessible Cabins		No
Dining Rooms 2		Sittings 2
Number of Elevators 4		Door Width 31"
Electric Current in Cabins		110 AC
Casino No		Slot Machines No
Swimming Pools Outside 2		Inside No
Whirlpools		No
Gymnasium Yes	Sauna Yes	Massage Yes
Cinema/Theatre Yes		Number of Seats 144
Cabin TV No		Library Yes
Children's Facilities/Playroom		Yes

Ratings

Ship Appearance/Condition	78	Shore Excursion Program	78
Interior Cleanliness	82	Entertainment	78
Passenger Space	82	Activities Program	76
Passenger Comfort Level	82	Cruise Director/Cruise Staff	76
Furnishings/Decor	81	Ship's Officers/Staff	80
Cruise Cuisine	78	Fitness/Sports Facilities	72
Food Service	80	Overall Ship Facilities	76
Beverages/Service	76	Value for Money	80
Accommodations	78	Total Cruise Experience	80
Cabin Service	80	**Overall Rating**	**1573**
Itineraries/Destinations	80	**Average**	**78.6**

Comments

Solidly constructed older ship is one of only a handful of two-funnel ships still operating/ expansive open deck space for sunning, with two outdoor pools/American-built, crewed and registered, this ship has spacious public rooms, though they're not as attractive as on sister ship *Constitution*/ wide range of cabins, each with ample closet and drawer space/casual atmosphere prevails throughout, with Aloha smiles/ dining room is set low down, and without an ocean view, but it's cheerful/food typically American-Polynesian in style/this ship will cruise you in comfort around the Hawaiian islands.

Island Princess ★★★★+

Principal Cruising Areas:
Alaska/Caribbean/Mexican Riviera

Ship	mv Island Princess	Passenger Space Ratio (basis 2)		32.0
Cruise Line/Operator	Princess Cruises	Passenger Space Ratio (all berths)		32.0
Former Names	Island Venture	Officers British	Service Staff International	
Gross Registered Tonnage	20,000	Total Cabins 316	Cabin Door Width 22–33"	
Built Rheinstahl Nordseewerke (W. Germany)		Outside 245	Inside 71	Single 6
First Entered Service	1971	Wheelchair Accessible Cabins		4
Last Refurbished	1984	Dining Rooms 1		Sittings 2
Country of Registry	Great Britain	Number of Elevators 4	Door Width 37"	
Radio Call Sign	GBBM	Electric Current in Cabins		110 AC
Satellite Telephone Number	1440214	Casino Yes	Slot Machines Yes	
Length 550 ft./167.6 m. Beam 80 ft./24.3 m.		Swimming Pools Outside 2	Inside No	
Engines	2×GMT diesels	Whirlpools		No
Passenger Decks	7	Gymnasium Yes Sauna Yes	Massage Yes	
Number of Crew	350	Cinema/Theatre Yes	Number of Seats 250	
Passenger Capacity (basis 2)	624	Cabin TV No	Library Yes	
Passenger Capacity (all berths)	624	Children's Facilities/Playroom		No

Ratings

Ship Appearance/Condition	86	Shore Excursion Program	82
Interior Cleanliness	88	Entertainment	87
Passenger Space	86	Activities Program	79
Passenger Comfort Level	86	Cruise Director/Cruise Staff	81
Furnishings/Decor	85	Ship's Officers/Staff	81
Cruise Cuisine	85	Fitness/Sports Facilities	80
Food Service	84	Overall Ship Facilities	85
Beverages/Service	83	Value for Money	85
Accommodations	82	Total Cruise Experience	86
Cabin Service	83	**Overall Rating**	**1679**
Itineraries/Destinations	85	**Average**	**83.9**

Comments

Very attractive profile/ship has nice lines, although the superstructure is high/extremely spacious public areas/gracious lobby/very tasteful decor throughout/suites are extremely spacious/other cabins have ample room, are well appointed, and have plenty of closet and drawer space/ lovely dining room, with excellent service from the attentive Italian staff/food is very good indeed/quality prevails aboard this ship/sharply-dressed crew at all times/ this ship is elegant, and will provide discerning passengers with an excellent cruise experience from start to finish.

Ivan Franko ★★

Principal Cruising Areas:
Baltic/Mediterranean/Scandinavia

Ship	ms Ivan Franko	Passenger Space Ratio (basis 2)	39.4
Cruise Line/Operator	Black Sea Shipping	Passenger Space Ratio (all berths)	30.4
Former Names	–	Officers Soviet	Service Staff East European
Gross Registered Tonnage	19,860	Total Cabins 273	Cabin Door Width 26"
Built	Mathias Thesen Werft (E. Germany)	Outside 273 Inside No	Single No
First Entered Service	1965	Wheelchair Accessible Cabins	No
Last Refurbished	1975	Dining Rooms 2	Sittings 1
Country of Registry	USSR	Number of Elevators 3	Door Width 32"
Radio Call Sign	USLI	Electric Current in Cabins	220 AC
Satellite Telephone Number	–	Casino No	Slot Machines No
Length 580 ft./176.7 m.	Beam 77 ft./23.4 m.	Swimming Pools Outside 1	Inside 1
Engines	2×Sulzer diesels	Whirlpools	No
Passenger Decks	8	Gymnasium Yes Sauna Yes	Massage Yes
Number of Crew	370	Cinema/Theatre Yes	Number of Seats 130
Passenger Capacity (basis 2)	504	Cabin TV No	Library Yes
Passenger Capacity (all berths)	650	Children's Facilities/Playroom	No

Ratings

Ship Appearance/Condition	74	Shore Excursion Program	72
Interior Cleanliness	68	Entertainment	73
Passenger Space	75	Activities Program	69
Passenger Comfort Level	74	Cruise Director/Cruise Staff	72
Furnishings/Decor	73	Ship's Officers/Staff	74
Cruise Cuisine	73	Fitness/Sports Facilities	73
Food Service	74	Overall Ship Facilities	75
Beverages/Service	72	Value for Money	75
Accommodations	75	Total Cruise Experience	74
Cabin Service	77	**Overall Rating**	**1470**
Itineraries/Destinations	78	**Average**	**73.5**

Comments

Classic lines and traditional ship profile/ black hull with white superstructure looking tired/ship is not very clean/interior decor also looks tired and well worn, but the wood paneling does add a little warmth/ cabins are almost all outside, but are rather spartan in nature—some have no private facilities/dining room operated more like a cafeteria/food is heavy and choice is limited/service is completely unrefined/this ship is in need of a major refurbishment program/good for families on a low budget, but there's no finesse—anywhere.

Jason ★★★

Principal Cruising Areas:
Aegean/Bahamas/Mediterranean

Ship	mts Jason	Passenger Space Ratio (basis 2)	18.9
Cruise Line/Operator	Epirotiki Lines	Passenger Space Ratio (all berths)	16.9
Former Names	Eros	Officers Greek	Service Staff Greek
Gross Registered Tonnage	5,250	Total Cabins 139	Cabin Door Width 24"
Built	Cantieri Riuniti dell'Adriatico (Italy)	Outside 103 Inside 36	Single No
First Entered Service	1965	Wheelchair Accessible Cabins	No
Last Refurbished	1967	Dining Rooms 1	Sittings 2
Country of Registry	Greece	Number of Elevators 1	Door Width 30"
Radio Call Sign	SZLZ	Electric Current in Cabins	220 DC
Satellite Telephone Number	1130175	Casino Yes	Slot Machines Yes
Length 346 ft./105.4 m.	Beam 61 ft./18.5 m.	Swimming Pools Outside 1	Inside No
Engines	2×Sulzer diesels	Whirlpools	No
Passenger Decks	6	Gymnasium No Sauna No	Massage No
Number of Crew	120	Cinema/Theatre No	Number of Seats –
Passenger Capacity (basis 2)	278	Cabin TV No	Library Yes
Passenger Capacity (all berths)	310	Children's Facilities/Playroom	No

Ratings

Ship Appearance/Condition	79	Shore Excursion Program	78
Interior Cleanliness	83	Entertainment	76
Passenger Space	76	Activities Program	74
Passenger Comfort Level	77	Cruise Director/Cruise Staff	74
Furnishings/Decor	80	Ship's Officers/Staff	79
Cruise Cuisine	79	Fitness/Sports Facilities	62
Food Service	81	Overall Ship Facilities	75
Beverages/Service	78	Value for Money	75
Accommodations	79	Total Cruise Experience	80
Cabin Service	80	**Overall Rating**	**1545**
Itineraries/Destinations	80	**Average**	**77.2**

Comments

Charming little ship with traditional profile/warm ambiance filters from officers and crew through to passengers/tasteful interior decor is in orange and gold/there is a small fortune in artworks aboard this vessel/well-stocked library/lovely dining room has big picture windows, and some precious tapestries/continental cuisine, with some excellent Greek dishes/cabins are small, but cozy and inviting, with sofa bed that converts to daytime sitting area/service is very good throughout/this ship will provide a most pleasant and intimate cruise experience in comfort and classical style, at a very fair price.

Jubilee ★★★★

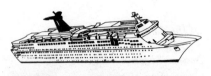

Principal Cruising Areas:
Caribbean

Ship	ms Jubilee
Cruise Line/Operator	Carnival Cruise Lines
Former Names	–
Gross Registered Tonnage	47,262
Built	Kockums (Sweden)
First Entered Service	1986
Last Refurbished	–
Country of Registry	Liberia
Radio Call Sign	ELFK6
Satellite Telephone Number	1240503
Length 748 ft./227.9 m.	Beam 92 ft./28.0 m.
Engines	2×Sulzer diesels
Passenger Decks	10
Number of Crew	670
Passenger Capacity (basis 2)	1500
Passenger Capacity (all berths)	1850

Passenger Space Ratio (basis 2)	31.5
Passenger Space Ratio (all berths)	25.5
Officers Italian	Service Staff International
Total Cabins 750	Cabin Door Width 22"
Outside 460 Inside 290	Single No
Wheelchair Accessible Cabins	No
Dining Rooms 2	Sittings 2
Number of Elevators 8	Door Width 33"
Electric Current in Cabins	110 AC
Casino Yes	Slot Machines Yes
Swimming Pools Outside 2	Inside No
Whirlpools	2
Gymnasium Yes Sauna Yes	Massage Yes
Cinema/Theatre No	Number of Seats –
Cabin TV Yes	Library Yes
Children's Facilities/Playroom	Yes

Ratings

Ship Appearance/Condition	85
Interior Cleanliness	86
Passenger Space	85
Passenger Comfort Level	85
Furnishings/Decor	83
Cruise Cuisine	76
Food Service	78
Beverages/Service	75
Accommodations	84
Cabin Service	82
Itineraries/Destinations	80

Shore Excursion Program	77
Entertainment	82
Activities Program	81
Cruise Director/Cruise Staff	81
Ship's Officers/Staff	81
Fitness/Sports Facilities	83
Overall Ship Facilities	85
Value for Money	85
Total Cruise Experience	83
Overall Rating	**1637**
Average	**81.8**

Comments

Bold, squarish, high-rise, yet attractive large ship with short, rakish bow/distinctive swept-back wing-tipped funnel/numerous public rooms on two decks/double-wide promenade deck/overwhelming multi-tiered showroom has huge stage/flamboyant colors in all public rooms except for elegant Churchill's Library/huge casino has non-stop action/cabins are quite spacious, with pretty decor/ especially nice are ten large suites/outside cabins feature large picture windows/two dining rooms are attractive, but have low ceilings/food needs upgrading/service is hurried/constant entertainment and activities/this ship provides novice cruisers with an excellent first cruise experience in very comfortable surroundings/fun-filled and stimulating/excellent for families and singles.

Jupiter ★★★

Principal Cruising Areas:
Aegean/Mediterranean

Ship	mts Jupiter	Passenger Space Ratio (basis 2)	24.1
Cruise Line/Operator	Epirotiki Lines	Passenger Space Ratio (all berths)	17.9
Former Names	Moledet/Alexandros	Officers Greek	Service Staff Greek
Gross Registered Tonnage	9,000	Total Cabins 187	Cabin Door Width 26"
Built Ateliers et Chantiers de Bretagne (France)		Outside 143 Inside 44	Single No
First Entered Service	1961	Wheelchair Accessible Cabins	No
Last Refurbished	1971	Dining Rooms 1	Sittings 2
Country of Registry	Greece	Number of Elevators 1	Door Width 30"
Radio Call Sign	SXGS	Electric Current in Cabins	110 AC/220 DC
Satellite Telephone Number	1133137	Casino No	Slot Machines No
Length 415 ft./126.4 m. Beam 65 ft./19.8 m.		Swimming Pools Outside 1	Inside No
Engines 2×Pielstick diesels		Whirlpools	No
Passenger Decks	7	Gymnasium No Sauna Yes	Massage No
Number of Crew	212	Cinema/Theatre Yes	Number of Seats 110
Passenger Capacity (basis 2)	374	Cabin TV No	Library Yes
Passenger Capacity (all berths)	501	Children's Facilities/Playroom	No

Ratings

Ship Appearance/Condition	76	Shore Excursion Program	78
Interior Cleanliness	78	Entertainment	76
Passenger Space	76	Activities Program	76
Passenger Comfort Level	78	Cruise Director/Cruise Staff	78
Furnishings/Decor	79	Ship's Officers/Staff	78
Cruise Cuisine	79	Fitness/Sports Facilities	66
Food Service	79	Overall Ship Facilities	77
Beverages/Service	77	Value for Money	78
Accommodations	77	Total Cruise Experience	79
Cabin Service	80	**Overall Rating**	**1542**
Itineraries/Destinations	77	**Average**	**77.1**

Comments

Typical '60s profile, with average good looks/good open deck and sunning space for ship size/plenty of charm, with homely interior decor/lovely tapestries and other artworks/small dining room is set low down, but is quite charming and tastefully decorated/food typically continental/ attentive service with a smile/cabins are compact, yet comfortable and quite adequate, with convertible sofa beds for daytime use/this ship provides a good cruise experience in comfortable, but not elegant, surroundings, to some classical destinations, at a very fair price.

Kazakhstan ★★★

Principal Cruising Areas:
Mediterranean / Scandinavia

Ship	ms Kazakhstan
Cruise Line/Operator	Black Sea Shipping
Former Names	–
Gross Registered Tonnage	16,631
Built	Wartsila (Finland)
First Entered Service	1976
Last Refurbished	1984
Country of Registry	USSR
Radio Call Sign	ULSB
Satellite Telephone Number	–
Length 515 ft./156.9 m.	Beam 72 ft./21.9 m.
Engines	2×Pielstick diesels
Passenger Decks	7
Number of Crew	250
Passenger Capacity (basis 2)	470
Passenger Capacity (all berths)	600

Passenger Space Ratio (basis 2)		35.3
Passenger Space Ratio (all berths)		27.7
Officers Soviet	Service Staff East European	
Total Cabins 335	Cabin Door Width 26"	
Outside 117	Inside 118	Single No
Wheelchair Accessible Cabins		No
Dining Rooms 2		Sittings 1
Number of Elevators 1	Door Width 30"	
Electric Current in Cabins		220 AC
Casino No	Slot Machines No	
Swimming Pools Outside 1		Inside No
Whirlpools		No
Gymnasium Yes	Sauna Yes	Massage Yes
Cinema/Theatre Yes	Number of Seats 143	
Cabin TV No		Library Yes
Children's Facilities/Playroom		No

Ratings

Ship Appearance/Condition	80	Shore Excursion Program	70
Interior Cleanliness	79	Entertainment	72
Passenger Space	78	Activities Program	70
Passenger Comfort Level	80	Cruise Director/Cruise-Staff	74
Furnishings/Decor	79	Ship's Officers/Staff	75
Cruise Cuisine	76	Fitness/Sports Facilities	78
Food Service	78	Overall Ship Facilities	78
Beverages/Service	76	Value for Money	82
Accommodations	77	Total Cruise Experience	79
Cabin Service	78	**Overall Rating**	**1541**
Itineraries/Destinations	82	**Average**	**77.0**

Comments

Fairly sleek-looking ship with contemporary profile and squarish funnel/extensive refurbishment added a cinema, new nightclub, foyer, "Troika Bar" and more cabins/8 new suites on Boat Deck are quite spacious, have full bathtubs, and good closet and drawer space/other cabins are small and sparingly furnished, but adequate/two dining rooms are decorated nicely, with one wall containing a multi-color, multi-image contemporary glass mural/service somewhat perfunctory/excellent itineraries/German-language ship/this ship provides a good cruise experience at a fair price, but there's no finesse.

La Palma ★★

Principal Cruising Areas:
Aegean/Mediterranean

Ship	mv La Palma		Passenger Space Ratio (basis 2)		17.6
Cruise Line/Operator	Intercruise		Passenger Space Ratio (all berths)		14.7
Formerly	Delphi/La Perla/Ferdinand de Lessop		Officers Greek		Service Staff Greek
Gross Registered Tonnage	11,608		Total Cabins 326	Cabin Door Width 24"	
Built	Chantiers de la Gironde (France)		Outside 176	Inside 150	Single 5
First Entered Service	1953		Wheelchair Accessible Cabins		No
Last Refurbished	1986		Dining Rooms 1		Sittings 2
Country of Registry	Cyprus		Number of Elevators 0		Door Width –
Radio Call Sign	P3AT		Electric Current in Cabins		110/220 AC
Satellite Telephone Number	1100201		Casino Yes		Slot Machines Yes
Length 475 ft./143.7 m.	Beam 64 ft./19.6 m.		Swimming Pools Outside 1		Inside No
Engines	2×B&W diesels		Whirlpools		No
Passenger Decks	7		Gymnasium Yes	Sauna No	Massage No
Number of Crew	230		Cinema/Theatre Yes	Number of Seats 120	
Passenger Capacity (basis 2)	660		Cabin TV No		Library Yes
Passenger Capacity (all berths)	790		Children's Facilities/Playroom		No

Ratings

Ship Appearance/Condition	75		Shore Excursion Program	68
Interior Cleanliness	78		Entertainment	73
Passenger Space	74		Activities Program	70
Passenger Comfort Level	76		Cruise Director/Cruise Staff	73
Furnishings/Decor	76		Ship's Officers/Staff	75
Cruise Cuisine	76		Fitness/Sports Facilities	72
Food Service	78		Overall Ship Facilities	70
Beverages/Service	74		Value for Money	72
Accommodations	76		Total Cruise Experience	76
Cabin Service	78		**Overall Rating**	**1485**
Itineraries/Destinations	75		**Average**	**74.2**

Comments

Traditional older styling, with low funnel profile/basically a well-maintained vessel/plenty of open deck and sunning space—even an isolated nudist deck/cheerful interior decor, with plenty of wood and wood trim throughout/dining room is set low down, but is quite cozy/food is continental, and moderately good/service comes with a smile/five suites are spacious for ship size/other cabins are moderately so, and all have private facilities/this is a high-density ship that caters well to young families and active singles on a modest budget/mostly European passengers.

Leonid Brezhnev ★★★

Principal Cruising Areas:
Baltic / Mediterranean / Scandinavia /
World Cruise

Ship	Leonid Brezhnev
Cruise Line / Operator	Black Sea Shipping
Former Names	Kareliya
Gross Registered Tonnage	16,900
Built	Wartsila (Finland)
First Entered Service	1975
Last Refurbished	1983
Country of Registry	USSR
Radio Call Sign	UIDO
Satellite Telephone Number	–
Length 515 ft. / 156.9 m.	Beam 72 ft. / 21.9 m.
Engines	2 × Pielstick diesels
Passenger Decks	7
Number of Crew	250
Passenger Capacity (basis 2)	486
Passenger Capacity (all berths)	775

Passenger Space Ratio (basis 2)		34.7
Passenger Space Ratio (all berths)		21.8
Officers Soviet	Service Staff East European	
Total Cabins 243	Cabin Door Width 26"	
Outside 124	Inside 119	Single No
Wheelchair Accessible Cabins		No
Dining Rooms 2		Sittings 2
Number of Elevators 2	Door Width 30"	
Electric Current in Cabins		220 AC
Casino Yes	Slot Machines Yes	
Swimming Pools Outside 1		Inside No
Whirlpools		No
Gymnasium Yes	Sauna Yes	Massage Yes
Cinema / Theatre Yes	Number of Seats 100	
Cabin TV No		Library No
Children's Facilities / Playroom		No

Ratings

Ship Appearance / Condition	81
Interior Cleanliness	81
Passenger Space	80
Passenger Comfort Level	80
Furnishings / Decor	81
Cruise Cuisine	76
Food Service	78
Beverages / Service	74
Accommodations	78
Cabin Service	78
Itineraries / Destinations	81

Shore Excursion Program	68
Entertainment	74
Activities Program	70
Cruise Director / Cruise Staff	72
Ship's Officers / Staff	76
Fitness / Sports Facilities	78
Overall Ship Facilities	78
Value for Money	82
Total Cruise Experience	82
Overall Rating	**1549**
Average	**77.4**

Comments

Smart-looking vessel with large squarish funnel / very pleasing interior decor / extensive refurbishment has added a new nightclub, casino, cinema and more cabins / 12 suites on Boat Deck are large and nicely appointed / other cabins are on the small side, but more than adequate / two dining rooms are homely, with dining family-style / food choice limited / service is good, and the staff do try hard, even though there's no finesse / this ship caters primarily to European passengers wanting a decent, but not elegant, cruise experience at modest cost.

Majestic ★ ★ ★ +

Principal Cruising Areas:
Alaska/Caribbean/Mexican Riviera

Ship	star ship Majestic	Passenger Space Ratio (basis 2)	25.3
Cruise Line/Operator	Premier Cruise Lines	Passenger Space Ratio (all berths)	24.3
Former Names	Sun Princess/Spirit of London	Officers British	Service Staff International
Gross Registered Tonnage	17,270	Total Cabins 349	Cabin Door Width 24"
Built Cantieri Navale del Tirreno e Riuniti (Italy)		Outside 234	Inside 115	Single 12
First Entered Service	1972	Wheelchair Accessible Cabins	No
Last Refurbished	1984	Dining Rooms 1	Sittings 2
Country of Registry	Great Britain	Number of Elevators 4	Door Width 22–35"
Radio Call Sign	GBFT	Electric Current in Cabins	110 AC
Satellite Telephone Number	1440213	Casino Yes	Slot Machines Yes
Length 535 ft./163.0 m.	Beam 75 ft./22.8 m.	Swimming Pools Outside 1	Inside No
Engines	2×GMT diesels	Whirlpools	No
Passenger Decks	7	Gymnasium Yes Sauna Yes	Massage Yes
Number of Crew	370	Cinema/Theatre Yes	Number of Seats 186
Passenger Capacity (basis 2)	686	Cabin TV No	Library Yes
Passenger Capacity (all berths)	712	Children's Facilities/Playroom	No

Ratings

Ship Appearance/Condition	81	Shore Excursion Program	80
Interior Cleanliness	80	Entertainment	78
Passenger Space	78	Activities Program	77
Passenger Comfort Level	81	Cruise Director/Cruise Staff	81
Furnishings/Decor	81	Ship's Officers/Staff	82
Cruise Cuisine	81	Fitness/Sports Facilities	60
Food Service	82	Overall Ship Facilities	79
Beverages/Service	80	Value for Money	78
Accommodations	78	Total Cruise Experience	82
Cabin Service	80	**Overall Rating**	**1581**
Itineraries/Destinations	82	**Average**	**79.0**

Comments

Clean, contemporary profile with rakish superstructure/well-maintained vessel/inboard lifeboats/open deck and sunning space good/much-upgraded interior decor features tasteful earth tones/comfortable public rooms, except when full/some public rooms, including showroom, need refur-bishing/charming dining room/good service throughout/good food, with fine pasta dishes/deluxe suites quite spacious/other cabins on the small side, but well equipped/this ship will cruise you in very comfortable surroundings, and a fun atmosphere. (Rated as *Sun Princess*.)

Mardi Gras ★ ★ ★ +

Principal Cruising Areas:
Bahamas

Ship	tss Mardi Gras	Passenger Space Ratio (basis 2)	30.1
Cruise Line/Operator	Carnival Cruise Lines	Passenger Space Ratio (all berths)	22.0
Former Names	Empress of Canada	Officers Italian	Service Staff International
Gross Registered Tonnage	27,250	Total Cabins 457	Cabin Door Width 26–30"
Built	Vickers Armstrong (UK)	Outside 193 Inside 264	Single No
First Entered Service	1962	Wheelchair Accessible Cabins	No
Last Refurbished	1985	Dining Rooms 1	Sittings 2
Country of Registry	Panama	Number of Elevators 4	Door Width 36"
Radio Call Sign	3EQN	Electric Current in Cabins	110/220 AC
Satellite Telephone Number	–	Casino Yes	Slot Machines Yes
Length 650 ft./198.1 m. Beam 87 ft./26.5 m.		Swimming Pools Outside 1	Inside 1
Engines	2×Parsons steam turbines	Whirlpools	No
Passenger Decks	9	Gymnasium Yes Sauna Yes	Massage Yes
Number of Crew	550	Cinema/Theatre Yes	Number of Seats 200
Passenger Capacity (basis 2)	906	Cabin TV No	Library No
Passenger Capacity (all berths)	1240	Children's Facilities/Playroom	Yes

Ratings

Ship Appearance/Condition	79	Shore Excursion Program	76
Interior Cleanliness	78	Entertainment	76
Passenger Space	77	Activities Program	75
Passenger Comfort Level	80	Cruise Director/Cruise Staff	78
Furnishings/Decor	78	Ship's Officers/Staff	78
Cruise Cuisine	76	Fitness/Sports Facilities	80
Food Service	78	Overall Ship Facilities	74
Beverages/Service	75	Value for Money	80
Accommodations	79	Total Cruise Experience	81
Cabin Service	78	**Overall Rating**	**1553**
Itineraries/Destinations	75	**Average**	**77.6**

Comments

Solidly constructed former ocean liner has midships funnel in Carnival's distinctive colors/well maintained throughout, even with heavy use from three- and four-day cruises/lots of lovely original woods and polished brass throughout/has enclosed promenade decks/public rooms not as numerous as sister ship *Carnivale*/two-level Grand Ballroom is lovely/cabins are quite large, and all have private facilities/some upper grade cabins are each done in different woods/lively casino action/this ship provides an excellent short cruise experience in very comfortable old-world surroundings/ideal for the active set seeking fun in the sun at a fair price.

Maxim Gorki ★★★+

Principal Cruising Areas:
Mediterranean/Scandinavia/World Cruise

Ship	ts Maxim Gorki	Passenger Space Ratio (basis 2)	41.7
Cruise Line/Operator	Black Sea Shipping	Passenger Space Ratio (all berths)	34.3
Former Names	Hanseatic/Hamburg	Officers Soviet Service Staff East European	
Gross Registered Tonnage	25,022	Total Cabins 319 Cabin Door Width 27"	
Built	Deutsche Werft (W. Germany)	Outside 204 Inside 115 Single No	
First Entered Service	1969	Wheelchair Accessible Cabins	No
Last Refurbished	1988	Dining Rooms 3 Sittings 1	
Country of Registry	USSR	Number of Elevators 4 Door Width 36"	
Radio Call Sign	UYAD	Electric Current in Cabins	220 AC
Satellite Telephone Number	–	Casino No Slot Machines No	
Length 642 ft./195.6 m. Beam 88.5 ft./26.9 m.		Swimming Pools Outside 1 Inside 1	
Engines	2×AEG turbines	Whirlpools	No
Passenger Decks	10	Gymnasium Yes Sauna Yes Massage Yes	
Number of Crew	340	Cinema/Theatre Yes Number of Seats 290	
Passenger Capacity (basis 2)	600	Cabin TV No Library Yes	
Passenger Capacity (all berths)	728	Children's Facilities/Playroom	No

Ratings

Ship Appearance/Condition	81	Shore Excursion Program	72
Interior Cleanliness	81	Entertainment	76
Passenger Space	80	Activities Program	70
Passenger Comfort Level	82	Cruise Director/Cruise Staff	78
Furnishings/Decor	80	Ship's Officers/Staff	79
Cruise Cuisine	77	Fitness/Sports Facilities	78
Food Service	78	Overall Ship Facilities	80
Beverages/Service	76	Value for Money	82
Accommodations	80	Total Cruise Experience	82
Cabin Service	79	**Overall Rating**	**1574**
Itineraries/Destinations	83	**Average**	**78.7**

Comments

Gleaming white ship with pleasing lines and outer styling, except for platform-topped funnel/quite well maintained/excellent open deck and sunning space/well-designed public rooms/good woods used throughout/especially nice is the intimate Zhiguli Club/three nicely decorated restaurants are set low down/food is moderately good/attentive, but somewhat starchy service/ delightful Russian Tea Ceremony on each cruise/spacious cabins, with wood paneling, and large bathrooms with full bathtub in each/superb deluxe cabins are fully equipped, and have huge picture windows/ mostly German and northern European passengers/this ship provides an excellent cruise experience in very comfortable, almost elegant, surroundings, at a modest price.

Maxim's des Mers

Principal Cruising Areas:
Mediterranean

Ship	Maxim's des Mers		Passenger Space Ratio (basis 2)		49.9
Cruise Line/Operator	Cruise and Charm		Passenger Space Ratio (all berths)		49.9
Former Names	–		Officers French		Service Staff French
Gross Registered Tonnage	1,590		Total Cabins 16		Cabin Door Width –
Built	(U.S.A.)		Outside 16	Inside No	Single No
First Entered Service	1944		Wheelchair Accessible Cabins		No
Last Refurbished	1987		Dining Rooms 1		Sittings 1
Country of Registry	Bahamas		Number of Elevators 0		Door Width –
Radio Call Sign	C6BC4		Electric Current in Cabins		220 AC
Satellite Telephone Number	1104261		Casino No		Slot Machines No
Length 178 ft./57.5 m.	Beam 34.7 ft./11.2 m.		Swimming Pools Outside 1		Inside No
Engines	–		Whirlpools		1
Passenger Decks	5		Gymnasium No	Sauna No	Massage Yes
Number of Crew	32		Cinema/Theatre No		Number of Seats –
Passenger Capacity (basis 2)	32		Cabin TV Yes		Library No
Passenger Capacity (all berths)	32		Children's Facilities/Playroom		No

Ratings

Ship Appearance/Condition	–		Shore Excursion Program	–
Interior Cleanliness	–		Entertainment	–
Passenger Space	–		Activities Program	–
Passenger Comfort Level	–		Cruise Director/Cruise Staff	–
Furnishings/Decor	–		Ship's Officers/Staff	–
Cruise Cuisine	–		Fitness/Sports Facilities	–
Food Service	–		Overall Ship Facilities	–
Beverages/Service	–		Value for Money	–
Accommodations	–		Total Cruise Experience	–
Cabin Service	–		**Overall Rating**	**–**
Itineraries/Destinations	–		**Average**	**–**

Comments

Cute little vessel with small, squat funnel/ incredibly lavish, somewhat gaudy but utterly colorful interior is decorated totally in art-deco style by Pierre Cardin/marble, rich polished woods and oriental rugs are everywhere/painted glass ceiling in dining salon is exquisite/excellent food as at Maxim's in Paris/wonderful cabins, each decorated in a different style and color scheme/Bernhardt, Chevalier and Mistinguett suites have whirlpool baths and private terraces, and are irresistibly grand/highly personal service by charming bilingual staff/this little ship is a mix of vintage Paris and Palm Beach at sea/wonderful for an eccentric week or two. (Not rated at press time.)

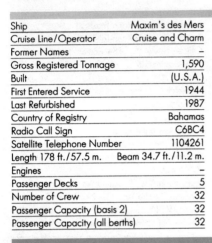

Mermoz ★★★★

Principal Cruising Areas:
Worldwide

Ship	ms Mermoz
Cruise Line/Operator	Paquet Cruises
Former Names	Jean Mermoz
Gross Registered Tonnage	13,691
Built	Chantiers de l'Atlantique (France)
First Entered Service	1957
Last Refurbished	1985
Country of Registry	Bahamas
Radio Call Sign	C6BB3
Satellite Telephone Number	1104216
Length 527 ft./161.7 m.	Beam 65 ft./19.7 m.
Engines	2×B&W diesels
Passenger Decks	10
Number of Crew	230
Passenger Capacity (basis 2)	530
Passenger Capacity (all berths)	745

Passenger Space Ratio (basis 2)		25.8
Passenger Space Ratio (all berths)		18.3
Officers French	Service Staff French/Indonesian	
Total Cabins 301	Cabin Door Width 24"	
Outside 240	Inside 61	Single 33
Wheelchair Accessible Cabins		No
Dining Rooms 2		Sittings 2
Number of Elevators 2	Door Width 30"	
Electric Current in Cabins		110/220 AC
Casino Yes	Slot Machines Yes	
Swimming Pools Outside 2		Inside No
Whirlpools		No
Gymnasium Yes	Sauna Yes	Massage Yes
Cinema/Theatre Yes	Number of Seats 260	
Cabin TV No		Library Yes
Children's Facilities/Playroom		No

Ratings

Ship Appearance/Condition	79		Shore Excursion Program	78
Interior Cleanliness	81		Entertainment	80
Passenger Space	81		Activities Program	76
Passenger Comfort Level	82		Cruise Director/Cruise Staff	78
Furnishings/Decor	81		Ship's Officers/Staff	80
Cruise Cuisine	85		Fitness/Sports Facilities	79
Food Service	81		Overall Ship Facilities	76
Beverages/Service	82		Value for Money	80
Accommodations	79		Total Cruise Experience	82
Cabin Service	80		**Overall Rating**	**1601**
Itineraries/Destinations	81		**Average**	**80.0**

Comments

Traditional ship profile/delightful interior decor, with earth tone color scheme throughout/tastefully and typically French in ambiance and service/very fine cuisine that is utterly creative, especially on the special theme cruises/Classical Music Festival cruise is spectacular/cabins are not large, but are tastefully furnished, cozy and comfortable, with solid fixtures and wood everywhere/ample closet and drawer space/bathrobes are provided for everyone/this ship has a wonderful European character, and is for those who enjoy being with the French, at a moderate price.

Mikhail Sholokhov ★★★

Principal Cruising Areas:
Orient

Ship	ms Mikhail Sholokhov	Passenger Space Ratio (basis 2)	42.2
Cruise Line/Operator	Far Eastern Shipping	Passenger Space Ratio (all berths)	23.9
Former Names	–	Officers Soviet	Service Staff East European
Gross Registered Tonnage	9,878	Total Cabins 117	Cabin Door Width 24″
Built	Adolf Warski Werft (Poland)	Outside 71 Inside 46	Single No
First Entered Service	1986	Wheelchair Accessible Cabins	No
Last Refurbished	–	Dining Rooms 1	Sittings 1
Country of Registry	USSR	Number of Elevators 1	Door Width 30″
Radio Call Sign	UKSK	Electric Current in Cabins	220 AC
Satellite Telephone Number	–	Casino No	Slot Machines No
Length 441 ft./134.4 m.	Beam 69 ft./21.0 m.	Swimming Pools Outside 1	Inside No
Engines	4×Sulzer diesels	Whirlpools	No
Passenger Decks	7	Gymnasium Yes Sauna Yes	Massage Yes
Number of Crew	168	Cinema/Theatre No	Number of Seats –
Passenger Capacity (basis 2)	234	Cabin TV No	Library Yes
Passenger Capacity (all berths)	412	Children's Facilities/Playroom	No

Ratings

Ship Appearance/Condition	78	Shore Excursion Program	74
Interior Cleanliness	79	Entertainment	74
Passenger Space	77	Activities Program	73
Passenger Comfort Level	79	Cruise Director/Cruise Staff	75
Furnishings/Decor	78	Ship's Officers/Staff	76
Cruise Cuisine	76	Fitness/Sports Facilities	75
Food Service	75	Overall Ship Facilities	77
Beverages/Service	74	Value for Money	79
Accommodations	77	Total Cruise Experience	80
Cabin Service	77	**Overall Rating**	**1533**
Itineraries/Destinations	80	**Average**	**76.6**

Comments

Boxy-looking profile with squared-off stern, stubby bow and huge, squat funnel/fully-enclosed bridge/one of a new series of five built in Poland/interior decor is reasonably pleasant, but somewhat spartan/limited public rooms/cabins are small, space-efficient units that have little warmth/good open deck and sunning space/dining room is cheerful, and dining is family-style/food is reasonable, no more/operates mainly in the Indonesian islands/this ship provides a reasonable cruise experience that is definitely for the budget-conscious.

Monterey ★★★ +

Principal Cruising Areas:
Hawaii

Ship	ss Monterey	Passenger Space Ratio (basis 2)	29.2
Cruise Line/Operator	Aloha Pacific Cruises	Passenger Space Ratio (all berths)	27.5
Former Names	Free State Mariner	Officers American	Service Staff American
Gross Registered Tonnage	21,051	Total Cabins 300	Cabin Door Width 26″
Built	Bethlehem Steel Corp. (USA)	Outside 171 Inside 129	Single No
First Entered Service	1952	Wheelchair Accessible Cabins	No
Last Refurbished	1988	Dining Rooms 1	Sittings 2
Country of Registry	USA	Number of Elevators 2	Door Width 30″
Radio Call Sign	KFCN	Electric Current in Cabins	110 AC
Satellite Telephone Number	–	Casino No	Slot Machines No
Length 563 ft./171.8 m. Beam 80.5 ft./24.5 m.		Swimming Pools Outside 1	Inside No
Engines	2×Bethlehem turbines	Whirlpools	2
Passenger Decks	5	Gymnasium Yes Sauna Yes Massage Yes	
Number of Crew	277	Cinema/Theatre Yes Number of Seats 107	
Passenger Capacity (basis 2)	600	Cabin TV No	Library Yes
Passenger Capacity (all berths)	638	Children's Facilities/Playroom	No

Ratings

Ship Appearance/Condition	81	Shore Excursion Program	80
Cleanliness	85	Entertainment	79
Passenger Space	81	Activities Program	79
Passenger Comfort Level	83	Cruise Director/Cruise Staff	80
Furnishings/Decor	82	Ship's Officers/Staff	81
Cruise Cuisine	82	Fitness/Sports Facilities	76
Food Service	81	Overall Ship Facilities	81
Beverages/Service	81	Value for Money	81
Accommodations	81	Total Cruise Experience	83
Cabin Service	80	**Overall Rating**	**1597**
Itineraries/Destinations	80	**Average**	**79.8**

Comments

Traditional ocean liner profile, with almost vertical bow/completely refurbished, with new sports deck added atop ship/American-built, owned, registered and crewed/good sheltered and open deck space/wide choice of cabins—top three categories have full bathtub/suites are extremely spacious/cabins are very roomy, well-appointed units, but those forward on Boat Deck have view obstructed by lifeboats/good conference facilities/dining room set low down, and decorated in soft earth tones/food is nouvelle American cuisine/service is friendly and attentive/this new entry will cruise you in reasonably elegant style around the Hawaiian islands, but do leave the children at home.

Neptune ★★★

Principal Cruising Areas:
Aegean/Mediterranean/Indian Ocean/
Orient

Ship	mv Neptune	Passenger Space Ratio (basis 2)	21.5
Cruise Line/Operator	Epirotiki Lines	Passenger Space Ratio (all berths)	18.7
Former Names	Meteor	Officers Greek	Service Staff Greek
Gross Registered Tonnage	4,000	Total Cabins 97	Cabin Door Width 22"
Built	Aalborg Vaerft (Denmark)	Outside 73 Inside 24	Single 6
First Entered Service	1955	Wheelchair Accessible Cabins	No
Last Refurbished	1972	Dining Rooms 1	Sittings 1
Country of Registry	Greece	Number of Elevators 0	Door Width –
Radio Call Sign	SXOS	Electric Current in Cabins	220 AC/220 DC
Satellite Telephone Number	–	Casino No	Slot Machines No
Length 277 ft./84.4 m.	Beam 45 ft./13.7 m.	Swimming Pools Outside 1	Inside No
Engines	2×B&W diesels	Whirlpools	No
Passenger Decks	6	Gymnasium No Sauna No	Massage No
Number of Crew	97	Cinema/Theatre No	Number of Seats –
Passenger Capacity (basis 2)	186	Cabin TV No	Library Yes
Passenger Capacity (all berths)	213	Children's Facilities/Playroom	No

Ratings

Appearance/Condition	76	Shore Excursion Program	75
Cleanliness	81	Entertainment	72
Passenger Space	70	Activities Program	70
Passenger Comfort Level	76	Cruise Director/Cruise Staff	70
Furnishings/Decor	80	Ship's Officers/Staff	74
Cruise Cuisine	78	Fitness/Sports Facilities	66
Food Service	77	Overall Ship Facilities	72
Beverages/Service	76	Value for Money	78
Accommodations	80	Total Cruise Experience	81
Cabin Service	79	**Overall Rating**	**1509**
Itineraries/Destinations	78	**Average**	**75.4**

Comments

Charming little ship, with traditional profile and clean, tidy lines/warm, intimate atmosphere/good sunning space for ship size, with real wooden deck loungers/limited public rooms have pleasant decor, and feature some interesting artworks/especially noticeable is the mosaic at poolside/well-stocked library/dining room is high up and has big picture windows/typically Mediterranean cuisine/apart from three large suite rooms that have full bathtub, cabins are compact but quite comfortable/ship is often chartered/will provide an intimate, highly personalized cruise experience in comfortable, but not elegant, surroundings, at a very fair price.

Nieuw Amsterdam ★★★★ +

Principal Cruising Areas:
Alaska/Caribbean

Ship	ms Nieuw Amsterdam	Passenger Space Ratio (basis 2)	27.9
Cruise Line/Operator	Holland America Line	Passenger Space Ratio (all berths)	25.1
Former Names	–	Officers Dutch Service Staff Filipino/Indonesian	
Gross Registered Tonnage	33,930	Total Cabins 603 Cabin Door Width 27"	
Built	Chantiers de l'Atlantique (France)	Outside 409 Inside 194 Single No	
First Entered Service	1983	Wheelchair Accessible Cabins	No
Last Refurbished	–	Dining Rooms 1 Sittings 2	
Country of Registry	Netherlands Antilles	Number of Elevators 7 Door Width 30"	
Radio Call Sign	PJCH	Electric Current in Cabins	110/220 AC
Satellite Telephone Number	1750103	Casino Yes Slot Machines Yes	
Length 704 ft./214.5 m.	Beam 89 ft./27.1 m.	Swimming Pools Outside 2 Inside No	
Engines	2×Sulzer diesels	Whirlpools	1
Passenger Decks	10	Gymnasium Yes Sauna Yes Massage Yes	
Number of Crew	542	Cinema/Theatre Yes Number of Seats 230	
Passenger Capacity (basis 2)	1214	Cabin TV Yes Library Yes	
Passenger Capacity (all berths)	1350	Children's Facilities/Playroom No	

Ratings

Ship Appearance/Condition	85	Shore Excursion Program	84
Interior Cleanliness	90	Entertainment	82
Passenger Space	86	Activities Program	81
Passenger Comfort Level	89	Cruise Director/Cruise Staff	84
Furnishings/Decor	89	Ship's Officers/Staff	83
Cruise Cuisine	85	Fitness/Sports Facilities	83
Food Service	86	Overall Ship Facilities	86
Beverages/Service	84	Value for Money	85
Accommodations	86	Total Cruise Experience	86
Cabin Service	86	**Overall Rating**	**1703**
Itineraries/Destinations	83	**Average**	**85.1**

Comments

Long, squat, angular profile, balanced by raked bow/plenty of open deck space/spacious, luxurious interior design, with pleasant colors/much use of polished teak and rosewood paneling/delightful Explorers' Lounge is relaxing for after-meal coffee and live chamber music/balconied main lounge/large, yet intimate, dining room, with plenty of space/international nouvelle cuisine/excellent service from Indonesian waiters/cabins are spacious and well appointed with quality fittings/top three categories have full bathtubs/several cabins have king- or queen-sized beds/some cabins on Boat and Navigation Decks have obstructed views/this ship is recommended for seasoned travelers wanting a quality (but affordable) cruise in elegant surroundings.

Noordam ★★★★+

Principal Cruising Areas:
Alaska/Caribbean

Ship	ms Noordam	Passenger Space Ratio (basis 2)	27.9
Cruise Line/Operator	Holland America Line	Passenger Space Ratio (all berths)	25.1
Former Names	–	Officers Dutch Service Staff Filipino/Indonesian	
Gross Registered Tonnage	33,930	Total Cabins 605 Cabin Door Width 27"	
Built Chantiers de l'Atlantique (France)		Outside 411 Inside 194 Single No	
First Entered Service	1984	Wheelchair Accessible Cabins	No
Last Refurbished	–	Dining Rooms 1 Sittings 2	
Country of Registry	Netherlands Antilles	Number of Elevators 7 Door Width 30"	
Radio Call Sign	PJCO	Electric Current in Cabins 110/220 AC	
Satellite Telephone Number	1750105	Casino Yes Slot Machines Yes	
Length 704 ft./214.5 m. Beam 89 ft./27.1 m.		Swimming Pools Outside 2 Inside No	
Engines	2×Sulzer diesels	Whirlpools 1	
Passenger Decks	10	Gymnasium Yes Sauna Yes Massage Yes	
Number of Crew	530	Cinema/Theatre Yes Number of Seats 230	
Passenger Capacity (basis 2)	1214	Cabin TV Yes Library Yes	
Passenger Capacity (all berths)	1350	Children's Facilities/Playroom No	

Ratings

Ship Appearance/Condition	85	Shore Excursion Program	84
Interior Cleanliness	91	Entertainment	82
Passenger Space	83	Activities Program	82
Passenger Comfort Level	90	Cruise Director/Cruise Staff	85
Furnishings/Decor	89	Ship's Officers/Staff	84
Cruise Cuisine	85	Fitness/Sports Facilities	84
Food Service	86	Overall Ship Facilities	86
Beverages/Service	83	Value for Money	85
Accommodations	86	Total Cruise Experience	87
Cabin Service	86	**Overall Rating**	**1706**
Itineraries/Destinations	83	**Average**	**85.3**

Comments

Identical exterior to *Nieuw Amsterdam* with same angular design/interior decor different/wonderful artworks from 17th and 18th centuries/superb choice of public rooms/Crow's Nest observation lounge is my favorite retreat/Explorers' Lounge is lovely for after-dinner coffee with live chamber music/large, but charming and spacious, dining room/excellent service—always with a smile from Indonesian staff/international nouvelle cuisine/spacious, well-appointed cabins/top three categories have full-length bathtubs/some cabins on Boat and Navigation Decks have obstructed views/excellent in-cabin video programming/this ship will cruise you (leave the children at home) in style, but at a very affordable, realistic price/highly recommended.

Nordic Prince ★★★★

Principal Cruising Areas:
Bermuda/Caribbean

Ship	ms Nordic Prince		Passenger Space Ratio (basis 2)		22.4
Line/Operator	Royal Caribbean Cruise Line		Passenger Space Ratio (all berths)		19.9
Former Names	–		Officers Norwegian	Service Staff International	
Gross Registered Tonnage	23,200		Total Cabins 535	Cabin Door Width 25″	
Built	Wartsila (Finland)		Outside 347	Inside 188	Single No
First Entered Service	1971		Wheelchair Accessible Cabins		No
Last Refurbished	1980		Dining Rooms 1		Sittings 2
Country of Registry	Norway		Number of Elevators 4	Door Width 35″	
Radio Call Sign	LAPJ		Electric Current in Cabins		110 AC
Satellite Telephone Number	–		Casino Yes	Slot Machines Yes	
Length 637 ft./194.1 m.	Beam 80 ft./24.3 m.		Swimming Pools Outside 1		Inside No
Engines	4×Sulzer diesels		Whirlpools		No
Passenger Decks	8		Gymnasium Yes Sauna Yes	Massage Yes	
Number of Crew	400		Cinema/Theatre No	Number of Seats –	
Passenger Capacity (basis 2)	1038		Cabin TV No		Library No
Passenger Capacity (all berths)	1168		Children's Facilities/Playroom		No

Ratings

Ship Appearance/Condition	83		Shore Excursion Program	82
Cleanliness	87		Entertainment	82
Passenger Space	84		Activities Program	81
Passenger Comfort Level	85		Cruise Director/Cruise Staff	82
Furnishings/Decor	82		Ship's Officers/Staff	82
Cruise Cuisine	84		Fitness/Sports Facilities	80
Food Service	85		Overall Ship Facilities	83
Beverages/Service	82		Value for Money	85
Accommodations	78		Total Cruise Experience	86
Cabin Service	81		**Overall Rating**	**1656**
Itineraries/Destinations	82		**Average**	**82.8**

Comments

Contemporary '70s look with long, sleek lines, raked bow and distinctive cantilevered Viking Crown Lounge set high on funnel/ "stretched" sister to *Song of Norway*/ expansive open deck space for sunning/ nicely polished decks and rails/good interior layout/Scandinavian decor is clean and bright, but becoming dated/good wood paneling and trim used throughout/cabins small and very compact, with only just enough closet space/good dining room operation and choice of food/very attentive, polished service, but pressure too high from waiters for good passenger comments/caters to novice and repeat passengers with well-programmed flair, and a fine-tuned cruise product in high-density, yet comfortable, surroundings.

Norway ★★★★

Principal Cruising Areas:
Bahamas/Caribbean

Ship	ss Norway	Passenger Space Ratio (basis 2)	37.9
Cruise Line/Operator	Norwegian Cruise Line	Passenger Space Ratio (all berths)	29.7
Former Names	France	Officers Norwegian Service Staff International	
Gross Registered Tonnage	70,202	Total Cabins 885 Cabin Door Width 28"	
Built	Chantiers de l'Atlantique (France)	Outside 517 Inside 368 Single No	
First Entered Service	1961	Wheelchair Accessible Cabins	10
Last Refurbished	1987	Dining Rooms 2 Sittings 2	
Country of Registry	Bahamas	Number of Elevators 9 Door Width 30"	
Radio Call Sign	NCLEX	Electric Current in Cabins	110 AC
Satellite Telephone Number	1104166	Casino Yes Slot Machines Yes	
Length 1,035 ft./315.4 m. Beam 110 ft./33.5 m.		Swimming Pools Outside 2 Inside 1	
Engines	2×CEM Parsons turbines	Whirlpools	No
Passenger Decks	10	Gymnasium Yes Sauna Yes Massage Yes	
Number of Crew	800	Cinema/Theatre Yes Number of Seats 555	
Passenger Capacity (basis 2)	1850	Cabin TV Yes Library Yes	
Passenger Capacity (all berths)	2356	Children's Facilities/Playroom Yes	

Ratings

Appearance/Condition	84	Shore Excursion Program	81
Cleanliness	82	Entertainment	94
Passenger Space	85	Activities Program	86
Passenger Comfort Level	86	Cruise Director/Cruise Staff	84
Furnishings/Decor	81	Ship's Officers/Staff	82
Cruise Cuisine	79	Fitness/Sports Facilities	88
Food Service	81	Overall Ship Facilities	87
Beverages/Service	77	Value for Money	87
Accommodations	81	Total Cruise Experience	85
Cabin Service	81	**Overall Rating**	**1667**
Itineraries/Destinations	76	**Average**	**83.3**

Comments

Former giant ocean liner *France*/superb transformation into cruise ship/two giant funnels/large landing craft provide efficient transportation ashore/Club International is most elegant public room/excellent theatre and shows/large, active casino/two dining rooms—nicest is the Windward, with its domed ceiling/service is good/wide range of cabins/two suites on Viking Deck feature two bedrooms and lounge/all cabins have high ceilings, long beds, plenty of space/new cabins added where Leeward Dining Room balcony was/first-class dazzle and sizzle entertainment/highly recommended for families with children/ship will provide an action-packed, sun-filled cruise experience in extremely comfortable surroundings, at a decent price.

Ocean Islander ★★★★

Principal Cruising Areas:
Caribbean/Mediterranean/Orinoco

Ship	mv Ocean Islander	Passenger Space Ratio (basis 2)	24.7
Cruise Line/Operator	Ocean Cruise Lines	Passenger Space Ratio (all berths)	24.7
Former Names	San Georgio/City of Andros	Officers Greek	Service Staff European
Gross Registered Tonnage	6,179	Total Cabins 123	Cabin Door Width 29″
Built	Cantieri Riuniti dell'Adriatico (Italy)	Outside 85	Inside 38	Single No
First Entered Service	1956	Wheelchair Accessible Cabins	No
Last Refurbished	1984	Dining Rooms 1	Sittings 2
Country of Registry	Bahamas	Number of Elevators 1	Door Width 25″
Radio Call Sign	C6CF4	Electric Current in Cabins	110 AC
Satellite Telephone Number	1104407	Casino Yes	Slot Machines Yes
Length 396.6 ft./112.6 m.	Beam 51 ft./15.5 m.	Swimming Pools Outside 1	Inside No
Engines	2×GMT diesels	Whirlpools	No
Passenger Decks	5	Gymnasium Yes	Sauna Yes	Massage Yes
Number of Crew	140	Cinema/Theatre No	Number of Seats –
Passenger Capacity (basis 2)	250	Cabin TV No	Library Yes
Passenger Capacity (all berths)	250	Children's Facilities/Playroom	No

Ratings

Ship Appearance/Condition	83	Shore Excursion Program	79
Interior Cleanliness	84	Entertainment	77
Passenger Space	79	Activities Program	76
Passenger Comfort Level	83	Cruise Director/Cruise Staff	81
Furnishings/Decor	84	Ship's Officers/Staff	82
Cruise Cuisine	82	Fitness/Sports Facilities	77
Food Service	82	Overall Ship Facilities	77
Beverages/Service	81	Value for Money	84
Accommodations	81	Total Cruise Experience	86
Cabin Service	82	**Overall Rating**	**1624**
Itineraries/Destinations	84	**Average**	**81.2**

Comments

Utterly charming little vessel, with well-balanced profile/suited best for cruising in sheltered areas/extremely clean and tidy throughout/warm, intimate and highly personable ambiance/ample open deck space for sunning/contemporary interior decor that is pleasing to the eye/cabins are quite large for ship size, nicely decorated with fine quality fabrics/good closet and drawer space/charming dining room, with good service and international cuisine/this ship provides a most enjoyable cruise experience in very comfortable, yacht-style surroundings, at an extremely realistic price/very highly recommended.

Ocean Pearl ★★★★

Principal Cruising Areas:
Orient

Ship	ms Ocean Pearl
Cruise Line/Operator	Ocean Cruise Lines
Former Names	Pearl of Scandinavia/Finnstar
Gross Registered Tonnage	12,456
Built	Wartsila (Finland)
First Entered Service	1967
Last Refurbished	1988
Country of Registry	Bahamas
Radio Call Sign	C6DC
Satellite Telephone Number	1104105
Length 514 ft./156.5 m.	Beam 66 ft./20.1 m.
Engines	4×Sulzer diesels
Passenger Decks	9
Number of Crew	235
Passenger Capacity (basis 2)	495
Passenger Capacity (all berths)	610

Passenger Space Ratio (basis 2)			25.1
Passenger Space Ratio (all berths)			20.4
Officers Scand.	Service Staff Europ./Filipino
Total Cabins 256		Cabin Door Width 24"
Outside 202	Inside 54		Single 23
Wheelchair Accessible Cabins			No
Dining Rooms 1			Sittings 2
Number of Elevators 2		Door Width 31"
Electric Current in Cabins			n/a
Casino Yes		Slot Machines Yes
Swimming Pools Outside 1			Inside No
Whirlpools			2
Gymnasium Yes	Sauna Yes		Massage Yes
Cinema/Theatre Yes		Number of Seats 62
Cabin TV No			Library Yes
Children's Facilities/Playroom			No

Ratings

Ship Appearance/Condition	82	Shore Excursion Program	86
Interior Cleanliness	88	Entertainment	80
Passenger Space	80	Activities Program	78
Passenger Comfort Level	85	Cruise Director/Cruise Staff	82
Furnishings/Decor	83	Ship's Officers/Staff	82
Cruise Cuisine	84	Fitness/Sports Facilities	82
Food Service	84	Overall Ship Facilities	81
Beverages/Service	83	Value for Money	84
Accommodations	82	Total Cruise Experience	85
Cabin Service	83	**Overall Rating**	**1662**
Itineraries/Destinations	88	**Average**	**83.1**

Comments

New, more attractive profile after extensive recent refurbishment program included structural alterations and a new, contemporary funnel/spotlessly clean/outstanding itineraries/new layout gives better passenger flow/tasteful decor includes many earth tones/lovely refinished woods throughout/new Marco Polo Lounge is vast improvement/new forward dining room is lovely, with good ocean views/food is very creative/excellent staff provide personal service with a smile/Explorer's suites are superb/all cabins are very spacious, and are well equipped, with lots of closet, drawer and storage space, but beware of low ceiling height/this ship provides a fine way to see the Orient in true comfort and style, and at a realistic price.

Ocean Princess ★★★★

Principal Cruising Areas:
Caribbean / Scandinavia / South America

Ship	mv Ocean Princess	Passenger Space Ratio (basis 2)	24.1
Cruise Line / Operator	Ocean Cruise Lines	Passenger Space Ratio (all berths)	22.2
Former Names	Italia / Princess Italia	Officers European	Service Staff European
Gross Registered Tonnage	11,126	Total Cabins 249	Cabin Door Width 24"
Built	Cantieri Navale Felszegi (Italy)	Outside 129	Inside 120 — Single No
First Entered Service	1967	Wheelchair Accessible Cabins	No
Last Refurbished	1984	Dining Rooms 1	Sittings 2
Country of Registry	Bahamas	Number of Elevators 3	Door Width 23"
Radio Call Sign	C6CF5	Electric Current in Cabins	110 AC
Satellite Telephone Number	1104410	Casino Yes	Slot Machines Yes
Length 492 ft. / 149.8 m.	Beam 71 ft. / 21.6 m.	Swimming Pools Outside 1	Inside No
Engines	2 × Sulzer diesels	Whirlpools	No
Passenger Decks	8	Gymnasium Yes — Sauna Yes	Massage Yes
Number of Crew	250	Cinema / Theatre Yes	Number of Seats 186
Passenger Capacity (basis 2)	460	Cabin TV No	Library No
Passenger Capacity (all berths)	500	Children's Facilities / Playroom	No

Ratings

Ship Appearance / Condition	83	Shore Excursion Program	80
Interior Cleanliness	83	Entertainment	80
Passenger Space	81	Activities Program	78
Passenger Comfort Level	83	Cruise Director / Cruise Staff	80
Furnishings / Decor	82	Ship's Officers / Staff	82
Cruise Cuisine	82	Fitness / Sports Facilities	80
Food Service	82	Overall Ship Facilities	80
Beverages / Service	81	Value for Money	82
Accommodations	81	Total Cruise Experience	85
Cabin Service	81	**Overall Rating**	**1629**
Itineraries / Destinations	83	**Average**	**81.4**

Comments

Long, sleek lines and swept-back funnel provide a very attractive profile / inboard lifeboats / heated outdoor pool / contemporary interior decor with attractive colors adds warmth / lovely, though noisy, dining room, with art deco feel, has raised center ceiling and beautiful etched glass dividers / excellent, attentive service / good international cuisine / good open deck space for sunning / cabins are reasonably sized, and have very pleasing decor, furnishings and fittings / all have tiled bathrooms / this ship will cruise you to some fascinating destinations in fine style and comfort, and the realistic price of this product is a real plus.

Oceanic ★★★★

Principal Cruising Areas:
Bahamas

Ship	star ship Oceanic	Passenger Space Ratio (basis 2)	34.4
Cruise Line/Operator	Premier Cruise Lines	Passenger Space Ratio (all berths)	26.1
Former Names	–	Officers Greek	Service Staff International
Gross Registered Tonnage	39,241	Total Cabins 569	Cabin Door Width 28"
Built	Cantieri Riuniti dell'Adriatico (Italy)	Outside 246 Inside 323	Single No
First Entered Service	1965	Wheelchair Accessible Cabins	No
Last Refurbished	1986	Dining Rooms 1	Sittings 2
Country of Registry	Panama	Number of Elevators 5	Door Width 30"
Radio Call Sign	HOOE	Electric Current in Cabins	110 AC
Satellite Telephone Number	1120520	Casino Yes	Slot Machines Yes
Length 782 ft./238.4 m.	Beam 96 ft./29.4 m.	Swimming Pools Outside 2	Inside No
Engines	4×De Laval turbines	Whirlpools	No
Passenger Decks	10	Gymnasium Yes Sauna No	Massage Yes
Number of Crew	530	Cinema/Theatre Yes	Number of Seats 420
Passenger Capacity (basis 2)	1138	Cabin TV No	Library No
Passenger Capacity (all berths)	1500	Children's Facilities/Playroom	Yes

Ratings

Ship Appearance/Condition	81	Shore Excursion Program	74
Interior Cleanliness	81	Entertainment	81
Passenger Space	82	Activities Program	80
Passenger Comfort Level	81	Cruise Director/Cruise Staff	81
Furnishings/Decor	81	Ship's Officers/Staff	81
Cruise Cuisine	81	Fitness/Sports Facilities	81
Food Service	82	Overall Ship Facilities	83
Beverages/Service	80	Value for Money	85
Accommodations	82	Total Cruise Experience	83
Cabin Service	82	**Overall Rating**	**1618**
Itineraries/Destinations	76	**Average**	**80.9**

Comments

Sleek-looking ship with classic, flowing lines/ excellent refurbishment/plenty of open deck space for sunning/swimming pool atop ship has magrodome roof/contemporary interior decor and bright colors/delightful enclosed promenades/balconied Sun Deck suites are superb and spacious/wide choice of other cabins/all cabins have heavy-duty furniture and come well equipped/many feature double beds/dining room is cheerful but crowded/good food and service/ busy casino action, but access for children should cease/wonderful for families with children, with counselors galore/special Disney cruise-stay package is recommended/this ship provides an excellent family-oriented cruise at an incredibly good price.

Oceanos ★★★ +

Principal Cruising Areas:
Aegean / Caribbean / Mediterranean

Ship	mts Oceanos	Passenger Space Ratio (basis 2)	27.2
Cruise Line / Operator	Epirotiki Lines	Passenger Space Ratio (all berths)	23.1
Formerly Eastern Princess / Ancona / Jean Laborde		Officers Greek	Service Staff Greek
Gross Registered Tonnage	14,000	Total Cabins 258	Cabin Door Width 26"
Built Ateliers et Chantiers de la Gironde (France)		Outside 176 Inside 82	Single 3
First Entered Service	1953	Wheelchair Accessible Cabins	No
Last Refurbished	1978	Dining Rooms 1	Sittings 2
Country of Registry	Greece	Number of Elevators 1	Door Width 30"
Radio Call Sign	SZPK	Electric Current in Cabins	110 AC
Satellite Telephone Number	1130604	Casino Yes	Slot Machines Yes
Length 500 ft. / 152.4 m. Beam 65 ft. / 19.8 m.		Swimming Pools Outside 1	Inside No
Engines	2×B&W diesels	Whirlpools	No
Passenger Decks	6	Gymnasium No Sauna Yes	Massage No
Number of Crew	250	Cinema / Theatre Yes Number of Seats 110	
Passenger Capacity (basis 2)	513	Cabin TV No	Library Yes
Passenger Capacity (all berths)	605	Children's Facilities / Playroom	No

Ratings

Ship Appearance / Condition	77	Shore Excursion Program	79
Interior Cleanliness	81	Entertainment	78
Passenger Space	78	Activities Program	76
Passenger Comfort Level	79	Cruise Director / Cruise Staff	76
Furnishings / Decor	81	Ship's Officers / Staff	78
Cruise Cuisine	80	Fitness / Sports Facilities	71
Food Service	81	Overall Ship Facilities	76
Beverages / Service	78	Value for Money	76
Accommodations	78	Total Cruise Experience	79
Cabin Service	80	**Overall Rating**	**1560**
Itineraries / Destinations	78	**Average**	**78.0**

Comments

One of the larger ships in the Epirotiki fleet, this has pleasing lines and a low, squat funnel / generous open deck and sunning space / two sheltered promenade decks for strolling / tasteful public room decor, adorned with much original artwork / "Byzantine" dining room is set low down, but is quite elegant and cheerfully decorated / food is continental / friendly service lacks finesse / cabins have wood paneling and a decent amount of space / while not luxurious, you will cruise in comfortable surroundings, at a modest price.

Odessa ★★

Principal Cruising Areas:
Baltic / Mediterranean / Scandinavia

Ship	mv Odessa	Passenger Space Ratio (basis 2)	29.9
Cruise Line/Operator	Black Sea Shipping	Passenger Space Ratio (all berths)	24.6
Former Names	Copenhagen	Officers Soviet Service Staff East European	
Gross Registered Tonnage	13,757	Total Cabins 241 Cabin Door Width 22"	
Built	Swan, Hunter (UK)	Outside 241 Inside No Single No	
First Entered Service	1975	Wheelchair Accessible Cabins	No
Last Refurbished	1985	Dining Rooms 1 Sittings 2	
Country of Registry	USSR	Number of Elevators 5 Door Width 30"	
Radio Call Sign	EWBK	Electric Current in Cabins	220 AC
Satellite Telephone Number	–	Casino Yes Slot Machines Yes	
Length 447 ft./136.2 m. Beam 71 ft./21.6 m.		Swimming Pools Outside 1 Inside No	
Engines	2×Pielstick diesels	Whirlpools	No
Passenger Decks	7	Gymnasium Yes Sauna Yes Massage Yes	
Number of Crew	260	Cinema/Theatre Yes Number of Seats 190	
Passenger Capacity (basis 2)	460	Cabin TV No Library No	
Passenger Capacity (all berths)	560	Children's Facilities/Playroom	No

Ratings

Ship Appearance/Condition	76	Shore Excursion Program	71
Interior Cleanliness	75	Entertainment	72
Passenger Space	71	Activities Program	67
Passenger Comfort Level	77	Cruise Director/Cruise Staff	74
Furnishings/Decor	76	Ship's Officers/Staff	76
Cruise Cuisine	75	Fitness/Sports Facilities	76
Food Service	72	Overall Ship Facilities	77
Beverages/Service	73	Value for Money	76
Accommodations	79	Total Cruise Experience	79
Cabin Service	76	**Overall Rating**	**1496**
Itineraries/Destinations	78	**Average**	**74.8**

Comments

Attractive ship with traditional lines/maintenance needs improving, and so does cleanliness/good selection of public rooms, but uncomfortable low-back chairs are used in most/"Odessa" restaurant is set high, and is quite charming, with intricate artwork on integral columns/service is quite atten-tive, but rather inflexible/cabins are all-outside, but are small and simply furnished, with little storage space/German language spoken on board/this ship is for those who want to cruise on a very modest budget, in reasonably comfortable surroundings, and don't mind the lack of finesse.

Odysseus

Principal Cruising Areas:
Aegean/Mediterranean

Ship	mts Odysseus	Passenger Space Ratio (basis 2)	21.9
Cruise Line/Operator	Epirotiki Lines	Passenger Space Ratio (all berths)	19.9
Formerly Aquamarine/Marco Polo/Isabela		Officers Greek	Service Staff Greek
Gross Registered Tonnage	9,272	Total Cabins 211	Cabin Door Width 24''
Built Española Shipyard (Spain)		Outside 171 Inside 40	Single No
First Entered Service	1962	Wheelchair Accessible Cabins	No
Last Refurbished	1988	Dining Rooms 1	Sittings 2
Country of Registry	Greece	Number of Elevators 1	Door Width 30''
Radio Call Sign	n/a	Electric Current in Cabins	220 AC
Satellite Telephone Number	n/a	Casino Yes	Slot Machines Yes
Length 483 ft./147.3 m. Beam 61 ft./18.7 m.		Swimming Pools Outside 1	Inside No
Engines	2×diesels	Whirlpools	1
Passenger Decks	7	Gymnasium Yes Sauna Yes	Massage Yes
Number of Crew	225	Cinema/Theatre No	Number of Seats –
Passenger Capacity (basis 2)	422	Cabin TV No	Library Yes
Passenger Capacity (all berths)	465	Children's Facilities/Playroom	No

Ratings

Ship Appearance/Condition	–	Shore Excursion Program	–
Interior Cleanliness	–	Entertainment	–
Passenger Space	–	Activities Program	–
Passenger Comfort Level	–	Cruise Director/Cruise Staff	–
Furnishings/Decor	–	Ship's Officers/Staff	–
Cruise Cuisine	–	Fitness/Sports Facilities	–
Food Service	–	Overall Ship Facilities	–
Beverages/Service	–	Value for Money	–
Accommodations	–	Total Cruise Experience	–
Cabin Service	–	**Overall Rating**	**–**
Itineraries/Destinations	–	**Average**	**–**

Comments

Newly acquired by Epirotiki, this is an attractive-looking vessel/although laid up for several years, it is well maintained/now extensively refurbished/has ample open deck and sunning space/same interior designer as on *Pegasus*/twin teak-decked sheltered promenades/good public rooms feature pleasing Mediterranean decor/ Taverna is especially popular/attractive mostly outside cabins have convertible sofa-bed, good closet and drawer space, and wood trim/dining room is quite charming/food is typically continental, and features several Greek dishes/warm, attentive service in true Epirotiki style/this ship is for those who want to cruise at modest cost on a very comfortable vessel. (Not rated at press time)

Orient Express ★★★+

Principal Cruising Areas:
Iberia/Mediterranean

Ship	mv Orient Express
Cruise Line/Operator	Orient Express
Former Names	Club Sea/Silja Star/Bore Star
Gross Registered Tonnage	12,343
Built	Chantiers de l'Atlantique (France)
First Entered Service	1975
Last Refurbished	1988
Country of Registry	Bermuda
Radio Call Sign	VSBR3
Satellite Telephone Number	1105126
Length 496 ft./151.3 m.	Beam 72 ft./21.9 m.
Engines	4×Pielstick diesels
Passenger Decks	7
Number of Crew	200
Passenger Capacity (basis 2)	670
Passenger Capacity (all berths)	693

Passenger Space Ratio (basis 2)	18.4
Passenger Space Ratio (all berths)	17.8
Officers British	Service Staff International
Total Cabins 335*	Cabin Door Width 27"
Outside 159 Inside 176	Single No
Wheelchair Accessible Cabins	4
Dining Rooms 4	Sittings Open
Number of Elevators 3	Door Width 30"
Electric Current in Cabins	220 AC
Casino Yes	Slot Machines Yes
Swimming Pools Outside 1	Inside 1
Whirlpools	No
Gymnasium No Sauna Yes	Massage No
Cinema/Theatre No	Number of Seats –
Cabin TV No	Library Yes
Children's Facilities/Playroom	Yes

* 272 refurbished

Ratings

Ship Appearance/Condition	80	Shore Excursion Program	74
Interior Cleanliness	82	Entertainment	75
Passenger Space	80	Activities Program	75
Passenger Comfort Level	81	Cruise Director/Cruise Staff	78
Furnishings/Decor	81	Ship's Officers/Staff	82
Cruise Cuisine	82	Fitness/Sports Facilities	78
Food Service	82	Overall Ship Facilities	80
Beverages/Service	81	Value for Money	81
Accommodations	80	Total Cruise Experience	81
Cabin Service	82	**Overall Rating**	**1596**
Itineraries/Destinations	81	**Average**	**79.8**

Comments

Despite a decidedly ungainly, boxy look, this cruise-ferry has been tastefully converted inside/ocean-going sister to the famous train, but with more awkward layout and poor passenger flow/extremely well maintained and run/enables passengers to take their cars and enjoy a cruise/smart interior decor and quality furnishings/four restaurants to choose from, one with à la carte menu/food ranges from fair to excellent/service is very good/choice of six types of cabins, all well appointed/ten special cabins have been created, each named after a carriage on the famous pullman train of the same name/this ship gives car-carrying passengers flexibility combined with a fine cruise experience at a decent price.

Orpheus ★ ★ ★

Principal Cruising Areas:
Aegean / Mediterranean

Ship	mts Orpheus	Passenger Space Ratio (basis 2)		16.6
Cruise Line / Operator	Epirotiki Lines	Passenger Space Ratio (all berths)		14.7
Former Names	Thesus / Munster	Officers Greek		Service Staff Greek
Gross Registered Tonnage	5,092	Total Cabins 159	Cabin Door Width 24"	
Built	Harland & Wolff (UK)	Outside 117	Inside 42	Single 7
First Entered Service	1952	Wheelchair Accessible Cabins		No
Last Refurbished	1983	Dining Rooms 1		Sittings 2
Country of Registry	Greece	Number of Elevators 1	Door Width 30"	
Radio Call Sign	SXUI	Electric Current in Cabins		220 DC
Satellite Telephone Number	–	Casino Yes	Slot Machines Yes	
Length 353 ft. / 107.5 m.	Beam 51 ft. / 15.5 m.	Swimming Pools Outside 1		Inside No
Engines	2 × B&W diesels	Whirlpools		No
Passenger Decks	6	Gymnasium No Sauna No	Massage No	
Number of Crew	140	Cinema / Theatre No	Number of Seats –	
Passenger Capacity (basis 2)	306	Cabin TV No		Library Yes
Passenger Capacity (all berths)	346	Children's Facilities / Playroom		No

Ratings

Ship Appearance / Condition	76	Shore Excursion Program	76
Interior Cleanliness	80	Entertainment	77
Passenger Space	76	Activities Program	76
Passenger Comfort Level	78	Cruise Director / Cruise Staff	76
Furnishings / Decor	79	Ship's Officers / Staff	77
Cruise Cuisine	79	Fitness / Sports Facilities	66
Food Service	79	Overall Ship Facilities	75
Beverages / Service	77	Value for Money	80
Accommodations	78	Total Cruise Experience	81
Cabin Service	79	**Overall Rating**	**1543**
Itineraries / Destinations	78	**Average**	**77.1**

Comments

Traditional ship profile, with small, squat funnel / charming and well maintained / ample open deck and sunning space / neat water slide into swimming pool / very comfortable public rooms, with Mediterranean decor, and nice artworks / pretty dining room / attentive, friendly service / newly refurbished cabins are compact, but nicely appointed and more than adequate / homely ambiance to this small ship, which is chartered to Swan Hellenic for life-enrichment cruises / excellent guest lecturers give informed, but informal, presentations on all cruises / this ship will provide a very comfortable two-week cruise experience in informal style, at a very reasonable price.

Pacific Princess ★★★★+

Principal Cruising Areas:
Caribbean/Mediterranean/Scandinavia

Ship	mv Pacific Princess
Cruise Line/Operator	Princess Cruises
Former Names	Sea Venture
Gross Registered Tonnage	20,000
Built Rheinstahl Nordseewerke (W. Germany)	
First Entered Service	1971
Last Refurbished	1984
Country of Registry	Great Britain
Radio Call Sign	GBLF
Satellite Telephone Number	1440212
Length 550 ft./167.6 m.	Beam 80 ft./24.3 m.
Engines	4×GMT diesels
Passenger Decks	7
Number of Crew	350
Passenger Capacity (basis 2)	624
Passenger Capacity (all berths)	624

Passenger Space Ratio (basis 2)	32.0
Passenger Space Ratio (all berths)	32.0
Officers British	Service Staff International
Total Cabins 316	Cabin Door Width 22–33"
Outside 245	Inside 71 Single 6
Wheelchair Accessible Cabins	4
Dining Rooms 1	Sittings 2
Number of Elevators 4	Door Width 37"
Electric Current in Cabins	110 AC
Casino Yes	Slot Machines Yes
Swimming Pools Outside 2	Inside No
Whirlpools	No
Gymnasium Yes Sauna Yes	Massage Yes
Cinema/Theatre Yes	Number of Seats 250
Cabin TV No	Library Yes
Children's Facilities/Playroom	No

Ratings

Ship Appearance/Condition	86	Shore Excursion Program	82
Interior Cleanliness	89	Entertainment	86
Passenger Space	87	Activities Program	79
Passenger Comfort Level	86	Cruise Director/Cruise Staff	82
Furnishings/Decor	86	Ship's Officers/Staff	81
Cruise Cuisine	85	Fitness/Sports Facilities	80
Food Service	84	Overall Ship Facilities	84
Beverages/Service	83	Value for Money	84
Accommodations	82	Total Cruise Experience	86
Cabin Service	83	**Overall Rating**	**1680**
Itineraries/Destinations	85	**Average**	**84.0**

Comments

Although the superstructure is high, this is a very attractive ship, with graceful lines/ extremely spacious public areas, open deck and sunning spaces/one swimming pool has magrodome for inclement weather/ tasteful earth-toned decor throughout/ lovely theatre/suites and all other cabins are quite roomy, and well appointed/ dining room is set low down, but has light decor and is spacious/excellent Italian service and very good food/excellent production shows and entertainment/very smartly dressed officers and crew/this ship is elegant, and moderately expensive, but will cruise you in superb style and comfort.

Pegasus ★★★ +

Principal Cruising Areas:
Aegean/Mediterranean/South America

Ship	mts Pegasus	Passenger Space Ratio (basis 2)		25.5
Cruise Line/Operator	Epirotiki Lines	Passenger Space Ratio (all berths)		21.0
Former Names	Sun Dancer/Svea Corona	Officers Greek		Service Staff Greek
Gross Registered Tonnage	17,500	Total Cabins 343		Cabin Door Width 24"
Built	Chantiers de l'Atlantique (France)	Outside 190	Inside 153	Single 76*
First Entered Service	1975	Wheelchair Accessible Cabins		No
Last Refurbished	1986	Dining Rooms 1		Sittings 2
Country of Registry	Greece	Number of Elevators 4		Door Width 30"
Radio Call Sign	SWPL	Electric Current in Cabins		110 AC
Satellite Telephone Number	1130111	Casino Yes		Slot Machines Yes
Length 473 ft./144.1 m.	Beam 72 ft./21.9 m.	Swimming Pools Outside 1		Inside 1
Engines	4×Pielstick diesels	Whirlpools		2
Passenger Decks	9	Gymnasium Yes	Sauna Yes	Massage Yes
Number of Crew	230	Cinema/Theatre Yes (2) Number of Seats 40/25		
Passenger Capacity (basis 2)	686	Cabin TV No		Library Yes
Passenger Capacity (all berths)	832	Children's Facilities/Playroom		No
		* with added upper		

Ratings

Ship Appearance/Condition	81	Shore Excursion Program	80
Interior Cleanliness	82	Entertainment	77
Passenger Space	76	Activities Program	76
Passenger Comfort Level	81	Cruise Director/Cruise Staff	79
Furnishings/Decor	81	Ship's Officers/Staff	80
Cruise Cuisine	80	Fitness/Sports Facilities	78
Food Service	79	Overall Ship Facilities	80
Beverages/Service	78	Value for Money	82
Accommodations	78	Total Cruise Experience	81
Cabin Service	80	**Overall Rating**	**1590**
Itineraries/Destinations	81	**Average**	**79.5**

Comments

Gleaming white ship has rather ungainly, high-sided profile with stubby stern and tall funnels/good open deck and sunning space/extensively refurbished, now with smart, contemporary interior decor and colors/except for three large suites, most cabins are compact, but nicely appointed, with nice blond woods used in many/even the hospital has a name on this ship—"Hippocrates" of course/excellent indoor spa-fitness center/large dining room has very comfortable chairs and big picture windows/good service/continental cuisine/ this ship provides a fine cruise experience with most of the trimmings, at a down-to-earth price.

Polaris

Principal Cruising Areas:
Worldwide Expedition Cruises

Ship	ms Polaris	Passenger Space Ratio (basis 2)		27.3
Cruise Line/Operator	Special Expeditions	Passenger Space Ratio (all berths)		27.3
Former Names	Lindblad Polaris/Oresund	Officers Swedish	Service Staff Filipino	
Gross Registered Tonnage	2,214	Total Cabins 42	Cabin Door Width 24"	
Built	Aalborg Vaerft (Denmark)	Outside 42	Inside No	Single No
First Entered Service	1960	Wheelchair Accessible Cabins		No
Last Refurbished	1987	Dining Rooms 1	Sittings 1	
Country of Registry	Bahamas	Number of Elevators 0	Door Width –	
Radio Call Sign	C6CB8	Electric Current in Cabins		220 AC
Satellite Telephone Number	1104424	Casino No	Slot Machines No	
Length 238 ft./72.5 m.	Beam 43 ft./13.1 m.	Swimming Pools Outside No	Inside No	
Engines	2×Nohab Polar diesels	Whirlpools		No
Passenger Decks	4	Gymnasium No	Sauna Yes	Massage No
Number of Crew	40	Cinema/Theatre No	Number of Seats –	
Passenger Capacity (basis 2)	81	Cabin TV No	Library Yes	
Passenger Capacity (all berths)	81	Children's Facilities/Playroom		No

Ratings

Ship Appearance/Condition	–	Shore Excursion Program	–
Interior Cleanliness	–	Entertainment	–
Passenger Space	–	Activities Program	–
Passenger Comfort Level	–	Cruise Director/Cruise Staff	–
Furnishings/Decor	–	Ship's Officers/Staff	–
Cruise Cuisine	–	Fitness/Sports Facilities	–
Food Service	–	Overall Ship Facilities	–
Beverages/Service	–	Value for Money	–
Accommodations	–	Total Cruise Experience	–
Cabin Service	–	**Overall Rating**	–
Itineraries/Destinations	–	**Average**	–

Comments

Expedition cruise vessel of modest proportions has dark blue hull and gleaming white superstructure/completely refurbished recently/carries eight rubber Zodiacs for in-depth excursions and landings/elegant Scandinavian interior furnishings and decor, with lots of wood trim/restful, well-stocked library/cabins are quite roomy for ship size, and nicely appointed/friendly, intimate atmosphere on board/limited entertainment, of course, but the ship has a good library/really excellent food and service/this is a delightful vessel to choose for your expeditions cruise experience. Overall rating 4+ stars.

Queen Elizabeth 2 ★★★★★+ to ★★★★+

Principal Cruising Areas:
Scheduled Trans-Atlantic Service/Bermuda/Caribbean/Iberia/
Mediterranean/World Cruise

Ship	tsmv Queen Elizabeth 2	Passenger Space Ratio (basis 2)	36.6
Cruise Line/Operator	Cunard Line	Passenger Space Ratio (all berths)	35.5
Former Names	–	Officers British Service Staff: British/International	
Gross Registered Tonnage	66,451	Total Cabins 957 Cabin Door Width 26–31"	
Built	Upper Clyde Shipbuilders (UK)	Outside 672 Inside 285 Single 110	
First Entered Service	1969	Wheelchair Accessible Cabins	2
Last Refurbished	1987	Dining Rooms 4 Sittings 1	
Country of Registry	Great Britain	Number of Elevators 13 Door Width 36"	
Radio Call Sign	GBTT	Electric Current in Cabins 110/220 AC	
Satellite Telephone Number	1440301	Casino Yes Slot Machines Yes	
Length 963 ft./293.5 m. Beam 105 ft./32 m.		Swimming Pools Outside 2 Inside 2	
Engines	9×MAN B&W diesels	Whirlpools	4
Passenger Decks	13	Gymnasium Yes Sauna Yes Massage Yes	
Number of Crew	1015	Cinema/Theatre Yes Number of Seats 531	
Passenger Capacity (basis 2)	1814	Cabin TV Yes Library Yes	
Passenger Capacity (all berths)	1870	Children's Facilities/Playroom Yes	

Comments Trans-Atlantic Crossings

Constructed as a dual-purpose Trans-Atlantic superliner/also goes cruising in style/incredibly extensive refit exchanged steam turbines for diesel propulsion for even greater speed and more reliability/fastest passenger ship in service/at speeds over 30 knots some vibration is evident at the stern, as on any fast ship/features the most extensive facilities of any passenger ship afloat/QE2 is a veritable city at sea, and, like any city, there are several parts of town/although brochures give two classes for Trans-Atlantic travel, First-Class and Trans-Atlantic-Class, there are in fact *three* distinct classes: Grill-Class, First-Class and Trans-Atlantic-Class/Grill-Class accommodations consist of suites and luxury outside cabins, with dining in one of two Grill Rooms: Queen's Grill and Princess Grill (5+ and 5 stars)/First-Class accommodations consist of outside double cabins, and inside and outside single cabins, with dining in the Columbia Restaurant (4+ stars)/

Trans-Atlantic-Class accommodations feature lower-priced cabin grades, with dining in the Mauretania Restaurant (4 stars)/all passengers enjoy use of all public rooms, except Queen's Grill Lounge—reserved for Grill-Class passengers only/one sitting in all restaurants/expanded Queen's Grill (now too large, I feel) has separate galley, finest waiters and service, very formal atmosphere, and food that can be rated among the world's best when ordered off-menu/Princess Grill and Columbia Restaurant share same galley (special menu and Kosher food available), but service in the intimate Princess Grill is superior/beautiful Mauretania Restaurant has own galley, and much-improved menu, food and service/Grill-Class and First-Class passengers have separate deck space and assigned chairs/in Grill-Class and First-Class, this is truly the most refined, elegant way to cross the Atlantic.

Ratings

	(a)	(b)	(c)
Ship Appearance/Condition	92	92	90
Interior Cleanliness	95	93	86
Passenger Space	93	92	90
Passenger Comfort Level	95	94	90
Furnishings/Decor	93	92	90
Cruise Cuisine	95	91	87
Food Service	92	88	85
Beverages/Service	93	90	88
Accommodations	95	92	86
Cabin Service	90	88	84
Itineraries/Destinations	91	91	89

	(a)	(b)	(c)
Shore Excursion Program	87	87	87
Entertainment	87	87	87
Activities Program	85	85	85
Cruise Director/Cruise Staff	87	87	87
Ship's Officers/Staff	90	88	85
Fitness/Sports Facilities	88	88	88
Overall Ship Facilities	91	91	89
Value for Money	90	90	87
Total Cruise Experience	92	90	86
Overall Rating	1821	1796	1746
Average	91.0	89.8	87.3

(a) Grill-Class Accommodations 5 + stars
(b) First-Class Accommodations 5 stars
(c) Trans-Atlantic-Class Accommodations 4 + stars

Comments Cruises

After recent $130 million refurbishment, QE2's public rooms and passenger facilities are quite spectacular, and have better color coordination/cabins on Five Deck in need of refurbishing/twelve new penthouse suites added along extended art-deco passageway/dramatic Grand Lounge has three tiers, a horseshoe-shaped staircase and high-tech sound-and-light system/new Teen Center, Adult Center, and Sporting Center/new shopping concourse and extended deck/new executive Board Room/new Yacht Club is delightfully nautical—features a crystal-clear piano/new Safety Deposit Center and Passenger Accounts Office/new whirlpools added outside/new automated telephone system/completely refurbished: Queen's Room (chairs are ungainly), Theatre Bar, Midships Lobby, Beauty Salons, and all four restaurants (newly-named Mauretania Restaurant features superb vintage photos of former Cunarder of same name)/relocated Computer Center, Greenery (flower dispensary)/unchanged: superb Club Lido indoor-out-door center, elegant Midships Bar, Theatre, fine professionally run Library (books in five languages), Card Room, Player's Club Casino, Golden Door Spa/religious services, synagogue/British officers and seamanship, but hotel staff has changed to a British and multi-national mix, now quite attentive and service-oriented/consistently good entertainment and fine lecture-life enrichment programs/one class only for cruises, with dining room assigned according to accommodations chosen/one sitting in all dining rooms/much upgraded cuisine/better luncheon buffets, but midnight buffets poor/"Gold Card" credit system for all on-board purchases/excellent laundry and dry-cleaning facilities/wonderful English "nannies" and children's facilities/this ship offers truly refined living at sea for those able to travel in upper-grade accommodations/QE2 is the most perfectly integrated ship afloat, and she's fast/once you've cruised QE2—nothing else can compare, but the staff could still achieve better levels of service and attention.

Queen of Bermuda ★★★ +

Principal Cruising Areas:
Bermuda/Mexico

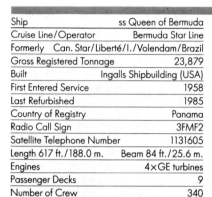

Ship	ss Queen of Bermuda	Passenger Space Ratio (basis 2)		33.3
Cruise Line/Operator	Bermuda Star Line	Passenger Space Ratio (all berths)		33.3
Formerly Can. Star/Liberté/I./Volendam/Brazil		Officers European	Service Staff International	
Gross Registered Tonnage	23,879	Total Cabins 358	Cabin Door Width 26"	
Built	Ingalls Shipbuilding (USA)	Outside 285	Inside 73	Single No
First Entered Service	1958	Wheelchair Accessible Cabins		No
Last Refurbished	1985	Dining Rooms 1		Sittings 2
Country of Registry	Panama	Number of Elevators 3	Door Width 30–33"	
Radio Call Sign	3FMF2	Electric Current in Cabins		110 AC
Satellite Telephone Number	1131605	Casino Yes	Slot Machines Yes	
Length 617 ft./188.0 m. Beam 84 ft./25.6 m.		Swimming Pools Outside 2		Inside No
Engines	4×GE turbines	Whirlpools		No
Passenger Decks	9	Gymnasium Yes Sauna Yes	Massage Yes	
Number of Crew	340	Cinema/Theatre Yes	Number of Seats 200	
Passenger Capacity (basis 2)	715	Cabin TV Yes		Library Yes
Passenger Capacity (all berths)	715	Children's Facilities/Playroom		No

Ratings

Ship Appearance/Condition	81	Shore Excursion Program	78
Interior Cleanliness	85	Entertainment	79
Passenger Space	80	Activities Program	78
Passenger Comfort Level	82	Cruise Director/Cruise Staff	75
Furnishings/Decor	83	Ship's Officers/Staff	78
Cruise Cuisine	78	Fitness/Sports Facilities	78
Food Service	80	Overall Ship Facilities	78
Beverages/Service	78	Value for Money	80
Accommodations	81	Total Cruise Experience	81
Cabin Service	80	**Overall Rating**	**1593**
Itineraries/Destinations	80	**Average**	**71.6**

Comments

Classic medium-size ocean liner profile/ extensively refurbished/beautifully finished outdoor teakwood decks/spacious promenade areas/public rooms are spacious and well appointed, with pleasing decor and colors/Polynesian Showplace is especially good/charming dining room now sports large windows/menu choice somewhat limited, but service is attentive and comes with a smile/large, but much underused, casino/plenty of sheltered and open sunning space/two outdoor pools/hot pink disco is downright ugly/cabins are of a generous size, with nice, heavy-duty furniture and fittings/this ship provides an enjoyable cruise experience in comfort, and at a very reasonable price that's hard to beat.

Regent Sea ★★★★

Principal Cruising Areas:
Alaska/Caribbean

Ship	mv Regent Sea	Passenger Space Ratio (basis 2)	32.0
Cruise Line/Operator	Regency Cruises	Passenger Space Ratio (all berths)	29.2
Former Names San Paolo/Navarino/Gripsholm		Officers European	Service Staff International
Gross Registered Tonnage	22,785	Total Cabins 355	Cabin Door Width 31"
Built	Ansaldo Sestri-Ponente (Italy)	Outside 328 Inside 27	Single No
First Entered Service	1957	Wheelchair Accessible Cabins	3
Last Refurbished	1985	Dining Rooms 1	Sittings 2
Country of Registry	Panama	Number of Elevators 4	Door Width 30"
Radio Call Sign	3EMU3	Electric Current in Cabins	110 AC
Satellite Telephone Number	1331736	Casino Yes	Slot Machines Yes
Length 620 ft./188.9 m. Beam 82 ft./24.9 m.		Swimming Pools Outside 1	Inside No
Engines	2×Gotaverken diesels	Whirlpools	1
Passenger Decks	9	Gymnasium Yes Sauna Yes	Massage Yes
Number of Crew	300	Cinema/Theatre Yes	Number of Seats 218
Passenger Capacity (basis 2)	712	Cabin TV No	Library Yes
Passenger Capacity (all berths)	780	Children's Facilities/Playroom	No

Ratings

Ship Appearance/Condition	82	Shore Excursion Program	77
Interior Cleanliness	82	Entertainment	78
Passenger Space	76	Activities Program	77
Passenger Comfort Level	82	Cruise Director/Cruise Staff	80
Furnishings/Decor	82	Ship's Officers/Staff	80
Cruise Cuisine	80	Fitness/Sports Facilities	80
Food Service	81	Overall Ship Facilities	81
Beverages/Service	78	Value for Money	82
Accommodations	82	Total Cruise Experience	81
Cabin Service	80	**Overall Rating**	**1601**
Itineraries/Destinations	80	**Average**	**80.0**

Comments

Well-constructed former ocean liner has classic lines and styling/one of only a handful of two-funnel ships/generous open deck and sunning space/rich, burnished wood trim in fine condition/distinct European flair evident in decor, furnishings and colors/welcoming public rooms are spacious and well appointed/dining room is bright and cheerful, and offers continental cuisine/mostly outside cabins are of generous proportions, with ample closet and drawer space/lively casino action/very attentive service/this ship will cruise you in fine style reminiscent of bygone days, and at a modest price.

Regent Star ★★★ +

Principal Cruising Areas:
Caribbean

Ship	mv Regent Star	Passenger Space Ratio (basis 2)	24.8
Cruise Line/Operator	Regency Cruises	Passenger Space Ratio (all berths)	24.2
Former Names	Statendam/Rhapsody	Officers European	Service Staff International
Gross Registered Tonnage	24,214	Total Cabins 487	Cabin Door Width 28"
Built	Wilton-Fijenoord (Holland)	Outside 300 Inside 187	Single No
First Entered Service	1957	Wheelchair Accessible Cabins	No
Last Refurbished	1987	Dining Rooms 1	Sittings 2
Country of Registry	Bahamas	Number of Elevators 2	Door Width 36"
Radio Call Sign	C6DY	Electric Current in Cabins	110 AC
Satellite Telephone Number	1104137	Casino Yes	Slot Machines Yes
Length 642 ft./195.6 m. Beam 79 ft./24.0 m.		Swimming Pools Outside 1	Inside 1
Engines	4×SWD diesels	Whirlpools	No
Passenger Decks	9	Gymnasium Yes Sauna Yes	Massage Yes
Number of Crew	450	Cinema/Theatre Yes	Number of Seats 330
Passenger Capacity (basis 2)	974	Cabin TV No	Library Yes
Passenger Capacity (all berths)	1000	Children's Facilities/Playroom	No

Ratings

Ship Appearance/Condition	80	Shore Excursion Program	78
Interior Cleanliness	81	Entertainment	78
Passenger Space	80	Activities Program	77
Passenger Comfort Level	82	Cruise Director/Cruise Staff	80
Furnishings/Decor	81	Ship's Officers/Staff	80
Cruise Cuisine	80	Fitness/Sports Facilities	81
Food Service	81	Overall Ship Facilities	79
Beverages/Service	78	Value for Money	81
Accommodations	79	Total Cruise Experience	81
Cabin Service	80	**Overall Rating**	**1597**
Itineraries/Destinations	80	**Average**	**79.8**

Comments

Well-constructed vessel with classic former ocean liner profile/recent extensive refurbishment has upgraded interior spaces and public rooms/reasonable amount of open deck and sunning space/good array of public rooms, with tasteful decor and colors/excellent indoor spa-fitness center/very comfortable dining room features raised center ceiling/European-style service and continental cuisine/outside cabins are quite roomy and nicely furnished/inside cabins are quite small/many cabins feature full bathtub/this ship offers a well-tuned cruise experience in very comfortable surroundings.

Regent Sun ★★★★

Principal Cruising Areas:
Alaska/Caribbean

Ship	ss Regent Sun
Cruise Line/Operator	Regency Cruises
Formerly	Royal Odyssey/Doric/Hanseatic
Gross Registered Tonnage	25,500
Built	Chantiers de l'Atlantique (France)
First Entered Service	1964
Last Refurbished	1988
Country of Registry	Greece
Radio Call Sign	SVBD
Satellite Telephone Number	1130406
Length 627 ft./191.1 m.	Beam 81 ft./24.6 m.
Engines	4×Parsons turbines
Passenger Decks	9
Number of Crew	360
Passenger Capacity (basis 2)	816
Passenger Capacity (all berths)	816

Passenger Space Ratio (basis 2)	31.2
Passenger Space Ratio (all berths)	31.2
Officers European	Service Staff International
Total Cabins 409	Cabin Door Width 27"
Outside 335	Inside 74 · Single 2
Wheelchair Accessible Cabins	No
Dining Rooms 1	Sittings 2
Number of Elevators 5	Door Width 29"
Electric Current in Cabins	110 AC
Casino Yes	Slot Machines Yes
Swimming Pools Outside 1	Inside 1
Whirlpools	No
Gymnasium Yes · Sauna Yes	Massage Yes
Cinema/Theatre Yes	Number of Seats 275
Cabin TV No	Library Yes
Children's Facilities/Playroom	No

Ratings

Ship Appearance/Condition	82
Interior Cleanliness	82
Passenger Space	82
Passenger Comfort Level	83
Furnishings/Decor	82
Cruise Cuisine	79
Food Service	80
Beverages/Service	78
Accommodations	82
Cabin Service	80
Itineraries/Destinations	80

Shore Excursion Program	78
Entertainment	78
Activities Program	77
Cruise Director/Cruise Staff	80
Ship's Officers/Staff	80
Fitness/Sports Facilities	81
Overall Ship Facilities	81
Value for Money	81
Total Cruise Experience	83
Overall Rating	**1609**
Average	**80.4**

Comments

Good-looking ship with classic profile and pleasing lines/spacious interior features two enclosed promenades and lots of public rooms to choose from/delightful, contemporary, yet elegant, decor and colors/all cabins are spacious, and come very nicely furnished, with plenty of closet, drawer and storage space/cabins on top deck have lifeboat-obstructed views/ attractive dining room/continental cuisine and service with a smile/this ship is the nicest of Regency's fleet of three, and will cruise you in fine style and comfort, but I wish they hadn't added those extra cabins.

Romanza ★★

Principal Cruising Areas:
Aegean / Mediterranean

Ship	mv Romanza	Passenger Space Ratio (basis 2)	13.4
Cruise Line/Operator	Chandris Fantasy Cruises	Passenger Space Ratio (all berths)	13.2
Former Names	Aurelia/Beaverbrae/Huscaran	Officers Greek	Service Staff International
Gross Registered Tonnage	7,537	Total Cabins 281	Cabin Door Width 22"
Built	Blohm & Voss (W. Germany)	Outside 135	Inside 146	Single 8
First Entered Service	1939	Wheelchair Accessible Cabins	No
Last Refurbished	1987	Dining Rooms 1	Sittings 2
Country of Registry	Panama	Number of Elevators 0	Door Width No
Radio Call Sign	HPKB	Electric Current in Cabins	220 AC
Satellite Telephone Number	–	Casino Yes	Slot Machines Yes
Length 488 ft./148.7 m.	Beam 60 ft./18.2 m.	Swimming Pools Outside 1	Inside No
Engines	3×MAN diesels	Whirlpools	No
Passenger Decks	7	Gymnasium No Sauna No	Massage No
Number of Crew	250	Cinema/Theatre Yes	Number of Seats 204
Passenger Capacity (basis 2)	562	Cabin TV No	Library Yes
Passenger Capacity (all berths)	570	Children's Facilities/Playroom	No

Ratings

Ship Appearance/Condition	66	Shore Excursion Program	70
Interior Cleanliness	74	Entertainment	75
Passenger Space	66	Activities Program	70
Passenger Comfort Level	72	Cruise Director/Cruise Staff	76
Furnishings/Decor	72	Ship's Officers/Staff	78
Cruise Cuisine	78	Fitness/Sports Facilities	54
Food Service	76	Overall Ship Facilities	64
Beverages/Service	76	Value for Money	78
Accommodations	69	Total Cruise Experience	80
Cabin Service	78	**Overall Rating**	**1448**
Itineraries/Destinations	76	**Average**	**72.4**

Comments

Well-constructed ship of vintage years; despite her age, she is well maintained/ reasonable open deck and sunning space/ high-density vessel is extremely popular with Europeans/good public rooms, but crowded when ship is full/interior decor is typically Mediterranean/cabins are very small/service is attentive/ship operates in four languages/constant announcements are irritating/charming dining room/reasonable food seldom arrives hot/this ship is ideal for those wanting to cruise the Mediterranean in reasonable comfort, at a great price.

Rotterdam ★★★★ +

Principal Cruising Areas:
Alaska / Caribbean

Ship	ss Rotterdam	Passenger Space Ratio (basis 2)		34.7
Cruise Line / Operator	Holland America Line	Passenger Space Ratio (all berths)		30.9
Former Names	–	Officers Dutch	Service Staff Filipino / Indonesian	
Gross Registered Tonnage	38,645	Total Cabins 575	Cabin Door Width 25–27"	
Built	Rotterdamsche Dry Dock (Holland)	Outside 307	Inside 268	Single 32
First Entered Service	1959	Wheelchair Accessible Cabins		No
Last Refurbished	1972	Dining Rooms 2		Sittings 2
Country of Registry	Netherlands Antilles	Number of Elevators 7	Door Width 31"	
Radio Call Sign	PJSU	Electric Current in Cabins		110 AC
Satellite Telephone Number	1750101	Casino Yes	Slot Machines Yes	
Length 748 ft. / 227.9 m.	Beam 94 ft. / 28.6 m.	Swimming Pools Outside 1	Inside 1	
Engines	6 × Parsons turbines	Whirlpools		No
Passenger Decks	10	Gymnasium Yes Sauna Yes	Massage Yes	
Number of Crew	603	Cinema / Theatre Yes	Number of Seats 620	
Passenger Capacity (basis 2)	1114	Cabin TV No	Library Yes	
Passenger Capacity (all berths)	1250	Children's Facilities / Playroom		No

Ratings

Ship Appearance / Condition	82	Shore Excursion Program	82
Interior Cleanliness	86	Entertainment	83
Passenger Space	86	Activities Program	82
Passenger Comfort Level	86	Cruise Director / Cruise Staff	82
Furnishings / Decor	82	Ship's Officers / Staff	84
Cruise Cuisine	85	Fitness / Sports Facilities	83
Food Service	86	Overall Ship Facilities	84
Beverages / Service	83	Value for Money	85
Accommodations	84	Total Cruise Experience	86
Cabin Service	85	**Overall Rating**	**1678**
Itineraries / Destinations	82	**Average**	**83.9**

Comments

Sturdily built ship has beautiful rounded lines / this grande dame is lovely—and loved / gracious and graceful, she is superbly maintained / expansive open deck space / numerous public rooms / gorgeous flower displays everywhere / acres of beautiful paneling and wood trim throughout / lovely balconied theatre / two-level Ritz Carlton is one of the most elegant art deco public rooms afloat / overly large casino seems completely out of place / two dining rooms offer refined dining, with excellent food and service / wide choice of cabin sizes and configurations, but all are comfortable, and well equipped / lots of cabins for single cruisers / a cruise on this ship fits as comfortably as a well-worn shoe, and the price is just right.

Royal Princess ★★★★★

Principal Cruising Areas:
Mediterranean/Trans-Canal

Ship	mv Royal Princess	Passenger Space Ratio (basis 2)		37.0
Cruise Line/Operator	Princess Cruises	Passenger Space Ratio (all berths)		35.2
Former Names	–	Officers British	Service Staff International	
Gross Registered Tonnage	44,348	Total Cabins 600	Cabin Door Width 24–30″	
Built	Wartsila (Finland)	Outside 600	Inside No	Single No
First Entered Service	1984	Wheelchair Accessible Cabins		No
Last Refurbished	–	Dining Rooms 1		Sittings 2
Country of Registry	Great Britain	Number of Elevators 6	Door Width 25–33″	
Radio Call Sign	GBRP	Electric Current in Cabins		110 AC
Satellite Telephone Number	1440211	Casino Yes	Slot Machines Yes	
Length 761 ft./231.9 m.	Beam 96 ft./29.2 m.	Swimming Pools Outside 4		Inside No
Engines	4×Pielstick diesels	Whirlpools		4
Passenger Decks	9	Gymnasium Yes	Sauna Yes	Massage Yes
Number of Crew	500	Cinema/Theatre Yes	Number of Seats 150	
Passenger Capacity (basis 2)	1200	Cabin TV Yes		Library Yes
Passenger Capacity (all berths)	1260	Children's Facilities/Playroom		No

Ratings

Ship Appearance/Condition	90	Shore Excursion Program	84
Interior Cleanliness	94	Entertainment	90
Passenger Space	92	Activities Program	83
Passenger Comfort Level	95	Cruise Director/Cruise Staff	84
Furnishings/Decor	92	Ship's Officers/Staff	86
Cruise Cuisine	86	Fitness/Sports Facilities	92
Food Service	83	Overall Ship Facilities	92
Beverages/Service	83	Value for Money	86
Accommodations	90	Total Cruise Experience	91
Cabin Service	88	**Overall Rating**	**1767**
Itineraries/Destinations	86	**Average**	**88.3**

Comments

Ultra-contemporary outer styling, with short, raked bow and angular stern/quality construction and materials/good deck space/excellent passenger flow/spacious passageways/all-outside cabins located above most public rooms are in unusual layout configurations/suites are simply gorgeous/all cabins are luxuriously equipped and have full bathtubs/some cabins on Baja and Caribe decks have views obstructed by lifeboats/beautifully appointed public rooms are all large/pity, but the ship has no small, intimate rooms/the Horizon Lounge has a superb vista/elegant dining room is set low down, adjacent to lobby/food and service excellent/this ship is beautiful, and will cruise you in spacious, elegant surroundings, at the appropriate price.

Royal Viking Sea ★★★★★ +

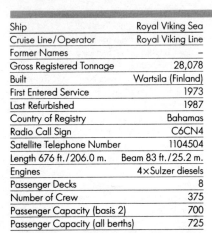

Principal Cruising Areas:
Worldwide

Ship	Royal Viking Sea	Passenger Space Ratio (basis 2)	40.1
Cruise Line/Operator	Royal Viking Line	Passenger Space Ratio (all berths)	38.7
Former Names	–	Officers Norwegian	Service Staff Scandinavian
Gross Registered Tonnage	28,078	Total Cabins 415	Cabin Door Width 24"
Built	Wartsila (Finland)	Outside 364 Inside 51	Single No
First Entered Service	1973	Wheelchair Accessible Cabins	No
Last Refurbished	1987	Dining Rooms 1	Sittings Open
Country of Registry	Bahamas	Number of Elevators 5	Door Width 35"
Radio Call Sign	C6CN4	Electric Current in Cabins	110/220 AC
Satellite Telephone Number	1104504	Casino Yes	Slot Machines Yes
Length 676 ft./206.0 m. Beam 83 ft./25.2 m.		Swimming Pools Outside 2	Inside No
Engines	4×Sulzer diesels	Whirlpools	No
Passenger Decks	8	Gymnasium Yes Sauna Yes	Massage Yes
Number of Crew	375	Cinema/Theatre Yes	Number of Seats 156
Passenger Capacity (basis 2)	700	Cabin TV Yes	Library Yes
Passenger Capacity (all berths)	725	Children's Facilities/Playroom	No

Ratings

Ship Appearance/Condition	91	Shore Excursion Program	92
Interior Cleanliness	95	Entertainment	91
Passenger Space	90	Activities Program	85
Passenger Comfort Level	95	Cruise Director/Cruise Staff	89
Furnishings/Decor	93	Ship's Officers/Staff	90
Cruise Cuisine	93	Fitness/Sports Facilities	90
Food Service	92	Overall Ship Facilities	91
Beverages/Service	92	Value for Money	88
Accommodations	93	Total Cruise Experience	92
Cabin Service	92	**Overall Rating**	**1829**
Itineraries/Destinations	95	**Average**	**91.4**

Comments

Contemporary profile, with well-balanced lines and beautifully raked bow/superbly maintained/excellent open deck and sunning space/elegant public rooms/improved fitness facilities/new casino with tasteful decor/lovely, spacious dining room provides distinguished dining and service in one unhurried sitting/cabins are extremely well appointed, and have ample closet, drawer and storage space/some bathrooms are awkward for access/bathrobes provided for all passengers/wonderful Scandinavian stewardesses/attention to detail apparent everywhere/this ship provides the discerning passenger with a superb cruise experience and utterly refined living at sea, at the appropriate price.

Royal Viking Sky ★★★★★ +

Principal Cruising Areas:
Worldwide

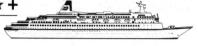

Ship	ms Royal Viking Sky	Passenger Space Ratio (basis 2)	40.1
Cruise Line/Operator	Royal Viking Line	Passenger Space Ratio (all berths)	38.7
Former Names	–	Officers Norwegian Service Staff Scandinavian	
Gross Registered Tonnage	28,078	Total Cabins 410 Cabin Door Width 24"	
Built	Wartsila (Finland)	Outside 359 Inside 51 Single No	
First Entered Service	1973	Wheelchair Accessible Cabins	No
Last Refurbished	1988	Dining Rooms 1 Sittings 2	
Country of Registry	Bahamas	Number of Elevators 5 Door Width 35"	
Radio Call Sign	C6CN3	Electric Current in Cabins	110/220 AC
Satellite Telephone Number	1104505/1104506	Casino Yes Slot Machines Yes	
Length 676 ft./206.0 m.	Beam 83 ft./25.2 m.	Swimming Pools Outside 2 Inside No	
Engines	4×Sulzer diesels	Whirlpools	No
Passenger Decks	8	Gymnasium Yes Sauna Yes Massage Yes	
Number of Crew	375	Cinema/Theatre Yes Number of Seats 156	
Passenger Capacity (basis 2)	700	Cabin TV Yes Library Yes	
Passenger Capacity (all berths)	725	Children's Facilities/Playroom	No

Ratings

Ship Appearance/Condition	91	Shore Excursion Program	92
Interior Cleanliness	95	Entertainment	91
Passenger Space	90	Activities Program	85
Passenger Comfort Level	95	Cruise Director/Cruise Staff	89
Furnishings/Decor	93	Ship's Officers/Staff	90
Cruise Cuisine	93	Fitness/Sports Facilities	90
Food Service	92	Overall Ship Facilities	91
Beverages/Service	92	Value for Money	88
Accommodations	93	Total Cruise Experience	92
Cabin Service	92	**Overall Rating**	**1829**
Itineraries/Destinations	95	**Average**	**91.4**

Comments

Twin sister to *Royal Viking Sea,* with same beautiful outer styling and good looks/recent refurbishment adds new casino location and excellent new fitness facilities/plenty of open deck and sunning space/tasteful Scandinavian decor throughout/lovely public rooms/elegant dining room provides setting for superb cuisine and true European service/penthouse suites are very spacious/all cabins are extremely well appointed, and have plenty of closet, drawer and storage space/some bathrooms awkward for access/fluffy cotton bathrobes provided/excellent Scandinavian stewardesses/worldwide cruising at its finest/this ship will cruise you in a truly elegant style, with finesse, grace, and everything that discriminating passengers would expect from a ship that is truly first-class.

Royal Viking Star ★★★★★

Principal Cruising Areas:
Worldwide

Ship	Royal Viking Star
Cruise Line/Operator	Royal Viking Line
Former Names	–
Gross Registered Tonnage	28,078
Built	Wartsila (Finland)
First Entered Service	1972
Last Refurbished	1981
Country of Registry	Bahamas
Radio Call Sign	C6CN2
Satellite Telephone Number	1104507/1104510
Length 676 ft./206.0 m.	Beam 83 ft./25.2 m.
Engines	4×Sulzer diesels
Passenger Decks	8
Number of Crew	375
Passenger Capacity (basis 2)	700
Passenger Capacity (all berths)	725

Passenger Space Ratio (basis 2)		40.1
Passenger Space Ratio (all berths)		38.7
Officers Norwegian	Service Staff Scandinavian	
Total Cabins 415	Cabin Door Width 24"	
Outside 367	Inside 48	Single No
Wheelchair Accessible Cabins		No
Dining Rooms 1		Sittings 1
Number of Elevators 5	Door Width 35"	
Electric Current in Cabins		110/220 AC
Casino Yes	Slot Machines Yes	
Swimming Pools Outside 2		Inside No
Whirlpools		No
Gymnasium Yes	Sauna Yes	Massage Yes
Cinema/Theatre Yes	Number of Seats 156	
Cabin TV Yes		Library Yes
Children's Facilities/Playroom		No

Ratings

Ship Appearance/Condition	91
Interior Cleanliness	92
Passenger Space	90
Passenger Comfort Level	93
Furnishings/Decor	92
Cruise Cuisine	90
Food Service	92
Beverages/Service	92
Accommodations	93
Cabin Service	92
Itineraries/Destinations	94

Shore Excursion Program	92
Entertainment	90
Activities Program	85
Cruise Director/Cruise Staff	88
Ship's Officers/Staff	90
Fitness/Sports Facilities	88
Overall Ship Facilities	90
Value for Money	88
Total Cruise Experience	91
Overall Rating	**1816**
Average	**90.8**

Comments

This ship, identical in outer styling to her sisters *Sea* and *Sky*, has enjoyed equal ratings and popularity/interior not refurbished however, due to her move to subsidiary company NCL's fleet/will be renamed Norwegian Star/to be converted for more popular-priced cruise service/as such, beginning in the spring of 1989, she will be less exclusive and less elegant/many more cabins to be added/present open dining to become two sittings/with a change of identity and personality, she'll never again be like her sister ships *Sea* and *Sky*. Rating reflects past facilities and service only.

Royal Viking Sun

Principal Cruising Areas:
Worldwide

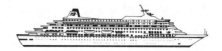

Ship	ms Royal Viking Sun		Passenger Space Ratio (basis 2)		51.3
Cruise Line/Operator	Royal Viking Line		Passenger Space Ratio (all berths)		49.3
Former Names	–		Officers Norwegian	Service Staff European	
Gross Registered Tonnage	38,000		Total Cabins 370	Cabin Door Width 31"	
Built	Wartsila (Finland)		Outside 355	Inside 15	Single No
First Entered Service	1988		Wheelchair Accessible Cabins		4
Last Refurbished	–		Dining Rooms 2	Sittings Open	
Country of Registry	Bahamas		Number of Elevators 4	Door Width 40"	
Radio Call Sign	C6DM3		Electric Current in Cabins		110 AC
Satellite Telephone Number	n/a		Casino Yes	Slot Machines Yes	
Length 673 ft./205.1 m.	Beam 92 ft./28.0 m.		Swimming Pools Outside 2	Inside No	
Engines	4×Sulzer diesels		Whirlpools		2
Passenger Decks	8		Gymnasium Yes	Sauna Yes	Massage Yes
Number of Crew	460		Cinema/Theatre Yes	Number of Seats 101	
Passenger Capacity (basis 2)	740		Cabin TV Yes	Library Yes	
Passenger Capacity (all berths)	770		Children's Facilities/Playroom		No

Ratings

Ship Appearance/Condition	–		Shore Excursion Program	–
Interior Cleanliness	–		Entertainment	–
Passenger Space	–		Activities Program	–
Passenger Comfort Level	–		Cruise Director/Cruise Staff	–
Furnishings/Decor	–		Ship's Officers/Staff	–
Cruise Cuisine	–		Fitness/Sports Facilities	–
Food Service	–		Overall Ship Facilities	–
Beverages/Service	–		Value for Money	–
Accommodations	–		Total Cruise Experience	–
Cabin Service	–		**Overall Rating**	**–**
Itineraries/Destinations	–		**Average**	**–**

Comments

Magnificent new vessel, unmistakably Royal Viking/ultra-contemporary ship has sleek, flowing lines, raked bow and well-rounded profile/incredibly spacious and well-designed interior/impressive public rooms/Observation Lounge is lovely/Grill Room high atop the ship is a sophisticated alternative dining spot/incredible penthouse suites/all cabins are big and have walk-in closets/wonderful Scandinavian stewardesses/the ship has it all for the discriminating passenger who demands the very finest in personal surroundings, food and service, regardless of price/this ship is simply beyond anything else in its class. (Not rated at press time, but will surpass *Sea* and *Sky*, based on shipyard inspection).

Sagafjord ★★★★★ +

Principal Cruising Areas:
Worldwide / World Cruise

Ship	ms Sagafjord	Passenger Space Ratio (basis 2)	41.5
Cruise Line / Operator	Cunard Line	Passenger Space Ratio (all berths)	39.5
Former Names	–	Officers Norwegian	Service Staff European
Gross Registered Tonnage	24,474	Total Cabins 321	Door Width 27"
Built	Forges et Chantiers (France)	Outside 298 Inside 23	Single 43
First Entered Service	1965	Wheelchair Accessible Cabins	13
Last Refurbished	1984	Dining Rooms 1	Sittings Open
Country of Registry	Bahamas	Number of Elevators 4	Door Width 28"
Radio Call Sign	C6ZU	Electric Current in Cabins	110 AC
Satellite Telephone Number	1104115	Casino Yes	Slot Machines Yes
Length 619 ft. / 188.6 m. Beam 82 ft. / 24.9 m.		Swimming Pools Outside 1	Inside 1
Engines	2 × Sulzer diesels	Whirlpools	1
Passenger Decks	7	Gymnasium Yes Sauna Yes	Massage Yes
Number of Crew	350	Cinema / Theatre Yes Number of Seats 181	
Passenger Capacity (basis 2)	589	Cabin TV Yes	Library Yes
Passenger Capacity (all berths)	620	Children's Facilities / Playroom	No

Ratings

Ship Appearance / Condition	95	Shore Excursion Program	92
Interior Cleanliness	93	Entertainment	86
Passenger Space	95	Activities Program	86
Passenger Comfort Level	95	Cruise Director / Cruise Staff	84
Furnishings / Decor	91	Ship's Officers / Staff	90
Cruise Cuisine	94	Fitness / Sports Facilities	90
Food Service	92	Overall Ship Facilities	92
Beverages / Service	92	Value for Money	90
Accommodations	92	Total Cruise Experience	95
Cabin Service	92	**Overall Rating**	**1829**
Itineraries / Destinations	93	**Average**	**91.4**

Comments

One of the most beautifully proportioned ships afloat / clean and graceful with well-rounded lines / superbly maintained and operated with pride / spacious interior, with ample public rooms to choose from / tasteful Scandinavian decor / finest quality furnishings and fittings throughout / sumptuous dining room / excellent, utterly creative cuisine using the finest ingredients / consistently supreme service in true European style / large, spacious suites and cabins, with superb appointments and every convenience / generous closet, drawer and storage space / soft cotton bathrobes provided / the *Sagafjord* will provide a sumptuous, truly refined life at sea for the most discriminating passenger, at the appropriate price.

Scandinavian Saga ★★

Principal Cruising Areas:
Bahamas/Nowhere

Ship	ms Scandinavian Saga	Passenger Space Ratio (basis 2)	37.5
Cruise Line/Operator	SeaEscape	Passenger Space Ratio (all berths)	9.5
Former Names	Castalia/Stena America	Officers Scandinavian Service Staff International	
Gross Registered Tonnage	10,000	Total Cabins 133 Cabin Door Width 23"	
Built	Kynoussaura Shipyard (Greece)	Outside 75 Inside 42 Single No	
First Entered Service	1975	Wheelchair Accessible Cabins No	
Last Refurbished	1988	Dining Rooms 1 Sittings 2	
Country of Registry	Bahamas	Number of Elevators 2 Door Width 29"	
Radio Call Sign	C6DP8	Electric Current in Cabins 220 AC	
Satellite Telephone Number	–	Casino Yes Slot Machines Yes	
Length 436 ft./132.8 m.	Beam 66 ft./20.1 m.	Swimming Pools Outside 1 Inside No	
Engines	2×Pielstick diesels	Whirlpools 1	
Passenger Decks	6	Gymnasium No Sauna No Massage No	
Number of Crew	200	Cinema/Theatre Yes Number of Seats n/a	
Passenger Capacity (basis 2)	266	Cabin TV No Library No	
Passenger Capacity (all berths)	1050	Children's Facilities/Playroom No	

Ratings

Ship Appearance/Condition	78	Shore Excursion Program	60
Interior Cleanliness	78	Entertainment	74
Passenger Space	76	Activities Program	73
Passenger Comfort Level	76	Cruise Director/Cruise Staff	70
Furnishings/Decor	76	Ship's Officers/Staff	75
Cruise Cuisine	76	Fitness/Sports Facilities	71
Food Service	76	Overall Ship Facilities	74
Beverages/Service	74	Value for Money	80
Accommodations	75	Total Cruise Experience	80
Cabin Service	76	**Overall Rating**	**1480**
Itineraries/Destinations	62	**Average**	**74.0**

Comments

Newest acquisition for SeaEscape, this handsome former cruise-ferry has a moderately raked bow and flat stern/car deck sensibly converted to a 540-seat showroom/public areas and cabins underwent major refurbishment/decor is contemporary and pleasing/expanded dining room now accommodates 440/theatre is the only real place to relax/fun ship for one-day and very short cruises, with non-stop entertainment and frivolity/extremely busy casino action/open deck and sunning space limited when ship full/food is Scandinavian in presentation, but choice is limited/tipping expected at each meal/caters to 1,050 day passengers, but has only 138 cabins/good value for money for a fun-filled day out, but it's not the same as a longer cruise.

Scandinavian Sky ★★

Principal Cruising Areas:
Bahamas/Nowhere

Ship	ms Scandinavian Sky
Cruise Line/Operator	SeaEscape
Former Names	Svea Regina/Odysseas Elytis
Gross Registered Tonnage	8,139
Built	Dubigeon-Normandie (France)
First Entered Service	1972
Last Refurbished	1985
Country of Registry	Bahamas
Radio Call Sign	C6BH4
Satellite Telephone Number	–
Length 416 ft./126.7 m.	Beam 64 ft./19.5 m.
Engines	2×Pielstick diesels
Passenger Decks	6
Number of Crew	230
Passenger Capacity (basis 2)	200
Passenger Capacity (all berths)	926

Passenger Space Ratio (basis 2)	40.6
Passenger Space Ratio (all berths)	8.7
Officers Scandinavian	Service Staff International
Total Cabins 100	Cabin Door Width 23″
Outside 58 Inside 42	Single No
Wheelchair Accessible Cabins	No
Dining Rooms 1	Sittings 2
Number of Elevators 2	Door Width 29″
Electric Current in Cabins	220 AC
Casino Yes	Slot Machines Yes
Swimming Pools Outside 1	Inside 1
Whirlpools	No
Gymnasium No Sauna No	Massage No
Cinema/Theatre No	Number of Seats –
Cabin TV No	Library No
Children's Facilities/Playroom	No

Ratings

Ship Appearance/Condition	74	Shore Excursion Program	62
Interior Cleanliness	77	Entertainment	73
Passenger Space	77	Activities Program	72
Passenger Comfort Level	78	Cruise Director/Cruise Staff	70
Furnishings/Decor	76	Ship's Officers/Staff	74
Cruise Cuisine	76	Fitness/Sports Facilities	69
Food Service	76	Overall Ship Facilities	76
Beverages/Service	74	Value for Money	80
Accommodations	74	Total Cruise Experience	80
Cabin Service	76	**Overall Rating**	**1480**
Itineraries/Destinations	66	**Average**	**74.0**

Comments

Former European passenger ferry has short bow, stubby stern, and twin tall funnels/only six lifeboats—not enough for full ship/open deck and sunning space limited when ship is full/fun ship for one-day or very short cruises, with non-stop entertainment and frivolity/constant action in casino/food is Scandinavian in presentation, but choice is limited/tipping expected at each meal/this ship caters to 1,000 day passengers, but has only 100 cabins/good value for money and fine for a quick fling, but it's not a real cruise.

Scandinavian Star ★★

Principal Cruising Areas:
Bahamas/Nowhere

Ship	ms Scandinavian Star	Passenger Space Ratio (basis 2)		38.0
Cruise Line/Operator	SeaEscape	Passenger Space Ratio (all berths)		10.5
Former Names	Massalia/Island Fiesta	Officers Scandinavian	Service Staff International	
Gross Registered Tonnage	10,513	Total Cabins 138	Cabin Door Width 24″	
Built	Dubigeon-Normandie (France)	Outside 65	Inside 73	Single No
First Entered Service	1972	Wheelchair Accessible Cabins		No
Last Refurbished	1984	Dining Rooms 1		Sittings 2
Country of Registry	Bahamas	Number of Elevators 2	Door Width 25″	
Radio Call Sign	C6BF	Electric Current in Cabins		220 AC
Satellite Telephone Number	–	Casino Yes	Slot Machines Yes	
Length 465 ft./141.8 m.	Beam 74 ft./22.7 m.	Swimming Pools Outside 1		Inside No
Engines	2×Pielstick diesels	Whirlpools		No
Passenger Decks	5	Gymnasium No Sauna No	Massage No	
Number of Crew	250	Cinema/Theatre No	Number of Seats –	
Passenger Capacity (basis 2)	276	Cabin TV No		Library No
Passenger Capacity (all berths)	1000	Children's Facilities/Playroom		No

Ratings

Ship Appearance/Condition	78	Shore Excursion Program	64
Interior Cleanliness	77	Entertainment	72
Passenger Space	76	Activities Program	71
Passenger Comfort Level	77	Cruise Director/Cruise Staff	70
Furnishings/Decor	76	Ship's Officers/Staff	74
Cruise Cuisine	76	Fitness/Sports Facilities	70
Food Service	76	Overall Ship Facilities	78
Beverages/Service	74	Value for Money	78
Accommodations	74	Total Cruise Experience	80
Cabin Service	76	**Overall Rating**	**1480**
Itineraries/Destinations	63	**Average**	**74.0**

Comments

Former European passenger ferry, with short bow, stubby stern and very tall twin funnels/open deck and sunning space cramped when ship is full/fun-filled action for one-day and very short cruises, with lively entertainment and frivolity/nowhere to relax/food is Scandinavian in presenta-tion, but choice is limited/tipping expected at each meal/very lively casino action/this ship caters to 1,000 day passengers but has only 143 cabins/good value for money for a day out, but it's nothing like a cruise of longer duration.

Scandinavian Sun ★★

Principal Cruising Areas:
Bahamas/Nowhere

Ship	Scandinavian Sun	Passenger Space Ratio (basis 2)	56.2
Cruise Line/Operator	SeaEscape	Passenger Space Ratio (all berths)	9.0
Formerly Freeport/Freeport I/Svea Star/Caribe		Officers Scandinavian Service Staff International	
Gross Registered Tonnage	9,903	Total Cabins 88 Cabin Door Width 24"	
Built Orenstein & Koppel (W. Germany)		Outside 75 Inside 13 Single 2	
First Entered Service	1968	Wheelchair Accessible Cabins No	
Last Refurbished	1982	Dining Rooms 1 Sittings 2	
Country of Registry	Bahamas	Number of Elevators 3 Door Width 24"	
Radio Call Sign	C6DN	Electric Current in Cabins 220 AC	
Satellite Telephone Number	–	Casino Yes Slot Machines Yes	
Length 441 ft./134.4 m. Beam 70 ft./21.3 m.		Swimming Pools Outside 1 Inside No	
Engines	2×Pielstick diesels	Whirlpools 1	
Passenger Decks	6	Gymnasium No Sauna No Massage No	
Number of Crew	250	Cinema/Theatre No Number of Seats –	
Passenger Capacity (basis 2)	176	Cabin TV No Library No	
Passenger Capacity (all berths)	1100	Children's Facilities/Playroom No	

Ratings

Ship Appearance/Condition	80	Shore Excursion Program	64
Interior Cleanliness	76	Entertainment	73
Passenger Space	76	Activities Program	72
Passenger Comfort Level	77	Cruise Director/Cruise Staff	71
Furnishings/Decor	74	Ship's Officers/Staff	74
Cruise Cuisine	76	Fitness/Sports Facilities	64
Food Service	76	Overall Ship Facilities	77
Beverages/Service	74	Value for Money	80
Accommodations	74	Total Cruise Experience	80
Cabin Service	76	**Overall Rating**	**1480**
Itineraries/Destinations	66	**Average**	**74.0**

Comments

Former European passenger ferry, then cruise ship, this nice-looking vessel has a pleasing profile/open deck and sunning space cramped when full/fun-filled activities and non-stop entertainment for day out or very short cruises but there's nowhere to relax/very lively casino action/food is Scandinavian in presentation, but choice is limited/tipping expected at each meal, even though it's buffet-style, which means long lines/caters to 1,100 day passengers, but has only 88 cabins/good value for money for a day's entertainment in the sun, but it is by no means like a cruise of longer duration, merely an attraction.

Sea Cloud ★★★★★

Principal Cruising Areas:
Caribbean/Mediterranean

Ship	sy Sea Cloud
Cruise Line/Operator	Sea Cloud Cruises
Former Names	Antaria/Patria/Angelita/Hussar
Gross Registered Tonnage	2,517
Built	Krupp Werft (W. Germany)
First Entered Service	1931
Last Refurbished	1984
Country of Registry	Malta
Radio Call Sign	9HOM2
Satellite Telephone Number	1756222
Length 316 ft./96.3 m.	Beam 49 ft./14.9 m.
Engines	4×Enterprise diesels/sail power
Passenger Decks	3
Number of Crew	60
Passenger Capacity (basis 2)	69
Passenger Capacity (all berths)	69

Passenger Space Ratio (basis 2)		36.4
Passenger Space Ratio (all berths)		36.4
Officers European	Service Staff European	
Total Cabins 37	Cabin Door Width 26"	
Outside 37	Inside No	Single No
Wheelchair Accessible Cabins		No
Dining Rooms 1		Sittings 1
Number of Elevators 0	Door Width –	
Electric Current in Cabins		110/220 AC
Casino No	Slot Machines No	
Swimming Pools Outside No		Inside No
Whirlpools		No
Gymnasium No	Sauna No	Massage No
Cinema/Theatre No	Number of Seats –	
Cabin TV No		Library Yes
Children's Facilities/Playroom		No

Ratings

Ship Appearance/Condition	–	Shore Excursion Program	–
Interior Cleanliness	–	Entertainment	–
Passenger Space	–	Activities Program	–
Passenger Comfort Level	–	Cruise Director/Cruise Staff	–
Furnishings/Decor	–	Ship's Officers/Staff	–
Cruise Cuisine	–	Fitness/Sports Facilities	–
Food Service	–	Overall Ship Facilities	–
Beverages/Service	–	Value for Money	–
Accommodations	–	Total Cruise Experience	–
Cabin Service	–	**Overall Rating**	–
Itineraries/Destinations	–	**Average**	–

Comments

This is the most beautiful tall ship sailing, and the largest private yacht ever built/ original owner was Marjorie Merriweather Post/30 sails cover an area of 34,000 square feet/assisted by diesel engines when not under sail/plenty of deck space/ incredibly fine handcrafted interior, with antique furniture, original oil paintings/ gorgeous wood paneling everywhere/two owner's suites are lavish, with Chippendale furniture, gilt detailing, a real fireplace, and Italian marble bathrooms/this is a special ship like no other, and is for the discerning few to relish the uncompromising comfort and elegance of a bygone era. Overall rating 5 stars, although scoring by categories above is not possible.

Sea Goddess I ★★★★★+

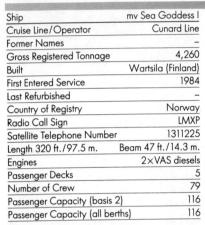

Principal Cruising Areas:
Baltic/Caribbean/Mediterranean/
Scandinavia

Ship	mv Sea Goddess I
Cruise Line/Operator	Cunard Line
Former Names	–
Gross Registered Tonnage	4,260
Built	Wartsila (Finland)
First Entered Service	1984
Last Refurbished	–
Country of Registry	Norway
Radio Call Sign	LMXP
Satellite Telephone Number	1311225
Length 320 ft./97.5 m.	Beam 47 ft./14.3 m.
Engines	2×VAS diesels
Passenger Decks	5
Number of Crew	79
Passenger Capacity (basis 2)	116
Passenger Capacity (all berths)	116

Passenger Space Ratio (basis 2)		36.7
Passenger Space Ratio (all berths)		36.7
Officers Norwegian	Service Staff Scandinavian	
Total Cabins 58	Cabin Door Width 24"	
Outside 58	Inside No	Single No
Wheelchair Accessible Cabins		No
Dining Rooms 1		Sittings Open
Number of Elevators 1	Door Width 31"	
Electric Current in Cabins		110/220 AC
Casino Yes		Slot Machines Yes
Swimming Pools Outside 1		Inside No
Whirlpools		1
Gymnasium Yes	Sauna Yes	Massage Yes
Cinema/Theatre No	Number of Seats –	
Cabin TV Yes		Library Yes
Children's Facilities/Playroom		No

Ratings

Ship Appearance/Condition	95
Interior Cleanliness	95
Passenger Space	88
Passenger Comfort Level	95
Furnishings/Decor	95
Cruise Cuisine	96
Food Service	94
Beverages/Service	96
Accommodations	95
Cabin Service	93
Itineraries/Destinations	93

Shore Excursion Program	85
Entertainment	85
Activities Program	83
Cruise Director/Cruise Staff	86
Ship's Officers/Staff	88
Fitness/Sports Facilities	88
Overall Ship Facilities	87
Value for Money	90
Total Cruise Experience	95
Overall Rating	**1822**
Average	**91.1**

Comments

Dramatic, ultra-sleek profile/meticulously maintained/has stern watersports platform/private club atmosphere/flowers everywhere/elegant, chic, public rooms and decor/finest quality furnishings and fabrics used throughout/elegant dining room, with leather-bound menus, beautiful crystalware and supremely attentive, highly personal service—or you can dine in-cabin at any time/plenty of superb caviar/cabins are fully-equipped, all-outside suites/refined, unstructured, private living at sea is the hallmark of a cruise on this vessel, and everything's included—even liquor and wine/this is lavish, civilized living at its best.

Sea Goddess II ★★★★★+

Principal Cruising Areas:
Mediterranean/Orient

Ship	mv Sea Goddess II		Passenger Space Ratio (basis 2)		36.7
Cruise Line/Operator	Cunard Line		Passenger Space Ratio (all berths)		36.7
Former Names	–		Officers Norwegian	Service Staff Scandinavian	
Gross Registered Tonnage	4,260		Total Cabins 58	Cabin Door Width 24"	
Built	Wartsila (Finland)		Outside 58	Inside No	Single No
First Entered Service	1985		Wheelchair Accessible Cabins		No
Last Refurbished	–		Dining Rooms 1		Sittings Open
Country of Registry	Norway		Number of Elevators 1		Door Width 31"
Radio Call Sign	LNQX		Electric Current in Cabins		110/220 AC
Satellite Telephone Number	1311235		Casino Yes		Slot Machines Yes
Length 320 ft./97.5 m.	Beam 47 ft./14.3 m.		Swimming Pools Outside 1		Inside No
Engines	2×VAS diesels		Whirlpools		1
Passenger Decks	5		Gymnasium Yes	Sauna Yes	Massage Yes
Number of Crew	79		Cinema/Theatre No	Number of Seats –	
Passenger Capacity (basis 2)	116		Cabin TV Yes		Library Yes
Passenger Capacity (all berths)	116		Children's Facilities/Playroom		No

Ratings

Ship Appearance/Condition	95		Shore Excursion Program	85
Interior Cleanliness	95		Entertainment	85
Passenger Space	88		Activities Program	83
Passenger Comfort Level	95		Cruise Director/Cruise Staff	86
Furnishings/Decor	95		Ship's Officers/Staff	88
Cruise Cuisine	96		Fitness/Sports Facilities	88
Food Service	94		Overall Ship Facilities	87
Beverages/Service	96		Value for Money	90
Accommodations	95		Total Cruise Experience	95
Cabin Service	93		**Overall Rating**	**1822**
Itineraries/Destinations	93		**Average**	**91.1**

Comments

Dramatic, ultra-sleek, contemporary profile/ immaculately run and maintained/lovely public rooms feature highest quality furnishings and decor throughout/charming, very elegant dining room/only the very freshest, highest-grade ingredients used/eat in-cabin or in the dining room/superb caviar, and plenty of it/lovely all-outside suites come fully equipped/finest personal service you can find today/this ship is for the discriminating person requiring an elegant environment in which to cruise in truly pampered, highly personal style/I can't think of a nicer or more sophisticated way to go cruising.

Sea Princess ★★★★ +

Principal Cruising Areas:
Alaska / Australasia / Orient / South Pacific

Ship	mv Sea Princess
Cruise Line/Operator	Princess Cruises
Former Names	Kungsholm
Gross Registered Tonnage	27,670
Built	John Brown & Co (UK)
First Entered Service	1966
Last Refurbished	1986
Country of Registry	Great Britain
Radio Call Sign	GBBA
Satellite Telephone Number	1440320
Length 660 ft./201.1 m.	Beam 87 ft./26.5 m.
Engines	2×Gotaverken diesels
Passenger Decks	8
Number of Crew	380
Passenger Capacity (basis 2)	730
Passenger Capacity (all berths)	730

Passenger Space Ratio (basis 2)		37.9
Passenger Space Ratio (all berths)		37.9
Officers British	Service Staff International	
Total Cabins 365	Cabin Door Width 25–27"	
Outside 295	Inside 70	Single 21
Wheelchair Accessible Cabins		10
Dining Rooms 1		Sittings 2
Number of Elevators 4	Door Width 32"	
Electric Current in Cabins		110 AC
Casino Yes	Slot Machines Yes	
Swimming Pools Outside 2		Inside 1
Whirlpools		1
Gymnasium Yes	Sauna Yes	Massage Yes
Cinema/Theatre Yes	Number of Seats 289	
Cabin TV No		Library Yes
Children's Facilities/Playroom		No

Ratings

Ship Appearance/Condition	84
Interior Cleanliness	90
Passenger Space	84
Passenger Comfort Level	90
Furnishings/Decor	90
Cruise Cuisine	85
Food Service	84
Beverages/Service	83
Accommodations	90
Cabin Service	84
Itineraries/Destinations	86

Shore Excursion Program	84
Entertainment	86
Activities Program	82
Cruise Director/Cruise Staff	83
Ship's Officers/Staff	82
Fitness/Sports Facilities	84
Overall Ship Facilities	85
Value for Money	85
Total Cruise Experience	88
Overall Rating	**1709**
Average	**85.4**

Comments

Handsome, solidly built ex-ocean liner with flowing, rounded lines and well-balanced profile/excellent open deck and sunning space/this ship is endowed with numerous lovely public rooms that are very spacious and gracious, with fine quality furnishings and fabrics throughout, trimmed with acres of fine woods/roomy cabins have enormous closet and drawer space, and fine woods everywhere/European-style dining room is really elegant, with old-world traditions and charm/good food and excellent service/entertainment is first-rate/altogether a thoroughly professional operation/you'll have a most enjoyable cruise experience on this ship, with extra attention to detail, and real European finesse at the appropriate price.

Sea Venture

Principal Cruising Areas:
Alaska / Mediterranean / Tahiti

Ship	mv Sea Venture	Passenger Space Ratio (basis 2)		23.6
Cruise Line/Operator	Sea Venture Cruises	Passenger Space Ratio (all berths)		22.3
Former Names	Taygetos	Officers European	Service Staff European	
Gross Registered Tonnage	8,500	Total Cabins 180	Cabin Door Width n/a	
Built	(Greece)	Outside 180	Inside No	Single No
First Entered Service	1980	Wheelchair Accessible Cabins		No
Last Refurbished	1988	Dining Rooms 1	Sittings 1	
Country of Registry	Greece	Number of Elevators 4	Door Width n/a	
Radio Call Sign	n/a	Electric Current in Cabins	110 AC	
Satellite Telephone Number	n/a	Casino Yes	Slot Machines Yes	
Length 424 ft./129.2 m. Beam 56 ft./17.0 m.		Swimming Pools Outside 1	Inside No	
Engines	2×diesels	Whirlpools		2
Passenger Decks	6	Gymnasium Yes Sauna Yes	Massage Yes	
Number of Crew	240	Cinema/Theatre No	Number of Seats –	
Passenger Capacity (basis 2)	360	Cabin TV Yes	Library Yes	
Passenger Capacity (all berths)	380	Children's Facilities/Playroom		No

Ratings

Ship Appearance/Condition	–	Shore Excursion Program	–
Interior Cleanliness	–	Entertainment	–
Passenger Space	–	Activities Program	–
Passenger Comfort Level	–	Cruise Director/Cruise Staff	–
Furnishings/Decor	–	Ship's Officers/Staff	–
Cruise Cuisine	–	Fitness/Sports Facilities	–
Food Service	–	Overall Ship Facilities	–
Beverages/Service	–	Value for Money	–
Accommodations	–	Total Cruise Experience	–
Cabin Service	–	**Overall Rating**	–
Itineraries/Destinations	–	**Average**	–

Comments

Striking, innovative and sleek design, instantly recognizable by its unique twin-level observation lounge built directly above the bow/carries glass-enclosed *Baby Sea Venture* from stern davits/ice-hardened hull for future adventure cruising/public rooms have a feel of casual elegance, with warm, inviting colors/all-outside cabins have bleached oak cabinets and archways, large picture windows, separate sitting room, refrigerated mini-bar, safe, entertainment center, and tiled bathroom with full bathtub/over half have private balcony/dining room is lovely, decorated in rose and cream/European staff and service/this new ship of modest size will provide elegant surroundings for the discerning passenger. (Not rated at press time.)

Seabourn Pride

Principal Cruising Areas:
Mediterranean/South America/
Trans-Canal/West Africa

Ship	ms Seabourn Pride
Cruise Line/Operator	Seabourn Cruise Line
Former Names	–
Gross Registered Tonnage	9,000
Built	Seebeckwerft (W. Germany)
First Entered Service	1988
Last Refurbished	–
Country of Registry	Norway
Radio Call Sign	n/a
Satellite Telephone Number	n/a
Length 440 ft./134.1 m.	Beam 63 ft./19.2 m.
Engines	2×Bergen diesels
Passenger Decks	6
Number of Crew	140
Passenger Capacity (basis 2)	212
Passenger Capacity (all berths)	212

Passenger Space Ratio (basis 2)		42.4
Passenger Space Ratio (all berths)		42.4
Officers Norwegian		Service Staff European
Total Cabins 106	Cabin Door Width 25–31"	
Outside 106	Inside No	Single No
Wheelchair Accessible Cabins		4
Dining Rooms 4		Sittings Open
Number of Elevators 4		Door Width 39"
Electric Current in Cabins		110/220 AC
Casino Yes		Slot Machines Yes
Swimming Pools Outside 1		Inside No
Whirlpools		2
Gymnasium Yes	Sauna Yes	Massage Yes
Cinema/Theatre No		Number of Seats –
Cabin TV Yes		Library Yes
Children's Facilities/Playroom		No

Ratings

Ship Appearance/Condition	–	Shore Excursion Program	–
Interior Cleanliness	–	Entertainment	–
Passenger Space	–	Activities Program	–
Passenger Comfort Level	–	Cruise Director/Cruise Staff	–
Furnishings/Decor	–	Ship's Officers/Staff	–
Cruise Cuisine	–	Fitness/Sports Facilities	–
Food Service	–	Overall Ship Facilities	–
Beverages/Service	–	Value for Money	–
Accommodations	–	Total Cruise Experience	–
Cabin Service	–	**Overall Rating**	–
Itineraries/Destinations	–	**Average**	–

Comments

Contemporary outer styling for this new, small, luxury cruise vessel/like *Sea Goddess I & II*, this has sleek swept-back lines/ship features the finest in furnishings and fittings/observation lounge has great views/dining room set low down, and features portholes/haute cuisine for the discerning traveler/expect service with a capital "S" for supreme/cabin doors are angled away from passageway/cabins are beautifully equipped all-outside all-suite rooms/walk-in closets/marble bathtubs/not for the budget-minded, this ship is strictly for those desiring a supremely elegant, yet intimate, yacht-like cruise experience in the finest of surroundings, no matter what the price/no tipping allowed. (Not rated at press time.)

SeaBreeze ★★★+

Principal Cruising Areas:
Bahamas

Ship	star ship SeaBreeze	Passenger Space Ratio (basis 2)	26.2
Cruise Line/Operator	Dolphin Cruise Line	Passenger Space Ratio (all berths)	18.2
Former Names	Royale/Federico "C"	Officers Greek	Service Staff International
Gross Registered Tonnage	21,900	Total Cabins 417	Cabin Door Width 30"
Built	Ansaldo Sestri-Ponente (Italy)	Outside 243 Inside 174	Single No
First Entered Service	1958	Wheelchair Accessible Cabins	No
Last Refurbished	1984	Dining Rooms 1	Sittings 2
Country of Registry	Panama	Number of Elevators 4	Door Width 27"
Radio Call Sign	3FGV2	Electric Current in Cabins	110/220 AC
Satellite Telephone Number	–	Casino Yes	Slot Machines Yes
Length 606 ft./184.6 m.	Beam 79 ft./24 m.	Swimming Pools Outside 1	Inside No
Engines	24	Whirlpools	3
Passenger Decks	8	Gymnasium Yes Sauna No	Massage Yes
Number of Crew	500	Cinema/Theatre Yes	Number of Seats 170
Passenger Capacity (basis 2)	834	Cabin TV No	Library No
Passenger Capacity (all berths)	1197	Children's Facilities/Playroom	Yes

Ratings

Ship Appearance/Condition	80	Shore Excursion Program	78
Interior Cleanliness	81	Entertainment	82
Passenger Space	79	Activities Program	80
Passenger Comfort Level	80	Cruise Director/Cruise Staff	80
Furnishings/Decor	80	Ship's Officers/Staff	78
Cruise Cuisine	81	Fitness/Sports Facilities	70
Food Service	82	Overall Ship Facilities	76
Beverages/Service	80	Value for Money	86
Accommodations	80	Total Cruise Experience	86
Cabin Service	78	**Overall Rating**	**1592**
Itineraries/Destinations	75	**Average**	**79.6**

Comments

Classic old liner styling and lines, with forthright profile/flamboyant red hull/open deck and sunning space is crowded when full/awkward layout hinders passenger flow/public rooms are bright and cheerful/excessive use of mirrors is hard on the eyes/dining room has bright decor, and tables are close together/both food and service are very good/wide variety of cabins in many configurations/many cabins can accommodate five—ideal for families/this ship caters so well to families with children, and the Disney package is unbeatable, as is the excellent value.

Seaward ★★★★ +

Principal Cruising Areas:
Bahamas / Caribbean

Ship	ms Seaward	Passenger Space Ratio (basis 2)	27.5
Cruise Line/Operator	Norwegian Cruise Line	Passenger Space Ratio (all berths)	23.5
Former Names	–	Officers Norwegian Service Staff International	
Gross Registered Tonnage	42,276	Total Cabins 767 Cabin Door Width 27"	
Built	Wartsila (Finland)	Outside 521 Inside 246 Single No	
First Entered Service	1988	Wheelchair Accessible Cabins	4
Last Refurbished	–	Dining Rooms 4 Sittings Open	
Country of Registry	Bahamas	Number of Elevators 6 Door Width 35"	
Radio Call Sign	C6DM2	Electric Current in Cabins	110 AC
Satellite Telephone Number 1104601/1104602		Casino Yes Slot Machines Yes	
Length 714 ft./216.3 m. Beam 95 ft./29.0 m.		Swimming Pools Outside 2 Inside No	
Engines	4×Sulzer diesels	Whirlpools	2
Passenger Decks	10	Gymnasium Yes Sauna Yes Massage Yes	
Number of Crew	624	Cinema/Theatre Yes Number of Seats 740	
Passenger Capacity (basis 2)	1534	Cabin TV Yes Library No	
Passenger Capacity (all berths)	1798	Children's Facilities/Playroom No	

Ratings

Ship Appearance/Condition	90	Shore Excursion Program	85
Interior Cleanliness	91	Entertainment	90
Passenger Space	90	Activities Program	84
Passenger Comfort Level	90	Cruise Director/Cruise Staff	85
Furnishings/Decor	90	Ship's Officers/Staff	84
Cruise Cuisine	83	Fitness/Sports Facilities	81
Food Service	84	Overall Ship Facilities	86
Beverages/Service	83	Value for Money	90
Accommodations	84	Total Cruise Experience	91
Cabin Service	83	**Overall Rating**	**1728**
Itineraries/Destinations	84	**Average**	**86.4**

Comments

Stunning new ship with contemporary European cruise-ferry profile and well-raked bow/sleek mast and funnel/interior designed to remind you of sea and sky/striking two-deck-high lobby with unique crystal and water sculpture/two glass-walled stairways/romantic, intimate 82-seat Palm Tree restaurant offers haute cuisine dining for surcharge/two main dining rooms are quite lovely/Gatsby's wine bar is a popular gathering place/striking theatre-showroom has dazzle and sizzle shows/cabins are of average size, but tastefully appointed, and quite comfortable—hairdryers included in bathroom/this ship is among the finest in the Caribbean, and is proving a popular favorite among NCL's passengers, at a sensible, competitive price.

Shota Rustaveli ★★★

Principal Cruising Areas:
Mediterranean

Ship	ms Shota Rustaveli	Passenger Space Ratio (basis 2)		40.9
Cruise Line/Operator	Black Sea Shipping	Passenger Space Ratio (all berths)		33.7
Former Names	–	Officers Soviet	Service Staff East European	
Gross Registered Tonnage	20,499	Total Cabins 250	Cabin Door Width 26"	
Built Mathias Thesen Werft (E. Germany)		Outside 250	Inside No	Single No
First Entered Service	1966	Wheelchair Accessible Cabins		No
Last Refurbished	1983	Dining Rooms 1		Sittings 2
Country of Registry	USSR	Number of Elevators 3	Door Width 32"	
Radio Call Sign	UUGF	Electric Current in Cabins		220 AC
Satellite Telephone Number	–	Casino No	Slot Machines No	
Length 580 ft./176.7 m. Beam 77 ft./23.4 m.		Swimming Pools Outside 2		Inside No
Engines	2×Sulzer diesels	Whirlpools		No
Passenger Decks	8	Gymnasium Yes Sauna Yes	Massage Yes	
Number of Crew	380	Cinema/Theatre Yes	Number of Seats 130	
Passenger Capacity (basis 2)	500	Cabin TV No		Library Yes
Passenger Capacity (all berths)	608	Children's Facilities/Playroom		Yes

Ratings

Ship Appearance/Condition	80	Shore Excursion Program		71
Interior Cleanliness	79	Entertainment		75
Passenger Space	83	Activities Program		71
Passenger Comfort Level	81	Cruise Director/Cruise Staff		72
Furnishings/Decor	77	Ship's Officers/Staff		75
Cruise Cuisine	75	Fitness/Sports Facilities		75
Food Service	76	Overall Ship Facilities		76
Beverages/Service	74	Value for Money		80
Accommodations	76	Total Cruise Experience		80
Cabin Service	79	**Overall Rating**		**1535**
Itineraries/Destinations	80	**Average**		**76.7**

Comments

Good-looking traditional ship styling with all-white profile/good open deck space for sunning/very spacious ship with interior decor quite pleasant/lots of wood paneling and trim/ship's all-outside cabins are small, but quite comfortable, with attractive wood accents and solid fixtures/many portholes actually open/dining room has lots of plants, and is set family-style/food is reasonable, that's all/service is attentive but somewhat inflexible/best for the passenger on a low budget who doesn't expect luxury, but wants a pleasant, well-organized cruise experience.

Sky Princess ★★★★ +

Principal Cruising Areas:
Amazon/Canada/Caribbean/
South America/Trans-Canal

Ship	ss Sky Princess
Cruise Line/Operator	Princess Cruises
Former Names	FairSky
Gross Registered Tonnage	46,314
Built	C.N.I.M. (France)
First Entered Service	1984
Last Refurbished	–
Country of Registry	Liberia
Radio Call Sign	ELDK9
Satellite Telephone Number	1240744
Length 789 ft./240.4 m.	Beam 92 ft./28.0 m.
Engines	2×GE turbines
Passenger Decks	11
Number of Crew	550
Passenger Capacity (basis 2)	1212
Passenger Capacity (all berths)	1350

Passenger Space Ratio (basis 2)		38.2
Passenger Space Ratio (all berths)		34.3
Officers Italian	Service Staff European	
Total Cabins 606	Cabin Door Width 23"	
Outside 388	Inside 218	Single No
Wheelchair Accessible Cabins		6
Dining Rooms 2		Sittings 2
Number of Elevators 6	Door Width 43"	
Electric Current in Cabins		115 AC
Casino Yes		Slot Machines Yes
Swimming Pools Outside 3		Inside No
Whirlpools		1
Gymnasium Yes	Sauna Yes	Massage Yes
Cinema/Theatre Yes	Number of Seats 237	
Cabin TV Yes		Library Yes
Children's Facilities/Playroom		Yes

Ratings

Ship Appearance/Condition	91
Interior Cleanliness	88
Passenger Space	88
Passenger Comfort Level	90
Furnishings/Decor	88
Cruise Cuisine	82
Food Service	81
Beverages/Service	80
Accommodations	88
Cabin Service	82
Itineraries/Destinations	84

Shore Excursion Program	80
Entertainment	82
Activities Program	80
Cruise Director/Cruise Staff	80
Ship's Officers/Staff	83
Fitness/Sports Facilities	85
Overall Ship Facilities	84
Value for Money	84
Total Cruise Experience	86
Overall Rating	**1681**
Average	**84.0**

Comments

Well-designed contemporary vessel has short, but sharply raked bow and swept-back funnel/lovely enclosed Promenade Deck/tasteful interior decor, though non-carpeted stairwells are sterile/superb showroom, with good visibility from all seats/Horizon Lounge is restful at night/popular Pizzeria/split casino configuration poor/good health spa/two dining rooms are brightly lit, but feature good food, with plenty of pasta/Italian service attentive/cabins are spacious and well appointed/outstanding are the large Lido Deck suites/high repeaters rate/this ship provides a well-balanced cruise experience for the mature passenger, at a moderate rate.

Skyward ★★★ +

Principal Cruising Areas:
Caribbean/Mexico

Ship	ms Skyward	Passenger Space Ratio (basis 2)	20.4
Cruise Line/Operator	Norwegian Cruise Line	Passenger Space Ratio (all berths)	17.6
Former Names	–	Officers Norwegian	Service Staff International
Gross Registered Tonnage	16,254	Total Cabins 397	Cabin Door Width 23″
Built	Seebeckwerft (W. Germany)	Outside 238	Inside 159	Single No
First Entered Service	1969	Wheelchair Accessible Cabins	No
Last Refurbished	1984	Dining Rooms 1	Sittings 2
Country of Registry	Bahamas	Number of Elevators 4	Door Width 29″
Radio Call Sign	C6CM5	Electric Current in Cabins	110/220 AC
Satellite Telephone Number	1104164	Casino Yes	Slot Machines Yes
Length 525 ft./160.0 m.	Beam 75 ft./22.8 m.	Swimming Pools Outside 1	Inside No
Engines	2×MAN diesels	Whirlpools	No
Passenger Decks	8	Gymnasium Yes Sauna Yes Massage Yes	
Number of Crew	330	Cinema/Theatre Yes	Number of Seats 180
Passenger Capacity (basis 2)	794	Cabin TV No	Library Yes
Passenger Capacity (all berths)	920	Children's Facilities/Playroom	No

Ratings

Ship Appearance/Condition	79	Shore Excursion Program	80
Interior Cleanliness	82	Entertainment	81
Passenger Space	76	Activities Program	78
Passenger Comfort Level	80	Cruise Director/Cruise Staff	80
Furnishings/Decor	82	Ship's Officers/Staff	81
Cruise Cuisine	81	Fitness/Sports Facilities	74
Food Service	82	Overall Ship Facilities	76
Beverages/Service	80	Value for Money	81
Accommodations	80	Total Cruise Experience	82
Cabin Service	80	**Overall Rating**	**1596**
Itineraries/Destinations	81	**Average**	**79.8**

Comments

Attractive-looking all-white ship with distinctive daytime lounge set high and forward against the ship's mast/newly refurbished interior features light, airy decor in clean, tidy colors/"Mayan Temple" on Sun Deck looks tacky, but adds to Mexican theme of itinerary/cabins are small, yet quite adequate for seven-day cruises, despite limited closet, drawer and storage space/attractive dining room/cheerful, but hurried service/this ship is ideal for active passengers wanting a decent cruise experience at a fair price, in comfortable, but not elegant, surroundings.

Society Explorer

Principal Cruising Areas:
Worldwide Expedition Cruises

Ship	mv Society Explorer	Passenger Space Ratio (basis 2)	23.9
Cruise Line/Operator	Society Expeditions	Passenger Space Ratio (all berths)	23.9
Former Names	Lindblad Explorer	Officers German Service Staff European/Filipino	
Gross Registered Tonnage	2,398	Total Cabins 54 Cabin Door Width 30"	
Built Nystad Varv Shipyard (Finland)		Outside 54 Inside No Single No	
First Entered Service	1969	Wheelchair Accessible Cabins No	
Last Refurbished	1985	Dining Rooms 1 Sittings 1	
Country of Registry	Bahamas	Number of Elevators 0 Door Width –	
Radio Call Sign	C6BA2	Electric Current in Cabins 220 AC	
Satellite Telephone Number	1104207	Casino No Slot Machines No	
Length 234 ft./72.8 m. Beam 45.5 ft./14.0 m.		Swimming Pools Outside 1 Inside No	
Engines	2×MWM diesels	Whirlpools No	
Passenger Decks	6	Gymnasium Yes Sauna Yes Massage Yes	
Number of Crew	65	Cinema/Theatre No Number of Seats –	
Passenger Capacity (basis 2)	100	Cabin TV No Library Yes	
Passenger Capacity (all berths)	100	Children's Facilities/Playroom No	

Ratings

Ship Appearance/Condition	–	Shore Excursion Program	–
Interior Cleanliness	–	Entertainment	–
Passenger Space	–	Activities Program	–
Passenger Comfort Level	–	Cruise Director/Cruise Staff	–
Furnishings/Decor	–	Ship's Officers/Staff	–
Cruise Cuisine	–	Fitness/Sports Facilities	–
Food Service	–	Overall Ship Facilities	–
Beverages/Service	–	Value for Money	–
Accommodations	–	Total Cruise Experience	–
Cabin Service	–	**Overall Rating**	**–**
Itineraries/Destinations	–	**Average**	**–**

Comments

Neat-looking specialist expedition cruise vessel with ice-hardened hull has nicely balanced profile and is extremely maneuverable/well fitted out with all necessary equipment, including 8 Zodiac rubber landing craft/cabins are small, but more than adequate/bathrooms, however, are really tiny/tasteful interior decor in public rooms/large reference library/intimate dining room/food is excellent, so is the wine list/smiling, attentive and genuinely friendly service/this is cruising for the serious adventurer who wants to be close to the earth and its fascinating peoples, yet have many of the creature comforts of home within reach. Overall rating 4 + stars, although category ratings above not relevant.

Song of America ★★★★

Principal Cruising Areas:
Caribbean

Ship	ms Song of America	Passenger Space Ratio (basis 2)	26.5
Line/Operator	Royal Caribbean Cruise Line	Passenger Space Ratio (all berths)	23.8
Former Names	–	Officers Norwegian	Service Staff International
Gross Registered Tonnage	37,584	Total Cabins 707	Cabin Door Width 25"
Built	Wartsila (Finland)	Outside 407 Inside 300	Single No
First Entered Service	1982	Wheelchair Accessible Cabins	No
Last Refurbished	–	Dining Rooms 1	Sittings 2
Country of Registry	Norway	Number of Elevators 7	Door Width 35"
Radio Call Sign	LENA	Electric Current in Cabins	110 AC
Satellite Telephone Number	–	Casino Yes	Slot Machines Yes
Length 703.7 ft./214.5 m. Beam 93.2 ft./28.4 m.		Swimming Pools Outside 2	Inside No
Engines	4×Sulzer diesels	Whirlpools	No
Passenger Decks	11	Gymnasium Yes Sauna Yes	Massage Yes
Number of Crew	500	Cinema/Theatre Yes	Number of Seats 204
Passenger Capacity (basis 2)	1414	Cabin TV No	Library Yes
Passenger Capacity (all berths)	1577	Children's Facilities/Playroom	No

Ratings

Ship Appearance/Condition	85	Shore Excursion Program	81
Interior Cleanliness	87	Entertainment	82
Passenger Space	85	Activities Program	81
Passenger Comfort Level	86	Cruise Director/Cruise Staff	81
Furnishings/Decor	84	Ship's Officers/Staff	82
Cruise Cuisine	84	Fitness/Sports Facilities	83
Food Service	84	Overall Ship Facilities	84
Beverages/Service	82	Value for Money	85
Accommodations	80	Total Cruise Experience	85
Cabin Service	81	**Overall Rating**	**1663**
Itineraries/Destinations	81	**Average**	**83.1**

Comments

Contemporary-looking ship has rounded lines and sharply raked bow/striking Viking Crown Lounge wrapped around funnel is the line's trademark/good open deck and sunning space/beautifully polished wooden decks and rails/public rooms are spacious, but musical-themed decor seems somewhat redundant/dining room is large, but low ceiling creates high noise level/ cabins are very small, yet most passengers seem happy with them/in typical RCCL fashion, the ship caters superbly to passengers in the public entertainment rooms/ attentive, polished service throughout/this ship caters to the novice and repeat passenger with well-programmed flair/provides a consistently good product in comfortable surroundings at a decent price.

Song of Norway ★★★★

Principal Cruising Areas:
Caribbean

Ship	ms Song of Norway	Passenger Space Ratio (basis 2)	22.5
Cruise Line	Royal Caribbean Cruise Line	Passenger Space Ratio (all berths)	20.2
Former Names	–	Officers Norwegian	Service Staff International
Gross Registered Tonnage	23,005	Total Cabins 535	Cabin Door Width 25"
Built	Wartsila (Finland)	Outside 352 Inside 185	Single No
First Entered Service	1970	Wheelchair Accessible Cabins	No
Last Refurbished	1986	Dining Rooms 1	Sittings 2
Country of Registry	Norway	Number of Elevators 4	Door Width 35"
Radio Call Sign	LNVP	Electric Current in Cabins	110 AC
Satellite Telephone Number	–	Casino Yes	Slot Machines Yes
Length 637 ft./194.1 m.	Beam 80 ft./24.3 m.	Swimming Pools Outside 1	Inside No
Engines	4×Sulzer diesels	Whirlpools	No
Passenger Decks	8	Gymnasium Yes Sauna No	Massage No
Number of Crew	400	Cinema/Theatre No	Number of Seats –
Passenger Capacity (basis 2)	1022	Cabin TV No	Library No
Passenger Capacity (all berths)	1140	Children's Facilities/Playroom	No

Ratings

Ship Appearance/Condition	84	Shore Excursion Program	81
Interior Cleanliness	88	Entertainment	82
Passenger Space	84	Activities Program	81
Passenger Comfort Level	85	Cruise Director/Cruise Staff	81
Furnishings/Decor	82	Ship's Officers/Staff	82
Cruise Cuisine	84	Fitness/Sports Facilities	80
Food Service	85	Overall Ship Facilities	83
Beverages/Service	82	Value for Money	85
Accommodations	78	Total Cruise Experience	86
Cabin Service	80	**Overall Rating**	**1654**
Itineraries/Destinations	81	**Average**	**82.7**

Comments

Contemporary '70s look with long, sleek lines, sharply raked bow and distinctive cantilevered Viking Crown Lounge set high on funnel/"stretched" sister to *Nordic Prince*/high-density ship with expansive open deck and sunning space/beautifully-polished wooden decks and rails/good interior layout/Scandinavian decor clean and bright, but becoming dated/nice wood trim in passageways/cabins are very small, with limited closet and drawer space/very good dining room operation/very attentive, polished service, but pressure high from waiters for good passenger comments/this ship caters to novice and repeat passengers with well-programmed flair, and provides a fine-tuned cruise product in comfortable surroundings.

Southward ★ ★ ★ ★

Principal Cruising Areas:
Mexican Riviera

Ship	ms Southward
Cruise Line/Operator	Norwegian Cruise Line
Former Names	–
Gross Registered Tonnage	16,607
Built Cantieri Navale del Tirreno et Riuniti (Italy)	
First Entered Service	1971
Last Refurbished	1985
Country of Registry	Bahamas
Radio Call Sign	C6CM6
Satellite Telephone Number	1104165
Length 541 ft./163.3 m.	Beam 75 ft./22.8 m.
Engines	2×GMT diesels
Passenger Decks	9
Number of Crew	325
Passenger Capacity (basis 2)	774
Passenger Capacity (all berths)	918

Passenger Space Ratio (basis 2)	21.4
Passenger Space Ratio (all berths)	18.0
Officers Norwegian Service Staff International	
Total Cabins 387 Cabin Door Width 24–28"	
Outside 266 Inside 121 Single No	
Wheelchair Accessible Cabins	No
Dining Rooms 1	Sittings 2
Number of Elevators 4 Door Width 26"	
Electric Current in Cabins	110 AC
Casino Yes Slot Machines Yes	
Swimming Pools Outside 1	Inside No
Whirlpools	No
Gymnasium Yes Sauna Yes Massage Yes	
Cinema/Theatre Yes Number of Seats 198	
Cabin TV No	Library Yes
Children's Facilities/Playroom	No

Ratings

Ship Appearance/Condition	81	Shore Excursion Program	80
Interior Cleanliness	82	Entertainment	81
Passenger Space	78	Activities Program	79
Passenger Comfort Level	82	Cruise Director/Cruise Staff	80
Furnishings/Decor	82	Ship's Officers/Staff	81
Cruise Cuisine	81	Fitness/Sports Facilities	75
Food Service	82	Overall Ship Facilities	78
Beverages/Service	80	Value for Money	81
Accommodations	80	Total Cruise Experience	82
Cabin Service	81	**Overall Rating**	**1607**
Itineraries/Destinations	81	**Average**	**80.3**

Comments

Clean, contemporary profile with rakish superstructure, dual funnels and inboard lifeboats/high-density vessel tends to feel crowded when full/open deck and sunning space limited/very comfortable public rooms with bright, modern decor/favorite is the Crow's Nest Nightclub, set high atop the ship by the forward mast/charming dining room with warm colors/ten suites on Boat Deck are quite spacious, and have full bathtubs/other cabins are compact but tidy, with good closet space for short cruise/food and service good, that's all/ship provides all the right ingredients for an active, fun-filled vacation in the sun, at the right price.

Sovereign of the Seas ★★★★ +

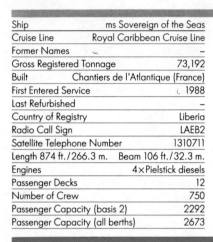

Principal Cruising Areas:
Caribbean

Ship	ms Sovereign of the Seas	Passenger Space Ratio (basis 2)		32.0
Cruise Line	Royal Caribbean Cruise Line	Passenger Space Ratio (all berths)		27.3
Former Names	–	Officers Norwegian	Service Staff International	
Gross Registered Tonnage	73,192	Total Cabins 1141	Cabin Door Width 23"	
Built	Chantiers de l'Atlantique (France)	Outside 723	Inside 418	Single No
First Entered Service	1988	Wheelchair Accessible Cabins		12
Last Refurbished	–	Dining Rooms 2		Sittings 2
Country of Registry	Liberia	Number of Elevators 18	Door Width 39"	
Radio Call Sign	LAEB2	Electric Current in Cabins		110 AC
Satellite Telephone Number	1310711	Casino Yes	Slot Machines Yes	
Length 874 ft./266.3 m.	Beam 106 ft./32.3 m.	Swimming Pools Outside 2		Inside No
Engines	4×Pielstick diesels	Whirlpools		1
Passenger Decks	12	Gymnasium Yes	Sauna Yes	Massage Yes
Number of Crew	750	Cinema/Theatre 2	Number of Seats 146/146	
Passenger Capacity (basis 2)	2292	Cabin TV Yes		Library Yes
Passenger Capacity (all berths)	2673	Children's Facilities/Playroom		Yes

Ratings

Ship Appearance/Condition	93	Shore Excursion Program	82
Interior Cleanliness	96	Entertainment	86
Passenger Space	95	Activities Program	86
Passenger Comfort Level	94	Cruise Director/Cruise Staff	85
Furnishings/Decor	92	Ship's Officers/Staff	85
Cruise Cuisine	85	Fitness/Sports Facilities	84
Food Service	85	Overall Ship Facilities	88
Beverages/Service	84	Value for Money	90
Accommodations	84	Total Cruise Experience	88
Cabin Service	83	**Overall Rating**	**1747**
Itineraries/Destinations	82	**Average**	**85.6**

Comments

Spectacular new megaship has nicely rounded lines despite high superstructure/open deck space adequate, no more/striking Viking Crown Lounge/stunning, trend-setting five-deck-high "Centrum" lobby, with cascading stairways/public rooms are spacious and elegant but layout is awkward/congested passenger flow in some areas/needs more intimate spaces/two-level showroom/delightful array of classy shops/two dining rooms feature well-presented food and good service/no tables for two/12 suites large/other cabins are very small/all are tastefully decorated but have little closet and drawer space/interactive video information system in all cabins/this floating resort is spectacular for one-week Caribbean cruises, but is somewhat impersonal.

Star Princess

Principal Cruising Areas:
Alaska/Caribbean

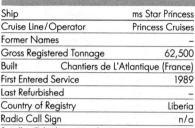

Ship	ms Star Princess	Passenger Space Ratio (basis 2)	42.5
Cruise Line/Operator	Princess Cruises	Passenger Space Ratio (all berths)	38.5
Former Names	–	Officers Italian	Service Staff European
Gross Registered Tonnage	62,500	Total Cabins 735	Cabin Door Width 23–32"
Built	Chantiers de L'Atlantique (France)	Outside 560 Inside 165	Single No
First Entered Service	1989	Wheelchair Accessible Cabins	10
Last Refurbished	–	Dining Rooms 2	Sittings 2
Country of Registry	Liberia	Number of Elevators 9	Door Width 43"
Radio Call Sign	n/a	Electric Current in Cabins	115 AC
Satellite Telephone Number	n/a	Casino Yes	Slot Machines Yes
Length 804 ft./245.0 m. Beam 102 ft./31.0 m.		Swimming Pools Outside 3	Inside No
Engines	4×MAN diesels	Whirlpools	4
Passenger Decks	13	Gymnasium Yes Sauna Yes	Massage Yes
Number of Crew	563	Cinema/Theatre Yes	Number of Seats 202
Passenger Capacity (basis 2)	1470	Cabin TV Yes	Library Yes
Passenger Capacity (all berths)	1620	Children's Facilities/Playroom	Yes

Ratings

Ship Appearance/Condition	–	Shore Excursion Program	–
Interior Cleanliness	–	Entertainment	–
Passenger Space	–	Activities Program	–
Passenger Comfort Level	–	Cruise Director/Cruise Staff	–
Furnishings/Decor	–	Ship's Officers/Staff	–
Cruise Cuisine	–	Fitness/Sports Facilities	–
Food Service	–	Overall Ship Facilities	–
Beverages/Service	–	Value for Money	–
Accommodations	–	Total Cruise Experience	–
Cabin Service	–	**Overall Rating**	–
Itineraries/Destinations	–	**Average**	–

Comments

Long, sleek lines for this striking, elegant new ship/squat funnel/innovative styling mixed with traditional shipboard features/inboard lifeboats/spacious public rooms/noteworthy horseshoe-shaped balconied showroom/domed forward observation lounge/lovely three-deck-high lobby-foyer/neat wine bar and pizzeria/in-pool bar/multi-tiered main restaurant has two-deck-high center ceiling/ancillary indoor-outdoor buffet restaurant/good food and service/spacious, superbly equipped cabins with large, modular bathrooms/interactive cabin video system/this ship will provide a traditional approach to cruising for the discerning repeat passenger liking crowds and a certain anonymity/I expect it to be superb. (Not rated at press time)

Stardancer ★★★★

Principal Cruising Areas:
Alaska/Mexican Riviera

Ship	ms Stardancer	Passenger Space Ratio (basis 2)	26.8
Cruise Line/Operator	Admiral Cruises	Passenger Space Ratio (all berths)	16.7
Former Names	Scandinavia	Officers Scandinavian Service Staff International	
Gross Registered Tonnage	26,746	Total Cabins 484	Cabin Door Width 23"
Built	Dubigeon-Normandie (France)	Outside 284 Inside 200	Single No
First Entered Service	1982	Wheelchair Accessible Cabins	1
Last Refurbished	1985	Dining Rooms 1	Sittings 2
Country of Registry	Bahamas	Number of Elevators 5	Door Width 35"
Radio Call Sign	C6CP	Electric Current in Cabins	110 AC
Satellite Telephone Number	1104204	Casino Yes	Slot Machines Yes
Length 608 ft./185.3 m. Beam 88.5 ft./26.9 m.		Swimming Pools Outside 1	Inside No
Engines	2×B&W diesels	Whirlpools	2
Passenger Decks	7	Gymnasium Yes Sauna Yes	Massage Yes
Number of Crew	380	Cinema/Theatre No	Number of Seats –
Passenger Capacity (basis 2)	996	Cabin TV Yes	Library Yes
Passenger Capacity (all berths)	1600	Children's Facilities/Playroom	Yes

Ratings

Ship Appearance/Condition	81	Shore Excursion Program	81
Interior Cleanliness	84	Entertainment	81
Passenger Space	81	Activities Program	80
Passenger Comfort Level	83	Cruise Director/Cruise Staff	81
Furnishings/Decor	82	Ship's Officers/Staff	82
Cruise Cuisine	80	Fitness/Sports Facilities	85
Food Service	81	Overall Ship Facilities	83
Beverages/Service	79	Value for Money	85
Accommodations	81	Total Cruise Experience	83
Cabin Service	81	**Overall Rating**	**1635**
Itineraries/Destinations	81	**Average**	**81.7**

Comments

This high-sided, shoebox-like cruise ship can also carry 350 vehicles on two lower decks/ generous open deck and sunning space/ excellent health spa facilities/public rooms are very chic, with lovely soft decor, tasteful colors and quality furnishings/compact cabins are very well appointed, and have ample closet space/dining room is large, but very attractive, and well laid out/good food and choice/very attentive service/ good for families with children/unusual concept that deserves praise/this ship provides an excellent cruise experience in tasteful surroundings, at an incredibly low price— and you can take your car.

Starward ★★★★

Principal Cruising Areas:
Bahamas/Caribbean

Ship	ms Starward	Passenger Space Ratio (basis 2)		20.7
Cruise Line/Operator	Norwegian Cruise Line	Passenger Space Ratio (all berths)		18.1
Former Names	–	Officers Norwegian	Service Staff International	
Gross Registered Tonnage	16,107	Total Cabins 389	Cabin Door Width 23"	
Built	A.G. Weser (W. Germany)	Outside 229	Inside 160	Single No
First Entered Service	1968	Wheelchair Accessible Cabins		No
Last Refurbished	1984	Dining Rooms 1		Sittings 2
Country of Registry	Bahamas	Number of Elevators 4	Door Width 32"	
Radio Call Sign	C6CM4	Electric Current in Cabins		110 AC
Satellite Telephone Number	1104163	Casino Yes	Slot Machines Yes	
Length 525 ft./160.0 m.	Beam 75 ft./22.8 m.	Swimming Pools Outside 2		Inside No
Engines	2×MAN diesels	Whirlpools		No
Passenger Decks	7	Gymnasium Yes Sauna Yes	Massage Yes	
Number of Crew	310	Cinema/Theatre Yes	Number of Seats 204	
Passenger Capacity (basis 2)	778	Cabin TV No		Library Yes
Passenger Capacity (all berths)	888	Children's Facilities/Playroom		No

Ratings

Ship Appearance/Condition	81	Shore Excursion Program		80
Interior Cleanliness	82	Entertainment		81
Passenger Space	78	Activities Program		80
Passenger Comfort Level	82	Cruise Director/Cruise Staff		79
Furnishings/Decor	82	Ship's Officers/Staff		80
Cruise Cuisine	81	Fitness/Sports Facilities		75
Food Service	82	Overall Ship Facilities		78
Beverages/Service	80	Value for Money		81
Accommodations	80	Total Cruise Experience		82
Cabin Service	80	**Overall Rating**		**1604**
Itineraries/Destinations	80	**Average**		**80.2**

Comments

Contemporary profile with swept-back funnel/reasonable open deck and sunning space/high-density vessel is noticeably crowded when full/plenty of public rooms/upbeat, cheerful decor throughout public rooms/charming dining room, with some tables overlooking the stern and ship's wash/reasonably good cruise food and service comes with a smile/except for five larger suites, cabins are compact units that are comfortable, with bright, contemporary colors/excellent ship for a fine-tuned Caribbean cruise in comfortable, but not elegant, surroundings, at a decent price.

Stella Maris ★★★★

Principal Cruising Areas:
Aegean/Mediterranean

Ship	ms Stella Maris
Cruise Line/Operator	Sun Line Cruises
Former Names	Bremerhaven
Gross Registered Tonnage	4,000
Built	Alder Werft (W. Germany)
First Entered Service	1960
Last Refurbished	1967
Country of Registry	Greece
Radio Call Sign	SZPS
Satellite Telephone Number	–
Length 300 ft./91.4 m.	Beam 45 ft./13.7 m.
Engines	2×Deutz diesels
Passenger Decks	4
Number of Crew	110
Passenger Capacity (basis 2)	180
Passenger Capacity (all berths)	180

Passenger Space Ratio (basis 2)	22.2
Passenger Space Ratio (all berths)	22.2
Officers Greek	Service Staff Greek
Total Cabins 93	Cabin Door Width 24″
Outside 80 Inside 13	Single No
Wheelchair Accessible Cabins	No
Dining Rooms 1	Sittings 1
Number of Elevators 0	Door Width –
Electric Current in Cabins	220 AC
Casino No	Slot Machines No
Swimming Pools Outside 1	Inside No
Whirlpools	No
Gymnasium No Sauna No	Massage No
Cinema/Theatre No	Number of Seats –
Cabin TV No	Library Yes
Children's Facilities/Playroom	No

Ratings

Ship Appearance/Condition	84	Shore Excursion Program	80
Interior Cleanliness	85	Entertainment	78
Passenger Space	80	Activities Program	78
Passenger Comfort Level	82	Cruise Director/Cruise Staff	81
Furnishings/Decor	82	Ship's Officers/Staff	82
Cruise Cuisine	84	Fitness/Sports Facilities	60
Food Service	83	Overall Ship Facilities	80
Beverages/Service	82	Value for Money	76
Accommodations	81	Total Cruise Experience	84
Cabin Service	82	**Overall Rating**	**1604**
Itineraries/Destinations	80	**Average**	**80.2**

Comments

Charming little ship with an intimate, yacht-like atmosphere/well maintained and spotlessly clean, neat and tidy/excellent service from attentive, considerate staff who are pleased to serve with a smile/very tasteful decor in public rooms/charming dining room, decorated in sunshine yellow and brown/fine food and wines/fresh flowers are everywhere/cabins are quite spacious for ship size, and well appointed/very warm and intimate ambiance/this ship will cruise you in sophisticated, very comfortable surroundings, with attention to detail that makes for a highly personable, and well-recommended experience.

Stella Oceanis ★★★+

Principal Cruising Areas:
Aegean/Caribbean/Mediterranean

Ship	ms Stella Oceanis	Passenger Space Ratio (basis 2)		20.0
Cruise Line Operator	Sun Line Cruises	Passenger Space Ratio (all berths)		16.3
Former Names	Aphrodite	Officers Greek		Service Staff Greek
Gross Registered Tonnage	6,000	Total Cabins 159		Cabin Door Width 24"
Built	Cantieri Riuniti dell'Adriatico (Italy)	Outside 113	Inside 46	Single No
First Entered Service	1965	Wheelchair Accessible Cabins		No
Last Refurbished	1967	Dining Rooms 1		Sittings 2
Country of Registry	Greece	Number of Elevators 1		Door Width 30"
Radio Call Sign	SZLX	Electric Current in Cabins		220 AC
Satellite Telephone Number	1130471	Casino No		Slot Machines No
Length 350 ft./106.6 m.	Beam 53 ft./16.1 m.	Swimming Pools Outside 1		Inside No
Engines	2×Sulzer diesels	Whirlpools		No
Passenger Decks	6	Gymnasium No	Sauna No	Massage No
Number of Crew	140	Cinema/Theatre No		Number of Seats –
Passenger Capacity (basis 2)	300	Cabin TV No		Library Yes
Passenger Capacity (all berths)	369	Children's Facilities/Playroom		No

Ratings

Ship Appearance/Condition	80	Shore Excursion Program	80
Interior Cleanliness	82	Entertainment	77
Passenger Space	79	Activities Program	76
Passenger Comfort Level	78	Cruise Director/Cruise Staff	80
Furnishings/Decor	80	Ship's Officers/Staff	81
Cruise Cuisine	82	Fitness/Sports Facilities	60
Food Service	82	Overall Ship Facilities	78
Beverages/Service	81	Value for Money	76
Accommodations	78	Total Cruise Experience	81
Cabin Service	80	**Overall Rating**	**1573**
Itineraries/Destinations	82	**Average**	**78.6**

Comments

Tidy-looking ship with clean, rounded lines/ well maintained/intimate atmosphere/limited public rooms, but nicely decorated/ a favorite is the Plaka Taverna, decorated in rich woods/cabins are small and more plain than on her smaller sister/dining room tastefully decorated/fine food and wines/ very good service from a dedicated and attentive staff/this ship lacks the sophistication of the other ships in the fleet, but is nonetheless quite charming/Sun Line provides a fine cruise experience.

Stella Solaris ★★★★

Principal Cruising Areas:
Aegean/Caribbean/Mediterranean/
South America

Ship	ss Stella Solaris
Cruise Line/Operator	Sun Line Cruises
Former Names	Stella V/Camboge
Gross Registered Tonnage	17,832
Built	Ateliers et Chantiers de France (France)
First Entered Service	1953
Last Refurbished	1985
Country of Registry	Greece
Radio Call Sign	SYWT
Satellite Telephone Number	1130403
Length 544 ft./165.8 m.	Beam 72 ft./21.9 m.
Engines	2×Parsons turbines
Passenger Decks	8
Number of Crew	330
Passenger Capacity (basis 2)	620
Passenger Capacity (all berths)	700

Passenger Space Ratio (basis 2)		28.8
Passenger Space Ratio (all berths)		25.5
Officers Greek		Service Staff Greek
Total Cabins 329		Cabin Door Width 24"
Outside 250	Inside 79	Single No
Wheelchair Accessible Cabins		No
Dining Rooms 1		Sittings 2
Number of Elevators 3		Door Width 31"
Electric Current in Cabins		110/220 AC
Casino Yes		Slot Machines Yes
Swimming Pools Outside 1		Inside No
Whirlpools		No
Gymnasium Yes	Sauna Yes	Massage Yes
Cinema/Theatre Yes		Number of Seats 275
Cabin TV No		Library Yes
Children's Facilities/Playroom		No

Ratings

Ship Appearance/Condition	86	Shore Excursion Program	81
Interior Cleanliness	86	Entertainment	81
Passenger Space	82	Activities Program	79
Passenger Comfort Level	86	Cruise Director/Cruise Staff	80
Furnishings/Decor	83	Ship's Officers/Staff	82
Cruise Cuisine	87	Fitness/Sports Facilities	77
Food Service	86	Overall Ship Facilities	82
Beverages/Service	83	Value for Money	84
Accommodations	82	Total Cruise Experience	86
Cabin Service	83	**Overall Rating**	**1660**
Itineraries/Destinations	84	**Average**	**83.0**

Comments

Traditional ship profile, with attractive funnel amidships/spotlessly clean and well maintained throughout/superb itineraries/plenty of open deck space/attractive twin pools and sunning area/elegant public rooms have quality furniture and fixtures/lovely dining room features excellent food, wine and European service/fresh flowers are everywhere/cabins are spacious and very well appointed—many have full bathtub/those located on Sapphire Deck and midships on Emerald Deck subject to engine noise/Lido Deck suites are delightful/this ship is for the discerning passenger who seeks a relaxed, unhurried cruise experience in fine surroundings, at reasonable cost/highly recommended.

Sun Viking ★★★★

Principal Cruising Areas:
Carribean

Ship	ms Sun Viking
Line/Operator	Royal Caribbean Cruise Line
Former Names	–
Gross Registered Tonnage	18,556
Built	Wartsila (Finland)
First Entered Service	1972
Last Refurbished	1983
Country of Registry	Norway
Radio Call Sign	LIZA
Satellite Telephone Number	–
Length 563 ft./171.6 m.	Beam 80 ft./24.3 m.
Engines	4×Sulzer diesels
Passenger Decks	7
Number of Crew	320
Passenger Capacity (basis 2)	728
Passenger Capacity (all berths)	800

Passenger Space Ratio (basis 2)		25.5
Passenger Space Ratio (all berths)		23.2
Officers Norwegian	Service Staff International	
Total Cabins 380	Cabin Door Width 25"	
Outside 262	Inside 118	Single No
Wheelchair Accessible Cabins		No
Dining Rooms 1		Sittings 2
Number of Elevators 4	Door Width 35"	
Electric Current in Cabins		110 AC
Casino Yes	Slot Machines Yes	
Swimming Pools Outside 1		Inside No
Whirlpools		No
Gymnasium Yes	Sauna Yes	Massage Yes
Cinema/Theatre No	Number of Seats –	
Cabin TV No		Library Yes
Children's Facilities/Playroom		No

Ratings

Ship Appearance/Condition	84
Interior Cleanliness	88
Passenger Space	80
Passenger Comfort Level	83
Furnishings/Decor	80
Cruise Cuisine	83
Food Service	82
Beverages/Service	81
Accommodations	80
Cabin Service	81
Itineraries/Destinations	83

Shore Excursion Program	81
Entertainment	83
Activities Program	83
Cruise Director/Cruise Staff	84
Ship's Officers/Staff	82
Fitness/Sports Facilities	80
Overall Ship Facilities	81
Value for Money	82
Total Cruise Experience	83
Overall Rating	**1644**
Average	**82.2**

Comments

Well-proportioned ship with contemporary styling/cantilevered Viking Crown Lounge set atop funnel housing provides an impressive view/smallest and most intimate ship in the RCCL fleet/good deck and sunning space/public rooms decorated in Scandinavian modern style and colors, and named after musicals/charming, friendly ambiance throughout/cabins are small and moderately comfortable, but there's not enough closet and drawer space/good food and service/this ship caters to passengers wanting a more intimate cruise, with all the RCCL trimmings at a fair price.

Sunward II ★★★+

Principal Cruising Areas:
Bahamas

Ship	ms Sunward II
Cruise Line/Operator	Norwegian Cruise Line
Former Names	Cunard Adventurer
Gross Registered Tonnage	14,155
Built	Rotterdamsche Dry Dock (Holland)
First Entered Service	1971
Last Refurbished	1984
Country of Registry	Bahamas
Radio Call Sign	C6CM3
Satellite Telephone Number	1104162
Length 485 ft./147.8 m.	Beam 70 ft./21.3 m.
Engines	4×SWD diesels
Passenger Decks	7
Number of Crew	315
Passenger Capacity (basis 2)	706
Passenger Capacity (all berths)	859

Passenger Space Ratio (basis 2)	20.0
Passenger Space Ratio (all berths)	16.4
Officers Norwegian	Service Staff International
Total Cabins 353	Cabin Door Width 22"
Outside 236 Inside 117	Single No
Wheelchair Accessible Cabins	No
Dining Rooms 1	Sittings 2
Number of Elevators 2	Door Width 32"
Electric Current in Cabins	110/220 AC
Casino Yes	Slot Machines Yes
Swimming Pools Outside 1	Inside No
Whirlpools	No
Gymnasium Yes Sauna Yes	Massage Yes
Cinema/Theatre Yes	Number of Seats 100
Cabin TV No	Library No
Children's Facilities/Playroom	No

Ratings

Ship Appearance/Condition	80	Shore Excursion Program	74
Interior Cleanliness	81	Entertainment	79
Passenger Space	80	Activities Program	78
Passenger Comfort Level	82	Cruise Director/Cruise Staff	80
Furnishings/Decor	80	Ship's Officers/Staff	80
Cruise Cuisine	80	Fitness/Sports Facilities	76
Food Service	81	Overall Ship Facilities	75
Beverages/Service	79	Value for Money	85
Accommodations	80	Total Cruise Experience	82
Cabin Service	80	**Overall Rating**	**1584**
Itineraries/Destinations	72	**Average**	**79.2**

Comments

Smart kid sister ship of the NCL fleet, with sleek profile and deep clipper bow/very well maintained/excellent ship for 3/4 day cruises/good layout, with ample public rooms and contemporary decor/excellent nightclub with forward observation views/good open deck space for sunning/well-appointed cabins for ship size, even though they are small/very attractive, brightly colored dining room/attentive, cheerful service/this ship features fun cruises to the Bahamas for the young, active set, and provides excellent value for money with a well-delivered product.

Taras Shevchenko ★★

Principal Cruising Areas:
Baltic/Mediterranean/Scandinavia/
World Cruise

Ship	ms Taras Shevchenko	Passenger Space Ratio (basis 2)	36.4
Cruise Line/Operator	Black Sea Shipping	Passenger Space Ratio (all berths)	27.7
Former Names	–	Officers Soviet	Service Staff East European
Gross Registered Tonnage	20,027	Total Cabins 285	Cabin Door Width 26"
Built	Mathias Thesen Werft (E. Germany)	Outside 285 Inside No	Single No
First Entered Service	1965	Wheelchair Accessible Cabins	No
Last Refurbished	1985	Dining Rooms 2	Sittings 1
Country of Registry	USSR	Number of Elevators 3	Door Width 32"
Radio Call Sign	UKSA	Electric Current in Cabins	220 AC
Satellite Telephone Number	–	Casino No	Slot Machines No
Length 580 ft./176.7 m.	Beam 77 ft./23.4 m.	Swimming Pools Outside 1	Inside 1
Engines	2×Sulzer diesels	Whirlpools	No
Passenger Decks	8	Gymnasium Yes Sauna Yes	Massage No
Number of Crew	370	Cinema/Theatre Yes	Number of Seats 130
Passenger Capacity (basis 2)	550	Cabin TV No	Library Yes
Passenger Capacity (all berths)	724	Children's Facilities/Playroom	Yes

Ratings

Ship Appearance/Condition	77	Shore Excursion Program	70
Interior Cleanliness	77	Entertainment	70
Passenger Space	76	Activities Program	68
Passenger Comfort Level	76	Cruise Director/Cruise Staff	72
Furnishings/Decor	73	Ship's Officers/Staff	71
Cruise Cuisine	72	Fitness/Sports Facilities	73
Food Service	73	Overall Ship Facilities	75
Beverages/Service	71	Value for Money	75
Accommodations	73	Total Cruise Experience	78
Cabin Service	74	**Overall Rating**	**1473**
Itineraries/Destinations	79	**Average**	**73.6**

Comments

Solidly constructed vessel has nicely rounded lines and classic profile, now with all-white hull/good open deck and sunning space/pleasant, though spartan, interior decor/needs major upgrading and refurbishing/lacks warmth/plain ceilings everywhere/spacious music salon/ship features all-outside cabins with private facilities/

10 suites are very spacious, and quite well appointed/single-sitting dining room, like the food, is reasonable, nothing more/service attentive, yet somewhat perfunctory/ship not up to western standards, but will provide a reasonable cruise at a budget rate, nothing more.

Tropicale ★ ★ ★ ★

Principal Cruising Areas:
Mexican Riviera

Ship	ms Tropicale	Passenger Space Ratio (basis 2)	35.9
Cruise Line/Operator	Carnival Cruise Lines	Passenger Space Ratio (all berths)	26.2
Former Names	–	Officers Soviet — Service Staff East European	
Gross Registered Tonnage	36,674	Total Cabins 511 — Cabin Door Width 22"	
Built	Aalborg Vaerft (Denmark)	Outside 324 — Inside 187 — Single No	
First Entered Service	1982	Wheelchair Accessible Cabins — No	
Last Refurbished	–	Dining Rooms 1 — Sittings 2	
Country of Registry	Liberia	Number of Elevators 8 — Door Width 36"	
Radio Call Sign	ELBM9	Electric Current in Cabins — 110 AC	
Satellite Telephone Number	1240561	Casino Yes — Slot Machines Yes	
Length 672 ft./204.8 m. — Beam 86 ft./26.2 m.		Swimming Pools Outside 2 — Inside No	
Engines	2×Sulzer diesels	Whirlpools — No	
Passenger Decks	10	Gymnasium Yes — Sauna Yes — Massage Yes	
Number of Crew	570	Cinema/Theatre No — Number of Seats –	
Passenger Capacity (basis 2)	1022	Cabin TV Yes — Library Yes	
Passenger Capacity (all berths)	1400	Children's Facilities/Playroom — Yes	

Ratings

Ship Appearance/Condition	86	Shore Excursion Program	78
Interior Cleanliness	84	Entertainment	82
Passenger Space	84	Activities Program	80
Passenger Comfort Level	85	Cruise Director/Cruise Staff	80
Furnishings/Decor	82	Ship's Officers/Staff	81
Cruise Cuisine	76	Fitness/Sports Facilities	82
Food Service	78	Overall Ship Facilities	84
Beverages/Service	75	Value for Money	83
Accommodations	81	Total Cruise Experience	82
Cabin Service	81	**Overall Rating**	**1618**
Itineraries/Destinations	74	**Average**	**80.9**

Comments

Distinctive contemporary look, with large, wing-tipped funnel/well laid-out interior design, with good passenger flow/public rooms are decorated in stimulating colors/dining room is set low down, but is cheerful, brightly lit and decorated/food is typical Americana, with quantity, not quality/service good but lacks finesse/cabins are quite spacious, well appointed, and decorated in contemporary colors/very lively casino action/good ship for families with children, since Carnival goes out of its way to entertain young cruisers/this ship will provide novice cruisers with a well-proven product that is attractively packaged, at a reasonable price.

Universe ★★★

Principal Cruising Areas:
Alaska/South Pacific

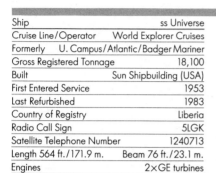

Ship	ss Universe		Passenger Space Ratio (basis 2)		33.5
Cruise Line/Operator	World Explorer Cruises		Passenger Space Ratio (all berths)		21.7
Formerly U. Campus/Atlantic/Badger Mariner			Officers Chinese	Service Staff Chinese/Filipino	
Gross Registered Tonnage	18,100		Total Cabins 313	Cabin Door Width 24"	
Built	Sun Shipbuilding (USA)		Outside 137	Inside 176	Single 25
First Entered Service	1953		Wheelchair Accessible Cabins		No
Last Refurbished	1983		Dining Rooms 1		Sittings 2
Country of Registry	Liberia		Number of Elevators 1	Door Width 26"	
Radio Call Sign	5LGK		Electric Current in Cabins		110 AC
Satellite Telephone Number	1240713		Casino No	Slot Machines No	
Length 564 ft./171.9 m.	Beam 76 ft./23.1 m.		Swimming Pools Outside 1		Inside No
Engines	2×GE turbines		Whirlpools		No
Passenger Decks	7		Gymnasium Yes Sauna No	Massage Yes	
Number of Crew	200		Cinema/Theatre Yes	Number of Seats 200	
Passenger Capacity (basis 2)	540		Cabin TV No	Library Yes	
Passenger Capacity (all berths)	831		Children's Facilities/Playroom		No

Ratings

Ship Appearance/Condition	76		Shore Excursion Program	76
Interior Cleanliness	81		Entertainment	70
Passenger Space	72		Activities Program	68
Passenger Comfort Level	78		Cruise Director/Cruise Staff	70
Furnishings/Decor .	76		Ship's Officers/Staff	76
Cruise Cuisine	80		Fitness/Sports Facilities	68
Food Service	79		Overall Ship Facilities	71
Beverages/Service	76		Value for Money	78
Accommodations	76		Total Cruise Experience	80
Cabin Service	78		**Overall Rating**	**1510**
Itineraries/Destinations	81		**Average**	**75.5**

Comments

Solidly constructed ship with cargo-liner profile/part floating campus (fall/winter) and part cruise ship (summer in Alaska)/life and ambiance is very casual/spacious public rooms with comfortable, conservative decor/excellent library and reference center of over 12,000 books/informal dining room is set low down, but is cozy and quite comfortable/cuisine is Asian-American/staff provide very attentive service with a smile/cultured entertainment consists of lectures and semi-classical music/caters particularly well to passengers of wisdom years who are seeking a leisurely two-week Alaska cruise in comfortable, but not glamorous, surroundings, at an extremely attractive price.

Vasco da Gama

Principal Cruising Areas:
Worldwide/World Cruise

Ship	ts Vasco da Gama	Passenger Space Ratio (basis 2)	38.9
Line	Arcalia Shipping/Neckermann Seereisen	Passenger Space Ratio (all berths)	32.6
Former Names	Infante Dom Henrique	Officers European	Service Staff Portuguese
Gross Registered Tonnage	24,562	Total Cabins 327	Cabin Door Width 31″
Built	Cockerill-Ougree (Belgium)	Outside 216	Inside 112	Single 34
First Entered Service	1961	Wheelchair Accessible Cabins	2
Last Refurbished	1988	Dining Rooms 2	Sittings 2
Country of Registry	Panama	Number of Elevators 4	Door Width 31″
Radio Call Sign	3EIY6	Electric Current in Cabins	220 AC
Satellite Telephone Number	1331251	Casino Yes	Slot Machines Yes
Length 641 ft./80 m.	Beam 80 ft./24.5 m.	Swimming Pools Outside 2	Inside No
Engines	4×Westinghouse turbines	Whirlpools	No
Passenger Decks	8	Gymnasium Yes Sauna Yes Massage Yes	
Number of Crew	250	Cinema/Theatre Yes Number of Seats 250	
Passenger Capacity (basis 2)	630	Cabin TV No	Library Yes
Passenger Capacity (all berths)	753	Children's Facilities/Playroom	Yes

Ratings

Ship Appearance/Condition	–	Shore Excursion Program	–
Interior Cleanliness	–	Entertainment	–
Passenger Space	–	Activities Program	–
Passenger Comfort Level	–	Cruise Director/Cruise Staff	–
Furnishings/Decor	–	Ship's Officers/Staff	–
Cruise Cuisine	–	Fitness/Sports Facilities	–
Food Service	–	Overall Ship Facilities	–
Beverages/Service	–	Value for Money	–
Accommodations	–	Total Cruise Experience	–
Cabin Service	–	**Overall Rating**	–
Itineraries/Destinations	–	**Average**	–

Comments

Extremely handsome profile with elegant lines/this former long-distance liner recently underwent a 10-month long complete refurbishment prior to being placed on exclusive charter to Neckermann Seereisen to replace the Maxim Gorki/nice long foredeck and raked bow/latest satellite navigation equipment installed/all cabins replaced with modular units/all public rooms completely redesigned/lovely wood paneling and trim throughout/fine teak decking/very spacious vessel/good sports facilities include squash and paddle-tennis courts/this ship is refurbished to a high standard and will provide a fine cruise experience in elegant surroundings, at a comfortable price. (Not rated at press time.)

Veracruz ★★

Principal Cruising Areas:
Caribbean/Mexico

Ship	ss Veracruz	Passenger Space Ratio (basis 2)		15.0
Cruise Line/Operator	Bermuda Star Line	Passenger Space Ratio (all berths)		13.1
Formerly Freeport/Carnival/Theodore Hertzl		Officers European	Service Staff International	
Gross Registered Tonnage	10,595	Total Cabins 363	Cabin Door Width 22″	
Built Deutsche Werft (W. Germany)		Outside 183	Inside 180	Single No
First Entered Service	1957	Wheelchair Accessible Cabins		No
Last Refurbished	1980	Dining Rooms 1		Sittings 2
Country of Registry	Panama	Number of Elevators 1	Door Width 30″	
Radio Call Sign	3FAQ	Electric Current in Cabins		110 AC
Satellite Telephone Number	–	Casino Yes	Slot Machines Yes	
Length 487 ft./148.4 m. Beam 64 ft./19.5 m.		Swimming Pools Outside 1		Inside No
Engines	4×DR diesels	Whirlpools		No
Passenger Decks	8	Gymnasium No Sauna No	Massage No	
Number of Crew	250	Cinema/Theatre Yes	Number of Seats 85	
Passenger Capacity (basis 2)	703	Cabin TV No		Library No
Passenger Capacity (all berths)	806	Children's Facilities/Playroom		No

Ratings

Ship Appearance/Condition	76	Shore Excursion Program	76
Interior Cleanliness	81	Entertainment	74
Passenger Space	68	Activities Program	71
Passenger Comfort Level	73	Cruise Director/Cruise Staff	73
Furnishings/Decor	76	Ship's Officers/Staff	74
Cruise Cuisine	80	Fitness/Sports Facilities	62
Food Service	79	Overall Ship Facilities	69
Beverages/Service	78	Value for Money	69
Accommodations	74	Total Cruise Experience	78
Cabin Service	80	**Overall Rating**	**1487**
Itineraries/Destinations	76	**Average**	**74.3**

Comments

Smallish vessel with pleasing lines and large, rounded funnel/high-density ship that feels crowded even when not full/rather bright, yet plain, interior decor/cabins are really tiny, with little room to move, and limited closet and drawer space/dining room is cozy, and quite well decorated/ cuisine is reasonably good/service is friendly, though lacking finesse/good ship for short cruises, nothing more, and below the standard of the line's two other ships/ this ship provides a comfortable cruise experience at a real budget price.

The Victoria ★ ★ ★ +

Principal Cruising Areas:
Caribbean

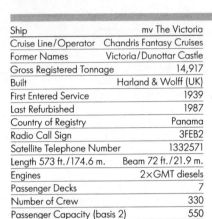

Ship	mv The Victoria	Passenger Space Ratio (basis 2)	27.1
Cruise Line/Operator	Chandris Fantasy Cruises	Passenger Space Ratio (all berths)	27.1
Former Names	Victoria/Dunottar Castle	Officers Greek	Service Staff International
Gross Registered Tonnage	14,917	Total Cabins 280	Cabin Door Width 26"
Built	Harland & Wolff (UK)	Outside 216	Inside 64	Single 8
First Entered Service	1939	Wheelchair Accessible Cabins	No
Last Refurbished	1987	Dining Rooms 1	Sittings 2
Country of Registry	Panama	Number of Elevators 3	Door Width 26"
Radio Call Sign	3FEB2	Electric Current in Cabins	115 AC
Satellite Telephone Number	1332571	Casino Yes	Slot Machines Yes
Length 573 ft./174.6 m.	Beam 72 ft./21.9 m.	Swimming Pools Outside 2	Inside No
Engines	2×GMT diesels	Whirlpools	No
Passenger Decks	7	Gymnasium Yes Sauna Yes	Massage Yes
Number of Crew	330	Cinema/Theatre Yes	Number of Seats 250
Passenger Capacity (basis 2)	550	Cabin TV No	Library Yes
Passenger Capacity (all berths)	550	Children's Facilities/Playroom	Yes

Ratings

Ship Appearance/Condition	78	Shore Excursion Program	76
Interior Cleanliness	80	Entertainment	76
Passenger Space	75	Activities Program	75
Passenger Comfort Level	78	Cruise Director/Cruise Staff	80
Furnishings/Decor	79	Ship's Officers/Staff	80
Cruise Cuisine	78	Fitness/Sports Facilities	72
Food Service	79	Overall Ship Facilities	75
Beverages/Service	76	Value for Money	80
Accommodations	76	Total Cruise Experience	80
Cabin Service	78	**Overall Rating**	**1551**
Itineraries/Destinations	80	**Average**	**77.5**

Comments

Solidly constructed vintage ship with classic profile/well maintained throughout/center stairway is real art deco-style/friendly ambiance aboard/public rooms limited for ship size/new Riviera Club is out of keeping with rest of ship's public rooms/good open deck space for sunning/small, but well-patronized, casino/dining room set low down, but comfortable, with superb two-deck-high center section/standard of cuisine is consistently good/cabins are quite spacious/suite rooms are cavernous, and large bathrooms come with deep, full bathtubs/attentive service throughout/this ship does an admirable job of providing a good cruise experience for novice cruisers, in pleasant surroundings/consistently good value, and far better than you might expect.

Viking Princess ★★

Principal Cruising Areas:
Bahamas/Nowhere

Ship	mv Viking Princess
Cruise Line/Operator	Crown Cruise Line
Former Names	Ilmatar
Gross Registered Tonnage	7,029
Built	Wartsila (Finland)
First Entered Service	1964
Last Refurbished	1979
Country of Registry	Panama
Radio Call Sign	3FNQ2
Satellite Telephone Number	–
Length 421 ft./128.3 m.	Beam 54 ft./16.4 m.
Engines	3×Sulzer diesels
Passenger Decks	6
Number of Crew	165
Passenger Capacity (basis 2)	210
Passenger Capacity (all berths)	470

Passenger Space Ratio (basis 2)		33.4
Passenger Space Ratio (all berths)		14.9
Officers Norwegian		Service Staff Filipino
Total Cabins 105	Cabin Door Width 26"	
Outside 85	Inside 20	Single No
Wheelchair Accessible Cabins		No
Dining Rooms 1		Sittings 2
Number of Elevators 1		Door Width 30"
Electric Current in Cabins		220 AC
Casino Yes		Slot Machines Yes
Swimming Pools Outside 1		Inside No
Whirlpools		No
Gymnasium Yes	Sauna Yes	Massage Yes
Cinema/Theatre No		Number of Seats –
Cabin TV No		Library No
Children's Facilities/Playroom		No

Ratings

Ship Appearance/Condition	78	Shore Excursion Program	60
Interior Cleanliness	80	Entertainment	73
Passenger Space	76	Activities Program	71
Passenger Comfort Level	76	Cruise Director/Cruise Staff	72
Furnishings/Decor	76	Ship's Officers/Staff	76
Cruise Cuisine	76	Fitness/Sports Facilities	70
Food Service	77	Overall Ship Facilities	76
Beverages/Service	75	Value for Money	79
Accommodations	75	Total Cruise Experience	80
Cabin Service	76	**Overall Rating**	**1482**
Itineraries/Destinations	60	**Average**	**74.1**

Comments

Squat, tidy-looking vessel with squarish funnel/good open deck and sunning space/ life-size chess game located forward of the funnel/interior decor quite attractive/ charming dining room set to the front, with good ocean views/food good, but choice limited/friendly service/very active casino set/cabins are small and compact, but clean and tidy, with attractive decor/this ship does not pretend to be glamorous, and features one- and two-day "getaway" cruises that are well organized, at a reasonable price, but it's not a real cruise.

Vistafjord ★ ★ ★ ★ ★ +

Principal Cruising Areas:
Worldwide

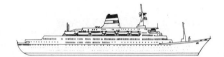

Ship	ms Vistafjord
Cruise Line/Operator	Cunard Line
Former Names	–
Gross Registered Tonnage	24,492
Built	Swan, Hunter (UK)
First Entered Service	1973
Last Refurbished	1983
Country of Registry	Bahamas
Radio Call Sign	C6ZV
Satellite Telephone Number	1104114
Length 626 ft./190.8 m.	Beam 82 ft./24.9 m.
Engines	2×Sulzer diesels
Passenger Decks	9
Number of Crew	384
Passenger Capacity (basis 2)	736
Passenger Capacity (all berths)	736

Passenger Space Ratio (basis 2)		33.2
Passenger Space Ratio (all berths)		33.2
Officers Norwegian	Service Staff European	
Total Cabins 387	Cabin Door Width 26"	
Outside 347	Inside 40	Single 36
Wheelchair Accessible Cabins		No
Dining Rooms 1	Sittings Open	
Number of Elevators 6	Door Width 29"	
Electric Current in Cabins		110 AC
Casino Yes	Slot Machines Yes	
Swimming Pools Outside 1	Inside 1	
Whirlpools		2
Gymnasium Yes	Sauna Yes	Massage Yes
Cinema/Theatre Yes	Number of Seats 250	
Cabin TV Yes	Library Yes	
Children's Facilities/Playroom		No

Ratings

Ship Appearance/Condition	95		Shore Excursion Program	92
Interior Cleanliness	95		Entertainment	84
Passenger Space	94		Activities Program	86
Passenger Comfort Level	94		Cruise Director/Cruise Staff	86
Furnishings/Decor	92		Ship's Officers/Staff	88
Cruise Cuisine	94		Fitness/Sports Facilities	90
Food Service	92		Overall Ship Facilities	93
Beverages/Service	91		Value for Money	90
Accommodations	92		Total Cruise Experience	94
Cabin Service	92		**Overall Rating**	**1826**
Itineraries/Destinations	92		**Average**	**91.3**

Comments

Finely proportioned ship with beautiful, flowing lines and classic profile/spotlessly clean/expansive open deck and sunning space/built with the finest quality materials inside and out/very spacious public rooms/tasteful Scandinavian decor throughout/quiet, elegant dining room, with superb, unhurried service/fine international cuisine with the highest quality ingredients/suites with balconies superb, but all cabins are well appointed/excellent Scandinavian stewardesses/conservative entertainment/this ship caters to the most discerning of passengers, in truly elegant style and supremely comfortable surroundings/in my opinion, this is one of the world's premier travel experiences.

Westerdam ★★★★+

Principal Cruising Areas:
Alaska / Caribbean

Ship	mv Westerdam
Cruise Line / Operator	Holland America Line
Former Names	Homeric
Gross Registered Tonnage	42,092
Built	Meyer Werft (W. Germany)
First Entered Service	1986
Last Refurbished	–
Country of Registry	Panama
Radio Call Sign	EELX
Satellite Telephone Number	1331766
Length 670 ft. / 204.2 m.	Beam 95 ft. / 28.9 m.
Engines	2×MAN diesels
Passenger Decks	8
Number of Crew	490
Passenger Capacity (basis 2)	1000
Passenger Capacity (all berths)	1060

Passenger Space Ratio (basis 2)		42.1
Passenger Space Ratio (all berths)		39.7
Officers Dutch	Service Staff Filipino / Indonesian	
Total Cabins 521	Cabin Door Width 25″	
Outside 348	Inside 173	Single 12
Wheelchair Accessible Cabins		No
Dining Rooms 1		Sittings 2
Number of Elevators 5	Door Width 39″	
Electric Current in Cabins		110 AC
Casino Yes	Slot Machines Yes	
Swimming Pools Outside 1		Inside 1
Whirlpools		No
Gymnasium Yes	Sauna Yes	Massage Yes
Cinema / Theatre Yes	Number of Seats 237	
Cabin TV Yes		Library Yes
Children's Facilities / Playroom		No

Ratings

Ship Appearance / Condition	88	Shore Excursion Program	81	
Interior Cleanliness	90	Entertainment	82	
Passenger Space	90	Activities Program	78	
Passenger Comfort Level	88	Cruise Director / Cruise Staff	81	
Furnishings / Decor	88	Ship's Officers / Staff	81	
Cruise Cuisine	83	Fitness / Sports Facilities	87	
Food Service	82	Overall Ship Facilities	86	
Beverages / Service	82	Value for Money	85	
Accommodations	88	Total Cruise Experience	86	
Cabin Service	83	**Overall Rating**	**1691**	
Itineraries / Destinations	82	**Average**	**84.5**	

Comments

Tall superstructure is well balanced, except for short, stubby bow / quality construction throughout / good passenger flow / elegant interior, with delightful public rooms decorated in pastel tones / high quality furnishings and fabrics / generous open deck space / excellent health and fitness center / cabins are generously proportioned, and equipped with ample closet, drawer and storage space / beautiful dining room, set low down, has raised center dome as well as portholes / service is superb / entertainment is good / this ship is delightful to cruise on, and provides an elegant setting for repeat passengers / an excellent acquisition for Holland America Line / 195 cabins to be added in a 140-feet "stretch" and extensive refit due in October, 1989.

Wind Song ★★★★★

Principal Cruising Areas:
Tahiti

Ship	yc Wind Song	Passenger Space Ratio (basis 2)		35.8
Cruise Line/Operator	Windstar Sail Cruises	Passenger Space Ratio (all berths)		31.2
Former Names	–	Officers Norwegian	Service Staff European	
Gross Registered Tonnage	5,307	Total Cabins 74	Cabin Door Width 25"	
Built Ateliers et Chantiers du Havre (France)		Outside 74	Inside No	Single No
First Entered Service	1987	Wheelchair Accessible Cabins		No
Last Refurbished	–	Dining Rooms 1		Sittings Open
Country of Registry	Bahamas	Number of Elevators 0		Door Width –
Radio Call Sign	C6CB2	Electric Current in Cabins		110 AC
Satellite Telephone Number	1104270	Casino Yes		Slot Machines Yes
Length 440 ft./134.1 m. Beam 52 ft./15.8 m.		Swimming Pools Outside 1		Inside No
Engines 2×Wartsila diesels/sail power		Whirlpools		No
Passenger Decks	4	Gymnasium Yes Sauna Yes		Massage Yes
Number of Crew	84	Cinema/Theatre No	Number of Seats –	
Passenger Capacity (basis 2)	148	Cabin TV Yes		Library Yes
Passenger Capacity (all berths)	170	Children's Facilities/Playroom		No

Ratings

Ship Appearance/Condition	90	Shore Excursion Program	85
Interior Cleanliness	92	Entertainment	84
Passenger Space	84	Activities Program	84
Passenger Comfort Level	92	Cruise Director/Cruise Staff	84
Furnishings/Decor	92	Ship's Officers/Staff	86
Cruise Cuisine	90	Fitness/Sports Facilities	88
Food Service	88	Overall Ship Facilities	88
Beverages/Service	86	Value for Money	86
Accommodations	91	Total Cruise Experience	90
Cabin Service	90	**Overall Rating**	**1755**
Itineraries/Destinations	85	**Average**	**87.7**

Comments

Long, sleek-looking craft that is part yacht-part cruise ship, with four giant masts and computer-controlled sails/one of three identical vessels/beautifully crafted interior with fine, light woods used, together with soft, complementary decor/open deck and sunning space adequate/elegant dining room has ocean views from large picture windows/nouvelle cuisine, but could be improved/fine European service/cabins are all-outside one-price suites and come completely equipped/watersports platform at stern/vessel carries windsurfers, water-ski boat/distinct European ambiance/this ship will cruise you in luxury, yet provide a relaxing cruise experience that's just right for seven idyllic days in sheltered areas/lovely way to unwind/gratuities included.

Wind Spirit ★★★★

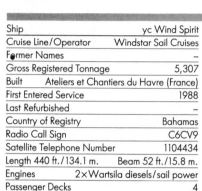

Principal Cruising Areas:
Caribbean

Ship	yc Wind Spirit	Passenger Space Ratio (basis 2)	35.8
Cruise Line/Operator	Windstar Sail Cruises	Passenger Space Ratio (all berths)	31.2
Former Names	–	Officers Norwegian	Service Staff European
Gross Registered Tonnage	5,307	Total Cabins 74	Cabin Door Width 25″
Built Ateliers et Chantiers du Havre (France)		Outside 74 Inside No	Single No
First Entered Service	1988	Wheelchair Accessible Cabins	No
Last Refurbished	–	Dining Rooms 1	Sittings Open
Country of Registry	Bahamas	Number of Elevators 0	Door Width –
Radio Call Sign	C6CV9	Electric Current in Cabins	110 AC
Satellite Telephone Number	1104434	Casino Yes	Slot Machines Yes
Length 440 ft./134.1 m. Beam 52 ft./15.8 m.		Swimming Pools Outside 1	Inside No
Engines 2×Wartsila diesels/sail power		Whirlpools	No
Passenger Decks	4	Gymnasium Yes Sauna Yes	Massage Yes
Number of Crew	84	Cinema/Theatre No	Number of Seats –
Passenger Capacity (basis 2)	148	Cabin TV Yes	Library Yes
Passenger Capacity (all berths)	170	Children's Facilities/Playroom	No

Ratings

Ship Appearance/Condition	90	Shore Excursion Program	85
Interior Cleanliness	92	Entertainment	84
Passenger Space	84	Activities Program	84
Passenger Comfort Level	92	Cruise Director/Cruise Staff	84
Furnishings/Decor	92	Ship's Officers/Staff	86
Cruise Cuisine	90	Fitness/Sports Facilities	88
Food Service	88	Overall Ship Facilities	88
Beverages/Service	86	Value for Money	86
Accommodations	91	Total Cruise Experience	90
Cabin Service	90	**Overall Rating**	**1755**
Itineraries/Destinations	85	**Average**	**87.7**

Comments

Twin sister to *Wind Song* and *Wind Spirit*/ part yacht-part cruise ship, with four giant masts and computer-controlled sails/ beautifully crafted interior with fine, light woods everywhere, and soft, complementary colors/adequate amount of open deck and sunning space due to sail machinery/ lovely dining room features nouvelle cuisine, but quality could be improved/cabins are all-outside one-price mini-suites and are beautifully appointed/stern watersports platform/vessel carries windsurfers and water-ski boat/distinct European ambiance/ this sail-cruise ship will cruise you in relaxed, refined luxury in the Mediterranean, providing seven idyllic days of superb living, with gratuites included.

Wind Star ★★★★

Principal Cruising Areas:
Caribbean

Ship	yc Wind Star	Passenger Space Ratio (basis 2)	35.8
Cruise Line/Operator	Windstar Sail Cruises	Passenger Space Ratio (all berths)	31.2
Former Names	–	Officers Norwegian	Service Staff European
Gross Registered Tonnage	5,307	Total Cabins 74	Cabin Door Width 25"
Built	Ateliers et Chantiers du Havre (France)	Outside 74 Inside No	Single No
First Entered Service	1986	Wheelchair Accessible Cabins	No
Last Refurbished	–	Dining Rooms 1	Sittings Open
Country of Registry	Bahamas	Number of Elevators 0	Door Width –
Radio Call Sign	C6CA9	Electric Current in Cabins	110 AC
Satellite Telephone Number	1104266	Casino Yes	Slot Machines Yes
Length 440 ft./134.1 m.	Beam 52 ft./15.8 m.	Swimming Pools Outside 1	Inside No
Engines	2×Wartsila diesels/sail power	Whirlpools	No
Passenger Decks	4	Gymnasium Yes Sauna Yes	Massage Yes
Number of Crew	84	Cinema/Theatre No	Number of Seats –
Passenger Capacity (basis 2)	148	Cabin TV Yes	Library Yes
Passenger Capacity (all berths)	170	Children's Facilities/Playroom	No

Ratings

Ship Appearance/Condition	90	Shore Excursion Program	85
Interior Cleanliness	92	Entertainment	84
Passenger Space	84	Activities Program	84
Passenger Comfort Level	92	Cruise Director/Cruise Staff	84
Furnishings/Decor	92	Ship's Officers/Staff	86
Cruise Cuisine	90	Fitness/Sports Facilities	88
Food Service	88	Overall Ship Facilities	88
Beverages/Service	86	Value for Money	86
Accommodations	91	Total Cruise Experience	90
Cabin Service	90	**Overall Rating**	**1755**
Itineraries/Destinations	85	**Average**	**87.7**

Comments

One of three identical sisters that is part yacht-part cruise ship, this high-tech vessel has four tall masts with computer-controlled sails/high quality interior is beautifully crafted/light woods used extensively throughout/lovely dining room has very comfortable seating, and ocean views/food is nouvelle cuisine, though not gourmet/Japanese sushi chef aboard/European service is excellent/all-outside suites are one price, and come beautifully appointed and finished/lots of wood trim everywhere/elegant main lounge/she's a very comfortable ship throughout, with emphasis on refined privacy, and will provide you with a wonderfully relaxing seven-day cruise experience, with gratuities included.

World Discoverer

Principal Cruising Areas:
Worldwide Expedition Cruises

Ship	World Discoverer	Passenger Space Ratio (basis 2)	22.5
Line	Discoverer Reederei/Society Expeditions	Passenger Space Ratio (all berths)	22.5
Former Names	–	Officers German Service Staff European/Filipino	
Gross Registered Tonnage	3,153	Total Cabins 78 Cabin Door Width 30"	
Built	Schichau-Unterweser (W. Germany)	Outside 78 Inside No Single No	
First Entered Service	1977	Wheelchair Accessible Cabins No	
Last Refurbished	1984	Dining Rooms 1 Sittings 1	
Country of Registry	Liberia	Number of Elevators 1 Door Width 36"	
Radio Call Sign	ELDU3	Electric Current in Cabins 110/220 AC	
Satellite Telephone Number	1242744	Casino No Slot Machines No	
Length 285 ft./86.8 m. Beam 50 ft./15.2 m.		Swimming Pools Outside 1 Inside No	
Engines	2×MAK diesels	Whirlpools No	
Passenger Decks	7	Gymnasium Yes Sauna No Massage Yes	
Number of Crew	75	Cinema/Theatre No Number of Seats –	
Passenger Capacity (basis 2)	140	Cabin TV No Library Yes	
Passenger Capacity (all berths)	140	Children's Facilities/Playroom No	

Ratings

Ship Appearance/Condition	–	Shore Excursion Program	–
Interior Cleanliness	–	Entertainment	–
Passenger Space	–	Activities Program	–
Passenger Comfort Level	–	Cruise Director/Cruise Staff	–
Furnishings/Decor	–	Ship's Officers/Staff	–
Cruise Cuisine	–	Fitness/Sports Facilities	–
Food Service	–	Overall Ship Facilities	–
Beverages/Service	–	Value for Money	–
Accommodations	–	Total Cruise Experience	–
Cabin Service	–	**Overall Rating**	–
Itineraries/Destinations	–	**Average**	–

Comments

Sophisticated, small but supremely comfortable vessel built expressly for adventure cruising has sleek, well-proportioned profile/features ice-hardened hull/extremely maneuverable/well equipped for in-depth expedition cruising/elegant and impressive public rooms and interior decor/cozy dining room/excellent cuisine and service/cabins are of good proportions, are comfortable, and tastefully furnished/expert lecturers and nature specialists escort every expedition/this ship provides the best setting for expedition cruising to some of the most remote destinations in the world/it's expensive, but worth it for discerning, well-traveled passengers/finest expedition cruise vessel of its type in service today. Overall rating 5 stars, although category ratings not relevant.

World Renaissance ★★★ +

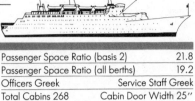

Principal Cruising Areas:
Aegean/Amazon/Caribbean/
Mediterranean

Ship	ms World Renaissance
Cruise Line/Operator	Epirotiki Lines
Formerly	Renaissance/Homeric Renaissance
Gross Registered Tonnage	11,724
Built	Chantiers de l'Atlantique (France)
First Entered Service	1966
Last Refurbished	1978
Country of Registry	Greece
Radio Call Sign	SYXQ
Satellite Telephone Number	1130440
Length 492 ft./149.9 m.	Beam 69 ft./21.0 m.
Engines	2×B&W diesels
Passenger Decks	8
Number of Crew	220
Passenger Capacity (basis 2)	536
Passenger Capacity (all berths)	609

Passenger Space Ratio (basis 2)		21.8
Passenger Space Ratio (all berths)		19.2
Officers Greek		Service Staff Greek
Total Cabins 268		Cabin Door Width 25"
Outside 228	Inside 40	Single 5
Wheelchair Accessible Cabins		No
Dining Rooms 1		Sittings 2
Number of Elevators 2		Door Width 33"
Electric Current in Cabins		110 AC
Casino Yes		Slot Machines Yes
Swimming Pools Outside 2		Inside No
Whirlpools		No
Gymnasium Yes	Sauna Yes	Massage Yes
Cinema/Theatre Yes		Number of Seats 115
Cabin TV No		Library Yes
Children's Facilities/Playroom		No

Ratings

Ship Appearance/Condition	78		Shore Excursion Program	77
Interior Cleanliness	81		Entertainment	77
Passenger Space	77		Activities Program	76
Passenger Comfort Level	81		Cruise Director/Cruise Staff	78
Furnishings/Decor	80		Ship's Officers/Staff	76
Cruise Cuisine	78		Fitness/Sports Facilities	75
Food Service	78		Overall Ship Facilities	78
Beverages/Service	76		Value for Money	81
Accommodations	80		Total Cruise Experience	81
Cabin Service	80		**Overall Rating**	**1568**
Itineraries/Destinations	82		**Average**	**78.4**

Comments

Traditional styling and profile topped by a slender funnel/charming vessel has yacht-like intimacy and ambiance/generous open deck and sunning space/beautiful wood paneling in cabins, which are homely and quite spacious for ship size/bathrooms are tiled/public rooms are few, but main lounge is very comfortable/Xenia Tavern is colonial in style and decor, and functions as setting for both intimate classical concerts as well as ship's disco/library-quiet room is restful/dining room is quite pleasant/continental cuisine is predominantly Greek/good service throughout/this ship will cruise you in comfortable surroundings, at a very fair price.

New ships to debut in 1989/1990

In addition to those ship profiles already included in this edition, the following are confirmed orders for new ships due to debut—up to June 1990.

Date due in service: Mar 1989
Name of ship: Star Princess
Company: Princess Cruises
Tonnage: 62,500 grt
Length: 804 feet
Passenger capacity: 1,470
Passenger space ratio: 42.5
Cost of ship: $150 m
Cost per cabin: $88,500
Where built: Chantiers de l'Atlantique (France)

Date due in service: Apr 1989
Name of ship: Oceanic Grace
Company: Oceanic Cruises
Tonnage: 5,050 grt
Length: 337 feet
Passenger capacity: 120
Passenger space ratio: 42.0
Cost of ship: $40 m
Cost per cabin: $666,666
Where built: Nippon Kokan (Japan)

Date due in service: Apr 1989
Name of ship: unnamed
Company: Yachtship Italy
Tonnage: 3,500 grt
Length: 289 feet
Passenger capacity: 100
Passenger space ratio: 35.0
Cost of ship: $28 m
Cost per cabin: $280,000
Where built: Ferrari (Italy)

Date due in service: July 1989
Name of ship: Vistamar
Company: Hoteles Marinos Reederei/Jahn Reisen
Tonnage: 7,300 grt
Length: 396 feet
Passenger capacity: 330
Passenger space ratio: 22.1
Cost of ship: $32 m
Cost per cabin: $213,333
Where built: Union Navale de Levante (Spain)

Date due in service: July 1989
Name of ship: unnamed
Company: Delfin Cruises
Tonnage: 5,700 grt
Length: 355 feet

Passenger capacity: 300
Passenger space ratio: 19.0
Cost of ship: $45 m
Cost per cabin: $300,000
Where built: Rauma–Repola (Finland)

Date due in service: Aug 1989
Name of ship: unnamed
Company: Yachtship Italy
Tonnage: 3,500 grt
Length: 289 feet
Passenger capacity: 100
Passenger space ratio: 35.0
Cost of ship: $28 m
Cost per cabin: $280,000
Where built: Ferrari (Italy)

Date due in service: Oct 1989
Name of ship: Fantasy
Company: Carnival Cruise Lines
Tonnage: 70,000 grt
Length: 865 feet
Passenger capacity: 2,600
Passenger space ratio: 26.9
Cost of ship: $200 m
Cost per cabin: $195,121
Where built: Wartsila (Finland)

Date due in service: Nov 1989
Name of ship: Seabourn Spirit
Company: Seabourn Cruise Line
Tonnage: 10,000 grt
Length: 440 feet
Passenger capacity: 212
Passenger space ratio: 47.1
Cost of ship: $50 m
Cost per cabin: $471,698
Where built: Seebeckwerft (W. Germany)

Date due in service: Dec 1989
Name of ship: unnamed
Company: Yachtship Italy
Tonnage: 3,500 grt
Length: 289 feet
Passenger capacity: 100
Passenger space ratio: 35.0
Cost of ship: $28 m
Cost per cabin: $280,000
Where built: Ferrari (Italy)

Date due in service: Dec 1989
Name of ship: unnamed
Company: Marflet Vacationes
Tonnage: 27,000 grt
Length: n/a
Passenger capacity: 1,200
Passenger space ratio: 22.5
Cost of ship: $125 m
Cost per cabin: $208,333
Where built: Astilleros Españoles (Spain)

Date due in service: Dec 1989
Name of ship: Van Gogh
Company: Goliath Transport
Tonnage: 4,000 grt
Length: 355 feet
Passenger capacity: 80
Passenger space ratio: 50.0
Cost of ship: $30 m
Cost per cabin: $750,000
Where built: De Hoop, Merwede (Holland)

Date due in service: Dec 1989
Name of ship: Rembrandt
Company: Goliath Transport
Tonnage: 4,000 grt
Length: 355 feet
Passenger capacity: 80
Passenger space ratio: 50.0
Cost of ship: $30 m
Cost per cabin: $750,000
Where built: De Hoop, Merwede (Holland)

Date due in service: Jan 1990
Name of ship: unnamed
Company: Princess Cruises
Tonnage: 70,000 grt
Length: 804 feet
Passenger capacity: 1,650
Passenger space ratio: 42.4
Cost of ship: $150 m
Cost per cabin: $181,818
Where built: Fincantieri (Italy)

Date due in service: Jan 1990
Name of ship: Crown Monarch
Company: Crown Cruise Line
Tonnage: 16,000 grt
Length: 500 feet
Passenger capacity: 560
Passenger space ratio: 28.5
Cost of ship: $73 m
Cost per cabin: $251,724
Where built: Union Navale de Levante (Spain)

Date due in service: Apr 1990
Name of ship: Horizon
Company: Chandris Fantasy Cruises
Tonnage: 45,000 grt
Length: 682 feet
Passenger capacity: 1,360
Passenger space ratio: 33.0
Cost of ship: $150 m
Cost per cabin: $220,588
Where built: Meyer Werft (W. Germany)

Date due in service: Apr 1990
Name of ship: unnamed
Company: Yachtship Italy
Tonnage: 3,500 grt
Length: 289 feet
Passenger capacity: 100
Passenger space ratio: 35.0
Cost of ship: $28 m
Cost per cabin: $280,000
Where built: Ferrari (Italy)

Date due in service: Apr 1990
Name of ship: Future Seas
Company: Admiral Cruises
Tonnage: 45,000 grt
Length: 637 feet
Passenger capacity: 1,600
Passenger space ratio: 28.1
Cost of ship: $150 m
Cost per cabin: $187,500
Where built: Chantiers de l'Atlantique (France)

Date due in service: Apr 1990
Name of ship: CostaMarina
Company: Costa Cruises
Tonnage: 25,000 grt
Length: 572 feet
Passenger capacity: 1,000*
Passenger space ratio: 25.0
Cost of ship: $100 m
Cost per cabin: $200,000
Where built: Mariotti (Italy)

Date due in service: Jun 1990
Name of ship: unnamed
Company: Crystal Cruises
Tonnage: 49,000 grt
Length: 787 feet
Passenger capacity: 960
Passenger space ratio: 51.0
Cost of ship: $200 m
Cost per cabin: $416,666
Where built: Mitsubishi (Japan)

* This ship being converted from former container vessel.

268

Rating Results

The following pages list the results of the ratings and evaluations:

1) Alphabetically by name of ship
2) In order of points received (from top score downwards)
3) According to category (for explanation of category, see p. 275)

Ratings in Alphabetical Order

SHIP	CRUISE LINE	RATING	AVERAGE	STARS
Achille Lauro	Star Lauro Line	1415	70.7	★★
Adriana	Jadrolinija	1488	74.4	★★
Aegean Dolphin	Dolphin Hellas Shipping	1572	78.6	★★★+
Albatross	Dolphin Hellas Shipping	1568	78.4	★★★+
Alexandr Pushkin	Baltic Shipping	1522	76.1	★★★
Americana	Ivaran Lines	–	–	–
Amerikanis	Chandris Fantasy Cruises	1556	77.8	★★★+
Antonina Nezhdanova	Far Eastern Shipping	1489	74.4	★★
Argonaut	Epirotiki Lines	1531	76.5	★★★
Arkona	Deutsche Seereederei	1588	79.4	★★★+
Atalante	Mediterranean Sun Lines	1290	64.5	★
Atlantic	Premier Cruise Lines	1628	81.4	★★★★
Atlas	Epirotiki Lines	1543	77.1	★★★
Ausonia	Siosa Lines	1531	76.5	★★★
Azerbaydzhan	Black Sea Shipping	1534	76.7	★★★
The Azur	Chandris Fantasy Cruises	1583	79.1	★★★+
Azure Seas	Admiral Cruises	1501	75.0	★★★
Belorussiya	Black Sea Shipping	1542	77.1	★★★
Berlin	Deilmann Reederei	1608	80.4	★★★★
Bermuda Star	Bermuda Star Line	1565	78.2	★★★+
Black Prince	Fred Olsen Cruises	1575	78.7	★★★+
Britanis	Chandris Fantasy Cruises	1551	77.5	★★★+
Canberra	P&O Canberra Cruises	1602	80.1	★★★★
Carib Vacationer	Vacation Liners	1343	67.1	★
Caribe I	Commodore Cruise Lines	1539	76.9	★★★
Carla Costa	Costa Cruises	1560	78.0	★★★+
Carnivale	Carnival Cruise Lines	1551	77.5	★★★+
Celebration	Carnival Cruise Lines	1640	82.0	★★★★
City of Mykonos	Cycladic Cruises	1420	71.0	★★

SHIP	CRUISE LINE	RATING	AVERAGE	STARS
City of Rhodos	Cycladic Cruises	1373	68.6	★
Constitution	American Hawaii Cruises	1573	78.6	★★★+
CostaRiviera	Costa Cruises	1609	80.4	★★★★
Crown del Mar	Crown Cruise Line	–	–	–
Crown Odyssey	Royal Cruise Line	1788	89.4	★★★★★
Cunard Countess	Cunard Line	1597	79.8	★★★+
Cunard Princess	Cunard Line	1599	79.9	★★★+
Dalmacija	Jadrolinija	1428	71.4	★★
Danae	Costa Cruises	1609	80.4	★★★★
Daphne	Costa Cruises	1614	80.7	★★★★
Dawn Princess	Princess Cruises	1612	80.6	★★★★
Discovery I	Discovery Cruises	1480	74.0	★★
Dolphin IV	Dolphin Cruise Line	1534	76.7	★★★
Emerald Seas	Admiral Cruises	1544	77.2	★★★
Enrico Costa	Costa Cruises	1434	71.7	★★
Eugenio Costa	Costa Cruises	1573	78.6	★★★+
Europa	Hapag-Lloyd Line	1823	91.1	★★★★★+
Explorer Starship	Exploration Cruise Lines	1620	81.0	★★★★
Fair Princess	Princess Cruises	1610	80.5	★★★★
FairStar	P&O Sitmar Cruises	1509	75.4	★★★
Fedor Dostoyevsky	Black Sea Shipping	1686	84.3	★★★★+
Fedor Shalyapin	Black Sea Shipping	1464	73.2	★★
Festivale	Carnival Cruise Lines	1588	79.4	★★★+
Funchal	Fritidskryss	1554	77.7	★★★+
Galaxias	Global Cruises	1476	73.8	★★
Galileo	Chandris Fantasy Cruises	1598	79.9	★★★+
Golden Odyssey	Royal Cruise Line	1658	82.9	★★★★
Gruziya	Black Sea Shipping	1536	76.8	★★★
Holiday	Carnival Cruise Lines	1619	80.9	★★★★
Illiria	Blue Aegean Cruises	1606	80.3	★★★★
Independence	American Hawaii Cruises	1573	78.6	★★★+
Island Princess	Princess Cruises	1679	83.9	★★★★+
Ivan Franko	Black Sea Shipping	1470	73.5	★★
Jason	Epirotiki Lines	1545	77.2	★★★
Jubilee	Carnival Cruise Lines	1622	81.1	★★★★
Jupiter	Epirotiki Lines	1542	77.1	★★★
Kazakhstan	Black Sea Shipping	1541	77.0	★★★
La Palma	Intercruise	1485	74.2	★★
Leonid Brezhnev	Black Sea Shipping	1549	77.4	★★★
Majestic	Premier Cruise Lines	1581	79.0	★★★+
Mardi Gras	Carnival Cruise Lines	1553	77.6	★★★+
Maxim Gorki	Black Sea Shipping	1574	78.7	★★★+
Mermoz	Paquet Cruises	1601	80.0	★★★★

SHIP	CRUISE LINE	RATING	AVERAGE	STARS
Mikhail Sholokhov	Far Eastern Shipping	1533	76.6	★★★
Monterey	Aloha Pacific Cruises	1597	79.8	★★★+
Neptune	Epirotiki Lines	1509	75.4	★★★
Nieuw Amsterdam	Holland America Line	1703	85.1	★★★★+
Noordam	Holland America Line	1706	85.3	★★★★+
Nordic Prince	Royal Caribbean Cruise Line	1656	82.8	★★★★
Norway	Norwegian Cruise Line	1667	83.3	★★★★
Ocean Islander	Ocean Cruise Lines	1624	81.2	★★★★
Ocean Pearl	Ocean Cruise Lines	1662	83.1	★★★★
Ocean Princess	Ocean Cruise Lines	1629	81.4	★★★★
Oceanic	Premier Cruise Lines	1618	80.9	★★★★
Oceanos	Epirotiki Lines	1560	78.0	★★★+
Odessa	Black Sea Shipping	1496	74.8	★★
Odysseus	Epirotiki Lines	–	–	–
Orient Express	British Ferries	1596	79.8	★★★+
Orpheus	Epirotiki Lines	1543	77.1	★★★
Pacific Princess	Princess Cruises	1680	84.0	★★★★+
Pegasus	Epirotiki Lines	1590	79.5	★★★+
Polaris	Society Expeditions	–	–	–
Queen Elizabeth 2 (Grill Class)	Cunard Line	1821	91.0	★★★★★+
Queen Elizabeth 2 (First Class)	Cunard Line	1796	89.8	★★★★★
Queen Elizabeth 2 (Transatlantic Class)	Cunard Line	1746	87.3	★★★★+
Queen of Bermuda	Bermuda Star Line	1593	79.6	★★★+
Regent Sea	Regency Cruises	1601	80.0	★★★★
Regent Star	Regency Cruises	1597	79.8	★★★+
Regent Sun	Regency Cruises	1609	80.4	★★★★
Romanza	Chandris Fantasy Cruises	1448	72.4	★★
Rotterdam	Holland America Line	1678	83.9	★★★★+
Royal Princess	Princess Cruises	1767	88.3	★★★★★
Royal Viking Sea	Royal Viking Line	1829	91.4	★★★★★+
Royal Viking Sky	Royal Viking Line	1829	91.4	★★★★★+
Royal Viking Star	Royal Viking Line	1816	90.8	★★★★★
Royal Viking Sun	Royal Viking Line	–	–	–
Sagafjord	Cunard Line	1829	91.4	★★★★★+
Scandinavian Saga	SeaEscape	1480	74.0	★★
Scandinavian Sky	SeaEscape	1480	74.0	★★
Scandinavian Star	SeaEscape	1480	74.0	★★
Scandinavian Sun	SeaEscape	1480	74.0	★★
Sea Cloud	Sea Cloud Cruises	–	–	–
Sea Goddess I	Cunard Line	1822	91.1	★★★★★+
Sea Goddess II	Cunard Line	1822	91.1	★★★★★+

SHIP	CRUISE LINE	RATING	AVERAGE	STARS
Sea Princess	Princess Cruises	1709	85.4	★★★★+
Sea Venture	Sea Venture Cruises	–	–	–
Seabourn Pride	Seabourn Cruise Line	–	–	–
SeaBreeze	Dolphin Cruise Line	1592	79.6	★★★+
Seaward	Norwegian Cruise Line	1728	86.4	★★★★+
Shota Rustaveli	Black Sea Shipping	1535	76.7	★★★
Sky Princess	Princess Cruises	1681	84.0	★★★★+
Skyward	Norwegian Cruise Line	1596	79.8	★★★+
Society Explorer	Society Expeditions	–	–	–
Song of America	Royal Caribbean Cruise Line	1663	83.1	★★★★
Song of Norway	Royal Caribbean Cruise Line	1654	82.7	★★★★
Southward	Norwegian Cruise Line	1607	80.3	★★★★
Sovereign of the Seas	Royal Caribbean Cruise Line	1712	85.6	★★★★+
Star Princess	Princess Cruises	–	–	–
Stardancer	Admiral Cruises	1635	81.7	★★★★
Starward	Norwegian Cruise Line	1604	80.2	★★★★
Stella Maris	Sun Line Cruises	1604	80.2	★★★★
Stella Oceanis	Sun Line Cruises	1573	78.6	★★★+
Stella Solaris	Sun Line Cruises	1660	83.0	★★★★
Sun Viking	Royal Caribbean Cruise Line	1644	82.2	★★★★
Sunward II	Norwegian Cruise Line	1584	79.2	★★★+
Taras Shevchenko	Black Sea Shipping	1473	73.6	★★
Tropicale	Carnival Cruise Lines	1618	80.9	★★★★
Universe	World Explorer Cruises	1510	75.5	★★★
Vasco da Gama	Arcalia Shipping/Neckermann Seereisen	–	–	–
Veracruz	Bermuda Star Line	1487	74.3	★★
The Victoria	Chandris Fantasy Cruises	1551	77.5	★★★+
Viking Princess	Crown Cruise Line	1482	74.1	★★
Vistafjord	Cunard Line	1826	91.3	★★★★★+
Westerdam	Holland America Line	1691	84.5	★★★★+
Wind Song	Windstar Sail Cruises	1755	87.7	★★★★★
Wind Spirit	Windstar Sail Cruises	1755	87.7	★★★★★
Wind Star	Windstar Sail Cruises	1755	87.7	★★★★★
World Discoverer	Society Expeditions	–	–	–
World Renaissance	Epirotiki Lines	1570	78.5	★★★+

Ratings by Points and Stars

STARS	RATING	AVERAGE	SHIP
★★★★★+	1829	91.4	Royal Viking Sea
★★★★★+	1829	91.4	Royal Viking Sky
★★★★★+	1829	91.4	Sagafjord
★★★★★+	1826	91.3	Vistafjord
★★★★★+	1823	91.1	Europa
★★★★★+	1822	91.1	Sea Goddess I
★★★★★+	1822	91.1	Sea Goddess II
★★★★★+	1821	91.0	Queen Elizabeth 2 (Grill Class)
★★★★★	1816	90.8	Royal Viking Star
★★★★★	1796	89.8	Queen Elizabeth 2 (First Class)
★★★★★	1788	89.4	Crown Odyssey
★★★★★	1767	88.3	Royal Princess
★★★★★	1755	87.7	Wind Song
★★★★★	1755	87.7	Wind Spirit
★★★★★	1755	87.7	Wind Star
★★★★+	1746	87.3	Queen Elizabeth 2 (Transatlantic Class)
★★★★+	1728	86.4	Seaward
★★★★+	1712	85.6	Sovereign of the Seas
★★★★+	1709	85.4	Sea Princess
★★★★+	1706	85.3	Noordam
★★★★+	1703	84.5	Nieuw Amsterdam
★★★★+	1691	84.5	Westerdam
★★★★+	1686	84.3	Fedor Dostoyevsky
★★★★+	1681	84.0	Sky Princess
★★★★+	1680	84.0	Pacific Princess
★★★★+	1679	83.9	Island Princess
★★★★+	1678	83.9	Rotterdam
★★★★	1667	83.3	Norway
★★★★	1663	83.1	Song of America
★★★★	1662	83.1	Ocean Pearl
★★★★	1660	83.0	Stella Solaris
★★★★	1658	82.9	Golden Odyssey
★★★★	1656	82.8	Nordic Prince
★★★★	1654	82.7	Song of Norway
★★★★	1644	82.2	Sun Viking
★★★★	1640	82.0	Celebration
★★★★	1637	81.8	Jubilee
★★★★	1635	81.7	Stardancer
★★★★	1629	81.4	Ocean Princess
★★★★	1628	81.4	Atlantic
★★★★	1624	81.2	Ocean Islander
★★★★	1620	81.0	Explorer Starship
★★★★	1619	80.9	Holiday
★★★★	1618	80.9	Oceanic
★★★★	1618	80.9	Tropicale
★★★★	1614	80.7	Daphne
★★★★	1612	80.6	Dawn Princess
★★★★	1610	80.5	Fair Princess
★★★★	1609	80.4	Danae
★★★★	1609	80.4	CostaRiviera
★★★★	1609	80.4	Regent Sun
★★★★	1608	80.4	Berlin
★★★★	1607	80.3	Southward
★★★★	1606	80.3	Illiria
★★★★	1604	80.2	Starward
★★★★	1604	80.2	Stella Maris
★★★★	1602	80.1	Canberra
★★★★	1601	80.0	Mermoz
★★★★	1601	80.0	Regent Sea
★★★+	1599	79.9	Cunard Princess
★★★+	1598	79.9	Galileo
★★★+	1597	79.8	Cunard Countess
★★★+	1597	79.8	Monterey
★★★+	1597	79.8	Regent Star
★★★+	1596	79.8	Orient Express
★★★+	1596	79.8	Skyward
★★★+	1593	79.6	Queen of Bermuda
★★★+	1592	79.6	SeaBreeze
★★★+	1590	79.5	Pegasus
★★★+	1588	79.4	Arkona
★★★+	1588	79.4	Festivale
★★★+	1584	79.2	Sunward II
★★★+	1583	79.1	The Azur
★★★+	1581	79.2	Majestic
★★★+	1575	78.7	Black Prince
★★★+	1574	78.7	Maxim Gorki
★★★+	1573	78.6	Constitution
★★★+	1573	78.6	Eugenio Costa
★★★+	1573	78.6	Independence
★★★+	1573	78.6	Stella Oceanis
★★★+	1572	78.6	Aegean Dolphin
★★★+	1570	78.5	World Renaissance

STARS	RAT-ING	AVER-AGE	SHIP
★★★+	1568	78.4	Albatross
★★★+	1565	78.2	Bermuda Star
★★★+	1560	78.0	Carla Costa
★★★+	1560	78.0	Oceanos
★★★+	1556	77.8	Amerikanis
★★★+	1554	77.7	Funchal
★★★+	1553	77.6	Mardi Gras
★★★+	1551	77.5	Britanis
★★★+	1551	77.5	Carnivale
★★★+	1551	77.5	The Victoria
★★★	1549	77.4	Belorussiya
★★★	1549	77.4	Leonid Brezhnev
★★★	1545	77.2	Jason
★★★	1544	77.2	Emerald Seas
★★★	1543	77.1	Atlas
★★★	1543	77.1	Orpheus
★★★	1542	77.1	Jupiter
★★★	1541	77.0	Kazakhstan
★★★	1539	76.9	Caribe I
★★★	1536	76.8	Gruziya
★★★	1535	76.7	Shota Rustaveli
★★★	1534	76.7	Azerbaydzhan
★★★	1534	76.7	Dolphin IV
★★★	1533	76.6	Mikhail Sholokhov
★★★	1531	76.5	Argonaut
★★★	1531	76.5	Ausonia
★★★	1522	76.1	Alexandr Pushkin
★★★	1510	75.5	Universe
★★★	1509	75.4	Neptune
★★★	1509	75.4	FairStar
★★★	1501	75.0	Azure Seas
★★	1496	74.8	Odessa
★★	1489	74.4	Antonina Nezhdanova
★★	1488	74.4	Adriana
★★	1487	74.3	Veracruz
★★	1485	74.2	La Palma
★★	1482	74.1	Viking Princess
★★	1480	74.0	Discovery I
★★	1480	74.0	Scandinavian Saga
★★	1480	74.0	Scandinavian Sky
★★	1480	74.0	Scandinavian Star
★★	1480	74.0	Scandinavian Sun
★★	1476	73.8	Galaxias
★★	1473	73.6	Taras Shevchenko
★★	1470	73.5	Ivan Franko
★★	1464	73.2	Fedor Shalyapin
★★	1448	72.4	Romanza
★★	1434	71.7	Enrico Costa
★★	1428	71.4	Dalmacija
★★	1420	71.0	City of Mykonos
★★	1415	70.7	Achille Lauro
★	1373	68.6	City of Rhodos
★	1343	67.1	Carib Vacationer
★	1290	64.5	Atalante

Ratings by Category

CATEGORY	GRT
1	Up to 10,000
2	10,000–20,000
3	20,000–30,000
4	Over 30,000

Category 1

STARS	RATING	SHIP	LINE
★★★★★+	1822	Sea Goddess I	Cunard Line
★★★★★+	1822	Sea Goddess II	Cunard Line
★★★★★	1755	Wind Song	Windstar Sail Cruises
★★★★★	1755	Wind Spirit	Windstar Sail Cruises
★★★★★	1755	Wind Star	Windstar Sail Cruises
★★★★	1624	Ocean Islander	Ocean Cruise Lines
★★★★	1620	Explorer Starship	Exploration Cruise Lines
★★★★	1608	Berlin	Deilmann Reederei
★★★★	1606	Illiria	Blue Aegean Cruises
★★★★	1604	Stella Maris	Sun Line Cruises
★★★+	1573	Stella Oceanis	Sun Line Cruises
★★★+	1554	Funchal	Fritidskryss
★★★	1545	Jason	Epirotiki Lines
★★★	1543	Orpheus	Epirotiki Lines
★★★	1542	Jupiter	Epirotiki Lines
★★★	1533	Mikhail Sholokhov	Far Eastern Shipping
★★★	1531	Argonaut	Epirotiki Lines
★★★	1509	Neptune	Epirotiki Lines
★★	1489	Antonina Nezhdanova	Far Eastern Shipping
★★	1488	Adriana	Jadrolinija
★★	1487	Veracruz	Bermuda Star Line
★★	1482	Viking Princess	Crown Cruise Line
★★	1480	Scandinavian Saga	SeaEscape

STARS	RATING	SHIP	LINE
★★	1480	Scandinavian Sky	SeaEscape
★★	1480	Scandinavian Sun	SeaEscape
★★	1476	Galaxias	Global Cruises
★★	1448	Romanza	Chandris Fantasy Cruises
★★	1428	Dalmacija	Jadrolinija
★★	1420	City of Mykonos	Cycladic Cruises
★	1373	City of Rhodos	Cycladic Cruises
★	1343	Carib Vacationer	Vacation Liners

Category 2

STARS	RATING	SHIP	LINE
★★★★	1662	Ocean Pearl	Ocean Cruise Lines
★★★★	1660	Stella Solaris	Sun Line Cruises
★★★★	1658	Golden Odyssey	Royal Cruise Line
★★★★	1644	Sun Viking	Royal Caribbean Cruise Line
★★★★	1629	Ocean Princess	Ocean Cruise Lines
★★★★	1614	Daphne	Costa Cruises
★★★★	1609	Danae	Costa Cruises
★★★★	1607	Southward	Norwegian Cruise Line
★★★★	1604	Starward	Norwegian Cruise Line
★★★★	1601	Mermoz	Paquet Cruises
★★★+	1599	Cunard Princess	Cunard Line
★★★+	1597	Cunard Countess	Cunard Line
★★★+	1596	Orient Express	British Ferries
★★★+	1596	Skyward	Norwegian Cruise Line
★★★+	1590	Pegasus	Epirotiki Lines
★★★+	1588	Arkona	Deutsche Seereederei
★★★+	1584	Sunward II	Norwegian Cruise Line
★★★+	1583	The Azur	Chandris Fantasy Cruises
★★★+	1581	Majestic	Premier Cruise Lines
★★★+	1575	Black Prince	Fred Olsen Cruises
★★★+	1572	Aegean Dolphin	Dolphin Hellas Shipping
★★★+	1570	World Renaissance	Epirotiki Lines
★★★+	1568	Albatross	Dolphin Hellas Shipping
★★★+	1560	Oceanos	Epirotiki Lines
★★★+	1556	Amerikanis	Chandris Fantasy Cruises
★★★+	1551	The Victoria	Chandris Fantasy Cruises
★★★	1549	Leonid Brezhnev	Black Sea Shipping
★★★	1543	Atlas	Epirotiki Lines
★★★	1542	Belorussiya	Black Sea Shipping
★★★	1541	Kazakhstan	Delphin Seereisen
★★★	1536	Gruziya	Black Sea Shipping

STARS	RATING	SHIP	LINE
★★★	1534	Azerbaydzhan	Black Sea Shipping
★★★	1534	Dolphin IV	Dolphin Cruise Line
★★★	1531	Ausonia	Siosa Lines
★★★	1510	Universe	World Explorer Cruises
★★	1496	Odessa	Black Sea Shipping
★★	1485	La Palma	Intercruise
★★	1480	Discovery I	Discovery Cruises
★★	1480	Scandinavian Star	SeaEscape
★★	1434	Enrico Costa	Costa Cruises
★	1290	Atalante	Mediterranean Sun Lines

Category 3

STARS	RATING	SHIP	LINE
★★★★★+	1829	Royal Viking Sea	Royal Viking Line
★★★★★+	1829	Royal Viking Sky	Royal Viking Line
★★★★★+	1829	Sagafjord	Cunard Line
★★★★★+	1826	Vistafjord	Cunard Line
★★★★★	1816	Royal Viking Star	Royal Viking Line
★★★★+	1709	Sea Princess	Princess Cruises
★★★★+	1686	Fedor Dostoyevsky	Black Sea Shipping
★★★★+	1680	Pacific Princess	Princess Cruises
★★★★+	1679	Island Princess	Princess Cruises
★★★★	1656	Nordic Prince	Royal Caribbean Cruise Line
★★★★	1654	Song of Norway	Royal Caribbean Cruise Line
★★★★	1635	Stardancer	Admiral Cruises
★★★★	1612	Dawn Princess	Princess Cruises
★★★★	1610	Fair Princess	Princess Cruises
★★★★	1609	Regent Sun	Regency Cruises
★★★★	1601	Regent Sea	Regency Cruises
★★★+	1598	Galileo	Chandris Fantasy Cruises
★★★+	1597	Monterey	Aloha Pacific Cruises
★★★+	1597	Regent Star	Regency Cruises
★★★+	1593	Queen of Bermuda	Bermuda Star Line
★★★+	1592	SeaBreeze	Dolphin Cruise Line
★★★+	1574	Maxim Gorki	Black Sea Shipping
★★★+	1565	Bermuda Star	Bermuda Star Line
★★★+	1560	Carla Costa	Costa Cruises
★★★+	1553	Mardi Gras	Carnival Cruise Lines
★★★+	1551	Britanis	Chandris Fantasy Cruises
★★★+	1551	Carnivale	Carnival Cruise Line
★★★	1539	Caribe I	Commodore Cruise Lines
★★★	1535	Shota Rustaveli	Black Sea Shipping

STARS	RATING	SHIP	LINE
★★★	1522	Alexandr Pushkin	Baltic Shipping
★★★	1509	FairStar	P&O Sitmar Cruises
★★★	1501	Azure Seas	Admiral Cruises
★★	1473	Taras Shevchenko	Black Sea Shipping
★★	1470	Ivan Franko	Black Sea Shipping
★★	1464	Fedor Shalyapin	Black Sea Shipping
★★	1415	Achille Lauro	Star Lauro Line

Category 4

STARS	RATING	SHIP	LINE
★★★★★+	1823	Europa	Hapag-Lloyd Line
★★★★★+	1821	Queen Elizabeth 2	Cunard Line (Grill Class)
★★★★★	1796	Queen Elizabeth 2	Cunard Line (First Class)
★★★★★	1788	Crown Odyssey	Royal Cruise Line
★★★★★	1767	Royal Princess	Princess Cruises
★★★★+	1746	Queen Elizabeth 2	Cunard Line (Transatlantic Class)
★★★★+	1728	Seaward	Norwegian Cruise Line
★★★★+	1712	Sovereign of the Seas	Royal Caribbean Cruise Line
★★★★+	1706	Noordam	Holland America Line
★★★★+	1703	Nieuw Amsterdam	Holland America Line
★★★★+	1691	Westerdam	Holland America Line
★★★★+	1681	Sky Princess	Princess Cruises
★★★★+	1678	Rotterdam	Holland America Line
★★★★	1667	Norway	Norwegian Cruise Line
★★★★	1663	Song of America	Royal Caribbean Cruise Line
★★★★	1630	Celebration	Carnival Cruise Lines
★★★★	1628	Atlantic	Premier Cruise Lines
★★★★	1622	Jubilee	Carnival Cruise Lines
★★★★	1619	Holiday	Carnival Cruise Lines
★★★★	1618	Oceanic	Premier Cruise Lines
★★★★	1609	CostaRiviera	Costa Cruises
★★★★	1601	Canberra	P&O Canberra Cruises
★★★+	1588	Festivale	Carnival Cruise Lines
★★★+	1573	Constitution	American Hawaii Cruises
★★★+	1573	Eugenio Costa	Costa Cruises
★★★+	1573	Independence	American Hawaii Cruises
★★★	1544	Emerald Seas	Admiral Cruises
★★★	1473	Tropicale	Carnival Cruise Lines

Appendices

Outstanding Statistics

During the compilation of this book, the following statistics, based on the ocean-going cruise ships, came to light:

Total tonnage of all ships (grt)	3,121,531
Average tonnage for the "fleet"	21,091.4
Number of crew employed	47,717
Passenger capacity (basis 2)	96,606
Passenger capacity (all)	120,366
Number of passenger cabins	49,748
Number of outside cabins	33,103
Number of inside cabins	16,645
Age of "fleet" (in 1989)	3,214
Average age per ship	21.71

World's 10 largest cruise lines (in order of tonnage)

Company: Kloster Cruises (NCL + RVL)
Number of ships: 10
Norway/Seaward/Southward/Skyward/Starward/Sunward II/Royal Viking Sea/Royal Viking Sky/Royal Viking Star/Royal Viking Sun
Total number of cabins: 5,287
Total number of berths: 10,185
Gross Registered Tonnage: 297,835

Company: P&O Canberra Cruises/Princess Cruises/P&O Sitmar Cruises
Number of ships: 10
Canberra/Dawn Princess/Fair Princess/FairStar/Island Princess/Pacific Princess/Royal Princess/Sea Princess/Sky Princess/Star Princess
Total number of cabins: 5,124
Total number of berths: 11,582
Gross Registered Tonnage: 294,596

Company: Carnival Cruise Lines
Number of ships: 7
Carnivale/Celebration/Festivale/Holiday/Jubilee/Mardi Gras/Tropicale
Total number of cabins: 4,256
Total number of berths: 10,882
Gross Registered Tonnage: 269,925

Company: Royal Admiral Cruises (RCCL + Admiral)
Number of ships: 8
Azure Seas/Emerald Seas/Stardancer/Nordic Prince/Song of America/Song of Norway/Sovereign of the Seas/Sun Viking
Total number of cabins: 4,545
Total number of berths: 10,742
Gross Registered Tonnage: 248,227

Company: Holland America Line
Number of ships: 7
Nieuw Amsterdam/Noordam/Rotterdam/Westerdam/Windsong/Windspirit/Windstar
Total number of cabins: 2,538
Total number of berths: 5,248
Gross Registered Tonnage: 167,046

Company: Cunard Line
Number of ships: 7
Cunard Countess/Cunard Princess/Queen Elizabeth 2/Sagafjord/Sea Goddess I/Sea Goddess II/
Vistafjord
Total number of cabins: 2,582
Total number of berths: 5,376
Gross Registered Tonnage: 159,025

Company: Epirotiki Lines
Number of ships: 10
Argonaut/Atlas/Jason/Jupiter/Neptune/Oceanos/Odysseus/Orpheus/Pegasus/
World Renaissance
Total number of cabins: 2,039
Total number of berths: 4,854
Gross Registered Tonnage: 136,838

Company: Costa Cruises
Number of ships: 6
CarlaCosta/CostaRiviera/Danae/Daphne/EnricoCosta/EugenioCosta
Total number of cabins: 2,088
Total number of berths: 4,729
Gross Registered Tonnage: 131,669

Company: Chandris Fantasy Cruises
Number of ships: 6
Amerikanis/The Azur/Britanis/Galileo/Romanza/The Victoria
Total number of cabins: 2,208
Total number of berths: 4,474
Gross Registered Tonnage: 111,299

Company: Premier Cruise Lines
Number of ships: 3
Atlantic/Oceanic/Majestic
Total number of cabins: 1,467
Total number of berths: 3,812
Gross Registered Tonnage: 93,111

World's 10 longest and largest passenger ships (past and present) January 1989

SHIP	OWNER/OPERATOR	GRT	LENGTH (feet)
Queen Elizabeth	Cunard Line	83,673	1,031
Normandie	French Line	82,799	1,029
Queen Mary	Cunard Line	81,237	1,019
Sovereign of the Seas	Royal Caribbean Cruise Line	73,189	873
Norway (ex-France)	Norwegian Cruise Line (ex-French Line)	70,202 (66,348)	1,035
Queen Elizabeth 2	Cunard Line	66,451	963
Star Princess	Princess Cruises	62,500	804
Leviathan (ex-Vaterland)	United States Lines (ex-Hamburg-America Line)	59,957 (54,282)	950
Majestic	White Star Line	56,551	956
United States	United States Lines	53,329	990

World's 10 largest cruise ships – January 1989

SHIP	CRUISE LINE/OPERATOR	BUILT	GRT
Sovereign of the Seas	Royal Caribbean Cruise Line	1988	73,189
Norway	Norwegian Cruise Line	1962	70,202
Queen Elizabeth 2	Cunard Line	1969	66,451
Star Princess	Princess Cruises	1989	62,500
Celebration	Carnival Cruise Lines	1987	47,262
Jubilee	Carnival Cruise Lines	1986	47,262
Sky Princess	Princess Cruises	1984	46,314
Holiday	Carnival Cruise Lines	1985	46,052
Canberra	Canberra Cruises	1961	44,807
Royal Princess	Princess Cruises	1984	44,348

World's 10 longest cruise ships – January 1989

SHIP	CRUISE LINE/OPERATOR	LENGTH (feet)
Norway	Norwegian Cruise Line	1,035
Queen Elizabeth 2	Cunard Line	963
Sovereign of the Seas	Royal Caribbean Cruise Line	873
Canberra	Canberra Cruises	810
Star Princess	Princess Cruises	804
Sky Princess	Princess Cruises	789
Oceanic	Premier Cruise Lines	774
Royal Princess	Princess Cruises	761
Festivale	Carnival Cruise Lines	760
Celebration/Jubilee	Carnival Cruise Lines	750

World's newest cruise ships – July 1986 to January 1989

SHIP	CRUISE LINE	TONNAGE	COST	IN SERVICE
Star Princess	Princess Cruises	62,500	$153 m	Jan 1989
Royal Viking Sun	Royal Viking Line	38,000	$125 m	Dec 1988
Seabourn Pride	Seabourn Cruise Line	9,000	$ 46 m	Dec 1988
Crown del Mar***	Crown Cruise Line	10,000	$ 30 m	Nov 1988
Monterey**	Aloha Pacific Cruises	21,051	$ 40 m	Sep 1988
Crown Odyssey	Royal Cruise Line	34,242	$150 m	Jun 1988
Seaward	Norwegian Cruise Line	42,276	$127 m	Jun 1988
Yorktown Clipper	Clipper Cruise Line	99	$ 12 m	Apr 1988
Americana	Ivaran Lines	19,203	$ 30 m	Mar 1988
Albatross***	Dolphin Hellas Shipping	10,026	$ 15 m	Mar 1988
Aegean Dolphin*	Dolphin Hellas Shipping	11,200	$ 25 m	Mar 1988
Wind Spirit	Windstar Sail Cruises	5,307	$ 35 m	Mar 1988
Sovereign of the Seas	Royal Caribbean Cruise Line	73,192	$185 m	Jan 1988
Wind Song	Windstar Sail Cruises	5,307	$ 35 m	July 1987
Celebration	Carnival Cruise Lines	47,262	$150 m	Mar 1987
Astor	Astor Cruises	20,158	$109 m	Jan 1987
Wind Star	Windstar Sail Cruises	5,307	$ 35 m	Dec 1986
Explorer Starship*	Exploration Cruise Lines	8,282	$ 40 m	Aug 1986
Homeric	Home Lines Cruises	42,092	$150 m	May 1986
Jubilee	Carnival Cruise Lines	47,262	$150 m	July 1986

Key:
  * = this ship constructed using an existing hull
  ** = this ship refurbished and reintroduced into service with same name
  *** = this ship refurbished and reintroduced into service under a new name

For Your Interest:
The cost of constructing a brand new cruise ship is enormous. At present, it works out to an average of $80,000 per berth for large ships, ascending in direct proportion to the size of the vessel to more than $500,000 per berth for small ships. Hotels, on the other hand, are much cheaper to build, but they don't move!

World Weather Chart – Major Cruise Ports

	JANUARY			FEBRUARY			MARCH			APRIL			MAY			JUNE		
	DAY	NIGHT	SEA	DAY	NIGHT	SEA	DAY	NIGHT	SEA	DAY	NIGHT	SEA	DAY	NIGHT	SEA	DAY	NIGHT	SEA
Acapulco	29	22	24	29	22	24	31	22	24	32	22	25	33	24	26	33	24	27
Alexandria	18	9	17	19	10	16	21	11	16	24	14	18	27	17	20	28	20	23
Athens	14	7	14	14	7	14	16	8	14	20	11	15	25	16	18	30	20	22
Bali	30	23	28	30	23	28	30	23	28	31	23	29	31	23	28	30	23	28
Bangkok	32	20	26	33	23	27	34	24	27	35	26	28	34	25	28	33	25	28
Barbados	28	21	26	28	21	25	29	21	25	30	22	26	31	23	27	31	23	28
Bremerhaven	2	−2	4	3	−2	4	7	1	4	11	4	6	16	8	10	19	11	13
Casablanca	17	7	16	18	8	16	19	10	16	21	11	17	22	13	19	24	17	19
Colombo	30	22	27	31	22	27	31	23	28	31	24	28	30	25	29	30	25	29
Copenhagen	2	−2	3	2	−2	2	5	−1	3	10	3	5	16	8	9	20	11	14
Cozumel	26	20	26	27	20	26	28	22	26	30	24	26	31	25	27	30	26	27
Curacao	29	23	26	29	23	26	30	24	26	30	25	26	31	26	27	31	26	27
Dubrovnik	12	6	13	12	6	13	14	8	13	17	11	15	21	15	17	25	19	22
Genoa	10	6	13	12	6	12	14	9	13	18	12	14	21	15	16	25	19	20
Haifa	14	8	17	15	8	16	17	10	16	21	13	18	24	16	21	26	18	23
Hong Kong	18	13	18	18	13	18	20	15	21	24	19	24	28	23	25	30	26	26
Honolulu	25	20	24	25	20	24	25	20	24	25	21	25	26	22	26	27	22	26
Istanbul	9	3	8	9	2	8	11	3	8	16	7	11	21	12	15	26	16	20
Kusadasi	13	6	15	14	6	13	16	7	14	20	10	15	24	14	18	28	17	21
Leningrad	−5	−11	–	−4	−11	–	1	−7	–	7	−1	1	14	5	5	19	10	12
Lisbon	14	8	14	15	8	14	17	10	14	20	12	14	21	13	16	25	15	17
Martinique	28	21	26	29	21	25	29	21	26	30	21	26	31	23	27	30	23	27
Miami	23	18	22	24	18	23	25	19	24	26	21	25	28	23	28	30	25	30
Papeete	30	23	27	30	23	27	30	23	27	30	23	28	29	22	28	29	21	27
Rio de Janeiro	30	23	25	30	23	25	29	23	26	27	21	25	26	20	24	25	18	23
St. Lucia	28	21	26	28	21	25	29	21	26	31	22	26	31	23	27	31	23	27
San Francisco	13	7	11	15	8	11	16	9	12	17	10	12	17	11	13	18	12	14
San Juan	27	21	26	27	21	26	27	22	26	28	22	27	29	23	27	29	24	28
Shanghai	8	−1	10	8	0	8	13	4	9	19	9	12	24	14	16	28	19	20
Singapore	31	23	27	31	23	27	31	24	28	31	24	28	31	24	28	31	25	29
Southampton	7	2	8	8	2	8	11	3	8	14	5	9	18	8	11	20	11	13
Yokohama	9	0	14	9	0	14	12	3	14	17	8	16	21	13	18	24	17	21

Day Temperature = Maximum
Night Temperature = Minimum
Sea Temperature = Average
Temperatures in centigrade

Temperature

To convert centigrade into
degrees Fahrenheit, multiply
centigrade by 1.8 and add 32.

To convert degrees Fahrenheit
into centigrade, subtract 32
from Fahrenheit and divide
by 1.8.

	JULY			AUGUST			SEPTEMBER			OCTOBER			NOVEMBER			DECEMBER				
DAY	NIGHT	SEA		DAY	NIGHT	SEA		DAY	NIGHT	SEA		DAY	NIGHT	SEA		DAY	NIGHT	SEA		DAY	NIGHT	SEA			
33	24	28		32	24	28		31	24	28		31	24	27		31	22	26		30	21	25			
30	23	25		30	23	26		29	21	26		28	18	24		24	15	22		20	11	19			
33	23	24		33	23	24		29	19	23		23	15	21		19	12	19		15	9	16			
30	22	27		31	22	27		31	22	27		32	23	27		32	23	28		30	23	29			
32	25	28		32	24	28		32	24	28		31	24	27		31	23	27		31	20	27			
30	23	28		31	23	28		31	23	28		30	23	28		29	23	28		28	22	27			
21	14	17		21	14	17		18	11	16		13	7	12		8	3	8		4	0	6			
26	19	21		27	19	22		26	17	21		24	15	21		21	11	19		18	9	17			
29	25	28		29	25	27		30	25	27		29	24	28		29	23	27		30	22	27			
22	14	16		21	14	16		18	11	14		12	7	12		7	3	8		4	1	5			
30	25	28		31	25	29		30	25	29		29	24	28		28	23	27		26	22	26			
31	26	28		32	26	28		32	26	28		32	26	28		30	25	27		29	24	24			
28	21	23		28	21	24		25	18	22		21	14	20		17	10	18		13	7	15			
27	22	23		28	22	23		25	19	21		20	15	19		15	11	16		12	7	14			
28	21	26		28	22	27		27	21	27		26	19	25		22	15	22		17	10	19			
31	26	28		31	26	28		30	25	27		27	23	26		24	19	24		20	15	21			
28	23	27		28	23	27		28	23	27		28	23	27		27	22	26		25	21	25			
29	18	22		29	20	23		25	15	21		21	12	19		15	8	15		11	5	11			
30	20	23		30	19	23		26	16	22		22	13	20		19	11	17		15	8	16			
22	14	16		19	12	16		14	7	12		7	2	8		1	−3	4		−3	−8	1			
27	17	12		28	17	19		26	17	19		22	14	18		17	11	16		15	9	15			
30	23	28		31	23	28		31	23	28		31	23	28		30	22	27		29	22	27			
31	25	31		31	26	31		30	25	30		28	23	28		26	21	25		24	18	23			
28	20	26		28	20	26		28	21	26		29	21	26		29	22	27		29	23	27			
25	18	22		25	18	22		25	19	22		26	20	22		26	20	23		28	22	24			
31	23	28		31	23	28		31	23	28		31	22	28		29	22	27		28	21	27			
18	12	15		18	12	15		20	13	16		20	12	15		18	10	13		14	8	11			
29	24	28		29	24	28		30	24	29		30	24	29		28	23	28		27	22	27			
32	23	24		32	23	26		27	19	25		23	13	23		17	7	18		10	2	13			
31	25	28		31	24	28		30	24	28		31	24	28		30	24	28		30	23	27			
22	13	15		22	13	16		19	11	16		15	7	15		11	5	12		8	3	10			
28	21	23		29	22	24		26	19	24		20	13	21		16	8	18		11	2	14			

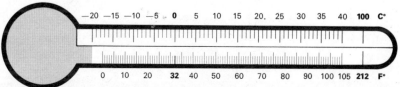

−20 −15 −10 −5   0   5   10   15   20   25   30   35   40 **100** C°

0   10   20   **32**   40   50   60   70   80   90   100 105 **212** F°

In order to fully evaluate the usefulness of this handbook, the International Cruise Passengers Association and the author would appreciate your comments. Any useful suggestion will be taken into consideration by the author during compilation of the next edition of this handbook.

Did you buy this book:

☐ because it contains comparative and analytical cruise ship ratings
☐ because it is informative
☐ on the recommendation of a friend or business associate
☐ on the recommendation of your cruise/travel agent
☐ after seeing it in a bookstore. If so, where _____
☐ after reading about it in a newspaper or periodical. If so, which _____

Have you taken a cruise before?   ☐ Yes   ☐ No

If yes, how many? _____
In which areas have you cruised? _____
Which is your favorite area? _____
Which is your favorite ship? _____
Which is your favorite cruise line? _____

What do you enjoy most about cruising?

☐ It's an inclusive-cost vacation
☐ The itinerary and port visits
☐ Being at sea, without newspapers, television and radio
☐ The food
☐ Being pampered and attended
☐ The entertainment and activities
☐ Having to pack and unpack only once

Did these revised ratings help you decide which ship to take on your next cruise vacation?   ☐ Yes   ☐ No

Have you found this handbook useful and informative?   ☐ Yes   ☐ No

What other information would you like to see included in future editions?

_____
_____
_____

Thank you for your valued time in completing this questionnaire. Please note that no correspondence will be entered into concerning the ship evaluations and ratings.
Please send this form to:
International Cruise Passengers Association, P.O. Box 886, F.D.R. Station, New York, N.Y. 10150–0886, U.S.A.